Trustworthiness in Mobile Cyber Physical Systems

Trustworthiness in Mobile Cyber Physical Systems

Editors

Kyungtae Kang
Junggab Son
Hyo-Joong Suh

MDPI • Basel • Beijing • Wuhan • Barcelona • Belgrade • Manchester • Tokyo • Cluj • Tianjin

Editors
Kyungtae Kang
Hanyang University
Korea

Junggab Son
Kennesaw State University
USA

Hyo-Joong Suh
The Catholic University of Korea
Korea

Editorial Office
MDPI
St. Alban-Anlage 66
4052 Basel, Switzerland

This is a reprint of articles from the Special Issue published online in the open access journal *Applied Sciences* (ISSN 2076-3417) (available at: https://www.mdpi.com/journal/applsci/special_issues/Trustworthiness_Mobile_CPS).

For citation purposes, cite each article independently as indicated on the article page online and as indicated below:

LastName, A.A.; LastName, B.B.; LastName, C.C. Article Title. *Journal Name* **Year**, *Volume Number*, Page Range.

ISBN 978-3-0365-1086-6 (Hbk)
ISBN 978-3-0365-1087-3 (PDF)

© 2021 by the authors. Articles in this book are Open Access and distributed under the Creative Commons Attribution (CC BY) license, which allows users to download, copy and build upon published articles, as long as the author and publisher are properly credited, which ensures maximum dissemination and a wider impact of our publications.

The book as a whole is distributed by MDPI under the terms and conditions of the Creative Commons license CC BY-NC-ND.

Contents

About the Editors vii

Hyo-Joong Suh, Junggab Son and Kyungtae Kang
Trustworthiness in Mobile Cyber-Physical Systems
Reprinted from: *Applied Sciences* **2021**, *11*, 1676, doi:10.3390/app11041676 1

Jeonghyun Lee and Sangkyun Lee
Robust CNN Compression Framework for Security-Sensitive Embedded Systems
Reprinted from: *Applied Sciences* **2021**, *11*, 1093, doi:10.3390/app11031093 7

Jin Hyun Kim, Hyo Jin Jo and Insup Lee
Model Checking Resiliency and Sustainability of In-Vehicle Network for Real-Time Authenticity
Reprinted from: *Applied Sciences* **2021**, *11*, 1068, doi:10.3390/aapp11031068 25

Hyeongmin Cho and Sangkyun Lee
Data Quality Measures and Efficient Evaluation Algorithms for Large-Scale High-Dimensional Data
Reprinted from: *Applied Sciences* **2021**, *11*, 472, doi:10.3390/app11020472 49

Hyundo Yoon, Soojung Moon, Youngki Kim, Changhee Hahn, Wonjun Lee and Junbeom Hur
SPEKS: Forward Private SGX-Based Public Key Encryption with Keyword Search
Reprinted from: *Applied Sciences* **2020**, *10*, 7842, doi:10.3390/app10217842 67

Youn Kyu Lee and Dohoon Kim
A Taxonomy for Security Flaws in Event-Based Systems
Reprinted from: *Applied Sciences* **2020**, *10*, 7338, doi:10.3390/app10207338 81

Yong-Il Jo, Seonah Lee, Wan Yeon Lee and Kyong Hoon Kim
Reducing Dynamic Power Consumption in Mixed-Critical Real-Time Systems
Reprinted from: *Applied Sciences* **2020**, *10*, 7256, doi:10.3390/app10207256 103

Seong Kyung Kwon, Hojin Jung and Kyoung-Dae Kim
Dynamic All-Red Signal Control Based on Deep Neural Network Considering Red Light Runner Characteristics
Reprinted from: *Applied Sciences* **2020**, *10*, 6050, doi:10.3390/app10176050 123

Seungmin Oh, Yoonsoo Choi, Sangdae Kim, Cheonyong Kim, Kwansoo Jung and Seok-Hun Kim
A Real-Time Data Delivery for Mobile Sinks Group on Mobile Cyber-Physical Systems
Reprinted from: *Applied Sciences* **2020**, *10*, 5950, doi:10.3390/app10175950 141

Daeho Choi, Tae-Wook Kim, and Jong-Chan Kim
AUTOSAR Runnable Periods Optimization for DAG-Based Complex Automobile Applications
Reprinted from: *Applied Sciences* **2020**, *10*, 5829, doi:10.3390/app10175829 153

About the Editors

Hyo-Joong Suh (Professor) is currently a professor at the School of Computer Science and Information Engineering, the Catholic University of Korea. He received his BS and MS degrees from Seoul National University in 1992 and 1994, respectively. He completed his PhD degree at the Department of Computer Engineering of Seoul National University in 2000. He is an expert in embedded and mobile systems, with extensive experience in scalable computer and wireless/mobile systems. His research extends from memory hierarchy optimization during MS and PhD research to the prototyping of various mobile devices from several communication companies as a professional service. His current research interest focuses on human behavior computing with personal identification using various sensors.

Junggab Son (Assistant Professor) is currently an Assistant Professor in the Department of Computer Science, College of Computing and Software Engineering, Kennesaw State University (KSU), Marietta, GA, USA. He was a limited-term Assistant Professor from January to May 2018 and was a research fellow/part-time assistant professor from October 2016 to December 2017 in the Department of Computer Science, KSU. Before joining KSU, he was a postdoctoral research associate in the Department of Mathematics and Physics, North Carolina Central University, Durham, NC, USA, from September 2014 to September 2016. He received his Ph.D. degree (August 2014) and M.S. degree (February 2011) in computer science and engineering from Hanyang University, Seoul, South Korea. He received his B.S. degree (February 2009) in computer science and engineering from Hanyang University, Ansan, South Korea. His research interests include applied cryptography, security, and privacy issues in significant applications, including cloud computing (Fog/Edge Computing), the internet of things (Future Internet), vehicular ad hoc networks, social network services, and bioinformatics.

Kyungtae Kang (Professor) received a B.S. degree in computer science and engineering, followed by M.S. and Ph.D. degrees in electrical engineering and computer science, from Seoul National University, Seoul, Korea, in 1999, 2001, and 2007, respectively. From 2008 to 2010, he was a postdoctoral research associate at the University of Illinois at Urbana-Champaign, IL, USA. In 2011, he joined the Department of Computer Science and Engineering at Hanyang University, where he is currently a tenured professor. His research interests lie primarily in systems, including operating systems, mobile systems, distributed systems, and real-time embedded systems. His recent research interest is in the interdisciplinary area of cyber-physical systems.

Editorial
Trustworthiness in Mobile Cyber-Physical Systems

Hyo-Joong Suh [1], Junggab Son [2] and Kyungtae Kang [3,*]

1 School of Computer Science and Information Engineering, The Catholic University of Korea, Bucheon 14662, Korea; hjsuh@catholic.ac.kr
2 Department of Computer Science, Kennesaw State University, Marietta, GA 30060, USA; json@kennesaw.edu
3 Department of Applied Artificial Intelligence, Hanyang University, Ansan 15588, Korea
* Correspondence: ktkang@hanyang.ac.kr; Tel.: +82-31-400-5235

Citation: Suh, H.-J.; Son, J.; Kang, K. Trustworthiness in Mobile Cyber-Physical Systems. *Appl. Sci.* **2021**, *11*, 1676. https://doi.org/10.3390/app11041676

Received: 8 February 2021
Accepted: 9 February 2021
Published: 13 February 2021

Publisher's Note: MDPI stays neutral with regard to jurisdictional claims in published maps and institutional affiliations.

Copyright: © 2021 by the authors. Licensee MDPI, Basel, Switzerland. This article is an open access article distributed under the terms and conditions of the Creative Commons Attribution (CC BY) license (https://creativecommons.org/licenses/by/4.0/).

1. Introduction

As they continue to become faster and cheaper, devices with enhanced computing and communication capabilities are increasingly incorporated into diverse objects and structures in the physical environment. Harnessing these capabilities will provide the basis for applications offering enormous societal impact and economic benefit, linking the cyber world of computing and communications with the physical world. Such applications are called cyber-physical systems (CPSs). It is evident that as direct interactions between real-world entities (including human activities) and cyber systems become more commonplace, the trustworthiness of such systems will become an increasingly important issue. Here, we use the term system trustworthiness in a broad sense to describe systems that demonstrate reliable functionality and are worthy of user confidence, such that they guarantee continuous service in response to internal errors or external attacks [1].

While CPSs traditionally involve static equipment and stable networks, the development of increasingly pervasive mobile devices has generated considerable attention in mobile CPSs (MCPSs). By exploiting the advantages of CPSs through mobile devices, such as the iPhone and Android phones, with their increasing processing power, range of sensors, and pervasive cellular connections, MCPSs provide expanded applicability, including access to networks comprising multiple mobile devices, such as vehicle networks. Owing to the instability of mobile networks and the variable computing power of individual mobile devices, many studies have been performed to address various aspects supporting the efficient cooperation and performance of MCPSs. In particular, the timeliness of data transferal is essential because delays and failures due to bottlenecks stemming from variable network environments can adversely affect the entire system.

The objective of this Special Issue is to contribute to the advancement of research on a wide variety of topics involved in the development of modern and future trustworthy MCPSs, including design, modeling, verification and validation, dependability, resilience, security, safety, and run-time resource optimization. It is imperative to address the issues that are critical to the mobility of MCPSs, report significant advances in the underlying science, and discuss the challenges facing the development and implementation of specific MCPS applications, including those associated with aerospace, autonomous automotive systems, automatic pilot avionics, smart grids, and distributed robotics. Such applications will empower the true vision of MCPSs, driving the evolution of human interactions with the physical world. Moreover, technologies utilizing CPSs will emerge as key drivers in the development of a future autonomous and smart-connected world.

As a side note, we focus on methods for integrating MCPSs with artificial intelligence (AI) without compromising the trustworthiness of the system. AI-enabled CPSs combine computational capabilities with the ability to control and sense physical space. For example, the behavior of autonomous CPSs, such as self-driving cars and autonomous drones in open environments is often determined by AI and machine learning algorithms. However, the use of data-driven deep learning techniques for perception and control in autonomous

CPSs has raised concerns regarding the safety and robustness of autonomous systems. When operating in a physical environment, the unexpected action of AI-enabled CPSs can inflict critical damage on the surrounding environment, including the potential endangerment of humans. Therefore, AI-enabled MCPSs should satisfy stringent regulations regarding their trustworthiness. Although sophisticated testing plays an important role in ensuring the safety and robustness of such systems, the complexity of modern autonomous CPSs means that evaluating trustworthiness via testing alone is insufficient. Formal verification reduces the burden on the testing process by ruling out large classes of errant behaviors at the design stage. Nevertheless, the introduction of a standard methodology for developing formal methods for autonomous AI-enabled CPSs is essential.

2. Review of Issue Contents

This Special Issue presents nine original papers covering the latest advances and technologies involved in the design of reliable, resilient, secure, and intelligent MCPSs. Moreover, each paper contributes research that offers insights regarding trustworthiness in MCPSs.

Artificial intelligence models, especially deep neural networks such as convolutional neural nets (CNNs), tend to have many learning parameters, thus making their integration into small embedded CPSs, such as mobile phones, challenging. In response to this issue, Lee et al. in [2] suggested a new model compression framework based on sparse coding and knowledge distillation with adversarial training, thereby producing compact CNN architectures that maintain robustness against adversarial perturbed inputs. Furthermore, the authors provide training algorithms based on the alternating direction method of multipliers (ADMM), which is more memory-efficient than existing CNN pruning methods and, therefore, more suitable for AI-enabled MCPSs.

In [3], Kim et al. propose two novel data quality measures suitable for large-scale high-dimensional data. As low-quality data can degrade prediction accuracy and inference bias, measuring the data quality is an important first step in successful AI applications. In MCPS, the use of AI often requires regular updates, while detecting inference bias when operating at the AI runtime is difficult; therefore, a data quality check is essential. This study also proposes efficient algorithms based on random projections and bootstrapping, enabling the suggested measures to be computed for large-scale and high-dimensional data, thus representing a departure from existing data quality measures.

Automotive systems are typical examples of CPSs in which embedded software is the main element controlling the mechanical components of the vehicle. Internet-connected software components can be victims of security attacks at any time, and CAN (Controller Area Networks), an in-vehicle network system connecting individual electronic control units (ECUs), serves as a breach point to break vehicle safety.

MAuth-CAN [4] is a new CAN authentication technique that protects ECUs from attacking messages based on a centralized node called an authenticator. It is secure against masquerade attacks by a compromised node and protects the authenticator node from bus-off attacks that can temporarily force an ECU to leave CAN. However, the use of a central node causes an additional authentication delay. Thus, in accordance with regulations such as ISO 26262, the efficacy of the MAuth-CAN must be formally verified before it can be used for commercial vehicles.

Cho et al. [5] present formal proof that MAuth-CAN is consistently resistant against message flooding and Bus-Off attacks and provide formal CAN models at various levels, which can be used to analyze CAN applications. Via model checking, the complicated behavior of CAN in the media access control level of the data link layer connecting to MAauth-CAN was checked exhaustively to prove its resilience and sustainability under such attacks. These results can be used to obtain safety certificates from regulatory authorities, while the methodology and the CAN models can be used to secure safety certificates regarding CAN applications.

Public key encryption with keyword search (PEKS) functionality enables users to search for encrypted data that has been outsourced to an untrusted server. Unfortunately, updates to the outsourced data may cause information leakage by exploiting the queries previously submitted in PEKS. Yoon et al. [6] address this by proposing a novel forward private PEKS scheme based on software guard extension (SGX), a trusted execution environment provided by Intel. By utilizing SGX, the proposed scheme presents substantial performance improvements compared with prior work. Owing to the readiness with which a trusted platform such as SGX can be integrated with many current CPSs, this research also has implications for security enhancements in CPS environments.

Event-based systems (EBSs) are prevalent in MCPS applications owing to their communication model, which uses implicit invocation and concurrency between components. However, the non-determinism of EBSs during event processing can introduce inherent security vulnerabilities into the system. Many types of attack can incapacitate and/or damage a target EBS by exploiting this event-based communication model. To minimize the security risks to EBSs, the security flaws of such systems, the relationships between these flaws, and feasible techniques for dealing with each flaw must be determined. However, existing security flaw taxonomies do not appropriately reflect the inherent security issues of EBSs. Therefore, Lee et al. [7] introduced a new taxonomy that defines and classifies the inherent security flaws of EBSs, which can serve as a basis for resolving its specific security problems. Moreover, the authors correlated their taxonomy with security attacks designed to target specific flaws and identified existing solutions for the prevention of such attacks.

In [8], Ali et al. describe an energy minimization technique for mixed-criticality real-time scheduling on a single-core system. The main contribution of the proposed technique is that it allows the processor frequency to be controlled dynamically depending on the system criticality mode. Through a series of simulations, they demonstrated and analyzed the effects caused by both low-and high-criticality modes in power-aware mixed-criticality systems. As safety and power awareness are both issues for MCPSs, this study offers valuable insights for power-aware safety-critical CPSs.

Safety and efficiency provide the focus in [9], in which Kwon et al. propose a system that dynamically controls the all-red signal length based on the driving characteristics of vehicles identified as red-light runners (RLRs) to improve the overall safety and efficiency of intersections in road networks. The proposed system uses a multi-channel deep convolutional neural network (MC-DCNN) to enable the online detection and classification of RLRs, which can be defined using clustering results acquired via dynamic time wrapping (DTW) and hierarchical clustering analysis (HCA). For dynamic all-red signal control, the proposed system uses a multi-level regression model to estimate the necessary all-red signal extension time more accurately, thereby improving the overall safety for intersection traffic as well as efficiency of the traffic flow.

By contrast, the study conducted by Oh et al. [10] concerns real-time data transmission to mobile equipment used by groups of workers, termed a mobile sink group (MSG), for which rapid and reliable data are vital to ensure the efficient operation of groups working on collaborative projects, which often involve multiple pieces of equipment where miscommunication could result in an industrial accident. The authors proposed a real-time data delivery mechanism based on a virtual grid structure to support MSGs. The main idea is to determine the farthest distance and calculate the minimum real-time data transmission speed required.

First, the proposed scheme models the MSG as a single center point and radius, and defines the end-to-end distance based on the member sink located furthest from the source node. Thus, the source node can calculate the transmission speed, which is maintained during the data transmission. The data transmission process is divided into two main phases: the main forwarding phase, which passes through the center of the mobile sinks from the source node, and the branch forwarding phase at the branch point, which receives data via the main forwarding phase. In addition, even if some mobile sinks deviate from the initial radius owing to environmental factors associated with MCPSs, the connection of the sinks is ensured through the inner/outer agent concept. Thus, the proposed scheme can deliver data to all member sinks in a timely manner and is superior to existing schemes in terms of real-time communication for MSGs.

Finally, in [11], Choi et al. address an important system optimization problem faced by automotive control systems. More specifically, a control application based on AUTOSAR (AUTomotive Open System Architecture) [12] is assumed, whereby fine granular schedule entities (i.e., runnables) are used to compose a control application. For this purpose, the authors propose a Lagrange multiplier-based runnable period optimization method that maximizes the level of system control, which is useful for the development of future MCPSs, where design optimization is a fundamental consideration.

3. Conclusions

This Special Issue presents new and innovative research addressing some of the many scientific challenges associated with improving the trustworthiness of MCPSs. We emphasize the need for a better understanding of the security and reliability of MCPS as well as the impacts of AI, and demonstrate procedures for solving the adverse effects caused by these impacts. As such, the studies contained within this volume provide a valuable basis for the protection and promotion of resilient MCPSs.

Author Contributions: Conceptualization, H.-J.S., J.S. and K.K.; methodology, H.-J.S. and K.K.; validation, J.S.; investigation, K.K.; writing—original draft preparation, K.K.; writing—review and editing, H.-J.S.; supervision, J.S. and K.K.; funding acquisition, H.-J.S. and K.K. All authors have read and agreed to the published version of the manuscript.

Funding: This research was supported by the National Research Foundation of Korea (2016R1D 1A1B01006716) and the Catholic University of Korea, Research Fund, 2020. This research was also supported by the Institute of Information & Communications Technology Planning & Evaluation (IITP) grant funded by the Korean government (Ministry of Science and ICT) (No.2020-0-01343, Artificial Intelligence Convergence Research Center (Hanyang University ERICA)).

Institutional Review Board Statement: Not applicable.

Informed Consent Statement: Not applicable.

Acknowledgments: This issue would not have been possible without the help of a variety of talented authors, professional reviewers, and the dedicated editorial team of Applied Sciences. First, we express our gratitude to the authors for their excellent contributions to this Special Issue on trustworthiness in mobile cyber-physical systems. We are also grateful to all the reviewers for their time and effort in examining these papers, and for their valuable comments and constructive suggestions. Finally, we appreciate the advice and support of the editorial team of Applied Sciences for their help in the publication process. We hope that this Special Issue will serve as a valuable reference for academicians, scientists, engineers, and practitioners working toward the design and implementation of trustworthy mobile cyber-physical systems.

Conflicts of Interest: The authors declare no conflict of interest.

References

1. Romanovsky, A.; Ishikawa, F. *Trustworthy Cyber-Physical Systems*, 1st ed.; Chapman & Hall/CRC: London, UK, 2017; pp. 2–22.
2. Lee, J.; Lee, S. Robust CNN Compression Framework for Security-Sensitive Embedded Systems. *Appl. Sci.* **2021**, *11*, 1093. [CrossRef]
3. Kim, J.H.; Jo, H.J.; Lee, I. Model Checking Resiliency and Sustainability of In-Vehicle Network for Real-Time Authenticity. *Appl. Sci.* **2021**, *11*, 1068. [CrossRef]
4. Jo, H.J.; Kim, J.H.; Choi, H.-Y.; Choi, W.C.; Lee, D.H.; Lee, I. MAuth-CAN: Masquerade-Attack-Proof Authentication for In-Vehicle Networks. *IEEE Trans. Veh. Technol.* **2020**, *69*, 2204–2218. [CrossRef]
5. Yoon, H.; Moon, S.; Kim, Y.; Hahn, C.; Lee, W.; Hur, J. SPEKS: Forward Private SGX-Based Public Key Encryption with Keyword Search. *Appl. Sci.* **2021**, *11*, 1068. [CrossRef]
6. Cho, H.; Lee, S. Data Quality Measures and Efficient Evaluation Algorithms for Large-Scale High-Dimensional Data. *Appl. Sci.* **2021**, *11*, 472. [CrossRef]
7. Yoon, H.; Moon, S.; Kim, Y.; Hahn, C.; Lee, W.; Hur, J. SPEKS: Forward Private SGX-Based Public Key Encryption with Keyword Search. *Appl. Sci.* **2020**, *10*, 7842. [CrossRef]

8. Lee, K.L.; Kim, D.A. Taxonomy for Security Flaws in Event-Based Systems. *Appl. Sci.* **2020**, *10*, 7338. [CrossRef]
9. Ali, I.; Jo, Y.-I.; Lee, S.; Lee, W.L.; Kim, K.H. Reducing Dynamic Power Consumption in Mixed-Critical Real-Time Systems. *Appl. Sci.* **2020**, *10*, 7256. [CrossRef]
10. Kwon, S.K.; Jung, H.; Kim, K.-D. Dynamic All-Red Signal Control Based on Deep Neural Network Considering Red Light Runner Characteristics. *Appl. Sci.* **2020**, *10*, 6050. [CrossRef]
11. Oh, S.; Choi, Y.; Kim, S.; Kim, C.; Jung, K.; Kim, S.-H. A Real-Time Data Delivery for Mobile Sinks Group on Mobile Cyber-Physical Systems. *Appl. Sci.* **2021**, *10*, 5950. [CrossRef]
12. Choi, D.; Kim, T.-W.; Kim, J.-K. AUTOSAR Runnable Periods Optimization for DAG-Based Complex Automobile Applications. *Appl. Sci.* **2021**, *10*, 5829. [CrossRef]

Article
Robust CNN Compression Framework for Security-Sensitive Embedded Systems

Jeonghyun Lee and Sangkyun Lee *

School of Cybersecurity, Korea University, Seoul 02841, Korea; nomar0107@korea.ac.kr
* Correspondence: sangkyun@korea.ac.kr

Abstract: Convolutional neural networks (CNNs) have achieved tremendous success in solving complex classification problems. Motivated by this success, there have been proposed various compression methods for downsizing the CNNs to deploy them on resource-constrained embedded systems. However, a new type of vulnerability of compressed CNNs known as the adversarial examples has been discovered recently, which is critical for security-sensitive systems because the adversarial examples can cause malfunction of CNNs and can be crafted easily in many cases. In this paper, we proposed a compression framework to produce compressed CNNs robust against such adversarial examples. To achieve the goal, our framework uses both pruning and knowledge distillation with adversarial training. We formulate our framework as an optimization problem and provide a solution algorithm based on the proximal gradient method, which is more memory-efficient than the popular ADMM-based compression approaches. In experiments, we show that our framework can improve the trade-off between adversarial robustness and compression rate compared to the existing state-of-the-art adversarial pruning approach.

Keywords: model compression; adversarial robustness; weight pruning; adversarial training; distillation; embedded system; secure AI

1. Introduction

In the past few years, convolutional neural networks (CNNs) have achieved great success in many applications including image classification and object detection. Despite the success, the excessively large amount of learning parameters and the vulnerability for the adversarial examples [1–8] are making it difficult to deploy CNNs especially on resource-constrained environments such as smartphones, automobiles, and wearable devices. To overcome this drawback, various model compression methods have been proposed, where many are based on weight pruning [9–17]. Weight pruning generates sparse learning weights by solving an optimization problem with sparsity constraints on the weights, and then the actual compression is accomplished by removing zero weights from a trained model. Although their approach is quite simple, state-of-the-art weight pruning methods [16,17] achieve a high compression rate with little drop in accuracy.

On the other hand, it has been reported that even the state-of-the-art CNNs are vulnerable to adversarial attacks [1–8]. Adversarial attacks are accomplished by using perturbed inputs which cause misclassification where modification is nearly imperceptibly small. Such perturbation can be easily produced by exploiting the gradient information of the target neural network [1,4,6]. Furthermore, some works show that adversary can even generate adversarial examples without knowing anything about the target neural network [5]. Adversarial training [1,6] has been proposed as a countermeasure to adversarial attacks bringing robustness to neural networks against adversarial inputs. This method trains a classifier not only with training examples but also with adversarial examples generated actively by the defender for known types of adversarial perturbations. In particular, projected gradient descent attack [6]-based adversarial training is known to provide high robustness against the first-order adversary [1,4,6]. However, it has been shown that adversarial training requires a significantly large capacity of the neural network to achieve high accuracy on both original and adversarial examples [6].

Recently, the vulnerability of the compressed neural network is raised as an issue [18]. As shown in Madry et al. [6] the adversarial robustness of compressed neural networks is hard to achieve due to the lack of its architectural capacity. This prevents the compressed neural network from being deployed to a trust-sensitive domain. Despite the seriousness of this problem, only a few methods have been proposed [19,20]. One notable technique is to consider adversarial robustness and model compression at the same time. Ye et al. [19] and Gui et al. [20] formulated an optimization problem by combining adversarial training with pruning and solved it with the alternating direction method of multiplier (ADMM) framework. These works demonstrated that considering weight pruning and adversarial training concurrently can show a better trade-off between robustness and compression rate than considering them separately. However, the ADMM framework requires two auxiliary tensors each of which has the same size as the learning parameters tensor of a CNN: this leads to a heavy memory burden for a resource-constrained environment. In this paper, we show that the joint optimization of pruning and adversarial training can be solved more memory efficiently using the proximal gradient method (PGM) without any auxiliary tensors.

Furthermore, we found that consistently providing information about the pretrained original network during adversarial training can improve the robustness of the resulting compressed network. With this intuition, we propose a novel robust pruning framework that jointly uses pruning and knowledge distillation [21] within the adversarial training procedure. Knowledge distillation is a technique to transfer the information of a network (teacher) to another network (student) by minimizing the gap between the SoftMax outputs of the two networks. In our framework, we use a pretrained original network as the teacher and provide its SoftMax output to a student network being compressed. We summarize our contribution as follows:

- We propose a new robust weight compression framework for CNNs that uses pruning and knowledge distillation jointly within the adversarial training procedure. Our method is described as an optimization problem which deals with pruning, knowledge distillation, and adversarial training concurrently.
- We show that our optimization problem can be solved with the proximal gradient method. Although the popular ADMM approach can also solve our optimization problem, it must keep two auxiliary tensors during optimization which can be a burden for a memory-constrained environment. Our proximal gradient-based approach solves the optimization problem without using any auxiliary tensor.
- In experiments, we demonstrated that the knowledge distillation in our framework improves the adversarial robustness of the compressed CNNs. In addition, our method showed a better trade-off between adversarial robustness and compression rate compared to the state-of-the-art methods [15,19,22].

2. Related Works
2.1. Adversarial Attacks

Adversarial attacks try to find allowable perturbations to change the prediction result of the target network. In the image classification domain, the set of allowable perturbations is generally defined by bounding the ℓ_p norm of perturbation to satisfy an imperceptibility constraint. Such perturbation can be generated by exploiting the information of the target network. According to the amount of this information, adversarial attacks are categorized into the black-box and white-box attacks. A black-box attack assumes a weak adversary who does not have any information about the target model. In this situation, the adversary must rely on query access for chosen input data [5] or the transferability of adversarial examples [2,3]. In a white-box setting, an adversary can access the details of the target model such as the structure, the parameters, the training dataset, etc. Based on the strong assumption, most white-box attack methods [1,4,6] exploit the first-order information of the target model to generate sophisticated perturbations. In this paper, we focus on the white-box attacks because it is important to study such attacks to implement effective defenses.

2.2. Adversarial Training

Adversarial training is a simple and intuitive learning strategy to enhance the robustness of a neural network against adversarial attacks. It generates adversarial examples using a first-order white-box attack [1,4,6] while training a neural network so that the network will correctly classify not only the training examples but also the generated examples. Adversarial training with a single-step attack such as the fast gradient sign method (FGSM) [1] is known to suffer from so-called label leaking [23] caused by the correlation between perturbation and true label. To prevent label leaking and to generate strong adversarial examples, Madry et al. [6] proposed projected gradient descent (PGD) attack-based adversarial training.

2.3. Weight Pruning

Weight pruning is a model compression technique to make unimportant learning weights to the zero value resulting in sparse weights, and thereby to remove redundant connections or components from a neural network. According to the unit of pruning, weight pruning is categorized into element-wise pruning and filter-wise pruning.

In their early stage, pruning methods focused on element-wise pruning that generates irregular sparsity patterns. To set the values of redundant weights to zero, element-wise pruning [9] measures the importance of weights usually by their absolute values. Han et al. [10] showed that this simple pruning process can be effectively combined with weight quantization and Huffman coding to achieve further compression.

Filter-wise pruning is getting more interest since it is more adequate for GPU acceleration as well as compressing convolution filters in CNNs. Some primary works prune the filters of CNN by measuring their importance by ℓ_2 norm [13] or by the number of effects on activation map [12]. Based on these works, several advanced filter pruning methods [14–17,24] have been proposed by varying the ways of measuring the importance of each filter and the composition of the pruning procedure.

2.4. Knowledge Distillation

The main idea of the knowledge distillation [21] is to transfer the knowledge of a trained teacher network to a student network by training the student network using the input and the SoftMax output of the teacher. In the early stage, it is usually applied for model compression and achieved by transferring the knowledge of an over-parameterized teacher model to a smaller student model. Bucila et al. [25] primarily used this strategy with unlabeled synthesized data to transfer the knowledge of a large ensemble teacher. Hinton et al. [21] formally defined the knowledge distillation loss with temperature and showed that distillation is effective for transferring knowledge with the original training dataset.

Distillation also can be used as a defense to adversarial examples. The defensive distillation [22] achieves adversarial robustness by applying distillation on student and teacher models which have the same structure. However, it has been shown that the defense can be easily broken [4].

Many methods have been proposed to improve the effectiveness of distillation. Distillation with boundary support samples [26] tries to improve the generalization performance of a student model by conducting the distillation with the adversarial examples near the decision boundary. Distillation with teacher assistant [27] fills the gap between student and teacher models by using intermediate models called teacher assistants.

2.5. Adversarially Robust Model Compression

To preserve the robustness of the compressed model, adversarial pruning can be applied in most cases which combines the ideas of adversarial training and pruning. Ye et al. [19] and Gui et al. [20] formulated an objective which includes both adversarial training and sparsity constraints, and showed that applying adversarial training and pruning concurrently generated better robustness than applying them separately. Xie et al. [28] used blind adversarial training [29] during adversarial pruning which generated adversarial examples dynamically during adversarial training to reduce the sensitivity to the budget of adversarial examples. Madaan et al. [30] proposed a new pruning criterion to reduce the vulnerability of latent space represented by the difference between the activation map of adversarial example and its original input.

Some works also considered the adversarial robustness of different types of compression to pruning. Bernhard et al. [31] observed that the change of adversarial robustness according to the different levels of quantization. Lin et al. [32] proposed a defensive quantization method that reduced the sensitivity to the input of the neural network. Goldblum et al. [33] used knowledge distillation to transfer the robustness of an over-parameterized model to a predefined smaller model.

3. Methods

The main objective of our suggested method is to preserve the adversarial robustness of CNNs during the pruning procedure. An adversarially robust CNN should demonstrate high generalization performance on both original and adversarial inputs. One existing approach to generate such a CNN is adversarial pruning, which is the combination of adversarial training and pruning. However, adversarial pruning alone is not enough to achieve the goal since the decision boundary of the original network is quickly collapsed during the initial stage of the pruning procedure due to the decrease of network capacity, which results in a large decrease in generalization performance on the original inputs. To solve this problem, we propose a novel robust pruning framework that combines adversarial pruning with knowledge distillation. Using the combination, we can provide information of the decision boundary of the original network consistently during adversarial pruning.

In this section, we first describe our definition of the adversary, and then formulate our entire framework as a single optimization problem showing that it can be solved efficiently by the proximal gradient method without using any auxiliary tensors.

3.1. The Attack Model

Before describing our proposed method, we first elaborate on the attack model. For the purpose, let us define the SoftMax output of a CNN with weight parameter $w \in \mathbb{R}^p$ as $f(\cdot; w)$. Let the data pairs $\{(x_i, y_i)\}_{i=1}^n$ be a training dataset. Here, $x_i \in \mathbb{R}^d$ is an input and $y_i \in \{0,1\}^k$ is the corresponding one-hot encoded true label. Then, the training procedure of CNN can be described as the following optimization problem.

$$w^* \in \underset{w \in \mathbb{R}^p}{\arg\min} \frac{1}{n} \sum_{i=1}^{n} \mathcal{L}(f(x_i; w), y_i). \tag{1}$$

Here, $\mathcal{L}$ is the cross-entropy loss [34] that indicates the gap between the SoftMax output and the true label. For the given discrete probability distribution p and q, the cross-entropy loss is defined as follows:

$$\mathcal{L}(q, p) = -\sum_{k} p_k \log q_k.$$

The objective of the adversary is changing the prediction result of the trained CNN by adding an imperceptible perturbation on the input image, which can be generated by both targeted attack and untargeted attack. In the targeted attack, the adversary generates perturbation that minimizes the cross-entropy between the SoftMax output and the predefined target label that is different from the true label. Given input data pair (x, y) and target label y_t, the targeted attack can be described as follows:

$$\min_{\delta \in \Delta} \mathcal{L}(f(x + \delta; w^*), y_t), \quad \text{such that } y_t \neq y. \tag{2}$$

Since the effectiveness of the targeted adversarial attack varies depending on the chosen target label, most robust pruning literature [19,20,30] focus on the untargeted attack for experimenting with adversarial examples, and we take the same approach. In untargeted adversarial attack, we generate adversarial examples by maximizing the cross-entropy between the SoftMax output and the true label:

$$\max_{\delta \in \Delta} \mathcal{L}(f(x + \delta; w^*), y). \tag{3}$$

Also, we suppose a white-box setting where the adversary has full knowledge about the target CNN. In this case, the adversary can solve (2) and (3) by exploiting the gradient of the target CNN.

3.2. Adversarial Pruning with Distillation

Adversarial training is a type of robust optimization procedure which can be stated by the following min-max problem:

$$w_{den}^* \in \arg\min_{w \in \mathbb{R}^p} \frac{1}{n} \sum_{i=1}^{n} \max_{\delta \in \Delta} \mathcal{L}(f(x_i + \delta; w), y_i). \tag{4}$$

To solve the inner maximization problem of (4), we consider the projected gradient descent (PGD) attack method [6] with an ℓ_∞-norm feasible set. For a given data pair (x, y), the PGD attack is defined as follows:

$$x^{t+1} = \Pi_{\mathcal{B}(x,\epsilon)}(x^t + \alpha \cdot \text{sgn}(\nabla_{x^t} \mathcal{L}(f(x^t + \delta; w), y))). \tag{5}$$

Here, $\Pi_{\mathcal{B}(x,\epsilon)}$ is a projection operation to the ℓ_∞-norm ball around x defined as $\mathcal{B}(x,\epsilon) := \{x + \delta : \|\delta\|_\infty \leq \epsilon\}$. Let us note that uniformly distributed random noise is added to x in the initial stage of the PGD attack to prevent the label leaking problem [23]. The solution of (4) which we denote as w_{den}^* is generally non-sparse since there is no sparse constraint on this optimization problem. By adding a sparse regularization term to (4), we can obtain the objective of adversarial pruning,

$$w_{spa}^* \in \arg\min_{w \in \mathbb{R}^p} \frac{1}{n} \sum_{i=1}^{n} \max_{\delta \in \Delta} \mathcal{L}(f(x_i + \delta; w), y_i) + \lambda \|w\|_0, \tag{6}$$

where $\lambda > 0$ is a hyperparameter to control the sparsity of w.

Generally, the solution of (1), denoted by w^*, is used as initial weights for solving (6). Here, our question is how we effectively preserve the accuracy of w^* on original inputs during adversarial pruning procedure. The accuracy on the original inputs is largely dropped during the adversarial pruning procedure since the one-hot encoded label y_i in (6) does not contain any information about the decision boundary of w^*.

To consistently provide the information of w^* during pruning, we combine the knowledge distillation idea with adversarial pruning. In our method, the pretrained network works as a teacher and provides SoftMax output $f^t(\cdot; w^*)$ on original input during adversarial pruning procedure. The proposed objective is formulated as follows:

$$\min_{w \in \mathbb{R}^p} \frac{1}{n} \sum_{i=1}^{n} (1 - \alpha) \mathcal{L}(f(x_i + \delta; w), y_i) + \alpha t^2 \mathcal{L}(f^t(x_i + \delta; w), f^t(x_i; w^*)) + \lambda \|w\|_0. \tag{7}$$

Here, δ is the solution of (3) and t is a distillation hyperparameter [21]. The t^2 is multiplied in front of the second term to prevent the shirking of gradient problem [21]. The second term in (7) is distillation loss which indicates the cross-entropy between SoftMax output of the currently pruned model $f(\cdot;w)$ and the teacher model $f(\cdot;w^*)$. The overall formulation of (7) can be interpreted as the linear combination of the adversarial pruning loss (6) and the distillation loss. By solving (7), we can obtain a sparse but robust solution that approximates the decision boundary of w^*. Our framework can be extended for filter pruning by replacing the third regularizer term with the number of non-zero filters as follows:

$$\min_{w\in\mathbb{R}^p} \frac{1}{n}\sum_{i=1}^{n}(1-\alpha)\mathcal{L}(f(x_i+\delta;w),y_i) + \alpha t^2 \mathcal{L}(f^t(x_i+\delta;w), f^t(x_i;w^*))$$
$$+\lambda \sum_{g=1}^{G} \mathbb{1}[\|w_g\|_2 \neq 0].$$

Here, G is the number of filters and w_g is the weight vector of gth filter.

3.3. Optimization

Most of the adversarial pruning approaches use the alternative direction method of multiplier (ADMM) method to solve the resulting optimization problem, for example, Ye et al. [19] and Gui et al. [20]. However, by construction, the ADMM requires using two additional tensors to the learning weights during optimization, which can be preventive on a resource-constrained environment with limited memory. Here, we suggest another algorithm based on the proximal gradient method to solve our proposed optimization problem (7) which does not require such auxiliary tensors. For simplicity, we denote the linear combination of two cross-entropy loss in (7) by $\mathcal{L}_{\text{APD}}$:

$$\mathcal{L}_{\text{APD}}(w) = \frac{1}{n}\sum_{i=1}^{n}(1-\alpha)\mathcal{L}(f(x_i+\delta;w),y_i) + \alpha t^2 \mathcal{L}(f^t(x_i+\delta;w), f^t(x_i+\delta;w^*)). \quad (8)$$

Here, APD stands for adversarial pruning with distillation. Then we can rewrite (7) as

$$\min_{w\in\mathbb{R}^p} \mathcal{L}_{\text{APD}}(w) + \lambda\|w\|_0. \quad (9)$$

By applying a second order Taylor approximation on w_k and Hessian approximation with $\nabla^2 \mathcal{L}_{apd}(w_k) \approx \frac{1}{\eta_k} I_{p\times p}$ for a $\eta_k > 0$ to (9), we obtain the following formulation:

$$\mathcal{L}_{\text{APD}}(w) \approx \mathcal{L}_{\text{APD}}(w_k) + \nabla \mathcal{L}_{\text{APD}}(w_k)^\top (w-w_k) + \frac{1}{2\eta_k}\|w-w_k\|^2.$$

Here, $I_{p\times p}$ indicates the identity matrix where the shape is $p\times p$. Based on this successive approximation result, the weight update can be formulated as follows:

$$w_{k+1} = \arg\min_{w\in\mathbb{R}^p} \mathcal{L}_{\text{APD}}(w_k) + \nabla \mathcal{L}_{\text{APD}}(w_k)^\top (w-w_k) + \frac{1}{2\eta_k}\|w-w_k\|^2 + \lambda\|w\|_0.$$

By removing the redundant parts of the above weight update equation, we can obtain

$$w_{k+1} = \arg\min_{w\in\mathbb{R}^p} \frac{1}{2\eta_k}\left(2\eta_k \nabla \mathcal{L}_{\text{APD}}(w_k)^\top w + \|w\|^2 - 2w^\top w_k\right) + \lambda\|w\|_0.$$

We can rewrite the above equation as follows:

$$w_{k+1} = \arg\min_{w\in\mathbb{R}^p} \frac{1}{2\eta_k}\left(\|w\|^2 - 2w^\top (w_k - \eta_k \nabla \mathcal{L}_{\text{APD}}(w_k))\right) + \lambda\|w\|_0.$$

By adding a constant $\|w_k - \eta_k \nabla \mathcal{L}_{\text{APD}}(w_k)\|^2$, we can obtain

$$w_{k+1} = \underset{w \in \mathbb{R}^p}{\arg\min} \frac{1}{2\eta_k} \left(\|w\|^2 - 2w^\top(w_k - \eta_k \nabla \mathcal{L}_{\text{APD}}(w_k)) + \|w_k - \eta_k \nabla \mathcal{L}_{\text{APD}}(w_k)\|^2 \right) + \lambda \|w\|_0.$$

Then, we can get the following equation:

$$w_{k+1} = \underset{w \in \mathbb{R}^p}{\arg\min} \frac{1}{2\eta_k} \|w - (w_k - \eta_k \nabla \mathcal{L}_{\text{APD}}(w_k))\|^2 + \lambda \|w\|_0.$$

This is exactly the form of proximal operator which is described as

$$w_{k+1} = \text{prox}_{\eta_k \lambda \|w\|_0}(w_k - \eta_k \nabla \mathcal{L}_{\text{APD}}(w_k)).$$

For each element, proximal operator with ℓ_0 regularization term can be computed as

$$(w_{k+1})_i = \begin{cases} (w_k - \eta_k \nabla \mathcal{L}_{\text{APD}}(w_k))_i, & |(w_k - \eta_k \nabla \mathcal{L}_{\text{APD}}(w_k))_i| > \sqrt{\lambda} \\ 0, & |(w_k - \eta_k \nabla \mathcal{L}_{\text{APD}}(w_k))_i| \leq \sqrt{\lambda} \end{cases}.$$

It is simply the thresholding operation which sets the updated weight parameter smaller than $\sqrt{\lambda}$ to zero. Let us note that by controlling the value of λ, we can explicitly manipulate the sparsity of network. The entire process of our method is described at Algorithm 1.

Algorithm 1: Adversarial Pruning with Distillation (APD)

Input: a distillation temperature t, a learning rate for the student η_s, a learning rate for the teacher η_t, the train dataset $\{(x_i, y_i)\}_{i=1}^n$ where $x_i \in \mathbb{R}^d$, $y_i \in \{0,1\}^k$, the ℓ_∞ bound ϵ for imperceptibility;

Initialize the student weight vector $w_s \in \mathbb{R}^p$;
Initialize the teacher weight vector $w_t \in \mathbb{R}^p$;
while w_t *not converged* **do**
    Sample a data pair (x,y) from the train dataset;
    Compute $\mathcal{L}(f(x; w_t), y)$;
    Weight Update: $w_t \leftarrow w_t - \eta_t \nabla \mathcal{L}(f(x; w_t), y)$;
end
while w_s *not converged* **do**
    Sample a data pair (x,y) from the train dataset;
    For each pixel of x, generate a uniformly random noise
    $\varepsilon = (\varepsilon_1, \cdots, \varepsilon_d) \sim \mathcal{U}(-\epsilon, \epsilon)$;
    $x_{adv} \leftarrow x + \varepsilon$;
    while x_{adv} *not converged* **do**
        Update: $x_{adv} = \Pi_{\mathcal{B}(x,\epsilon)}(x_{adv} + \alpha \cdot \text{sgn}(\nabla_{x_{adv}} \mathcal{L}(f(x_{adv}, w_s), y)))$;
    end
    Compute the teacher SoftMax output: $f^t(x; w_t)$;
    Compute the student SoftMax output: $f^t(x_{adv}; w_s)$;
    Compute $\mathcal{L}_{\text{APD}}(w_s)$ with (8);
    Update weight: $w_s = \text{prox}_{\eta_s \lambda \|\cdot\|_0}(w_s - \eta_s \nabla \mathcal{L}_{\text{APD}}(w_s))$
end
return w_s;

---

4. Experiments

To demonstrate that our method improves the adversarial robustness of the pruned network, we applied our method on three popular CNNs: LeNet [35] with the MNIST dataset, and VGG16 [36], ResNet18 [37] with the CIFAR10 dataset [38]. The MNIST dataset consists of 28×28 gray-scaled images with 60,000 trainset and 10,000 testset.

The CIFAR10 dataset has 32 × 32 color images with 50,000 trainset and 10,000 testset. As in Han et al. [10], we used the term "compression rate" to indicate the ratio of the number of zeros to the number of entire weight parameters in a CNN. We denoted the test accuracy on the original images as "original accuracy" and the test accuracy on the adversarial images as "adversarial accuracy". As in other literature [19,20,33], we consider that the robustness of the model is improved when both the original accuracy and the adversarial accuracy are improved. Otherwise, we consider a model with a higher mean value of the original and adversarial accuracy to be more robust. Given the time spent on the adversarial training for the large networks, we set the number of iterations of projected gradient descent (PGD) attack to 5 for the adversarial training of VGG16 and ResNet18. In this case, we evaluated the adversarial accuracy on both 10 iterations of PGD attack (denoted by PGD10) and 5 iterations of PGD attack (denoted by PGD5). We followed the parameters of Ye et al. [19] for the rest of the PGD attack parameters, which are strong enough to make the adversarial accuracy of the naturally trained LeNet, VGG16, and ResNet18 close to zero. The implementation of our method is available as open source (https://github.com/JEONGHYUN-LEE/APD).

4.1. The Effect of Knowledge Distillation

We compared the result of adversarial pruning (denoted by AP) (6) and our method (denoted by APD) (7) to show the effectiveness of the knowledge distillation, for both element-wise pruning and filter pruning. In this comparison, we set the value of α in (7) to 1 to maximize the effect of the SoftMax output of the teacher network. Also, we set the temperature t of the knowledge distillation to 10 for the MNIST dataset, and 100 for the CIFAR10 dataset for a similar reason.

4.1.1. Element-Wise Pruning

Generally, the element-wise pruning [9,10] can achieve higher sparsity with only a few accuracy drops compared to the filter pruning [11–15]. Therefore, we tested the element-wise pruning on the relatively high compression rates (×2, ×3, ×4) compared to the filter pruning [39]. As in Ye et al. [19], we applied the same sparsity for every convolution layer in the target neural network. For instance, if the compression rate of a given network is determined to ×2, we set the fraction of zero weights in every layer of this network equal to 0.5. With this pruning scheme, we compared the element-wise pruning result of our method (7) with adversarial pruning (6). Both methods were optimized with proximal gradient descent. With this comparison, we demonstrated how much improvement was achieved by the knowledge distillation of our method. The results on MNIST and CIFAR10 are summarized at Tables 1 and 2, respectively.

A popular small network LeNet [35] is enough to achieve a high accuracy on the MNIST dataset. Our baseline LeNet, trained by the original training process achieves the original accuracy of 99.34% and the adversarial accuracy of 0%. With LeNet, our method (APD) showed a large improvement in both original accuracy and adversarial accuracy over the adversarial pruning (AP). In the compression rate of ×2, APD improved the original accuracy by 1.01 and the adversarial accuracy by 2.28% over AP. In the relatively high compression rate of ×3 and ×4, APD achieved a larger improvement in both original accuracy and adversarial accuracy. In particular, the amount of improvement in the adversarial accuracy achieved by APD in the compression rate of ×3 and ×4 was over than 20%. Compared to the baseline performance, APD achieved the compression rate of ×4 with the adversarial accuracy of 94.25% while reducing the original accuracy by about 1%.

We also applied APD and AP to the two CNNs, VGG16 [36] and ResNet18 [37] with the CIFAR10 dataset. Achieving high adversarial robustness on the CIFAR10 dataset is more challenging since it requires a higher architectural capacity of the CNN compared to the MNIST dataset. Our baseline VGG16 achieved the original accuracy of 92.99% and the adversarial accuracy of 0%. Despite the difficulty, APD showed an improvement with VGG16 in the entire compression rates. For instance, in the compression rate of ×4, APD improved the original accuracy by 0.88% and the adversarial accuracy against both PGD5 and PGD10 by more than 1% over AP. Though ResNet18 consists of fewer parameters than VGG16 (11 M vs. 138 M), the generalization performance of Resnet18 for the CIFAR10 dataset is higher than that of VGG16. The baseline ResNet18 showed the original accuracy of 94.40% and the adversarial accuracy of 0.03%. With ResNet18, APD improved the original accuracy and adversarial accuracy against both PGD5 and PGD10 by more than 2% over AP in the entire compression rates. Based on those results, we can conclude that consistently providing the SoftMax output of the baseline CNN with the knowledge distillation improves the adversarial robustness of the element-wise pruning solution.

Table 1. Summary of element-wise pruning results of APD (ours) and AP on MNIST.

Network (Dataset)	Comp Rate	Method	Org Accuracy (%)	Adv Accuracy (%)
LeNet (MNIST)	×2	AP	97.82	92.83
		APD	**98.83**	**95.11**
	×3	AP	90.94	72.71
		APD	**98.55**	**94.51**
	×4	AP	94.45	71.63
		APD	**98.48**	**94.25**

Table 2. Summary of element-wise pruning results of APD (ours) and AP on CIFAR10.

Network (Dataset)	Comp Rate	Method	Org Acc (%)	PGD5 Adv Acc (%)	PGD10 Adv Acc (%)
VGG16 (CIFAR10)	×2	AP	81.67	49.20	40.91
		APD	**82.44**	**50.63**	**42.24**
	×3	AP	80.72	48.70	40.87
		APD	**81.77**	**50.30**	**42.31**
	×4	AP	79.69	48.77	40.97
		APD	**80.57**	**49.93**	**42.06**
ResNet18 (CIFAR10)	×2	AP	85.13	51.27	42.45
		APD	**87.56**	**54.65**	**45.55**
	×3	AP	84.67	51.79	42.64
		APD	**86.87**	**54.40**	**45.31**
	×4	AP	84.65	51.25	42.55
		APD	**86.73**	**54.23**	**45.61**

4.1.2. Filter Pruning

The filter pruning [11–15] generates the sparse patterns more adequate for GPU acceleration compared to the element-wise pruning [9,10]. However, the sparsity that the filter pruning can achieve is often lower than that of element-wise pruning [39]. Therefore, we set the smaller compression rates of ×1.5, ×2, and ×2.5 than those of the element-wise pruning. As with element-wise pruning, we set the same sparsity for each convolution layer. We compared our method (APD) with the adversarial pruning (AP) to show the effectiveness of the knowledge distillation on the filter pruning. The results on MNIST and CIFAR10 are summarized at Tables 3 and 4, respectively.

With LeNet, APD improved both original accuracy and adversarial accuracy in the entire compression rates. For instance, in the largest compression rate of ×2.5, APD improves the original accuracy by 0.36% and the adversarial accuracy by 1.44%. The improvement on the original accuracy tends to be smaller than the improvement on the adversarial accuracy since the original accuracy is already closed to that of the baseline network. APD also showed an improvement in both accuracy measures on the CIFAR10 dataset. With VGG16, APD improved the original accuracy significantly in high compression rate. For instance, in the compression rate of ×2.5, the original accuracy is improved by 5.23%. The adversarial accuracy against both PGD5 and PGD10 attacks is also improved by APD. In the compression rate of ×2.5, the adversarial accuracy increases by 2.09% against PGD5 attacks and 0.6% against PGD10 attacks. With ResNet18, APD also showed a consistent improvement on both original accuracy and adversarial accuracy in the entire compression rates. For instance, in the largest compression rate of ×2.5, APD improves the original accuracy by about 2% and adversarial accuracy by about 1% against both PGD5 and PGD10. Those results imply that the knowledge distillation in our method improves the adversarial robustness of the filter pruning solution.

Table 3. Summary of filter-wise pruning results of APD (ours) and AP on MNIST.

Network (Dataset)	Comp Rate	Method	Org Accuracy (%)	Adv Accuracy (%)
LeNet (MNIST)	×1.5	AP	98.91	95.26
		APD	**99.18**	**96.32**
	×2	AP	98.79	94.95
		APD	**99.17**	**96.21**
	×2.5	AP	98.68	94.58
		APD	**99.04**	**96.02**

Table 4. Summary of filter-wise pruning results of APD (ours) and AP on CIFAR10.

Network (Dataset)	Comp Rate	Method	Org Acc (%)	PGD5 Adv Acc (%)	PGD10 Adv Acc (%)
VGG16 (CIFAR10)	×1.5	AP	79.91	49.02	41.10
		APD	**81.01**	**50.18**	**42.62**
	×2	AP	73.69	47.11	40.56
		APD	**76.88**	**48.61**	**41.22**
	×2.5	AP	69.30	45.10	39.61
		APD	**74.53**	**47.19**	**40.21**
ResNet18 (CIFAR10)	×1.5	AP	84.57	51.42	42.35
		APD	**86.70**	**54.29**	**45.42**
	×2	AP	83.37	51.27	42.90
		APD	**85.55**	**53.32**	**45.59**
	×2.5	AP	82.09	51.65	43.21
		APD	**84.02**	**52.54**	**44.63**

4.2. The Convergence Behavior

To investigate the effect of the knowledge distillation on the convergence behavior of the adversarial pruning, we traced both original accuracy and adversarial accuracy of AP and APD on every epoch. The results on the epoch 0 indicate the initial performance of the currently pruned model where the weight parameters were initialized with the baseline model. We focused on the original accuracy of the early stage of the optimization to show how well APD preserved the original accuracy of the baseline model during the adversarial pruning.

4.2.1. Element-Wise Pruning

We traced both original accuracy and adversarial accuracy of AP and APD with the element-wise pruning scheme in the compression rate of ×2, ×3 and ×4. The results are described at Figure 1. Let us note that the adversarial accuracy is measured against PGD10. APD achieved a significant improvement in the original accuracy in the early stage of optimization with LeNet, VGG16, and ResNet18. With LeNet, the original accuracy of AP fell to lower than 20% on the first epoch whereas the original accuracy of APD was maintained above 90% across the entire optimization process. With VGG16, the original accuracy of both AP and APD was dropped on the first epoch. However, the amount of decrease in the original accuracy on the first epoch of APD was less than that of AP. For instance, in the compression rate of ×4, the original accuracy on the first epoch of APD was higher than that of AP by about 20%. Moreover, with LeNet and VGG16, APD improved the convergence behavior of both original accuracy and adversarial accuracy compared to AP. For instance, in the compression rate of ×3 with VGG16, APD only required 40 epochs for the average value of the original accuracy and the adversarial accuracy to reach 61.00% (the maximum average value achieved by AP), whereas AP required 46 epochs to achieve that. With ResNet18, APD reduced the drop of original accuracy on the first epoch by about 10% across the entire compression rates though the improvement in the convergence behavior of both original accuracy and adversarial accuracy is smaller than that of other networks.

4.2.2. Filter Pruning

We also traced both original accuracy and adversarial accuracy of AP and APD with the filter pruning scheme in the compression rate of ×1.5, ×2, and ×2.5. The results are described at Figure 2. APD improved the overall convergence behavior of the filter pruning. With LeNet, APD reduced the drop of the original accuracy on the first epoch about 5%. With VGG16, the improvement in the first epoch was more significant. For instance, in the compression rate of ×1.5, APD reduced the drop of the original accuracy on the first epoch by about 20%. Mitigating the drop of original accuracy in the first epoch led to an improvement in the overall convergence behavior. For instance, in the compression rate of ×1.5 with LeNet, APD required 49 epochs for the average value of the original accuracy and the adversarial accuracy to reach 96.63% (the maximum average value achieved by AP), whereas AP required 86 epochs to achieve that. In the compression rate ×1.5 with VGG16, APD required 33 epochs for the average value of both accuracies to reach 54.46% (the maximum average value achieved by AP), whereas AP required 59 epochs to achieve that. With ResNet18, APD also reduced the drop of original accuracy in the initial stage of pruning but the amount of improvement decreased in the high compression rate.

4.3. Comparison with the State-of-the-Art Methods

To show the relative benefit of our method (denoted as APD) compared to other state-of-the-art methods, we also compared APD to Defensive Distillation [22] (denoted as DD), Filter Pruning via Geometric Median [15] (denoted as FPGM), and Ye et al. [19]. The results are summarized at Table 5.

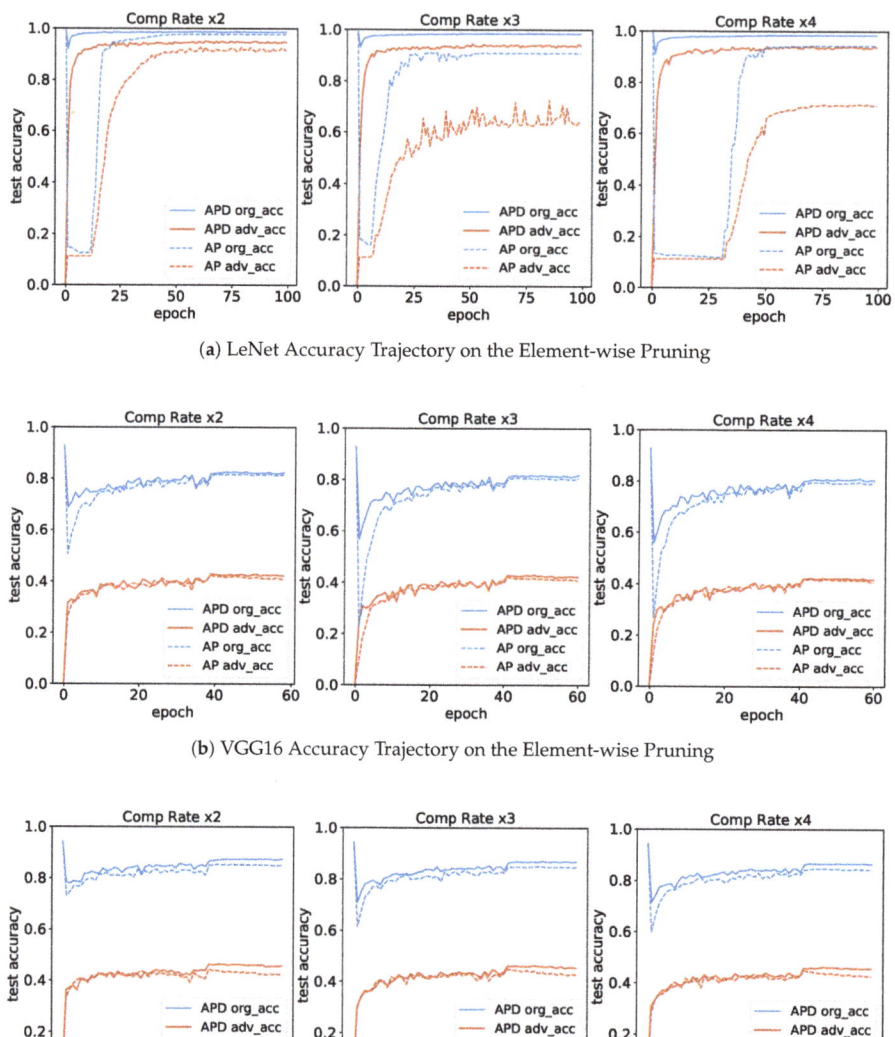

Figure 1. The original accuracy and the adversarial accuracy of AP and APD (ours) with respect to the epoch of the element-wise pruning procedure for (**a**) LeNet, (**b**) VGG16, and (**c**) ResNet18. The left of each row is the result in the compression rate of ×2, the middle of each row is the result in the compression rate of ×3, and the right side of each row is the result in compression rate of ×4. The blue line means the original accuracy and the red line indicates the adversarial accuracy. The solid line is the result of APD and the dashed line is the result of AP.

Table 5. Summary of filter-wise pruning results of APD (ours) and other state-of-the-art methods.

Network (Dataset)	Type	Method	Comp Rate	Org Acc (%)	Adv Acc (%)
VGG16 (CIFAR10)	Pruning	FPGM	×1.3	**93.13**	16.17
	Pruning + Defense	APD	×**1.5**	81.01	**42.62**
LeNet (MNIST)	Defense	DD	×1	93.15	86.57
	Pruning + Defense	APD	×**2**	**99.17**	**96.21**
LeNet (MNIST)	Pruning + Defense	Ye et al.	×2	99.01	95.44
	Pruning + Defense	APD	×2	**99.17**	**96.21**
	Pruning + Defense	Ye et al.	×4	98.87	94.77
	Pruning + Defense	APD	×4	**98.88**	**94.90**
	Pruning + Defense	Ye et al.	×8	98.07	89.95
	Pruning + Defense	APD	×8	**98.08**	**91.06**
ResNet18 (CIFAR10)	Pruning + Defense	Ye et al.	×2	81.83	48.00
	Pruning + Defense	APD	×2	**82.09**	**48.03**

DD is a well-known defense strategy that generates a robust model by using knowledge distillation. It trains a teacher model with a high temperature value in a modified SoftMax output and then applies knowledge distillation to a student model whose architecture is the same as that of the teacher model. We compared the original accuracy and the adversarial accuracy of APD and DD with LeNet in the compression rate of ×2. For DD, we set the temperature t as 40 and the number of epochs as 100. In comparison, APD showed about 6% higher original accuracy and 10% higher adversarial accuracy than DD.

FPGM is a SOTA filter pruning method that effectively prunes the redundant filters by measuring the Geometric Median [40] of each filter. To show that the pruning method only is not enough to generate sparse but robust solutions, we compared our pruned VGG16 with the compression rate of ×1.5 to FPGM's pruned VGG16 with the compression rate of ×1.3. APD showed 26.45% higher adversarial accuracy and 12.12% lower original accuracy compared to FPGM. The mean value of the original and the adversarial accuracy of APD is 61.82 and that of FPGM is 54.65. This result demonstrates that the model generated by the pruning method alone is vulnerable to adversarial attack.

Ye et al. is a SOTA robust pruning method. To solve the adversarial pruning (6) problem using alternative direction method of multipliers (ADMM), the method introduced two additional tensors for auxiliary parameters and Lagrangian multipliers. The size of those two tensors is exactly the same as the size of the weight parameters and therefore, it requires two times more memory than the memory required to store the weight parameters during the optimization procedure. On the other hand, APD solves our optimization problem (7) with the proximal gradient descent, which does not require any auxiliary tensor. We compared the result of APD and Ye et al with LeNet and ResNet18. VGG16 was excluded in this comparison since the exact values of the original accuracy and the adversarial accuracy with VGG16 are not available in the original paper of Ye et al. We set the compression rates to ×2, ×4, and ×8 for LeNet, and ×2 for ResNet18. With LeNet, APD slightly improved both original accuracy and adversarial accuracy over Ye et al. in entire compression rates. With ResNet18, APD improved the original accuracy by 0.26% and the adversarial accuracy by 0.03% compared to Ye et al. The adversarial robustness of APD appears to be similar to that of Ye et al.; however, APD requires far less memory that Ye et al. and therefore will be more suitable for generating robust models in memory-constrained environments as we discuss in the next section.

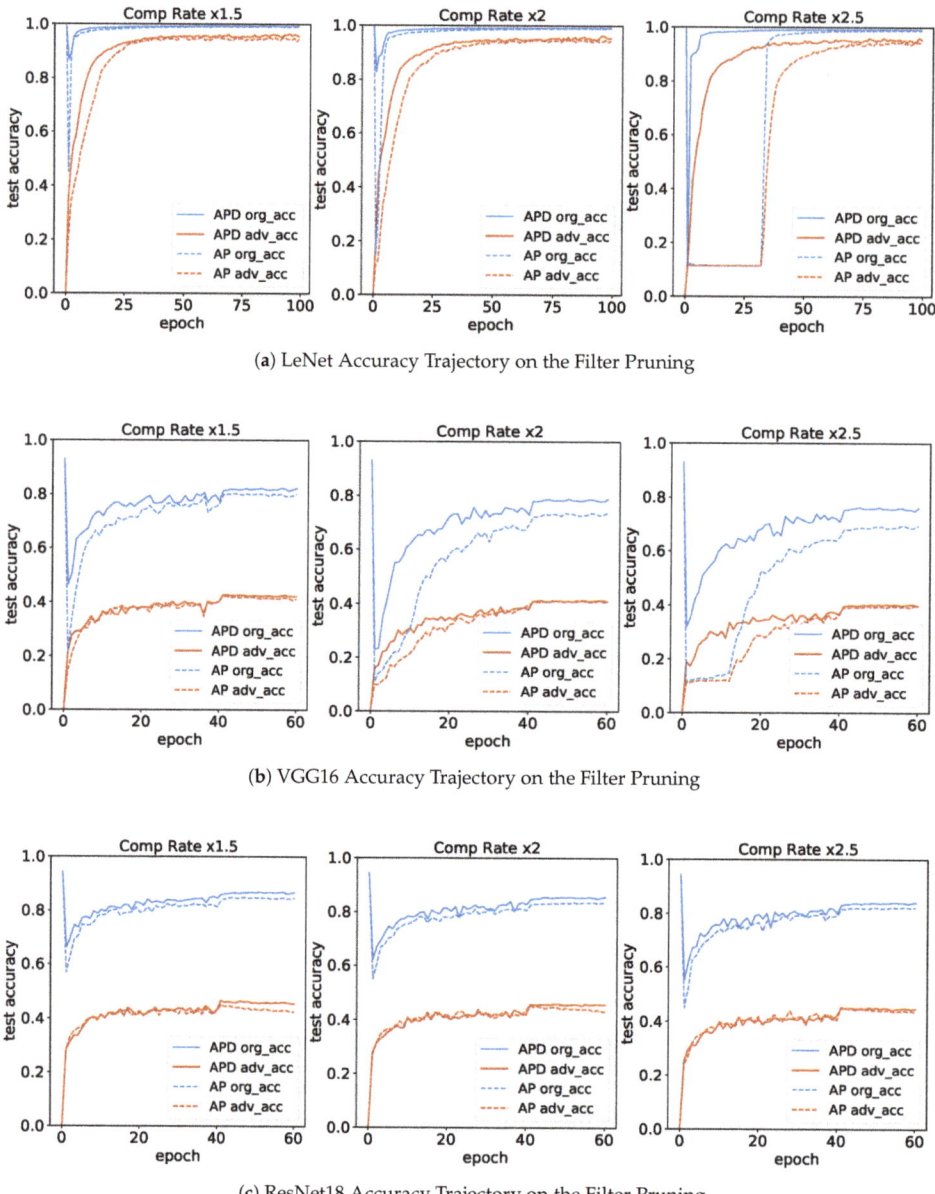

Figure 2. The original accuracy and the adversarial accuracy of AP and APD (ours) with respect to the epoch of the filter pruning procedure for (**a**) LeNet, (**b**) VGG16, and (**c**) ResNet18. The left of each row is the result in the compression rate of ×1.5, the middle of each row is the result in the compression rate of ×2, and the right side of each row is the result in compression rate of ×2.5. The blue line means the original accuracy and the red line indicates the adversarial accuracy. The solid line is the result of APD and the dashed line is the result of AP.

4.4. Computational and Space Complexity

To show the computational and memory efficiency of APD in comparison to other methods, here we provide a short analysis without big O notations. The most dominant part of the training procedure of CNNs in terms of computational complexity is the forward and backward operations. For a given network and input data, we denoted the amount of computation for a forward as F and the amount of computation for a backward as B. In addition, we supposed that the number of iterations for training given network is I_T and the number of iterations for generating adversarial example as I_A. Then, the computational complexity of most of the pruning methods such as FPGM is $I_T \times (F + B)$. DD contains additional forward operations for generating the SoftMax output of the teacher network resulting in $I_T \times (2F + B)$. A relatively large increase of computational complexity for APD and Ye et al. is inevitable since the adversarial training requires an iterative adversarial attack for every iteration. Considering this, the computational complexity of Ye et al. is $I_T \times (F + B + I_A \times F)$, where APD requires $I_T \times (2F + B + I_A \times F)$ since it contains both adversarial training and knowledge distillation.

On the other hand, the most dominant part of the space complexity of the training procedure is the number of learning parameters. To describe the space complexity, let us denote the number of weights of the given network as P. FPGM requires no additional parameter and therefore its complexity is P. The space complexity of DD and APD are $2P$ since they require a teacher and a student network to perform knowledge distillation. Ye et al. requires two additional parameters for ADMM and a large $3P$ space complexity in result. Compared to Ye et al., the analysis shows that APD requires far less memory with the cost of an additional forward step.

4.5. Effectiveness of Knowledge Distillation on Other Attack Methods

To test our method on the other adversarial attacks, we evaluated the adversarial accuracy of our PGD-based trained LeNet (MNIST) against Fast Gradient Sign Method (FGSM) attack [1] and Carlini–Wagner (CW) ℓ_2 attack [4]. For FGSM attack, we set the attack radius ϵ to 0.3. For CW attack, we used ℓ_2 bounded perturbation and set the maximum iterations to 1000. The baseline LeNet showed the original accuracy of 99.41% and the adversarial accuracy of 1.08% against FGSM and 0.48% against CW. The results are described in Table 6. The APD showed higher original accuracy and adversarial accuracy against both FGSM and CW ℓ_2 attacks compared to AP in the entire compression rates. In particular, the improvement on the adversarial accuracy against CW ℓ_2 attack is significant. Those results imply that our PGD-based approach is also effective on the other attack methods.

Table 6. Summary of AP and APD results against FGSM and CW ℓ_2 attacks on the MNIST dataset.

Network (Dataset)	CompRate	Method	Org Acc (%)	FGSM Adv Acc (%)	CW ℓ_2 Adv Acc (%)
LeNet (MNIST)	×1.5	AP	98.91	97.62	70.23
		APD	**99.18**	**98.27**	**91.01**
	×2	AP	98.79	97.48	69.77
		APD	**99.17**	**98.28**	**88.19**
	×2.5	AP	98.68	97.38	77.11
		APD	**99.04**	**98.15**	**93.30**

5. Conclusions

The adversarial robustness of the compressed CNNs is essential for deploying them to the real-world embedded systems. In this paper, we proposed a robust model compression framework for CNNs. Our framework used the knowledge distillation to improve the result of the existing adversarial pruning approach. In several experiments, our framework showed a significant improvement in the trade-off between the compression rate and the adversarial robustness on the two datasets, MNIST and CIFAR10. We found that the amount of improvement of our framework tends to decrease in the high compression rate. We expect that this phenomenon is due to the large gap in the architectural capacity between the teacher network and the student network. We hope that this phenomenon will be mitigated through future works.

Author Contributions: conceptualization, J.L. and S.L.; methodology, J.L. and S.L.; validation, J.L.; writing—original draft preparation, J.L.; writing—review and editing, S.L.; supervision, S.L. All authors have read and agreed to the published version of the manuscript.

Funding: This research was supported by Basic Science Research Program through the National Research Foundation of Korea (NRF) funded by the Ministry of Education (2018R1D1A1B07051383), and by the MSIT (Ministry of Science and ICT), Korea, under the ITRC(Information Technology Research Center) support program (IITP-2020-0-01749) supervised by the IITP (Institute of Information & Communications Technology Planning & Evaluation).

Data Availability Statement: The data presented in this study are openly available: MNIST (http://yann.lecun.com/exdb/mnist/) and CIFAR10 (https://www.cs.toronto.edu/~kriz/cifar.html).

Conflicts of Interest: The authors declare no conflict of interest.

References

1. Goodfellow, I.J.; Shlens, J.; Szegedy, C. Explaining and Harnessing Adversarial Examples. *arXiv* **2015**, arXiv:1412.6572.
2. Papernot, N.; McDaniel, P.; Goodfellow, I. *Transferability in Machine Learning: From Phenomena to Black-Box Attacks Using Adversarial Samples*; Technical Report; Pennsylvania State University: State College, PA, USA, 2016.
3. Papernot, N.; McDaniel, P.; Goodfellow, I.; Jha, S.; Celik, Z.B.; Swami, A. Practical Black-Box Attacks against Machine Learning. In Proceedings of the Asia Conference on Computer and Communications Security, New York, NY, USA, 2–6 April 2017.
4. Carlini, N.; Wagner, D. Towards Evaluating the Robustness of Neural Networks. In Proceedings of the 2017 IEEE Symposium on Security and Privacy (SP), San Jose, CA, USA, 22–26 May 2017.
5. Nitin Bhagoji, A.; He, W.; Li, B.; Song, D. Practical Black-box Attacks on Deep Neural Networks using Efficient Query Mechanisms. In *European Conference on Computer Vision*; Springer: Berlin/Heidelberg, Germany, 2018.
6. Madry, A.; Makelov, A.; Schmidt, L.; Tsipras, D.; Vladu, A. Towards Deep Learning Models Resistant to Adversarial Attacks. *arXiv* **2018**, arXiv:1706.06083.
7. Laidlaw, C.; Feizi, S. Functional Adversarial Attacks. In *Advances in Neural Information Processing Systems*; Curran Associates Inc.: Vancouver, BC, Canada, 2019.
8. Huang, Z.; Zhang, T. Black-Box Adversarial Attack with Transferable Model-based Embedding. *arXiv* **2020**, arXiv:1911.07140.
9. Han, S.; Pool, J.; Tran, J.; Dally, W.J. Learning both Weights and Connections for Efficient Neural Networks. *Adv. Neural Inf. Process. Syst.* **2015**, *28*, 1135–1143.
10. Han, S.; Mao, H.; Dally, W.J. Deep Compression: Compressing Deep Neural Networks with Pruning, Trained Quantization and Huffman Coding. *arXiv* **2016**, arXiv:1510.00149.
11. Wen, W.; Wu, C.; Wang, Y.; Chen, Y.; Li, H. Learning Structured Sparsity in Deep Neural Networks. *Adv. Neural Inf. Process. Syst.* **2016**, *29*, 2074–2082.
12. He, Y.; Zhang, X.; Sun, J. Channel Pruning for Accelerating Very Deep Neural Networks. In Proceedings of the IEEE International Conference on Computer Vision, Venice, Italy, 22–29 Ocotber 2017.
13. Li, H.; Kadav, A.; Durdanovic, I.; Samet, H.; Graf, H.P. Pruning Filters for Efficient ConvNets. *arXiv* **2017**, arXiv:1608.08710.
14. He, Y.; Kang, G.; Dong, X.; Fu, Y.; Yang, Y. Soft Filter Pruning for Accelerating Deep Convolutional Neural Networks. *arXiv* **2018**, arXiv:1808.06866.
15. He, Y.; Liu, P.; Wang, Z.; Hu, Z.; Yang, Y. Filter Pruning via Geometric Median for Deep Convolutional Neural Networks Acceleration. In Proceedings of the IEEE Conference on Computer Vision and Pattern Recognition, Long Beach, CA, USA, 16–20 June 2019.
16. Lin, M.; Ji, R.; Wang, Y.; Zhang, Y.; Zhang, B.; Tian, Y.; Shao, L. HRank: Filter Pruning using High-Rank Feature Map. In Proceedings of the IEEE/CVF Conference on Computer Vision and Pattern Recognition (CVPR), Seattle, WA, USA, 14–19 June 2020.
17. Chin, T.W.; Ding, R.; Zhang, C.; Marculescu, D. Towards Efficient Model Compression via Learned Global Ranking. In Proceedings of the IEEE/CVF Conference on Computer Vision and Pattern Recognition (CVPR), Seattle, WA, USA, 14–19 June 2020.
18. Wang, L.; Ding, G.W.; Huang, R.; Cao, Y.; Lui, Y.C. Adversarial Robustness of Pruned Neural Networks. In *ICLR Workshop Submission*; OpenReview.net: Vancouver, BC, Canada, 2018.

19. Ye, S.; Lin, X.; Xu, K.; Liu, S.; Cheng, H.; Lambrechts, J.H.; Zhang, H.; Zhou, A.; Ma, K.; Wang, Y. Adversarial Robustness vs. Model Compression, or Both? In Proceedings of the IEEE/CVF International Conference on Computer Vision (ICCV), Seoul, Korea, 27–28 October 2019; pp. 111–120.
20. Gui, S.; Wang, H.; Yu, C.; Yang, H.; Wang, Z.; Liu, J. Model Compression with Adversarial Robustness: A Unified Optimization Framework. In *Advances in Neural Information Processing Systems*; Curran Associates Inc.: Vancouver, BC, Canada, 2019.
21. Hinton, G.; Vinyals, O.; Dean, J. Distilling the Knowledge in a Neural Network. *arXiv* **2014**, arXiv:1503.02531.
22. Papernot, N.; McDaniel, P.; Wu, X.; Jha, S.; Swami, A. Distillation as a Defense to Adversarial Perturbations against Deep Neural Networks. In Proceedings of the IEEE Symposium on Security and Privacy (SP), San Jose, CA, USA, 23–25 May 2016.
23. Kurakin, A.; Goodfellow, I.; Bengio, S. Adversarial Machine Learning at Scale. *arXiv* **2017**, arXiv:1611.01236.
24. Lee, N.; Ajanthan, T.; Torr, P.H.S. SNIP: Single-shot Network Pruning based on Connection Sensitivity. *arXiv* **2019**, arXiv:1810.02340.
25. Bucila, C.; Caruana, R.; Niculescu-Mizil, A. Model compression. In Proceedings of the 12th ACM SIGKDD International Conference on Knowledge Discovery and Data Mining, Philadelphia, PA, USA, 20–23 August 2006.
26. Heo, B.; Lee, M.; Yun, S.; Choi, J.Y. Knowledge Distillation with Adversarial Samples Supporting Decision Boundary. *Proc. Aaai Conf. Artif. Intell.* **2019**, *33*, 3771–3778. [CrossRef]
27. Mirzadeh, S.I.; Farajtabar, M.; Li, A.; Levine, N.; Matsukawa, A.; Ghasemzadeh, H. Improved Knowledge Distillation via Teacher Assistant. *Proc. Aaai Conf. Artif. Intell.* **2020**, *34*, 5191–5198. [CrossRef]
28. Xie, H.; Qian, L.; Xiang, X.; Liu, N. Blind Adversarial Pruning: Balance Accuracy, Efficiency and Robustness. *arXiv* **2020**; arXiv:2004.05914.
29. Xie, H.; Xiang, X.; Liu, N.; Dong, B. Blind Adversarial Training: Balance Accuracy and Robustness. *arXiv* **2020**; arXiv:2004.05914.
30. Madaan, D.; Shin, J.; Hwang, S.J. Adversarial Neural Pruning with Latent Vulnerability Suppression. *arXiv* **2020**, arXiv:1908.04355.
31. Bernhard, R.; Moellic, P.A.; Dutertre, J.M. Impact of Low-bitwidth Quantization on the Adversarial Robustness for Embedded Neural Networks. In Proceedings of the International Conference on Cyberworlds (CW), Kyoto, Japan, 2–4 Ocotber 2019.
32. Lin, J.; Gan, C.; Han, S. Defensive Quantization: When Efficiency Meets Robustness. *arXiv* **2019**, arXiv:1904.08444.
33. Goldblum, M.; Fowl, L.; Feizi, S.; Goldstein, T. Adversarially Robust Distillation. *Proc. Aaai Conf. Artif. Intell.* **2020**, *34*, 3996–4003.
34. Cox, D. The Regression Analysis of Binary Sequences. *J. R. Stat. Soc. Ser. (Methodological)* **1958**, *20*, 1958. [CrossRef]
35. Lecun, Y.; Bottou, L.; Bengio, Y.; Haffner, P. Gradient-based learning applied to document recognition. *Proc. IEEE* **1998**, *86*, 2278–2324. [CrossRef]
36. Simonyan, K.; Zisserman, A. Very Deep Convolutional Networks for Large-Scale Image Recognition. *arXiv* **2015**, arXiv:1409.1556.
37. He, K.; Zhang, X.; Ren, S.; Sun, J. Deep Residual Learning for Image Recognition. In Proceedings of the IEEE Conference on Computer Vision and Pattern Recognition, Las Vegas, NV, USA, 27–30 June 2016; pp. 770–778.
38. Krizhevsky, A. *Learning Multiple Layers of Features from Tiny Images*; Technical Report, University of Toronto, Toronto, ON, Canada, 2009.
39. Renda, A.; Frankle, J.; Carbin, M. Comparing Rewinding and Fine-tuning in Neural Network Pruning. *arXiv* **2020**, arXiv:2003.02389.
40. Fletcher, P.T.; Venkatasubramanian, S.; Joshi, S. Robust statistics on Riemannian manifolds via the geometric median. In Proceedings of the 2008 IEEE Conference on Computer Vision and Pattern Recognition, Anchorage, AK, USA, 23–28 June 2008; pp. 1–8.

Article

Model Checking Resiliency and Sustainability of In-Vehicle Network for Real-Time Authenticity

Jin Hyun Kim [1,*], Hyo Jin Jo [2,*] and Insup Lee [3]

1 Department of Information and Communication, Gyeongsang National University, Jinju 52828, Korea
2 School of Software, Soongsil University, Seoul 06978, Korea
3 Department of Computer and Information Science, University of Pennsylvania, Philadelphia, PA 19104, USA; lee@cis.upenn.edu
* Correspondence: jin.kim@gnu.ac.kr (J.H.K.); hyojin.jo@ssu.ac.kr (H.J.J.); Tel.: +82-10-9253-1935 (J.H.K.); +82-10-4138-7957 (H.J.J.)

Featured Application: MAuth-CAN is a new CAN authentication mechanism, and the proposed CAN model and verification techniques are useful to analyze timing properties of CAN applications.

Abstract: The Controller Area Network (CAN) is the most common network system in automotive systems. However, the standardized design of a CAN protocol does not consider security issues, so it is vulnerable to various security attacks from internal and external electronic devices. Recently, in-vehicle network is often connected to external network systems, including the Internet, and can result in an unwarranted third-party application becoming an attack point. Message Authentication CAN (MAuth-CAN) is a new centralized authentication for CAN system, where two dual-CAN controllers are utilized to process message authentication. MAuth-CAN is designed to provide an authentication mechanism as well as provide resilience to a message flooding attack and sustainably protect against a bus-off attack. This paper presents formal techniques to guarantee critical timing properties of MAuth-CAN, based on model checking, which can be also used for safety certificates of vehicle components, such as ISO 26262. Using model checking, we prove sufficient conditions that MAuth-CAN is resilient and sustainable against message flooding and bus-off attacks and provide two formal models of MAuth-CAN in timed automata that are applicable for formal analysis of other applications running on CAN bus. In addition, we discuss that the results of model checking of those properties are consistent with the experiment results of MAuth-CAN implementation.

Keywords: controller area network bus; authentication; authenticity; resiliency; sustainability; formal verification; model checking; in-vehicle network

Citation: Kim, J.H.; Jo, H.J.; Lee, I. Model Checking Resiliency and Sustainability of In-Vehicle Network for Real-Time Authenticity. *Appl. Sci.* **2021**, *11*, 1068. https://doi.org/10.3390/app11031068

Academic Editor: Kyungtae Kang
Received: 13 December 2020
Accepted: 6 January 2021
Published: 25 January 2021

Publisher's Note: MDPI stays neutral with regard to jurisdictional claims in published maps and institutional affiliations.

Copyright: © 2021 by the authors. Licensee MDPI, Basel, Switzerland. This article is an open access article distributed under the terms and conditions of the Creative Commons Attribution (CC BY) license (https://creativecommons.org/licenses/by/4.0/).

1. Introduction

Advanced digital control technology provides more convenience, safety, and predictability to automotive systems. Recently, many vehicles would not only make use of local sensors, but also cooperate with other vehicles and infrastructures, such as the Intelligent Transport System (ITS). For instance, Right-turn Collision Caution (RtCC) cooperating with infrastructures can alert drivers in a risky situation hidden when they would make right turn. ITS monitors the situation about oncoming vehicles and pedestrians around intersections or a corner with poor visibility from drivers where a vehicle would make a right turn. It cooperates with the vehicle via road-to-vehicle communication so the information on potential approaching risk is conveyed by vehicle-to-vehicle communication with audio and visual alerts to warn the driver, and when necessary, the driver is alerted about the approach risk. The infrastructure uses a dedicated ITS frequency of 760 MHz for road-to-vehicle and vehicle-to-vehicle communication to gather information that cannot be obtained by vehicle sensors. In addition, various features, such as Communication Radar Cruise Control, Red Right Caution, and Emergency Vehicle Notification using network communication also helps drivers be more predictive against approaching risky situations so that their driving is safe and predictable.

However, the vehicle connecting to open networks can be vulnerable to security attacks. For instance, many studies such as [1–6] have shown that the adversary is able to easily access an in-vehicle network from the outside and control vehicles. Once an adversary compromises an ECU, it disguises itself as a normal node, breaches to other ECUs, and controls and disrupts normal driving function. In addition, DoS (Denial of Service) is also one of the most common attacks that exhausts data processing and communication resources.

To prevent the masquerade attack to a vehicle network, the most popular defense technologies are intrusion detection systems (IDS) and authentication systems. Most proposed IDS techniques are not, however, fast enough to protect the attack, i.e., the adversary can compromise the vehicle system before IDS detects the attack [7–13]. In order to address these issues, many authentication protocols have been studied, such as [14–20]. These works can be classified into two categories: authentication using group keys [14–17] or authentication using pairwise keys [18–20]. In case that CAN uses a group key for message authentication, the group key could be exploited if any node using the group key is compromised. In case of authentication using pairwise keys, CAN bus can be overflowed by authentication tags (e.g., message authentication code) if CAN bus uses a basic pairwise key-based authentication method where every destination node requires a unique authentication tag for verification of a CAN message. Thus, the work [18–20] adopts a centralized node-based authentication to deal with the overflow issue.

However, this centralized node-based authentication has two problems. First, the authentication by a centralized node can be delayed by DoS attack on the centralized node. Second, in case of the centralized authentication, the authenticator could miss a message if it is too slow to process every message. Thus, it should be guaranteed that the authentication is complete on time no matter how often the adversary sends an attack message.

To address the above problems, Jo et al. have proposed a new authentication protocol, named MAuth-CAN (Message Authentication-CAN), in [21]. MAuth-CAN uses an ECU node dedicated to authenticating each message over the CAN bus by using pairwise keys. For sharing the authentication result with other ECUs, the authenticator uses an authentication-fail error (AFR) message. The authentication fail report (i.e., AFR message) is transmitted and gives alerts to other nodes only when a message is authenticated. This minimizes the communication overload caused by a centralized authentication because the authentication fail report is transmitted only when a message cannot pass authentication. In addition, Jo et al. addresses Bus-off Attacks (BoAs) by introducing their centralized message authentication to dual-CAN controllers. Under the adversary's BoA to the authenticator, the AFR message from the authenticator can also be destroyed by the adversary, resulting in consecutive transmission errors. If the transmission error count of the authenticator steps over a threshold, it is enforced to leave CAN bus for a while and reset to recover the connection to CAN bus. Jo et al. adopts dual-CAN controllers for the authenticator to be more sustainable under BoA. Jo et al. [21] also showed that (1) MAuth-CAN is robust against the masquerade attack and BoA, (2) it requires approximately 46% less CAN bandwidth than a comparable protocol [19], and (3) it does not need to modify the current CAN controller to apply the CAN protocol.

However, they have not provided the proof of timing-related properties of MAuth-CAN that can be used for security proof and evidence for practical use of real applications. For instance, MAuth-CAN should prove that no adversary message is accepted by any node while authentication is in processing under DoS attack. It is related to a timeout for AFR, which delays message communication. Thus, it is necessary to check if such a timeout is bounded to check if the authentication delay meets the maximum acceptance communication delay.

In this paper, we show that the authentication of MAuth-CAN is resilient enough to prevent a masquerade attack for the given timing constraints and is sustainable under a DoS attack. In addition, we prove that the timeout for authentication can be bounded with respect to the message transmission time. In this paper, we apply formal methods of model checking to prove the timing properties of MAuth-CAN. We build formal models of CAN and MAuth-CAN using timed automata and perform model-checking to verify the critical timing properties of MAuth-CAN using UPPAAL SMC and UPPAAL MC. We present two formal models of CAN and MAuth-CAN. The first model abstracts MAuth-CAN by a producer-consumer model in terms of authenticator and attacker, so that it is proved that the authenticator in terms of a consumer addresses all attack messages from the attacker in terms of a producer. The second model details CAN in the level of MAC frame of the data link layer, so that the model of MAuth-CAN is shown to be valid in the data-link layer of CAN networking.

This paper presents sufficient conditions to ensure:

- The centralized authentication of MAuth-CAN never fails to make AFR messages reach individual ECUs within a specific bounded time,
- The authentication of MAuth-CAN can never be a victim of BoA.

The above conditions are relevant to (1) the size of reception queue of authenticator's CAN controller, (2) the relation between authentication time and CAN bus transmission time, and (3) the number of CAN controllers of the authenticator.

This paper presents the following three contributions:

- In terms of MAuth-CAN security, it shows that MAuth-CAN is resilient and sustainable against a message flooding attack and bus-off attack under the specific conditions this paper provides;
- It presents a usage of formal methods to obtain certificates of safety and security standards and regulations, such as ISO (International Organization for Standardization) 26262;
- It presents new formal models of CAN bus at the level of MAC (Media Access Control) of the data link layer that can be useful for verification of properties of other applications running on CAN bus.

The rest of the paper is organized as follows: Section 2 discusses the related work. Section 3 presents the background theory of this work. Section 4 overviews MAuth-CAN, a centralized CAN authentication, two attack scenarios i.e., masquerade attack and BoA attack, and MAuth-CAN's countermeasure to those attacks. Section 5 shows formal proof of our proposed sufficient conditions for MAuth-CAN resiliency to a masquerade attack and sustainability to BoA attack, using symbolic and statistical model checking techniques. Section 6 presents more results from the implementation of MAuth-CAN. In Section 7, we conclude this paper with the potential future work.

2. Related Work

In 2010, Koscher et al. were the first to demonstrate attacks on in-vehicle network using a real vehicle [1]. They introduced the CARSHARK tool, which makes it easy for an adversary to analyze and inject attack packets on in-vehicle network, i.e., CAN bus. After the first vehicle attack, many studies included new attack surfaces on an in-vehicle network [2–6]. To deal with these cyber-attacks on in-vehicle network, intrusion detection systems [7–13] and message authentication protocols [5,14–21] were studied.

In the work of [7–10], the transmission frequencies or sequences of CAN packets were used to detect the CAN traffic abnormality caused by in-vehicle network attacks. Recently, deep neural network (DNN) model-based intrusion detection systems that take transmission frequencies or sequences of CAN packets as input values have been proposed in [11,12]. However, these studies [7–12] cannot detect masquerade attacks by a compromised ECU because the compromised node can mimic the transmission frequencies or sequences of CAN packets to bypass intrusion detection algorithms.

To handle the masquerade attacks, Cho et al. proposed an ECU's clock-based intrusion detection system [13]. In this study, a clock skew for each ECU is profiled as a hardware fingerprint, which is unique for every ECU, and this inimitable value is used to identify a masquerading ECU. However, this study cannot be used to deal with masquerade attacks using aperiodic CAN messages generated from aperiodic vehicle operations, such as auto-parking, lane keeping aid (LKA), and adaptive cruise control (ACC) functions. Furthermore, this clock-based intrusion detection can be defeated by the clock emulation attack proposed in [22].

To address the limitations of existing intrusion detection systems, message authentication protocols for in-vehicle network have been designed. In general, message authentication protocols can be divided into two categories: a group key-based authentication [14–17] and a central node-based authentication [18–21]. In the group key-based authentication studies [14–17], one group key shared by all ECUs is used to generate authentication tags such as message authentication code. However, these studies cannot also handle masquerade attacks because one group key could be accessed by a compromised node. In light of this, centralized node-based authentication studies have been presented in [18–21] for handling masquerade attacks by compromised ECUs. Since the centralized node-based authentication does not share one group key with all ECUs, a compromised ECU cannot access the authentication keys stored in other ECUs. However, the methods [18,19] cannot be applied into legacy vehicles because the CAN-controller must be modified to include new functions that do not follow the CAN-standard or incurs network overhead that exceeds the maximum capacity of the CAN bus. Furthermore, the protocol [20] also has limitation that several bytes of a CAN message is not included in the authentication value generation process.

To handle these issues of authentication protocols, Jo et al. presented an authentication report-based message authentication [21]. This protocol does not incur network overhead nor require CAN controller modification, but there is a message authentication delay caused by an authentication report message. Even though the work of [21] evaluated the authentication delay by using CAN development boards, there is no formal analysis about the delay which could affect real-time operations of vehicles. Thus, this paper puts the authentication delay of [21] into formal analysis using UPPAAL SMC and UPPAAL MC.

In addition, we did the several Arduino-based authentication tests, which are related to what-if analysis and robustness checking defined in [23], by measuring the authentication delay of [21] in the worst case scenarios to show that the authentication delay is bounded within a certain amount of time even when there are DoS attacks such as message flooding and bus-off attacks on CAN.

3. Preliminaries

In this section, we give the overall of our approach and overview our formal techniques, model checking, UPPAAL and CAN communication, prior to MAuth-CAN in the following section.

3.1. Our Approach

The CAN authentication in MAuth-CAN meets two goals: (1) No receiver can open any message that does not go through a centralized authentication of MAuth-CAN, (2) The CAN controller for message authentication is never enforced to leave CAN bus by consecutive and numerous transmission errors by intention.

In this paper, we show why MAuth-CAN never fails to meet the above goals. To simplify the above goals, we present sufficient conditions in theorems, which should be satisfied to meet the goals (Section 4.4, and then prove them by model checking (Section 5)). We use a high-level model of MAuth-CAN, where the reaction of the authenticator to the attack message is highlighted (Section 5.1). Then, using model checking, we prove that the authenticator of MAuth-CAN passes no attack message without verification even under even consecutive attacks if the sufficient conditions in Theorem 1 consisting of Lemma 1 and Lemma 2 are satisfied. We present a low-level formal model of MAuth-CAN in the MAC level of the data link layer of CAN, which is detailed enough to be able to reflect actual behaviors of CAN. This model ensures our verification is practical enough to provide valid proofs of security of MAuth-CAN (Section 5.2). Then, we prove Theorem 2 by proving Lemma 3, which is the essential property of MAuth-CAN assumed by Theorem 2. Finally, we show that our verification results are consistent with the actual implementation of MAuth-CAN (Section 6).

In the following subsection, we present our model method technique, model checking using UPPAAL.

3.2. Model Checking

Model checking is a rigorous verification method that presents a mathematical proof for a given property of the system. It accepts a system model and properties that the system model should satisfies. During verification, model checking explores all states of the system by taking every symbolic computational step and exhaustively check if every state satisfies given properties. Since model checking explores thoroughly all states of the system, it requires numerous time and memories. It is used to obtain guarantee of given properties of safety critical systems by mathematical proving techniques.

In this paper, we apply UPPAAL, a model checker, to prove MAuth-CAN's properties. UPPAAL tool suite includes various analysis techniques such as symbolic model checking, statistical model checking, and simulation. Symbolic model checking of UPPAAL accepts timed automata (TA) [24] as modeling language and use CTL (Computational Tree Logic) for property specification. CTL in UPPAAL comprises path formulas and state formulas. A path formula consists of branch quantifiers and path quantifiers. A and E, branch quantifiers, denotes "all paths" and "any path", respectively. $\Box$ and $\Diamond$, path quantifiers, represent "all states" and "exist a state", respectively.

Let ϕ a state formula. A path formula along with a state formula is expressed by the grammar:

$$\varphi ::= \phi \mid A\Box\phi \mid E\Box\phi \mid A\Diamond\phi \mid E\Diamond\phi \mid \phi_1 \rightarrow \phi_2$$

Using such a formula, reachability, safety and liveness properties can be formulated in UPPAAL. Reachability properties are expressed by the path formula $E\Diamond\phi$, meaning that a state satisfying ϕ is reachable.

Safety properties are formulated by the path formula $A\Box$. For example, $A\Box\phi$ requires that ϕ should be true in all reachable states. Meanwhile, $E\Box\phi$ denotes that there exists a maximal path such that ϕ is always true. A maximal path is a path that is either infinite or where the last state has no outgoing transitions [25]. Liveness properties are formulated by the path formula $A\Diamond\phi$, which means that there exists a state satisfying ϕ in all the branches, i.e., ϕ is eventually satisfied. One of useful formulas is the leads to or response property, which are written $A\Box(\phi \rightarrow A\Diamond\psi)$. That means that whenever ϕ happens, ψ should hold eventually [25]. For instance, whenever a message is sent, that should always be acknowledged.

UPPAAL SMC accepts a network of stochastic timed automata (NSTA). A model of network of timed automata in UPPAAL is redefined by a network of stochastic timed automata where the non-determinism of behavior in a timed automata model is refined by a probability distribution, so that the property for a given model is characterized by a probability that an event happens or a property holds.

The specification of UPPAAL SMC is based on Metric Interval Temporal Logic [26]. For an NSTA M, $P_M(\mid\phi)$ denotes the probability that a random run of M satisfies ϕ. The problem of checking $P_M(\phi) \geq p$ ($p \in [0, 1]$) is undecidable. For this reason, for the sub-logic of cost-bounded reachability problem $P_M(\Diamond_{(x \leq C)} AP) \geq p$, where x is a clock, C is a time bound, and AP is a conjunction of predicates over the state of a NSTA, UPPAAL SMC approximates the answer using simulation-based algorithms [27]. In UPPAAL SMC, the following three types of questions can be answered:

1. Probability estimation: What is the probability $P_M(\Diamond_{(x \leq C)} AP)$ for a given M?
2. Hypothesis testing: Is the probability $P_M(\Diamond_{(x \leq C)} AP)$ for a given M greater or equal to p [0, 1]?
3. Probability comparison: Is the probability $P_M(\Diamond_{(x \leq C)} AP_1)$ greater than the probability $P_M(\Diamond_{(x \leq C)} AP_2)$?

$P_M(\lozenge_{(x\leq C)}AP)$ is expressed by "P[$\Leftarrow$ C](<> AP)" in UPPAAL. This formula omits x from the original formula assuming that the global clock is used implicitly by formula. Besides, the following two forms of queries to simulate a given model:

- simulate [bound; N] $\{E_1, E_2, \ldots, E_k\}$: Simulate a model and return results in $E_1, \ldots, E_k$ expressions. N represents the number of simulations.
- E[bound; N] (min | max: expr): Simulate a model N rounds of which each precedes up to bound time units and return the min or max of the expression expr.

where bound is a time bound on the simulation, E_k is an expression that would be monitored and visualized.

In this paper, we use both UPPAAL and UPPAAL MC for proving properties of MAuth-CAN and simulating our model of MAuth-CAN. In Section 5, we present MAuth-CAN model of TA and various properties specification in CTL and verification results from UPPAAL.

3.3. CAN (Controller Area Network)

A Controller Area Network (CAN) is a de-facto standard for an in-vehicle network. Basically, once a node using CAN releases a message onto CAN bus, CAN broadcasts the message to all nodes, and the message is selectively picked up by an ECU that is one of message's destinations. Table 1 shows the structure of the CAN packet frame.

Table 1. CAN packet frame (Unit: bits).

SOF	ID	Control	Data	CRC	ACK	EOF
1	11	6	0–64	16	1	7

Table 2 shows the individual frames of a CAN packet. Each node is given its own CAN ID, which plays a role as priority for CAN bus. Two or more nodes release messages into CAN bus at the same time, then one of them with the higher priority can transmit the message. In CAN bus, 0 (dominant bit) has a higher priority over 1 (recessive bit). That is, CAN controller permits 0 to flow over CAN bus rather than 1 when both are released at time same time. CAN causes various errors, such as bit, stuff, CRC, and ACK errors. Once a node on CAN bus encounters one of the errors, rest of nodes are informed the error simultaneously. Each node updates one of error counters, such as Receive Error Counter (REC) and Transmit Error Counter (TEC), according to error types error mode depending on error counter. For instance, a node transits into the passive error from the active error state when REC or TEC is over 126 (≥ 127). A node under the passive error state goes to bus-off state when TEC is over 255 (≥ 256), but the node is not driven to bus-off state by REC. Once a node is at bus-off state, it is enforced to leave the CAN bus for a specific time. TEC has different increasing and decreasing rates. Every time a transmission error happens, TEC increases by 8. Meanwhile, it decreases by 1 every time a transmission is successful.

Table 2. Symbol and variable definitions.

Var	UPPAAL Var	Description
ECU_i	nodid	ECU with id i
AUTH		Authenticator
$CANID_i$	canid	CAN id used by ECU_i
Msg_i		Message with absolute sequence id i
$AFR_{i,1|2}$		AFR message for message Msg_i
$Auth(Msg_i)$		Authentication of message Msg_i
$Tran(Msg_i)$		Transmission by CAN bus for message Msg_i
$Accept(Msg_i)$		Action of accepting message Msg_i by ECU
$TxMsg_i$	txMsg[i]	Message released by $CANID_i$
$RxMsg_i$	rxMsg[i]	Message read by $CANID_i$
CANBus	canstat	Predicate to indicate whether CAN bus is occupied or not

Table 2. Cont.

Var	UPPAAL Var	Description
T_{auth}	AUTU_TIME	Authentication processing time of authenticator
T_{tx}	TX_TIME	Transmission time of CAN bus
UCMsgCnt	AttkMsgCnt	The number of messages that remain unchecked by the authenticator
TB		A waiting time that CAN controller waits for AFR message
IQSizei	MAX_QSIZE$_i$	The reception queue size of CANID$_i$

4. MAuth-CAN

This section overviews MAuth-CAN, a new CAN authentication technology, and their properties for protection of masquerade attack and BoA. In addition, we formulate properties for model checking of MAuth-CAN. Prior to description of MAuth-CAN protocol and models, Table 2 defines symbols and variables for formal descriptions.

4.1. System and Adversary Assumptions

In this subsection, we provide the assumptions for CAN and adversary (attacker), in particular, their capability for defense and attack.

4.1.1. System Assumptions

First, the system dedicates to the authenticator an ECU with two CAN controllers for CAN message authentication. The dedicated ECU is assumed to be assigned to the highest priority CANID, which is open to anyone. Second, we assume that it is possible to compute the maximum acceptable communication delay for a given application running and communicating over CAN. Third, we assume that the ECU, i.e., the authenticator, for authentication is very hard for the attacker to compromise so as to drop the assumption that CAN is a victim of a single point failure (SPF) where all points lose a specific security once a point is compromised. This assumption can be achieved by applying lightweight tamper-resistance hardware such as SMART [28] and TrustLite [29] into the authenticator.

4.1.2. Adversary Assumptions

An adversary is subject to the following assumptions: First, any adversary reaches a node responsible for driving controls and can cause bad driving consequences. Second, two or more adversary nodes cannot perform DDoS (Distributed DoS), i.e., attacker cannot compromise more than one ECU node. Third, the information of CAN messages, such as source address, data, etc., transmitted on CAN bus can be fabricated, forged by adversary node. Fourth, the highest priority ID can be exploited by an adversary. Fifth, each ECU has a different CAN controller and the different number of the message receiving queues from the others. Sixth, each ECU is equipped with a single message buffer each for transmission and reception.

4.2. Attack Scenarios

4.2.1. Masquerade Attack

An adversary fabricates CAN messages with a normal CANID so that vehicle driving is illegally controlled by adversary's control messages. For example, the compromised ECU can transmit a CAN message using the CANID of an ECU related to the engine to control the vehicle's speed. According to [5], the CANID of 0x43F was transmitted by a compromised node to actuate the vehicle's engine.

4.2.2. Denial of Service Leading to Bus-Off

Figure 1 describes a scenario of an adversary's Denial of Service attack using BO. The adversary performs DoS attack with consecutive attack messages, in particular, while the authenticator needs to broadcast an authentication-fail report. When both the adversary and the authenticator attempt to send messages with the same identifier simultaneously, the AFR and the attack message collide with each other. As a result, the transmission error occurs and increases TEC on both sender and receiver. If the TEC of the authenticator goes behind the threshold of Passive Error mode, it has less chances to transmit messages than the attacker. This situation can continue by the crafty attacker until the authenticator becomes off CAN bus.

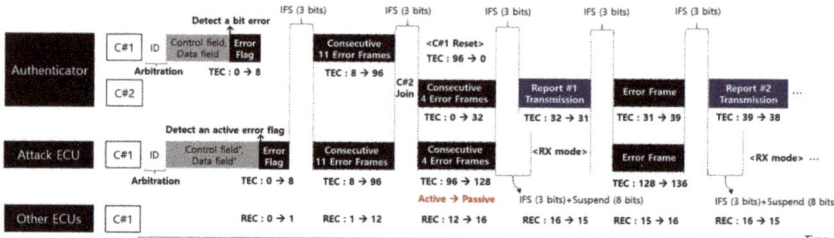

Figure 1. Bus-off attack scenarios from a single-point adversary (IFS: Interframe space, Suspend: Suspend transmission, RX mode: Reception mode, Active: Error active state, Passive: Error passive state, C#1: Controller #1, C#2: Controller #2).

4.3. Countermeasures of MAuth-CAN

To protect from the above attacks, MAuth-CAN performs the authentication using dual-CAN controllers as shown in Figure 2.

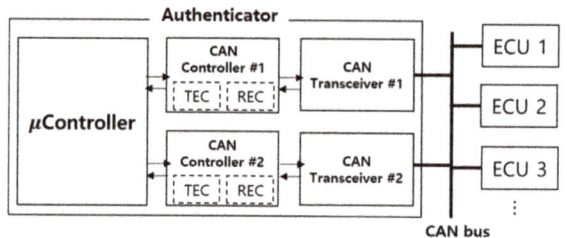

Figure 2. New authenticator model with dual CAN controllers.

As the authenticator uses two CAN controllers, the reception and transmission queues are doubled. The controller has its own transmission error counter (TEC) and receive error counter (REC), thus dual-CAN controllers have two TECs and RECs for authentication. In particular, TEC is the decisive variable that determines to expel a CAN controller from CAN bus.

4.3.1. Countermeasure to Masquerade Attack

To avoid masquerade attacks, MAuth-CAN performs the authentication for every single message via CAN bus, as shown in Figure 3. When an ECU transmits a message upon CAN bus, every CAN controller takes the message into its reception queue but delays in reading it until the authentication for the message is done. A CAN controller keeps a new message in its reception queue for T B time units, as shown in Figure 3. The controller reads a new message when the TB expires (Pass scenario in Figure 3). If a message does not pass authentication, then a CAN authenticator creates and broadcasts an error report i.e., an authentication-fail report (AFR) and ECUs discard the message (Fail scenario in Figure 3). MAuth-CAN uses the duration of the length of $4 \times T_{tx}$ for TB under the assumption that the transmission time is always greater than the authentication time. In this paper, we present the results of model checking for proving that the condition and the assumptions of MAuth-CAN authenticator are sufficient to protect masquerade attack to CAN system. The details regarding the AFR message is given in [21].

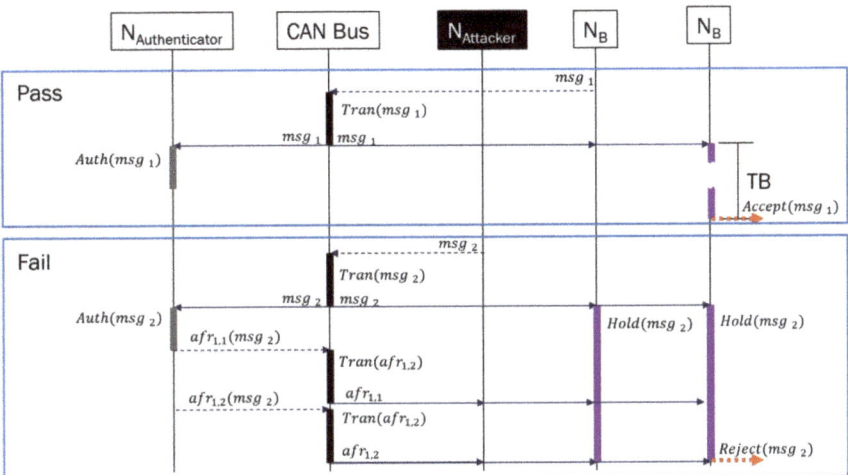

Figure 3. Basics of MAuth-CAN.

4.3.2. Countermeasure to DoS and Bus-Off Attacks

Figure 4 shows a scenario that MAuth-CAN performs CAN message authentication under BoA, and consequently sends all AFR messages to ECUs when a message cannot pass the authentication.

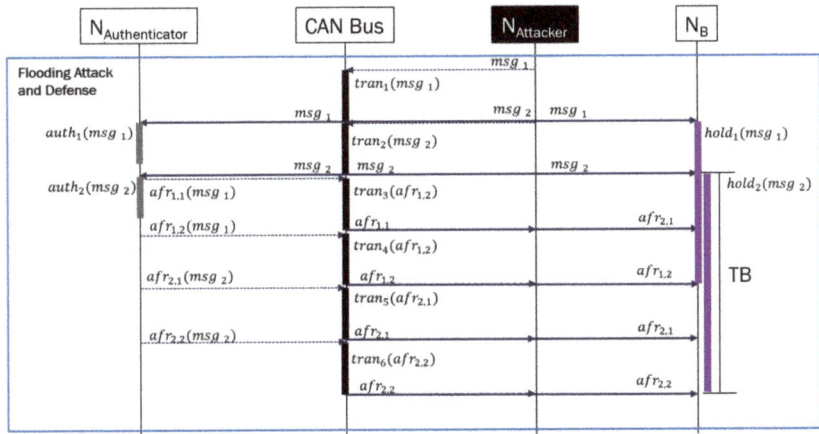

Figure 4. MAuth-CAN resistant against flooding.

AFR Flooding

Every time an unauthenticated message comes in, the authenticator instantiates and broadcasts an AFR. Ideally, if the authenticator always dominates CAN bus over any nodes including the attacker, every ECU under masquerade attack must receive the AFR message within $4 \times T_{tx}$ time units according to Figure 4. In order for the attacker not to be able to infer anything from AFR messages or reuse the previous AFR messages, the authenticator uses the reversed hash chain. An AFR message consists of two packets. Thus, the AFR message for the first adversary message can reach all nodes within $3 \times T_{tx}$ time unit, but the AFR message for the second adversary message can be delayed by the first AFR message. For this reason, the waiting time of ECU for authentication needs to be $4 \times \mathbf{T_{tx}}$ time units.

BO Avoidance

Both authenticator and attacker attempt to dominate CAN bus at the same time if the highest priority CANID is open. If they send messages simultaneously with the same ID, the transmission error occurs and increases TEC of message senders i.e., the authenticator and the attacker, here. If either of authenticator or attacker's TECs steps over a threshold of Active Error mode, it transits to Passive Error mode. When TEC goes over the limit of Passive Error mode, the ECU in Passive Error mode is enforced to leave CAN bus for a while.

To avoid this situation, the authenticator is equipped with two CAN controllers using two TECs of each CAN controllers. Consequently, both CAN controllers of the authentication cannot be enforced to enter into Passive Error mode at the same time.

MAuth-CAN is resilient to masquerade attacks if the authenticator leaves no missing message to verify at all. It is also sustainable under BoA because the attacker is disabled to send adversary messages faster than authenticator using two TECs in dual-CAN controllers.

4.4. Sufficient Conditions for MAuth-CAN Resiliency and Sustainability

CAN is resilient to masquerade attack if the authentication makes it to investigate every single message. Also, it is sustainable if the authentication is never disabled by BoA. MAuth-CAN achieves the above two goals by introducing a new authenticator equipped with two CAN controllers. In this paper, we show that MAuth-CAN achieves the above two goals with the following properties and prove them using model checking.

Theorem 1. *If MAuth-CAN authenticator uses a reception queue of size 2 for incoming new messages and the authentication time is always less than the message transmission time, it never fails to transmit AFR messages and the duration for ECUs to wait for AFR message needs no longer than $4 \times T_{tx}$.*

Theorem 1 emphasizes on the size of the reception queue for the CAN controller of the authenticator and the relation between the authentication time and the transmission time. The size of the CAN controller's reception queue is relevant to the resiliency of MAuth-CAN authenticator. The relation between the authentication time and the transmission time is relevant to the waiting time of ECUs for AFR messages.

Theorem 2. *MAuth-CAN authenticator is sustainable under BoA if it uses two CAN controllers.*

The sustainability of MAuth-CAN in Theorem 2 means that MAuth-CAN is never enforced to be off from CAN bus. In order to prove Theorem 2, we focus on TEC of authenticator's CAN controllers because TEC of the CAN controller goes over the threshold of Passive Error mode, then the CAN controller is enforced to leave CAN bus for a while. Thus, we will show that TEC of authenticator's CAN controllers never goes over the threshold of Passive Error mode even if that of attacker's CAN controller goes over the threshold. In next section, we will prove the above two theorems using model checking techniques.

5. Formal Analysis of MAuth-CAN

In this section, we present two formal models of CAN authentication in TA: An abstract CAN networking model and a detailed ECU model. The first model, the CAN networking model, captures the interlocking between three components: the authenticator, CAN bus, and ECUs. It focuses on verification of Theorem 1. The second model, the ECU model, details the behaviors of ECUs and bus at a bit-wise level so that the analysis can be done at a lower level. It focuses on verification of Theorem 2.

5.1. Model Checking Analysis of Theorem 1

To avoid the complexity of formal analysis, we abstract interaction between CAN components, as shown in Figure 5.

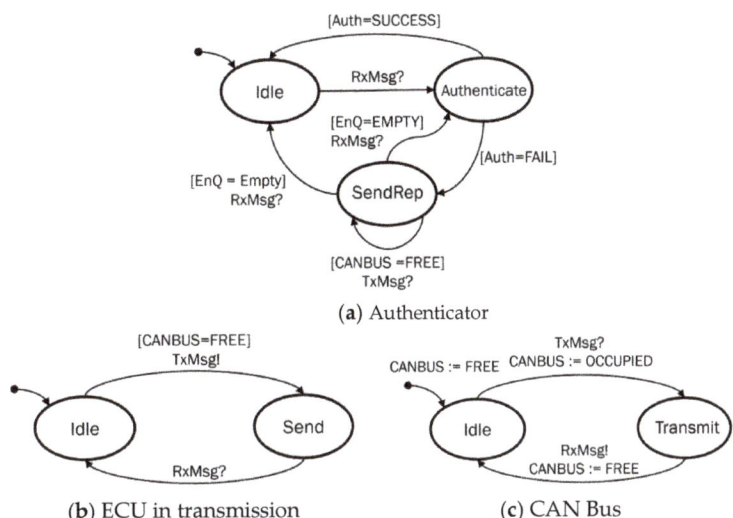

Figure 5. CAN networking model. (**a**) This figure shows the state transitions of the authenticator in MAuth-CAN. (**b**) It shows the state transitions of an ECU in data transmission. (**c**) It shows the state transitions of the CAN bus for data transmission.

The model of CAN interaction comprises authenticator, attacker, and CAN bus. The attacker model has the same behavior as normal ECUs, but the authenticator in our model responds to the message from the attack by broadcasting AFR messages. We do not include the behavior of the CAN controller of CAN message receiver nodes in our model since the authenticator model has the same behavior as CAN message receiver and we focus on the resiliency of MAuth-CAN's authentication that handles every attack message.

The authenticator model in Figure 5a waits for any message through CAN bus. When the authenticator reads a message (RxMsg) from CAN bus, the authenticator in Figure 5a transits into the location Authenticate for processing authentication. If the message passes the authentication, it returns to Idle state. Otherwise, it joins SendRep state. Then, it sends the AFR message for the unauthenticated message when CAN bus is available (CANBUS = FREE). The authenticator keeps any message in its reception queue (EnQ) when it is in authentication. If the queue is empty, the authenticator returns to the initial location Idle. Otherwise, it returns to Authenticate and performs authentication for another incoming message again.

The CAN controller model of an attacker in Figure 5b is simpler than the authenticator. If the CAN controller has a message to send and CAN bus is available, it just sends it through CAN bus. Notice that it returns to the initial location when the transmission of the message is acknowledged by CAN bus through the event RxMsg.

The CAN bus model in Figure 5c controls the permission for a CAN controller to access CAN bus. Initially, it allows any controller to use CAN bus by setting CAN-BUS:=FREE. If the CAN bus receives a message via TxMsg, it locks the key by setting CANBUS:=OCCUPIED, prohibits any node from using CAN bus, moves to Transmit location, and notifies the transmitting of a message. Finally, the CAN bus returns to the initial location Idle with unlocking the key with setting CANBUS:=FREE.

Based on the CAN networking model in Figure 5, Figure 6 captures CAN behavior models in TA. It also comprises three models: Authenticator, ECU and CAN bus. Four TA processes are instantiated for simulation and verification: Two authenticator processes from the authenticator model, one CAN attacker process from the ECU model, and one CAN bus process from the CAN bus.

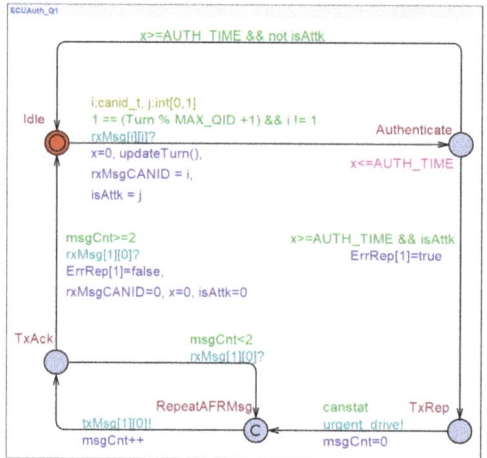
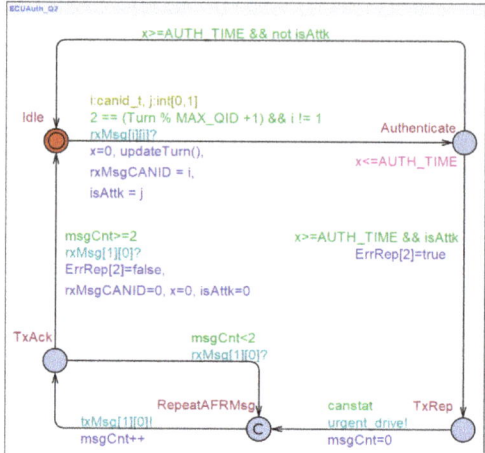

(**a**) CAN authentication using two buffers of the incoming queue in TA.

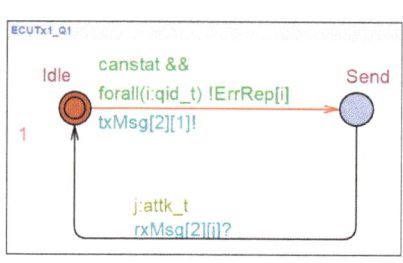
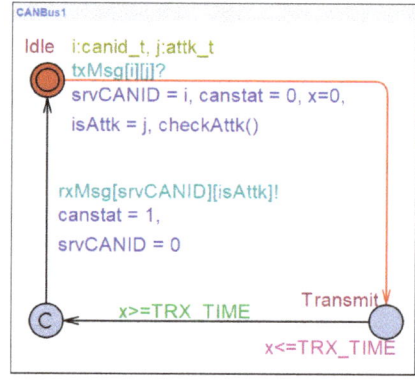

(**b**) ECU in TA (**c**) CAN bus in TA

Figure 6. Simulation of CAN networking in TA. (**a**) This figure shows two UPPAAL processes of message authenticator that individually process authentication of incoming message. (**b**) This figure shows an UPPAAL process of an ECU that continuously sends messages, simulating message flooding attack. (**c**) This figure shows an UPPAAL process of a CAN bus that simulates the message transmission in the synchronization with the sender ECU and the receiver ECU.

As shown in Figure 6a, two authenticator processes are instantiated from the authenticator model to capture message queuing behavior using the reception queue of size 2. It particularly highlights the concurrent behavior of the CAN controller's authentication, reception, and message transmission using the reception queue of size 2. When a new message arrives, authenticator's CAN controller checks the message and sends AFR messages for unauthenticated messages. While the authenticator is sending AFR, it can simultaneously receive another new message. It is because the reception queue and sending queue of a CAN controller are separate. However, only one of them can process authentication at the same time. The authenticator processes, ECUAuth_Q1 and ECUAuth_Q2, in Figure 6a have an invariant over Authenticate location, which limits the authentication time to a specific time bound AUTH_TIME. The authenticator process leaves Authenticate location after AUTH_TIME expires and transits to TxRep location so as to send one of AFR messages. In this interaction model, canstat represents the status of CAN bus. The authenticator process can send the AFR message through CAN bus when no node occupies CAN bus, then canstat value of CANBus1 is set to true (1). When TA authenticator enters RepeatAFRMsg location, it broadcasts two consecutive packets for one AFR message.

The ECU process in ECUTx1_Q1 of Figure 6b may send any attack message (txMsg[canid][attkid]) at any time if CAN bus is available. If the reception of the attack message is acknowledged by the authenticator i.e., rxMsg[canid][attkid] is received, it may send another message.

The CAN bus in CANBus1 of Figure 6c manages the permission for use of CAN bus using canstat. If the CAN bus process receives a message from an ECU and the authenticator, it sets canstat to false (0). Then, any CAN controller cannot occupy CAN bus. The transmission of messages is captured with the clock x and the invariant TRX_TIME over Transmit location. The CAN bus process stays over Transmit location for TRX_TIME time units, and then it leaves Transmit location with synchronizing the channel rxMsg and setting canstat to true (1). Particularly, The CAN bus model is designed to count the number of attack messages using the function checkAttk(). The number is denoted by AttMsgCnt. AttMsgCnt keeps increasing, meaning that the authenticator fails to check the attack message. If AttMsgCnt keeps below a specific number, particularly the reception queue size of the authenticator, it means that the authenticator succeeds in authenticating every attack message.

MAuth-CAN authenticator must not miss any message without verification, meaning that no ECU should not read unauthenticated message. All CAN controllers on ECUs temporarily store any incoming message in the reception queue during authentication. They postpone reading it until a predefined authentication time ends. However, when the AFR message arrives within the predefined authentication time, the CAN controller regards that the message in the reception queue fails the authentication and discards it. For the reasons, it is crucial to characterize the AFR waiting time TB i.e., the duration that an ECU waits for AFR message. Also, the CAN authenticator is capable of verifying consecutive adversary messages and transmit AFR messages within a predefined authentication time so as to protect every ECU from adversary messages. In terms of the authenticator, we prove the following lemma in order to characterize the CAN controller of the authenticator that can protect adversary messages in any forms:

Lemma 1. *If the CAN controller of the authenticator is given the reception queue of size 2 and the transmission time is less than the authentication time, it can always verify every new message and every ECU does not miss AFR.*

In order to prove Lamma 1, we model-check the CAN controller model of the authenticator and checks the number of delayed AFR messages in the transmission queue. If the variable AttkMsgCnt is not larger than the size of the reception queue, we can say that the authenticator has no remaining AFR to send. The following two CTL properties are checked by UPPAAL MC and the verification results are also shown in Table 3:

$$\text{CTL-Property-1: A[] not deadlock} \quad (1)$$

$$\text{CTL-Property-2: A[] AttkMsgCnt} \leq \text{IQSizeAUTH} \quad (2)$$

Table 3. Setting of the model checking for Lemma 1 and model-checking results.

Case	IQSize$_{AUTH}$	T_{auth}~T_{tx}	CTL-Property-2	Case	IQSize$_{AUTH}$	T_{auth}~T_{tx}	CTL-Property-2
1	1	=	Not Satisfied	4	2	=	Not Satisfied
2	1	<	Not Satisfied	5	2	<	*Satisfied*
3	1	>	Not Satisfied	6	2	>	Not Satisfied

CTL-Property-1 specifies that the system is put into no deadlock where no progress is made. CTL-Property-2 states that AttkMsgCnt is not larger than the maximum reception queue size of authenticator's CAN controller.

To prove Lemma 1, we have six different configurations in Table 3, where the maximum reception queue size of the authenticator, the authentication time, and transmission time are varied. The maximum reception queue size is either of one or two. The transmission time and the authentication time are also varied in such a way that $T_{auth} \sim T_{tx}$ where $\sim = \{<, =, >\}$.

In Table 3, T_{auth} and T_{tx} denote the authentication processing time and the transmission time, respectively. The results show that CAN authentication needs no more than two queues if the authentication time is less than the transmission time, so that no message is missed without verification.

To validate our models, we simulate the model using statistical model checking technique and the following query:

Sim-Property-1: simulate [≤100;1] CANBus1.srvCANID (3)

This query states which CANID preempts CAN bus over time.

Figure 7 shows a simulation of CAN authentication with different number of CAN controller. The x-axis represents the time and the y-axis represents the identifier of a CAN controller which makes it to transmit a message. Thus, Figure 7 shows which CAN controller makes it to transmit messages over time. The attacker's CANID is 2 and the authenticator's is 1.

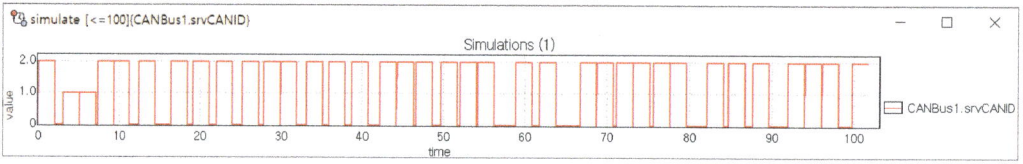

(a) Simulation of CAN authentication with a single buffer (size 1) of the incoming queue of CAN.

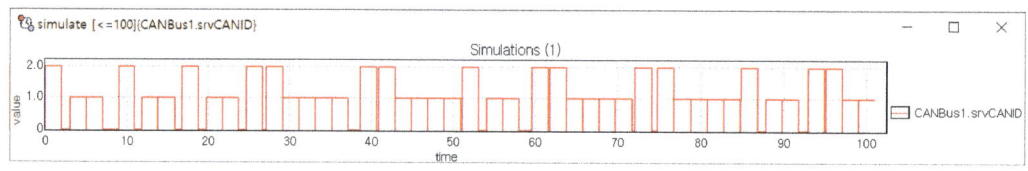

(b) Simulation of CAN authentication with two buffers (size 2) of the incoming queue of CAN.

Figure 7. Simulation of CAN authentication nodes. (a) This figure shows that the attack messages are overwhelming CAN bus by message flooding attack, and blocking all AFR messages from the authenticator. (b) This figure shows that two consecutive AFR messages for one attack message are transmitted on CAN bus without failure and the attack message cannot dominate CAN Bus.

Figure 7a shows the case where the authenticator's CAN controller uses a single buffer of a reception queue so it cannot handle no more than one message. The first two messages are adversary messages sent by the attacker. The third and fourth messages are the AFR messages sent by the authenticator after addressing the first adversary message. Note that authenticator's CAN controller succeeds in sending the AFR messages for the first adversary message, but not the rest of the adversary messages.

Meanwhile, the plot in Figure 7b shows different behavior of CAN authentication when authenticator's CAN controller 2 size of the reception queue. In Figure 7b, the first two transmissions are made by the attacker. The second adversary message transmission is possible while the authenticator is checking the first adversary message. However, the 4 transmissions following the first two adversary messages are made for AFR messages by the authenticator. That is consistent with Figure 4: Two attack messages can be consecutively transmitted over CAN bus, but AFR messages follow those attack messages. In following, all AFR messages are successfully sent following every attack message. No AFR message is delayed by adversary message, then no adversary message is adopted by ECUs due to AFR messages.

In order to compute the minimum TB, we present Lemma 2:

Lemma 2. *If the CAN authenticator makes it to address all consecutive attack messages, TB is not necessarily longer than $4 \times T_{tx}$.*

In our model, for a given authentication time, denoted by T_{auth}, and transmission time, denoted by T_{tx}, we can measure the maximum communication delay, using the clocks ECUAuth_Q1.x and ECUAuth_Q2.x on the locations ECUAuth_Q1.TxAck and ECUAuth_Q2.TxAck. For given $T_{auth} = 1$ and $T_{tx} = 2$, we check the worst-case time for the AFR message to arrive all ECUs. We use the following queries:

CTL-Property-3: sup{ECUAuth_Q1.TxAck}: ECUAuth_Q1.x (4)

CTL-Property-4: sup{ECUAuth_Q2.TxAck}: ECUAuth_Q2.x (5)

"sup{expr}: list" in UPPAAL MC returns the maximum value of variables in "list". That is, the expression in list is evaluated only on the states that satisfy expr (a state predicate) that acts like an observation.

Model checking shows that the worst-case response time of the AFR is always 8 ($4 \times T_{tx}$). That is consistent with the illustration in Figure 4, thus we can conclude that $4 \times T_{tx}$ is the minimum TB.

In the results of model-checking for CTL-Property-1, 2, 3, and 4, we prove Lemma 1 and Lemma 2. Consequently, Theorem 1 is proved by the proofs of Lemma 1 and Lemma 2.

In this section, we show that MAuth-CAN is resilient to masquerade attack using consecutive adversary messages if the authenticator reads incoming message using 2 size of reception queue and the authentication time is less than the message transmission time. In particular, it is shown that the consecutive two messages of AFR sent by the authenticator can prevent the flooding of adversary messages by preempting CAN bus. However, it is true only if the AFR messages is successfully transmitted to other nodes.

In next section, we will show that MAuth-CAN is sustainable to BoA even if CAN priority is not secure and attacker can utilize the highest priority of CAN.

5.2. Model Checking Analysis of Theorem 2

Recall the scenario that BoA enforces the CAN controller of the authenticator to leave CAN bus for a while. When the authenticator tries to transmit AFR messages, the attacker causes transmission error. The attacker with the same priority of CAN bus begins the attack message transmission at the same time when the authenticator begins message transmission. Then, two messages conflicts, resulting in transmission error. The repeated transmission errors accumulate up to a specific count, then CAN system gets rid of the attacker and the authenticator from CAN bus for a while. The CAN authentication should be designed to sustainable against this BoA.

In order to capture such a complicated situation, we present more concrete and detailed model of the CAN controller and bus in TA. Our CAN controller model in TA captures a detailed behavior of the CAN controller based on the CAN protocol in Figure 8. We capture CAN controller's behavior in a bit-wise level as if a simple protocol is captured by a TA as shown in Figure 9. In Figure 9, a frame consists of a specific number of bits and TA captures the behavior of such a frame with the same series of time units. Here, we do not consider the semantics of bits and focus on a bit-wise timing behavior of the protocol.

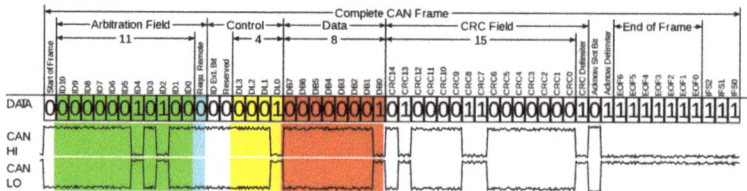

Figure 8. CAN-Frame in base format in bit levels [30].

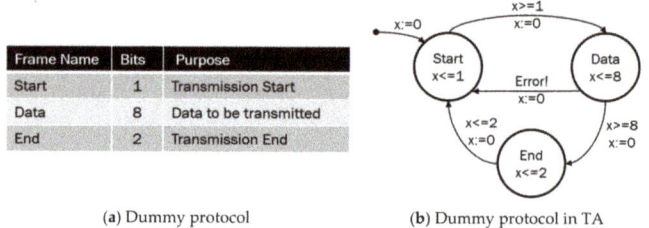

(**a**) Dummy protocol (**b**) Dummy protocol in TA

Figure 9. Modeling a dummy protocol into TA. (**a**) This figure gives an example of a simple protocol in packet frames. (**b**) This figure captures the simple protocol into a TA model in a bit-wise level.

If a protocol evolves from one frame to another frame, TA captures the frames transits from one location and to another location. Basically, a frame is captured by a location in our TA model, where our TA model stays for the same time units as the number of bits of a frame. For example, the Start frame using 1 bit in Figure 9 is captured by the Start location where TA stays for the same number of time units as 1 bit. A specific event occurring on a frame can be captured by an event causing a transition leaving off the location representing the frame. For example, if a Data frame in Figure 9 encounters an error and needs re-transmission, then TA captures it by a transition returning from Data location to Start location.

Figures 10 and 11 shows TA models of CAN bus and controller in the MAC level of the data link layer. The CAN controller has three modes: Receiving mode, transmission mode, and error handling mode. The receiving mode consists of receiving (Rxing) and error handing locations (RxErrRep, RxErrStuffing, RxErrDelimite). The transmission mode is composed of multiple transmissions of different frames, as shown in Figure 11. When a CAN controller needs data transmission, the CAN controller model at the location Rxing in Figure 10 checks if CAN bus is available by checking the condition variable canstat. The SOF frame of Figure 8 is modeled by the invariant $x \leq SOF$ over the location StartTrans and the guard $x==SOF$ on the transition leaving StartTrans in Figure 11. Note that the Arbitration Field frame needs an interaction of CAN controller with the CAN bus for CAN bus arbitration and such a scheduling responsibility is placed upon the CAN bus, so the Arbitration Field frame is modeled on the location CANArbitration in CAN bus model of Figure 10. The last 1 bit of Arbitration frame field and the first 2 bits of Control field are abstracted together by the location DestControl. When more than one CAN controller attempt to make any frame transmissions simultaneously, it may lead to a transmission error status of CAN controller and bus. The transmission error is captured by the transition leaving the location Txing of Figure 11 having no guard. The transition may be taken non-deterministically to leave the location Txing, and that implies that our CAN controller model of TA can go to a transmission error (handling) status at any time. When a transmission error occurs, the CAN controller is put into one of Active Error model, Passive Error mode, or Reset. When a transmission error happens, the CAN controller goes to at Active Error mode and an Active Error frame will be transmitted on the bus if TEC (Transmission Error Counter) is lesser than 128. If TEC is greater than 127 and lesser than

255, then the CAN controller is led to Passive Error mode and a Passive Error frame will be transmitted on the bus.

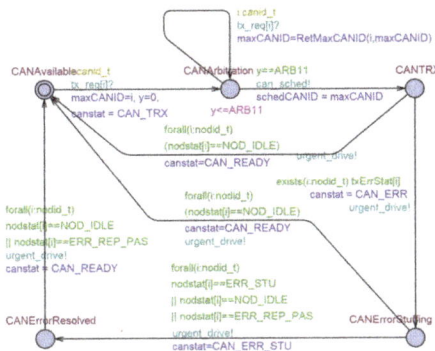

Figure 10. CAN bus model in TA.

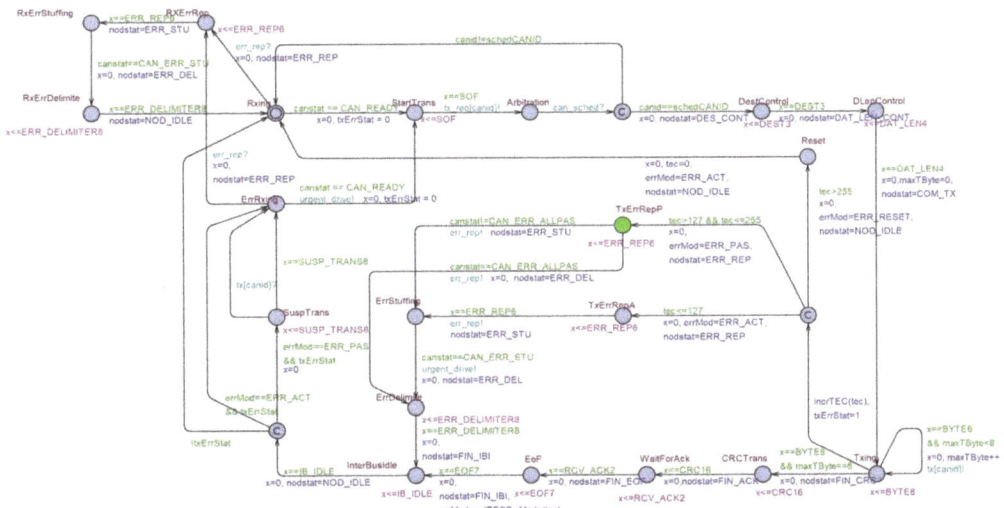

Figure 11. A CAN controller model in TA.

The CAN controller in Passive Error mode is given a penalty in such a way that it is more delayed to make transmission than the CAN controller in Active Error or Normal modes. The situation is captured by our CAN controller model of TA where the CAN controller in Passive Error mode should stay over SuspTrans location for 8 time-units. When TEC of a CAN controller is greater than 255, then the controller enters Bus Off state, where no frames cannot be transmitted by the controller [30]. We capture the BO situation with Reset location in Figure 11, where the CAN controller stays for a while without being able to send any message.

Now, we present the formal verification results of model checking for MAuth-CAN under BoA. In order to prove Theorem 1 that the CAN controller in charge of the authentication is sustainable to BoA, we need to verify if our dual-CAN controllers can never be put into Passive Error mode when the attacker crafts continually to cause transmission errors. We introduce to Lemma 3 as follows:

Lemma 3. *Dual-CAN controllers of MAuth-CAN authentication is never put into Passive Error mode together at the same time when the attacker is in Passive Error mode.*

We prove Lemma 3 by model checking as follows: In order to reduce the state space of our models, the TA authenticator model and the TA at-tacker model in Figures 12 and 13 are mutated from the CAN controller model of Figure 11 so that they terminate analysis when one of them goes into Passive Error mode. That is, when either of the authenticator controller or the attack controller goes to Passive Error mode first, then the analysis is over. We verify that both dual-CAN controllers for authentication never go to Passive Error mode at the same time. In this way, our model checking using the mutated CAN controller models can be less suffering state-explosion issue. We use the following queries to prove Lemma 3:

$$\text{CTL-Property-5: A[] not deadlock} \tag{6}$$

$$\text{CTL-Property-6: A[] CANContAttk3.errMod==ERR\_PAS imply}$$
$$\text{(CANContAuth1.errMod != ERR\_PAS or CANContAuth2.errMod != ERR\_PAS)} \tag{7}$$

$$\text{CTL-Property-7: A[] (CANContAuth1.errMod! = ERR\_PAS or CANContAuth2.errMod! = ERR\_PAS)} \tag{8}$$

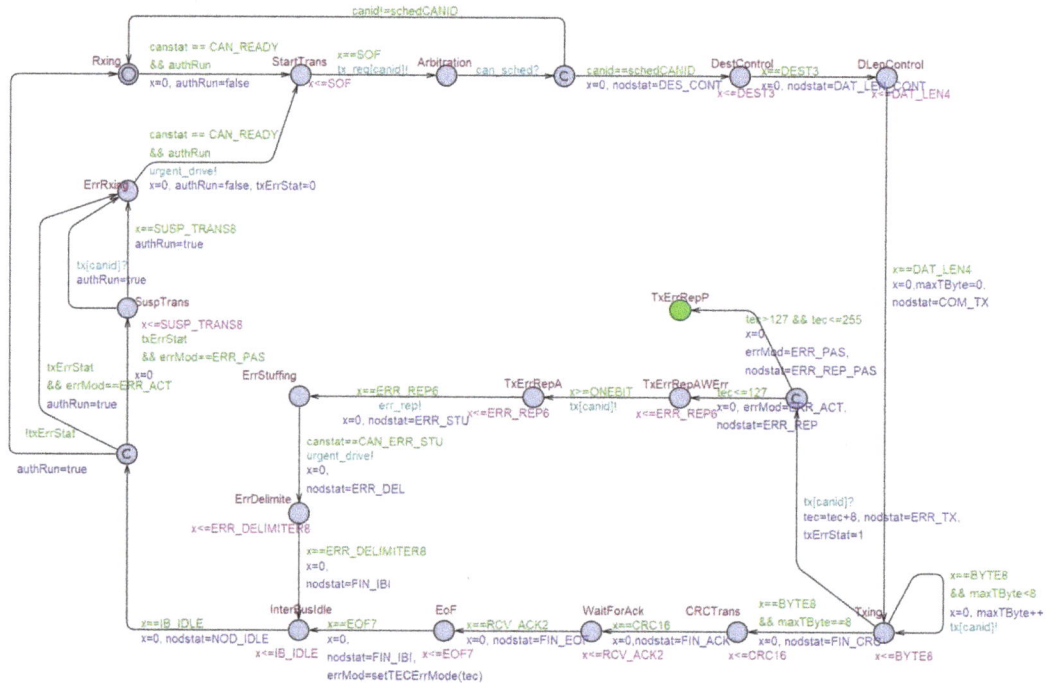

Figure 12. An ECU controller model of the authenticator in TA.

CTL-Property-5 specifies that the system model should never be in deadlock status in which every process stops running. We use it to check if our TA model is valid to check using model checking. CTL-Property-6 specifies that the error mode (errMod) of both authenticators (CANContAuth1 and CANContAuth2) would never be in Passive Error mode (ERR_PAS) together at the same time when the error mode (errMod) of the attacker (CANContAtt3) happens to be in Passive Error mode (ERR_PAS). Similarly, CTL-Property-7 is used to check if they can fall into Passive Error mode.

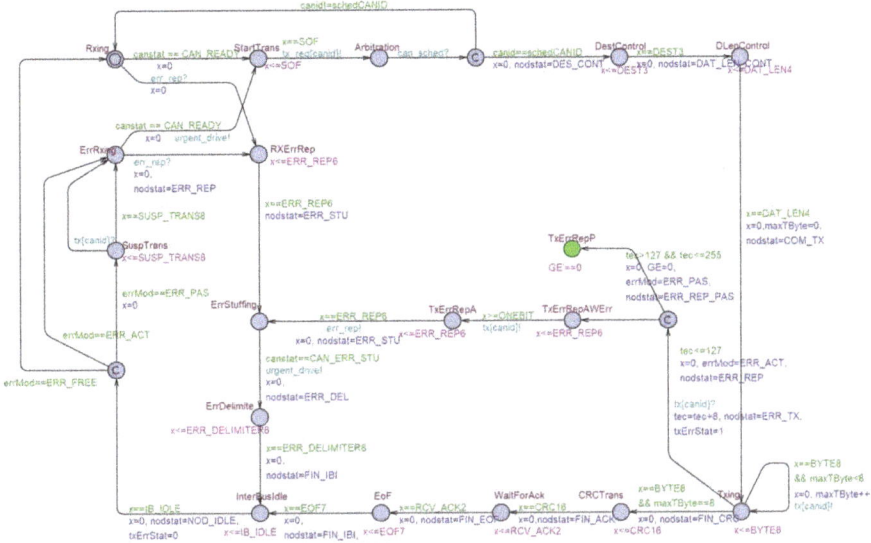

Figure 13. An ECU controller model of the attacker in TA.

Figure 14 shows that the properties above are met by our model, implying that Lemma 3 is proved by the model checking of the CTL properties. By proving Lemma 3, we conclude that Theorem 1 is proved and that our authentication using dual-CAN controllers is resilient to BoA even when the attacker can exploit the highest priority of CAN controller.

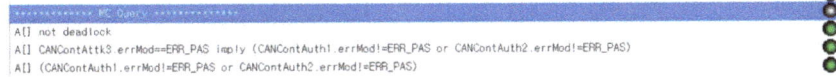

Figure 14. Model checking results for MAuth-CAN's resiliency to BoA.

Our model checking environment is as follows:
- Processor: Intel Core i7 CPU, 1.80GHz, 2.30GHz
- RAM: 16.0GB
- OS: Windows 10-64Bits

6. Implementation and Experiments

In this section, the implementation and experimental results of MAuth-CAN are provided to check whether Theorem 1 and 2 proved in the formal analysis are applicable to the CAN testbed considering real CAN traffic with message authentication. In the experiment of MAuth-CAN, we adopt the BLAKE2S algorithm with keyed mode for implementation of message authentication code, which is used to generate authentication tags for CAN messages and report messages. BLAKE2S is a cryptographic hash function which is faster than keccak (SHA3) in software implementations. The security proof of BLAKE2S with keyed mode is referred to [31]. We tested the implemented source codes on the Raspberry Pi 3 Model B and Arduino Zero that are assumed to be the authenticator and the normal ECUs, respectively.

6.1. Message Authentication Time

When an ECU transmits a CAN message, it always generates a message authentication tag (i.e., a MAC value). The CAN message then is verified by the authenticator and a report message (an AFR message) is generated if there is a verification failure. The normal ECUs verify an AFR message to see if it is transmitted by the authenticator only when they receive it. We tested each operation one hundred times, and the average the computation time and the corresponding standard deviation for individual cryptographic operations are presented in Table 4.

Table 4. Individual operations of MAuth-CAN (μs).

	Authenticator		ECU	
	Message Authentication (T^M_{Auth})	Report Generation (T^R_{Gen})	Message Generation (T^M_{Gen})	Report Verification (T^R_{Ver})
Mean	28.26	28.14	258.8	516.4
Std. Dev.	0.46	0.34	0.43	1.02

6.2. Reception Time of an AFR Message

We evaluate the reception time of an AFR message under the following two attacks: message flooding attack and BoA.

6.2.1. Reception Time of an AFR Message under Message Flooding Attacks

As shown in Table 4, the sum of T^M_{Auth} and T^R_{Gen} is approximately 56.4 μs and less than the transmission time of an AFR message, i.e., 444 μs = $\frac{Packet\_Size}{Bus\_Speed}$ = $2 \times \frac{111 \; bits}{500,000 \; bits/s}$ (111 bits is size of a CAN data frame with an 8 byte data field if the bit-stuffing rule of the CAN standard is ignored). Since the time to authenticate a CAN message and to generate a report message is less than the transmission time of the report message, the authenticator can authenticate all CAN messages without increasing its own message queue. Thus, every report message for an invalid CAN message can be transmitted successfully within a bounded time, which is the length of 4 × the transmission time as described in Theorem 1. According to our implementation result, the worst time of report reception under the flooding attacks is approximately 1012 μs, as shown in Figure 15a.

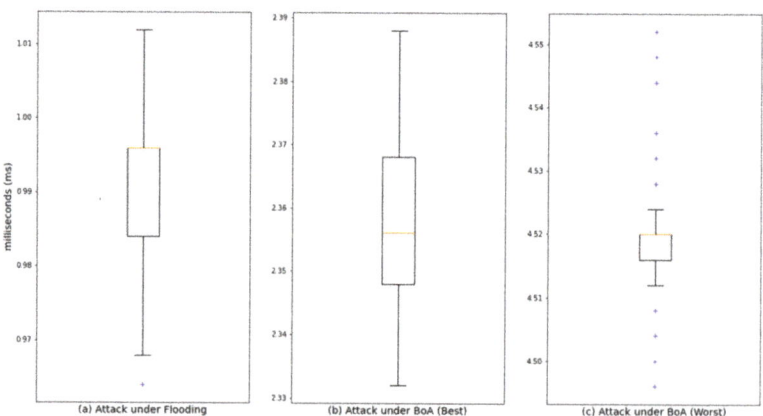

Figure 15. The reception time of an AFR message under attacks. (**a**) This figure shows the AFR reception time under message flooding. Note that the maximum time of AFRs is 1012 μs. (**b**) This figure shows the ARF reception time under BoA where the malicious ECU creates the bit-error at the FIRST bit position in the AFR message. (**c**) This figure shows the ARF reception time under BoA where the malicious ECU creates the bit-error at the LAST bit position in the AFR message.

The reception time shown in Figure 15a is slightly larger than 888 μs = $\frac{Packet\_Size}{Bus\_Speed}$ = $4 \times \frac{111 \text{ bits}}{500,000 \text{ bits}/s}$, which is the theoretical transmission time of four CAN packets. The reason is that this experimental time is affected by the bit stuffing rule for synchronization of CAN bus and the time measurement error originating from Arduino UNO. In order to maintain synchronization of CAN bus, a bit stuffing rule is defined in the CAN standard. In this rule, a bit of opposite value is inserted after every five consecutive bits of the same value. For example, if six consecutive dominant bits, 000000, are transmitted by the host controller of an ECU, the CAN controller of the ECU adds one recessive bit after every five consecutive dominant bits 0000010. This additional bit is automatically removed by the CAN controllers of receiver ECUs.

6.2.2. Reception Time of an AFR Message under BoA

BoA on the authenticator causes the transmission delay of an AFR message. In general, the continuous BoA can permanently interfere with the communication from an ECU. However, since the authenticator of MAuth-CAN has two CAN controllers, it is possible for the authenticator to put a malicious ECU that performs the BoA into Passive Error mode which allows the transmission of an AFR message from the authenticator.

The time it takes for the malicious node performing BoA to become the error passive state varies depending on the attack bit position for the BoA (i.e., a bit-error position in the data field of an AFR message). If the malicious node performing BoA creates the first bit-error at the first bit position in the data field of an AFR message, the reception time of an AFR message is approximately 2355 ms as shown in Figure 15b. In other hands, to maximize the transmission delay of an AFR message by the BoA, the malicious node performing BoA can create a bit-error at the last bit position (i.e., 64th bit position in the data field) of an AFR message. In this the worst case, the reception time of an AFR message is approximately 4495 ms as shown in Figure 15c.

Through this experiment, we show Theorem 2 by validating that Passive Error mode of the malicious node performing BoA on the authenticator allows the authenticator with dual CAN-controllers to transmit an AFR message within the bounded time and the worst case time is 4495 ms.

7. Conclusions

CAN is the most common in-vehicle network system. The latest automobiles developed recently are equipped with numerous ECUs. The ECU over CAN bus can be a victim of security attacks leading to critical risks of vehicle safety. In particular, in case that the infotainment system of unwarranted third party vendor and driving control systems share CAN bus, the security risk is dramatically escalated.

MAuth-CAN is a centralized authentication mechanism for CAN. In MAuth-CAN, the response timing is critical for the properties since a timeout works for the indication that a message passes authentication and ECUs accept a new message stored in its temporary queue when the timeout expires. MAuth-CAN utilizes two CAN controllers for fault-tolerance mechanism so that it continues its functionality under message flooding and bus-off attacks.

This paper presents the formal proofs of resiliency and sustainability of MAuth-CAN authentication against message flooding and bus-off attacks where timing is critical to maintain such properties. Also, this paper shows how model checking, a formal verification technique, works for safety and security certificates of in-vehicle network. In this paper, we present a novel CAN model in a formal model, which captures CAN's timing behavior in MAC level of the data-link layer and can thus be used for verification of safety properties of other CAN applications. Using this CAN model, we perform formal verification for the sufficient conditions of those properties of MAuth-CAN.

As conclusions, we show that MAuth-CAN authenticator is sufficiently resilient and sustainable against those two kinds of attacks if MAuth-CAN authenticator can handle two consecutive attack messages, the authentication time is less than the message transmission time, and MAuth-CAN authenticator uses two CAN controllers. Also, we conclude that $4 \times T_{tx}$ is the minimum and sufficient length of the timeout for ECUs to open incoming messages that have passed MAuth-CAN authentication. The experiment results from the implementation of MAuth-CAN are shown to be consistent with that propositions and conditions we have shown in this paper.

Author Contributions: Conceptualization, J.H.K., H.J.J. and I.L.; methodology, J.H.K.; validation, I.L. and H.J.J.; writing—original draft preparation, J.H.K. and H.J.J.; writing—review and editing, I.L.; supervision, I.L.; project administration, I.L.; funding acquisition, I.L., J.H.K., H.J.J. and All authors have read and agreed to the published version of the manuscript.

Funding: This work was supported in part by NRF-2020R1A2C1014855, NRF-2018R1C1B5086261, and ONR N00014-17-1-2012 and ONR N00014-20-1-2744.

Institutional Review Board Statement: Not applicable.

Informed Consent Statement: Not applicable.

Data Availability Statement: Data sharing not applicable.

Conflicts of Interest: The authors declare no conflict of interest.

References

1. Koscher, K.; Czeskis, A.; Roesner, F.; Patel, S.; Kohno, T.; Checkoway, S.; McCoy, D.; Kantor, B.; Anderson, D.; Shacham, H.; et al. Experimental Security Analysis of a Modern Automobile. In Proceedings of the 2010 IEEE Symposium on Security and Privacy, Berkeley, CA, USA, 22–25 May 2011; pp. 447–462. [CrossRef]
2. Checkoway, S.; McCoy, D.; Kantor, B.; Anderson, D.; Shacham, H.; Savage, S.; Koscher, K.; Czeskis, A.; Roesner, F.; Kohno, T. Comprehensive Experimental Analyses of Automotive Attack Surfaces. In *Proceedings of the 20th USENIX Conference on Security*; SEC'11; USENIX Association: Berkeley, CA, USA, 2011; p. 6.
3. Foster, I.; Prudhomme, A.; Koscher, K.; Savage, S. Fast and Vulnerable: A Story of Telematic Failures. In Proceedings of the 9th USENIX Workshop on Offensive Technologies (WOOT 15), Washington, DC, USA, 10–11 August 2015.
4. Miller, C.; Valasek, C. Remote Exploitation of an Unaltered Passenger Vehicle. *Black Hat USA* **2015**, *2015*, 91.
5. Woo, S.; Jo, H.; Lee, D. A Practical Wireless Attack on the Connected Car and Security Protocol for In-Vehicle CAN. *IEEE Intell. Transp. Syst.* **2015**, *16*, 993–1006. [CrossRef]
6. Jo, H.J.; Choi, W.; Na, S.Y.; Woo, S.; Lee, D.H. Vulnerabilities of Android OS-Based Telematics System. *Wirel. Pers. Commun.* **2017**, *92*, 1511–1530. [CrossRef]
7. Taylor, A.; Japkowicz, N.; Leblanc, S. Frequency-based anomaly detection for the automotive CAN bus. In Proceedings of the 2015 World Congress on Industrial Control Systems Security (WCICSS), London, UK, 14–16 December 2015; pp. 45–49. [CrossRef]
8. Song, H.M.; Kim, H.R.; Kim, H.K. Intrusion detection system based on the analysis of time intervals of CAN messages for in-vehicle network. In Proceedings of the 2016 IEEE International Conference on Information Networking (ICOIN), Kota Kinabalu, Malaysia, 13–15 January 2016; pp. 63–68. [CrossRef]
9. Tomlinson, A.; Bryans, J.; Shaikh, S.A.; Kalutarage, H.K. Detection of Automotive CAN Cyber-Attacks by Identifying Packet Timing Anomalies in Time Windows. In Proceedings of the 2018 48th Annual IEEE/IFIP International Conference on Dependable Systems and Networks Workshops (DSN-W), Luxembourg, 25–28 June 2018; pp. 231–238. [CrossRef]
10. Marchetti, M.; Stabili, D. Anomaly detection of CAN bus messages through analysis of ID sequences. In Proceedings of the 2017 IEEE Intelligent Vehicles Symposium (IV), Los Angeles, CA, USA, 11–14 June 2017; pp. 1577–1583. [CrossRef]
11. Kang, M.J.; Kang, J.W. Intrusion Detection System Using Deep Neural Network for In-Vehicle Network Security. *PLoS ONE* **2016**, *11*, 1–17. [CrossRef] [PubMed]
12. Song, H.M.; Woo, J.; Kim, H.K. In-vehicle network intrusion detection using deep convolutional neural network. *Veh. Commun.* **2020**, *21*, 1–13. [CrossRef]
13. Cho, K.T.; Shin, K.G. Fingerprinting Electronic Control Units for Vehicle Intrusion Detection. In Proceedings of the 25th USENIX Security Symposium (USENIX Security 16), Austin, TX, USA, 10–12 August 2016; pp. 911–927.
14. Hartkopp, O.; Reuber, C.; Schilling, R. MaCAN—Message Authenticated CAN. In Proceedings of the 10th International Conference on Embedded Security in Cars (Escar Euroupe 2012), Berlin, Germany, 28–29 November 2012.
15. Kang, K.D.; Baek, Y.; Lee, S.; Son, S.H. An Attack-Resilient Source Authentication Protocol in Controller Area Network. In Proceedings of the 2017 ACM/IEEE Symposium on Architectures for Networking and Communications Systems (ANCS), Beijing, China, 18–19 May 2017; pp. 109–118. [CrossRef]
16. Nürnberger, S.; Rossow, C. vatiCAN—Vetted, Authenticated CAN Bus. In Proceedings of the 18th International Conference on Cryptographic Hardware and Embedded Systems (CHES 2016), Santa Barbara, CA, USA, 17–19 August 2016; Springer: Berlin/Heidelberg, Germany, 2016; pp. 106–124. [CrossRef]

17. Radu, A.I.; Garcia, F.D. LeiA: A Lightweight Authentication Protocol for CAN. In Proceedings of the 21st European Symposium on Research in Computer Security (ESORICS 2016), Heraklion, Greece, 28–30 September 2016; Springer: Berlin/Heidelberg, Germany, 2016.
18. Kurachi, R.; Matsubara, Y.; Takada, H.; Adachi, N.; Miyashita, Y.; Horihata, S. CaCAN—Centralized Authentication System in CAN (Controller Area Network). In Proceedings of the 12th International Conference on Embedded Security in Cars (escar Euroupe 2014), Hamburg, Germany, 18–19 November 2014.
19. Groza, B.; Murvay, S.; Herrewege, A.V.; Verbauwhede, I. LiBrA-CAN: Lightweight Broadcast Authentication for Controller Area Networks. *ACM Trans. Embed. Comput. Syst.* **2017**, *16*, 1–28. [CrossRef]
20. Wang, E.; Xu, W.; Sastry, S.; Liu, S.; Zeng, K. Hardware Module-based Message Authentication in Intra-vehicle Networks. In Proceedings of the 8th International Conference on Cyber-Physical Systems, ICCPS '17, Pittsburgh, PA, USA, 18–20 April 2017; ACM: New York, NY, USA, 2017; pp. 207–216. [CrossRef]
21. Jo, H.J.; Kim, J.H.; Choi, H.; Choi, W.; Lee, D.H.; Lee, I. MAuth-CAN: Masquerade-Attack-Proof Authentication for In-Vehicle Networks. *IEEE Trans. Veh. Technol.* **2020**, *69*, 2204–2218. [CrossRef]
22. Sagong, S.U.; Ying, X.; Clark, A.; Bushnell, L.; Poovendran, R. Cloaking the Clock: Emulating Clock Skew in Controller Area Networks. In Proceedings of the 9th ACM/IEEE International Conference on Cyber-Physical Systems, ICCPS '18, Porto, Portugal, 11–13 April 2018; IEEE Press: Piscataway, NJ, USA, 2018; pp. 32–42. [CrossRef]
23. Testa, A.C.M.; Coronato, A. Heuristic strategies for assessing wireless sensor network resiliency: An event-based formal approach. *J. Heuristics* **2015**, *21*, 145–175. [CrossRef]
24. Bengtsson, J.; Yi, W. Timed automata: Semantics, algorithms and tools. *Lect. Notes Comput. Sci.* **2004**, *3098*, 87–124.
25. Behrmann, G.; David, A.; Larsen, K. A Tutorial on Uppaal. In *Formal Methods for the Design of Real-Time Systems*; Springer: Berlin/Heidelberg, Germany, 2004; pp. 33–35.
26. Alur, R.; Feder, T.; Henzinger, T.A. The benefits of relaxing punctuality. *JACM* **1996**, *43*, 116–146. [CrossRef]
27. David, A.; Larsen, K.G.; Legay, A.; Mikučionis, M.; Poulsen, D.B. Uppaal SMC tutorial. *Int. J. Softw. Tools Technol. Transf.* **2015**, *17*, 397–415. [CrossRef]
28. Eldefrawy, K.; Francillon, A.; Perito, D.; Tsudik, G. SMART: Secure and Minimal Architecture for (Establishing a Dynamic) Root of Trust. In Proceedings of the 19th Annual Network and Distributed System Security Symposium (NDSS 2012), San Diego, CA, USA, 5–8 February 2012.
29. Koeberl, P.; Schulz, S.; Sadeghi, A.R.; Varadharajan, V. TrustLite: A Security Architecture for Tiny Embedded Devices. In Proceedings of the Ninth European Conference on Computer Systems, EuroSys '14, Graz, Austria, 7–13 May 2006; ACM: New York, NY, USA, 2014; pp. 1–14. [CrossRef]
30. Wikipedia. CAN Bus. Available online: https://en.wikipedia.org/wiki/CAN_bus (accessed on 20 January 2021).
31. Luykx, A.; Mennink, B.; Neves, S. Security Analysis of BLAKE2's Modes of Operation. *IACR Trans. Symmetric Cryptol.* **2016**, *2016*, 158–176. [CrossRef]

Article

Data Quality Measures and Efficient Evaluation Algorithms for Large-Scale High-Dimensional Data

Hyeongmin Cho and Sangkyun Lee *

School of Cybersecurity, Korea University, Seoul 02841, Korea; whgudals159@korea.ac.kr
* Correspondence: sangkyun@korea.ac.kr

Abstract: Machine learning has been proven to be effective in various application areas, such as object and speech recognition on mobile systems. Since a critical key to machine learning success is the availability of large training data, many datasets are being disclosed and published online. From a data consumer or manager point of view, measuring data quality is an important first step in the learning process. We need to determine which datasets to use, update, and maintain. However, not many practical ways to measure data quality are available today, especially when it comes to large-scale high-dimensional data, such as images and videos. This paper proposes two data quality measures that can compute class separability and in-class variability, the two important aspects of data quality, for a given dataset. Classical data quality measures tend to focus only on class separability; however, we suggest that in-class variability is another important data quality factor. We provide efficient algorithms to compute our quality measures based on random projections and bootstrapping with statistical benefits on large-scale high-dimensional data. In experiments, we show that our measures are compatible with classical measures on small-scale data and can be computed much more efficiently on large-scale high-dimensional datasets.

Keywords: data quality; large-scale; high-dimensionality; linear discriminant analysis; random projection; bootstrapping

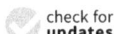

Citation: Cho, H.; Lee, S. Data Quality Measures and Efficient Evaluation Algorithms for Large-Scale High-Dimensional Data. *Appl. Sci.* **2021**, *11*, 472. https://doi.org/10.3390/app11020472

Received: 31 October 2020
Accepted: 4 January 2021
Published: 6 January 2021

Publisher's Note: MDPI stays neutral with regard to jurisdictional claims in published maps and institutional affiliations.

Copyright: © 2021 by the authors. Licensee MDPI, Basel, Switzerland. This article is an open access article distributed under the terms and conditions of the Creative Commons Attribution (CC BY) license (https://creativecommons.org/licenses/by/4.0/).

1. Introduction

We are witnessing the success of machine learning in various research and application areas, such as vision inspection, energy consumption estimation, and autonomous driving, just to name a few. One major contributor to the success is the fact that the datasets are continuously accumulated and openly published in several domains. Low data quality is very likely to cause inferior prediction performance of machine learning models, and therefore measuring data quality is an indispensable step in a machine learning process. Especially in real-time and mission-critical cyber-physical-system, defining appropriate data quality measures is critical since the low generalization performance of a deployed model can result in system malfunction and possibly catastrophic damages to the physical world. Despite the importance, there exist only a few works for measuring data quality where most of them are hard to evaluate on large-scale high-dimensional data due to computation complexity.

A popular early work on data quality measures includes Ho and Basu [1], proposing 12 types of quality measures which are simple but powerful enough to address different aspects of data quality. These measures have limitations, however, in that it is difficult to compute them for large-scale high-dimensional and multi-class datasets. Baumgartner and Somorjai [2] proposed a quality measure designed for high-dimensional biomedical datasets; however, it does not work efficiently on large-scale data. Recently, Branchaud-Charron et al. [3] proposed a quality measure for high-dimensional data using spectral clustering. Although this measure is adequate for large-scale high-dimensional data, it requires an embedding network which involves a large amount of computation time for training.

In this paper, we propose three new quality measures called M_{sep}, M_{var}, and M_{var_i}, and their computation methods that overcome the above limitations. Our approach is inspired by Fisher's linear discriminant analysis (LDA) [4], which is mathematically well-defined for finding a feature subspace that maximizes class separability. Our computation method makes use of the techniques from statistics, random projection [5] and bootstrapping [6], to compute the measure for large-scale high-dimensional data efficiently.

The contributions of our paper are summarized as follows:

- We propose three new data quality measures that can be compuated directly from a given dataset and can be compared across datasets with different numbers of classes, examples, and features. Although our approach takes ideas from LDA (linear discriminant analysis) and PCA (principal component analysis), the techniques by themselves do not produce single numbers that are comparable across different datasets.
- We provide efficient algorithms to approximate the suggested data quality measures, making them available for large-scale high-dimensional data.
- The proposed class separability measure M_{sep} is strongly correlated with the actual classification performance of linear and non-linear classifiers in our experiments.
- The proposed in-class variability measures M_{var} and M_{var_i} quantify the diversity of data within each class and can be used to analyze redundancy or outlier issues.

2. Related Work

In general, the quality of data can be measured by Kolmogorov complexity which is also known as the descriptive complexity for algorithmic entropy [7]. However, the Kolmogorov complexity is not computationally feasible; instead, an approximation is used in practice. To our knowledge, there are three main approaches for approximating the Kolmogorov complexity: descriptor-based, classifier-based, and graph-based approaches. We describe these three main categories below.

2.1. Descriptor-Based Approaches

Ho and Basu [1] proposed simple but powerful quality measures based on descriptors. They proposed 12 quality measures, namely F1, F2, F3, L1, L2, L3, N1, N2, N3, N4, T1, and T2. The F measures represent the amount of feature overlap. In particular, F1 measures the maximum Fisher's ratio which represents the maximum discriminant power of between features. F2 represents the volume of overlap region in the two-class conditional distributions. F3 captures the ratio of overlapping features using the maximum and minimum value. The L measures are for the linear separability of classes. L1 is a minimum error of linear programming (LP), L2 is an error rate of a linear classifier by LP, and L3 is an error rate of linear classifier after feature interpolation. The N measures represent mixture identifiability, the distinguishability of the data points belonging to two different classes. N1 represents the ratio of nodes connected to the different classes using the minimum spanning tree of all data points. N2 is the ratio of the average intra-class distance and average inter-class distance. N3 is the leave-one-out error rate of the nearest neighbor (1NN). N4 is an error rate of 1NN after feature interpolation. The T measure represents the topological characteristic of a dataset. T1 represents the number of hyperspheres adjacent to other class features. T2 is the average number of data points per dimension. These quality measures can capture various aspects of data quality; however, they are fixed for binary classification and not applicable for multi-class problems. Furthermore, quality measures, such as N1, N2, and N3, require a large amount of computation time on large-scale high-dimensional data.

Baumgartner and Somorjai [2] proposed a quality measure for high-dimensional but small biomedical datasets. They used singular value decomposition (SVD) with time complexity $\mathcal{O}(min(m^2n, mn^2))$, where m is the number of data points, and n is the number of features. Thus, it is computationally demanding to calculate their measures for the datasets with large m and n, such as recent image datasets.

There are other descriptor-based approaches, for example for meta learning [8,9], for classifier recommendation [10], and for synthetic data generation [11]. However, only a small number of data points in a low dimensional space have been considered in these works.

2.2. Graph-Based Approaches

Branchaud-Charron et al. [3] proposed a graph-based quality measure using spectral clustering. First, they compute a probabilistic divergence-based $K \times K$ class similarity matrix S, where K is the number of classes. Then, an adjacency matrix W is computed from the S matrix. The quality measure is defined as a cumulative sum of the eigenvalues gap which is called as cumulative spectral gradient (CSG), which represents the minimum cutting cost of the S. The authors also used a convolutional neural network-based auto-encoder and t-SNE [12,13] to find an embedding that can represent data points (images in their case) well. Although the method is designed for high-dimensional data, it requires to train a good embedding network to reach quality performance.

Duin and Pękalska [14] proposed a quality measure based on a dissimilarity matrix of data points. Since calculating the dissimilarity matrix is a time-consuming process, the method is not adequate for large-scale high-dimensional data.

2.3. Classifier-Based Approaches

Li et al. [15] proposed a classifier-based quality measure called an intrinsic dimension, which is the minimum number of solutions for certain problems. For example, in a neural network, the intrinsic dimension is the minimum number of parameters to reach the desired prediction performance.

The method has a benefit that it can be applied to many different types of data as long as one has trainable classifiers for the data; however, it often incurs high computation cost since it needs to change the number of classifier parameters iteratively during data quality evaluation.

Overall, the existing data quality measures are mostly designed for binary classification in low dimension spaces with a small number of data points. Due to their computation complexity, they tend to consume large amount of time when applied to large-scale high-dimensional data. In addition, the existing measures tend to focus only on the inter-class aspects of data quality. In this paper, we propose two new data quality measures suitable for large-scale high-dimensional data resolving the above mentioned issues.

3. Methods

In this section, we formally describe our data quality measures. We focus on multi-class classification tasks where each data point is associated with a class label out of c categories ($c \geq 2$). Our measures are created by adapting ideas from Fisher's LDA [4]. Fisher's LDA is a dimensionality reduction technique, finding a projection matrix that maximizes the between-class variance and minimizes the within-class variance at the same time. Motivated by the idea, we propose two types of data quality measures, class separability M_{sep} and in-class variability M_{var} and M_{var_i}. For efficient handling of large-scale high-dimensional data, we also propose techniques to reduce both computation and memory requirements taking advantage of statistical methods, bootstrapping [6] and random projection [5].

3.1. Fisher's LDA

The objective of Fisher's LDA [4] is to find the feature subspace which maximizes the linear separability of a given dataset. Fisher's LDA achieves the objective by minimizing the within-class variance and maximizing the between-class variance simultaneously.

To describe the Fisher's LDA formally, let us consider an input matrix $X \in \mathbb{R}^{m \times n}$ where m is the number of data points, n is the input dimension, and $x_{i,j} \in \mathbb{R}^n$ is a j-th data point in the i-th class. The within-class scatter matrix $S_w \in \mathbb{R}^{n \times n}$ is defined as follows:

$$S_w = \sum_{i=1}^{c} \sum_{j=1}^{m_i} (x_{i,j} - \overline{x}_i)(x_{i,j} - \overline{x}_i)^T.$$

Here, c is the number of classes, m_i is the number of data points in the i-th class, and $\overline{x}_i \in \mathbb{R}^n$ is the mean of data points in the i-th class. This formulation can be interpreted as the sum of class-wise scatter matrices. A small determinant of S_w indicates that data points in the same class exist densely in a narrow area, which may lead to high class separability.

Next, the between-class scatter matrix $S_b \in \mathbb{R}^{n \times n}$ is defined as follows:

$$S_b = \sum_{i=1}^{c} m_i (\overline{x}_i - \overline{x})(\overline{x}_i - \overline{x})^T,$$

where $\overline{x}$ is the mean of entire data points in the given dataset. A large determinant of S_b indicates that the mean vector $\overline{x}_i$ of each class is far from the $\overline{x}$, another condition hinting for high class separability.

Using these two matrices, we can describe the objective of Fisher's LDA as follows:

$$\Phi_{lda} \in \arg\max_{\Phi} \frac{|\Phi^T S_b \Phi|}{|\Phi^T S_w \Phi|}. \tag{1}$$

Here, $\Phi_{lda} \in \mathbb{R}^{n \times d}$ is the projection matrix where d is the dimension of feature subspace (in general, we choose $d \ll n$). The column vectors of projection matrix Φ_{lda} are the axes of feature subspace, which maximize the class separability. The term in the objective function is also known as the Fisher's criterion. By projecting X onto these axes, we obtain a d-dimensional projection of the original data $X' \in \mathbb{R}^{m \times d}$:

$$X' = X \Phi_{lda}.$$

In general, if S_w is an invertible matrix, we can calculate the projection matrix which maximizes the objective of the Fisher's LDA by eigenvalue decomposition.

3.2. Proposed Data Quality Measures

Motivated by the ideas in Fisher's LDA, we propose two types of new data quality measures: M_{sep} (class separability), M_{var} and M_{var_i} (in-class variability).

3.2.1. Class Separability

Our first data quality measure tries to capture the class separability of a dataset by combining the within-class variance and between-class variance, similarly to Fisher's LDA (1) but more efficiently for large-scale and high-dimensional data and comparable with other datasets.

We start from creating the normalized versions of the matrices S_w and S_b in Fisher's LDA (1) so that they will not be affected by the different numbers of examples in classes (m_i is the number of examples in the i-th class) across different datasets. The normalized versions are denoted by $\hat{S}_w$ and $\hat{S}_b$:

$$\hat{S}_w := \sum_{i=1}^{c} \frac{1}{m_i} \sum_{j=1}^{m_i} (x_{i,j} - \overline{x}_i)(x_{i,j} - \overline{x}_i)^T, \quad \hat{S}_b := \sum_{i=1}^{c} \frac{m_i}{\sum_{j=1}^{c} m_j} (\overline{x}_i - \overline{x})(\overline{x}_i - \overline{x})^T. \tag{2}$$

Considering the determinants of these $n \times n$ matrices as in the original Fisher's LDA will be too costly for a high-dimensional data where n is large, since the time complexity to compute the determinants will be proportional nearly to n^3. Instead, we consider the direction of maximum linear separation $v \in \mathbb{R}^n$ that maximizes the ratio of between-class variance to the within-class variance being projected onto the vector. Using the vector, we define our first data quality measure M_{sep} for class separability as follows:

$$M_{sep} := \max_{v \in \mathbb{R}^n : \|v\|=1} \frac{|v^T \hat{S}_b v|}{|v^T \hat{S}_w v|}. \tag{3}$$

This formulation is almost the same as (1) in Fisher's LDA except that (1) finds the projection matrix ϕ_{lda} which maximizes the Fisher's criterion, while, in (3), we will focus on finding the maximum value of Fisher's criterion itself. Unlike Fisher's criterion, our measure M_{sep} is comparable across datasets with different numbers of classes and examples due to normalization, to check the relative difficulty of linear classification.

Solving (3) directly will be preventive for a large n as in the original LDA. If $\hat{S}_w$ is invertible, we can calculate the vector which maximizes M_{sep} as follows using simple linear algebra. To find the vector v which maximizes the equation in (3), first differentiate it with respect to v to get:

$$(v^T \hat{S}_b v) \hat{S}_w v = (v^T \hat{S}_w v) \hat{S}_b v.$$

This leads us to the following generalized eigenvalue problem in the form of:

$$\hat{S}_w^{-1} \hat{S}_b v = \lambda v, \tag{4}$$

where $\lambda = \frac{v^T \hat{S}_b v}{v^T \hat{S}_w v}$ can be thought as an eigenvalue of the matrix $\hat{S}_w^{-1} \hat{S}_b$. The maximizer v is the eigenvector corresponding to the largest eigenvalue of $\hat{S}_w^{-1} \hat{S}_b$ which can be found rather efficiently by the Lanczos algorithm [16]. However, the overall time complexity for computation can be up to $\mathcal{O}(n^3)$, which makes it difficult to calculate the optimal vector for high-dimensional data, such as images. In Section 3.3, we provide an efficient algorithm to compute M_{sep} using random projection.

3.2.2. In-Class Variability

Our second data quality measure gauges the in-class variability. Figure 1 shows one of the motivating examples to consider in-class variability for data quality. In the figure, we have two photos of the Bongeunsa temple in Seoul, Korea, taken by the same photographer. The photographer had been asked to take photos of Korean objects from several different angles, and it turned out that quite a few of the photos were taken in only marginal angle differences. Since the data creation was a government-funded project providing data for developing object recognition systems in academia and industry, low data variability was definitely an issue.

Figure 1. An example of low in-class variability that similar images in the same class. The images are Bongeunsa temple in Seoul, Korea. (Source: Korean Type Object Image AI Training Dataset at http://www.aihub.or.kr/aidata/132, National Information Society Agency.)

Here, we define two types of in-class variability measure, the overall in-class variability of a given dataset M_{var} and the in-class variability of the i-th class, M_{var_i}. First, the overall in-class variability M_{var} tries to capture the minimum variance of data points being projected onto any direction, based on the matrix $\hat{S}_w$ defined in (2):

$$M_{var} := \min_{v \in \mathbb{R}^n : \|v\|=1} \frac{1}{c \cdot n} v^T \hat{S}_w v,$$

where c is the number of class and n is the dimension of data. Unlike class separability, we added additional normalization factors c and n, since the value $\hat{S}_w$ is affected by the number of class and the data dimension.

Second, the class-wise in-class variability M_{var_i} is based on the sample covariance matrix of each class:

$$\hat{S}_{w_i} := \frac{1}{m_i} \sum_{j=1}^{m_i} (x_{i,j} - \overline{x}_i)(x_{i,j} - \overline{x}_i)^T,$$

where m_i is the number of data points in the i-th class. The class-wise in-class variability measure M_{var_i} is defined as follows:

$$M_{var_i} := \min_{v \in \mathbb{R}^n : \|v\|=1} \frac{1}{c \cdot n} v^T \hat{S}_{w_i} v \ .$$

The normalization factors c and n are required for the same reason as in M_{var}. The measure M_{var_i} represents the smallest variance of the data points in the same class after being projected onto any direction.

As a matter of fact, M_{var} and M_{var_i} are the same as the smallest eigenvalue of $\frac{1}{c \cdot n} \hat{S}_w$ and $\frac{1}{c \cdot n} \hat{S}_{w_i}$ which can be computed for instance using the Lanczos algorithm [16] on the inverse of them with $\mathcal{O}(n^3)$ computation, which will be preventive for large data dimensions n. We discuss a more efficient way to estimate the value in the next section, which can be computed alongside with our first data quality measure without significant extra cost.

Using the M_{var} and M_{var_i}, we can analyze the variety or redundancy in a given dataset. For instance, a very small M_{var} and M_{var_i} would indicate that we may have a small diversity issue where data points in the invested class are mostly alike. On the other hand, the overly large M_{var} and M_{var_i} may indicate a noise issue in the class, possibly including incorrect labeling. The difference between M_{var} and M_{var_i} is that the M_{var} aggregates the information of diversity for each class, and the M_{var_i} represents the information of diversity for a specific class. Since the M_{var} aggregates the information of variability of data points in each class, we can use this for comparing the in-class variability between datasets. On the other hand, we can use M_{var_i} for the datasets analysis, i.e., data points of a specific class with less M_{var_i} than other classes may cause low generalization performance. We will discuss more details in Section 4.

3.3. Methods for Efficient Computation

One of the key properties required for data quality measures is that they should be computable in a reasonable amount of time and computation resources since the amount and the dimension of data are keep increasing as new advanced sensing technologies become available. In this section, we describe how we avoid a large amount of time and memory complexity to compute our suggested data quality measures.

3.3.1. Random Projection

Random projection [5] is a dimension reduction technique that can transform an n-dimensional vector into a k-dimensional vector ($k \ll n$), while preserving the critical information of the original vector. The idea behind of random projection is the Johnson-Lindenstrauss lemma [17]. That is, for any vectors $\{x, x'\} \in X$ from a set of m vectors in

$X \subset \mathbb{R}^n$ and for $\epsilon \in (0,1)$, there exists a linear mapping $f : \mathbb{R}^n \to \mathbb{R}^k$ such that the pairwise distances of vectors are almost preserved after projection in the sense that:

$$(1-\epsilon)\|x-x'\|_2^2 \leq \|f(x)-f(x')\|_2^2 \leq (1+\epsilon)\|x-x'\|_2^2,$$

where $k > 8\ln(m)/\epsilon^2$. It is known that when the original dimension n is large, a random projection matrix $P \in \mathbb{R}^{k \times n}$ can serve as the feature mapping f in the lemma, since random vectors in $\mathbb{R}^n$ tend to be orthogonal to each other as n increases [18].

Motivated by the above phenomenon, we use random projection to find a vector that satisfies (3) instead of calculating the eigenvalue decomposition to solve (4). The idea is that if the number of random vectors is sufficiently large, the maximum value of the Fisher's criterion calculated by random projection can approximate the behavior of a true solution.

Furthermore, random projection makes it unnecessary to explicitly store $\hat{S}_w$ and $\hat{S}_b$ since we can simply compute the denominator and numerator of (3) as follows:

$$w^T \hat{S}_w w = \sum_{i=1}^{c} \frac{1}{m_i} \sum_{j=1}^{m_i} w^T (x_{i,j} - \overline{x}_i)(x_{i,j} - \overline{x}_i)^T w,$$

$$w^T \hat{S}_b w = \sum_{i=1}^{c} \frac{m_i}{\sum_{j=1}^{c} m_j} w^T (\overline{x}_i - \overline{x})(\overline{x}_i - \overline{x})^T w,$$

where w is a random unit vector drawn from $\mathcal{N}(0,1)$. This technique is critical for dealing with high-dimensional data, such as images, in a memory-efficient way. In our experiments, ten random projection vectors were sufficient in most cases to accurately estimate our quality measures.

3.3.2. Bootstrapping

Bootstrapping [6] is a sampling-based technique that estimates the statistic of the population with little data using sampling with replacement. For instance, bootstrapping can be used to estimate the mean and the variance of a statistic from an unknown population. Let s_i is a statistic of interest that is calculated from a randomly drawn sample of an unknown population. The mean and variance of the statistic can be estimated as follows:

$$\hat{\mu} = \frac{1}{B}\sum_{i=1}^{B} s_i, \quad \hat{\sigma}^2 = \frac{1}{B}\sum_{i=1}^{B} s_i^2 - \left(\frac{1}{B}\sum_{i=1}^{B} s_i\right)^2,$$

where B is the number of bootstrap samples, $\hat{\mu}$ is a mean estimate of the statistic, and $\hat{\sigma}^2$ is the variability of the estimate. By using a small B, we can reduce the number of data points to be considered at once. We found that $B = 100$ and making each bootstrap sample to be 25% of a given dataset in size worked well overall our experiments. We summarized the above procedure in Algorithm 1 (The implementation is available here: https://github.com/Hyeongmin-Cho/Efficient-Data-Quality-Measures-for-High-Dimensional-Classification-Data).

Algorithm 1: Algorithm of class separability and in-class variability.

Result: M_{sep}, M_{var} and M_{var_i} score
Dataset = $\{(x_1, y_1), \ldots, (x_m, y_m)\}$
Args= the number of samples B, a sample ratio of each bootstrap sample against a given dataset R, the number of random vector used in each sample nv, an array storing the values of overall in-class variability A_{var}, an array storing the values of class-wise in-class variability A_{var_i} and an array storing the values of class separability A_{sep}.
$'\leftarrow'$ symbol stands for variable assignment

$i \leftarrow 1$
$A_{var} \leftarrow \{\}$
$A_{var_i} \leftarrow \{\}$
$A_{sep} \leftarrow \{\}$
while $i \leq B$ **do**
    $j \leftarrow 1$
    $i \leftarrow i + 1$
    Calculate the number of class c and data dimension n from the dataset
    Sampling with replacement using stratified sampling as much as R ratio from the dataset
    Standardize the sampled dataset
    while $j \leq nv$ **do**
        $j \leftarrow j + 1$
        $w \leftarrow$ a unit vector drawn from $\mathcal{N}(0, 1)$
        Compute $w^T \hat{S}_{w_{j,c}} w$
        $w^T \hat{S}_{w_j} w \leftarrow Sum(\{w^T \hat{S}_{w_{j,1}} w, \ldots, w^T \hat{S}_{w_{j,c}} w\})$
        $M_{var-j} \leftarrow w^T \hat{S}_{w_j} w$
        Compute $w^T \hat{S}_{b_j} w$
        $M_{sep-j} \leftarrow (w^T \hat{S}_{b_j} w) / (w^T \hat{S}_{w_j} w)$
    end
    A_{var_i}.insert($\{\frac{1}{c \cdot n} \min(w^T \hat{S}_{w_{1,1}} w, \ldots, w^T \hat{S}_{w_{nv,1}} w), \ldots, \frac{1}{c \cdot n} \min(w^T \hat{S}_{w_{1,c}} w, \ldots, w^T \hat{S}_{w_{nv,c}} w)\}$)
    A_{var}.insert($\frac{1}{c \cdot n} \min(M_{var-1}, \ldots, M_{var-nv})$)
    A_{sep}.insert($\max(M_{sep-1}, \ldots, M_{sep-nv})$)
end
$M_{sep} \leftarrow Mean(A_{sep})$
$M_{var} \leftarrow Mean(A_{var})$
$M_{var_i} \leftarrow ClassWiseMean(A_{var_i})$
Return $M_{sep}, M_{var}, M_{var_i}$

4. Experiment Results

In this section, we show that our method can evaluate the data quality of the large-scale high-dimensional dataset efficiently.

To verify the representative performance of M_{sep} for class separability, we calculated the correlation between the accuracy of chosen classifiers and M_{sep}. Classifiers used in our experiments are as follows: a perceptron, a multi-layer perceptron with one hidden layer and LeakyReLU (denoted by MLP-1), and a multi-layer perceptron with two hidden layers and LeakyReLU (denoted by MLP-2). To simplify the experiments, we trained the models with the following settings: 30 epochs, a batch size of 100, a learning rate of 0.002, the Adam optimizer, and the cross-entropy loss function. Additionally, we fixed the hyperparameters of Algorithm 1 as $B = 100$, $R = 0.25$, and $nv = 10$ since there was no big difference in performance when larger hyperparameter values were used.

For comparison with other quality measures, we chose F1, N1, and N3 from Ho and Basu [1] and CSG from Branchaud-Charron et al. [3]. Here, N1, N3, and CSG are known to be highly correlated with test accuracy of classifiers Branchaud-Charron et al. [3]. F1 is similar to our M_{sep} in its basic idea. Other quality measures suggested in Ho and Basu [1] showed very similar characteristics to $F1$, $N1$, $N3$, and CSG and are therefore not included in the results.

4.1. Datasets

To evaluate the representative performance of M_{sep} for class separability, we used various image datasets that are high-dimensional and popular in mobile applications. We chose ten benchmark image datasets for our experiments: MNIST, notMNIST, CIFAR10, Linnaeus, STL10, SVHN, ImageNet-1, ImageNet-2, ImageNet-3, and ImageNet-4. MNIST [19] consists of ten handwritten digits from 0 to 9. The dataset contains 60,000 training and 10,000 test data points. We sampled 10,000 data from the training data for a model training and measuring the quality, and we sampled 2500 data from the test data for assessing the model accuracy. The notMNIST [20] dataset is quite similar to MNIST, containing English letters from A to J in various fonts. It has 13,106 training and 5618 test samples. We sampled the data in the same way as MNIST. Linnaeus [21] consists of five classes: berry, bird, dog, flower, and others. Although the dataset is available in various image sizes, we chose 32×32 to reduce the computation time of $N1$, $N3$, and CSG. CIFAR10 [22] is for object recognition with ten general object classes. It consists of 50,000 training data and 10,000 test data points. We sampled the CIFAR10 dataset in the same way as MNIST. STL10 [23] is also for object recognition with ten classes, and it has 92×92 images: we resized the images into 32×32 to reduce the computation time for the $N1$, $N3$, and CSG. The dataset consists of 5000 training and 8000 test data points. We combined these two sets into a single dataset, and then sampled 10,000 data points from the combined set for model training and measuring quality. We also sampled 2500 data points from the combined set for assessing prediction model accuracy if necessary. SVHN [24] consists of street view house number images. The dataset contains 73,200 data points. We sampled 10,000 training data for a model training and measuring the quality, and we sampled 2500 data for assessing the model accuracy. ImageNet-1, ImageNet-2, ImageNet-3 and ImageNet-4 are subsets of Tiny ImageNet dataset [25]. The Tiny ImageNet dataset contains 200 classes, and each class has 500 images. They are consist of randomly selected ten classes of the Tiny ImageNet dataset (total 5000 data points). We used 4500 data points for model training and measuring the quality and 500 data points for assessing the model accuracy, respectively.

We summarized the details of datasets in Table 1. The accuracy values in the Table 1 are calculated from the MLP-2 model since it showed good overall performance compared to the perceptron and the MLP-1 models.

Table 1. Details of the datasets used in our experiments. The accuracy is from MLP-2, and M represents the total number of data used for training and evaluation.

Datasets	Accuracy	M	No. Classes	Description
MNIST	92.64%	12.5 k	10	Hand written digit
notMNIST	89.24%	12.5 k	10	Fonts and glyphs similar to MNIST
Linnaeus	45.50%	4.8 k	5	Botany and animal class images
CIFAR10	42.84%	12.5 k	10	Object recognition images
STL10	40.88%	12.5 k	10	Object recognition images
SVHN	45.60%	12.5 k	10	House number images
ImageNet-1	37.40%	5 k	10	Visual recognition images (Tiny ImageNet)
ImageNet-2	40.60%	5 k	10	Visual recognition images (Tiny ImageNet)
ImageNet-3	34.20%	5 k	10	Visual recognition images (Tiny ImageNet)
ImageNet-4	36.20%	5 k	10	Visual recognition images (Tiny ImageNet)

4.2. Representation Performance of the Class Separability Measure M_{Sep}

Here, we show in experiments that how well our first quality measure M_{sep} represents class separability, compared to simple but popular classifiers and the existing data quality measures.

4.2.1. Correlation with Classifier Accuracy

To demonstrate how well M_{sep} represents the class separability of given datasets, we compared the absolute value of Pearson correlation and Spearman rank correlation between quality measures M_{sep}, $N1$, $N3$, $F1$, and CSG to the prediction accuracy of three classification models: perceptron, MLP-1, and MLP-2. Table 2 summarizes the results.

In the case of the perceptron, M_{sep} has a similar Pearson correlation with the shortest computation time to the $N1$ and $N3$ which have the highest correlation with the accuracy of classifiers. Furthermore, M_{sep} and $F1$ have the highest Spearman rank correlation. This is because M_{sep} and $F1$ measure linear separability that is essentially the information captured by the linear classifier, the perceptron in our case. In the case of MLP-1 and MLP-2, M_{sep} also showed a sufficiently high correlation with classification accuracy although it is slightly lower in Pearson correlation compared to the case of the perceptron. On the other hand, CSG does not seem to have noticeable benefits considering its computation time. This is because CSG is affected by an embedding network which requires a large amount of training time.

In summary, the result shows that our measure M_{sep} can capture separability of data as good as the existing data quality measures, while reducing computation time significantly.

Table 2. The absolute Pearson and Spearman rank correlation between the quality measures and the accuracy of three classifiers on the ten image datasets (MNIST, CIFAR10, notMNIST, Linnaeus, STL10, SVHN, ImageNet-1, ImageNet-2, ImageNet-3, and ImageNet-4). The computation time of our method M_{sep} is the fastest.

Classifier	Quality Measure	Pearson Corr.	Spearman Corr.	Time (s)
Perceptron	$F1$	0.9386	0.7697	1253
	$N1$	0.9889	0.7333	5104
	$N3$	0.9858	0.7333	9858
	CSG	0.9452	0.8182	23,711
	M_{sep} (ours)	0.9693	0.8061	354
MLP-1	$F1$	0.9039	0.3455	1253
	$N1$	0.9959	0.9758	5104
	$N3$	0.9961	0.9030	9858
	CSG	0.9295	0.5879	23,711
	M_{sep} (ours)	0.9261	0.3818	354
MLP-2	$F1$	0.8855	0.3455	1253
	$N1$	0.9908	0.9273	5104
	$N3$	0.9912	0.8788	9858
	CSG	0.9127	0.5879	23,711
	M_{sep} (ours)	0.9117	0.4303	354

4.2.2. Correlation with Other Quality Measures

In order to check if our suggested data quality measure M_{sep} is compatible with the existing ones in quality, and therefore ours can be a faster alternative to the existing data quality measures, we computed the Pearson correlation between $F1$, $N1$, $N3$, CSG, and M_{sep}. The results are summarized in Table 3. Our measure M_{sep} showed a high correlation with all four existing measures $F1$, $N1$, $N3$, and CSG, indicating that M_{sep} is able to capture the data quality information represented by $F1$, $N1$, $N3$, and CSG.

Table 3. The absolute Pearson correlation between M_{sep} and other quality measures.

	M_{sep} (Ours)	F1	N1	N3	CSG
M_{sep} (ours)	1.0000	0.9673	0.9322	0.9245	0.9199
F1	0.9673	1.000	0.8909	0.8879	0.8806
N1	0.9322	0.8909	1.0000	0.9988	0.9400
N3	0.9245	0.8879	0.9988	1.000	0.9417
CSG	0.9199	0.8806	0.9400	0.9417	1.0000

4.2.3. Computation Time

As mentioned above, our quality measure M_{sep} represents the class separability well, but much faster in computation than F1, N1, N3, and CSG. Here, we show how the computation time changes according to data dimension and sample sizes, in order to show that our suggested data quality measure can be used for many big-data situations.

The computation time according to the data dimension is shown in Figure 2 and Table 4. In all dimensions, our measure M_{sep} was on average 3.8 times faster than F1, 13.1 times faster than N1, 25.9 times faster than N3, and 17.7 times faster than CSG. Since the N1, N3, and CSG have to calculate the MST and to train a 1NN classifier and embedding networks, respectively, it is inevitable that they would take a large amount of computation time (see more details in Sections 2.1 and 2.2). On the other hand, since M_{sep} utilizes random projection and bootstrapping to avoid eigenvalue decomposition problem and to deal with the big-data situations, the computation time of M_{sep} is shortest in all cases.

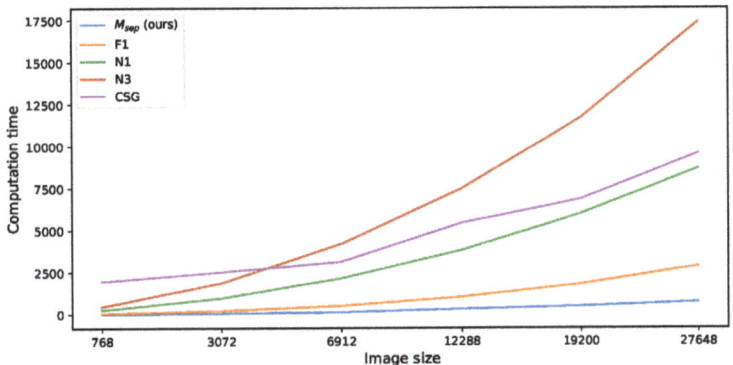

Figure 2. Data dimension vs. computation time (CIFAR10).

Table 4. Data dimension vs. computation time (CIFAR10) in detail (the values in the table represent seconds).

Image Size	Dimension	F1	N1	N3	CSG	M_{sep} (Ours)	Speedup
$16 \times 16 \times 3$	768	49	246	445	1963	17	$\times 2.9 \sim 115.5$
$32 \times 32 \times 3$	3072	203	947	1850	2513	57	$\times 3.6 \sim 44.1$
$48 \times 48 \times 3$	6912	492	2144	4182	3132	122	$\times 4.0 \sim 34.3$
$64 \times 64 \times 3$	12,288	1011	3810	7466	5427	303	$\times 3.3 \sim 24.6$
$80 \times 80 \times 3$	19,200	1783	5973	11,674	6838	461	$\times 3.9 \sim 25.3$
$96 \times 96 \times 3$	27,648	2850	8652	17,346	9550	700	$\times 4.1 \sim 24.8$

Figure 3 and Table 5 show how computation time changes for various sample sizes. Our measure M_{sep} was on average 2.8 times faster than F1, 47.0 times faster than N1, 94.5 times faster than N3, and 41.6 times faster than CSG. N1 and N3 show extremely increasing computation time with respect to the sample size, which is not suitable for large-scale high-dimensional datasets.

All the above results show that our measure M_{sep} is suitable for the big-data situations and compatible with other well-accepted data quality measures.

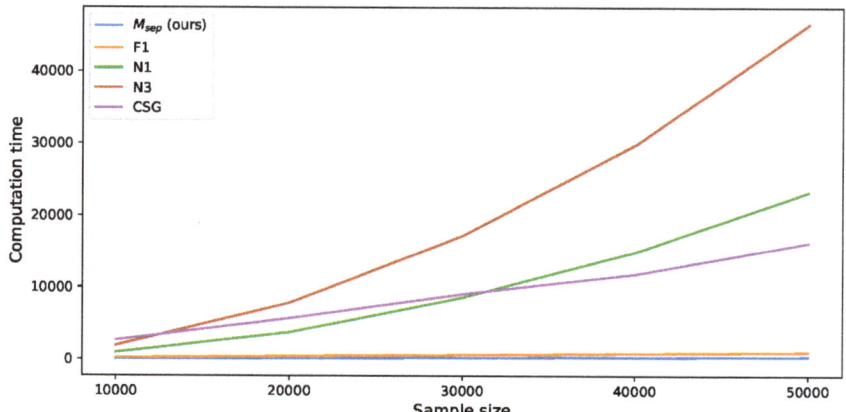

Figure 3. Sample size vs. computation time (CIFAR10).

Table 5. Sample size vs. computation time (CIFAR10) in detail (the values in the table represent seconds).

Sample Size	F1	N1	N3	CSG	M_{sep} (Ours)	Speedup
10,000	205	939	1904	2645	56	×3.7 ~ 47.2
20,000	411	3719	7797	5674	136	×3.0 ~ 57.3
30,000	605	8572	17,177	9065	220	×2.8 ~ 78.1
40,000	825	14,896	29,813	11,843	293	×2.8 ~ 101.8
50,000	1006	23,235	46,541	16,208	387	×2.6 ~ 120.3

4.2.4. Comparison to Exact Computation

In Section 3.2, we proposed to use random projections and bootstrapping for fast approximation of the solution of (4), which can be computed exactly as an eigenvalue. Here, we compare the values of M_{sep} using the proposed approximate computation (denoted by "Approx") and the exact computation (denoted by "Exact") due to an eigensolver in the Python scipy package. One thing is that, since we use only Gaussian random vectors for projection, it is likely that they may not match the true eigenvectors; therefore, the approximated quantity would differ from the exact value. However, we found that the approximate quantities match well the exact values in their correlation, as indicated in Table 6, and, therefore, can be used for fast comparison of data quality of high-dimensional large-scale datasets.

4.3. Class-Wise In-Class Variability Measure, M_{Var_i}

In fact, many of the existing data quality measures are designed to measure the difficulty of classification for a given dataset. However, we believe that the in-class variability of data must be considered as another important factor of data quality. One example to show the importance and usefulness of our in-class variability measure M_{var_i} is the generalization performance of a classifier.

Table 6. Comparison of Exact and Approx values and their correlations. Pearson and Spearman are the Pearson and Spearman rank correlation between the Exact and Approx.

	Exact	*Approx*
MNIST	0.1550	0.0535
CIFAR10	0.0331	0.0173
notMNIST	0.2123	0.0625
Linnaeus	0.0250	0.0118
STL10	0.0695	0.0207
SVHN	0.0004	0.0010
ImageNet-1	0.0062	0.0131
ImageNet-2	0.0293	0.0145
ImageNet-3	0.0191	0.0125
ImageNet-4	0.0092	0.0076
Pearson		0.9847
Spearman		0.9152

The generalization performance of the learning model is an important consideration especially in mission-critical AI-augmented systems. There are many possible reasons causing low generalization, and overfitting is one of the troublemakers. Although we have techniques to alleviate overfitting, e.g., checking the learning curve, regularization [26,27], and ensemble learning [28], it is critical to check if there is an issue in data to begin with which may lead to any inductive bias. For example, a very small value of M_{var_i} in a class compared to the others would indicate a lack of variability in the class, which can lead to low generalization due to, e.g., unchecked input noise, background signal, object occlusion, and angle/brightness/contrast differences during training. On the other hand, the overly large M_{var_i} may indicate outliers or even mislabeled data points likely to incur unwanted inductive bias in training.

To show the importance and usefulness of in-class variability, we created a degraded version of CIFAR10 (denoted by degraded-CIFAR10) by reducing the variability of a specific class. The degraded-CIFAR10 is created by the following procedure. First, we chose an image of the deer class in the training data, then selected the nine mostly similar images in the angular distance to the chosen one. Figure 4 shows the total ten images selected by the above procedure that have similar backgrounds and shapes. Next, we created 1000 images by sampling with replacement from the ten images, while adding random Gaussian noise with zero mean and unit variance, and we replaced the original deer class data with sampled degraded deer class data.

Table 7 shows that the value of M_{var_i} is significantly small on the degraded deer class compared to the other classes. That is, it can capture small in-class variability. In contrast, Table 8 shows that the existing quality measures *F1*, *N1*, *N3*, and *CSG* may not be enough to signify the degradation of the dataset. As we can see, all quality measures indicate that class separability increased in degraded-CIFAR10 compared to the original CIFAR10; however, the test accuracy from MLP-2 decreased. This is because the reduction in in-class variability is very likely to decrease the generalization performance. Therefore, class separability measures can deliver incorrect information regarding data quality in terms of in-class variability, which can be a critical problem for generating a trustworthy dataset or training a trustworthy model.

Figure 4. Ten similar selected images in the deer class on degraded-CIFAR10. Images with high similarity were selected using cosine similarity.

Table 7. Our in-class variability measure for the degraded-CIFAR10 dataset. A class with a smaller value than other classes has a lower variability.

Class	Measure $M_{var_i} \times 1000$
Airplane	0.1557
Automobile	0.2069
Bird	0.1394
Cat	0.1803
Deer	**0.0123**
Dog	0.1830
Frog	0.1344
Horse	0.1775
Ship	0.1472
Truck	0.1997

Table 8. Quality measures on the degraded-CIFAR10 dataset. The existing quality measures $F1$, $N1$, $N3$, and CSG only capture the class separability and fail to capture the degradation. Lower values of $N1$, $N3$, and CSG represent higher class separability, whereas lower values of $F1$ represent lower class separability. The test accuracy is from MLP-2 trained with original and degraded-CIFAR10, respectively, and tested on the original CIFAR10 test data.

Data \ Quality Measure	$F1$	$N1$	$N3$	CSG	Test Accuracy (%)
Original CIFAR10	0.2213	0.7909	0.7065	0.7030	42.84
Degraded-CIFAR10	0.2698	0.7035	0.6096	0.6049	41.28

As we showed above, the small value of M_{var_i} of a specific class represents that similar images do exist in the invested class, which can lead to low generalization performance of classifiers. Suppose we have generated a dataset for an autonomous driving object classification task. The dataset has been revealed that it has a high class separability through various quality measures. Moreover, the training accuracy was also high. Therefore, one may expect high generalization performance. Unfortunately, the exact opposite can happen. If the variability in the specific class is small as in the degraded-CIFAR10 example above, high generalization performance cannot be expected. For instance, if a car with new colors and new shapes that have never been trained is given as an input to the model, the probability of properly classifying the car will be low. This example indicates that in-class variability plays an important role in data quality evaluation.

4.4. Quality Ranking Using M_{Sep} and M_{Var}

As we mentioned before, quality measures M_{sep} and M_{var} can be compared among different datasets. The class separability M_{sep} represents the relative difficulty of linear classification, and the overall in-class variability M_{var} represents the average variability of data points in classes.

Figure 5 shows a data quality comparison plot of datasets in our experiments. The direction towards the lower-left corner indicates lower class separability and lower in-class variability, and the upper-right direction is for higher class separability and higher in-class variability. According to the plot, the MNIST and the notMNIST dataset show very high linear separability compared to other datasets, indicating that their classification might be easier than the other datasets. The SVHN dataset is at the lower-left corner, indicating low linear separability and possible redundancy issues (this could be just the reflection of the fact that many SVHN images contain changing digits but the same backgrounds). The four ImageNet datasets, Linnaeus, CIFAR10 and STL10 have similar class separability and in-class variability values. This appears to be understandable considering their similar data construction designed for object recognition.

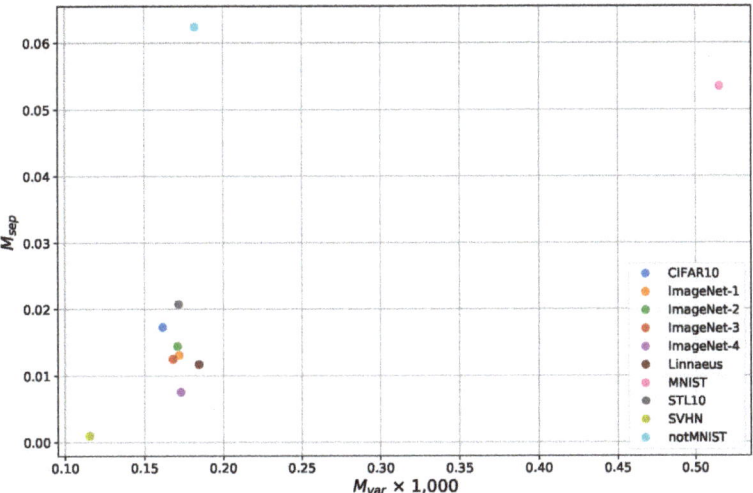

Figure 5. Data quality plot using the two proposed quality measures.

5. Conclusions

In this paper, we proposed data quality measures M_{sep}, M_{var} and M_{var_i}, which can be applied efficiently on large-scale high-dimensional datasets. Our measures are estimated using random projection and bootstrapping and therefore can be applied efficiently on large-scale high-dimensional data. We showed that M_{sep} can be used as a good alternative to the existing data quality measures capturing class separability, while reducing their computational overhead significantly. In addition, M_{var} and M_{var_i} measures in-class variability, which is another important factor to avoid unwanted inductive bias in trained models.

Author Contributions: Conceptualization, H.C. and S.L.; methodology, H.C. and S.L.; validation, H.C.; writing-original draft preparation, H.C.; writing-review and editing, S.L.; supervision, S.L. All authors have read and agreed to the published version of the manuscript.

Funding: This research was supported by Basic Science Research Program through the National Research Foundation of Korea(NRF) funded by the Ministry of Education(2018R1D1A1B07051383), and also by the MSIT(Ministry of Science and ICT), Korea, under the ITRC(Information Technology Research Center) support program(IITP-2020-0-01749) supervised by the IITP(Institute of Information & Communications Technology Planning & Evaluation).

Data Availability Statement: The data presented in this study are openly available: MNIST (http://yann.lecun.com/exdb/mnist/), notMNIST (https://www.kaggle.com/lubaroli/notmnist), Linnaeus (http://chaladze.com/l5/), CIFAR10 (https://www.cs.toronto.edu/~kriz/cifar.html), STL10 (https://ai.stanford.edu/~acoates/stl10/), SVHN (http://ufldl.stanford.edu/housenumbers/), and ImageNet (https://www.kaggle.com/c/tiny-imagenet).

Conflicts of Interest: The authors declare no conflict of interest.

References

1. Ho, T.K.; Basu, M. Complexity measures of supervised classification problems. *IEEE Trans. Pattern Anal. Mach. Intell.* **2002**, *24*, 289–300.
2. Baumgartner, R.; Somorjai, R. Data complexity assessment in undersampled classification of high-dimensional biomedical data. *Pattern Recognit. Lett.* **2006**, *27*, 1383–1389. [CrossRef]
3. Branchaud-Charron, F.; Achkar, A.; Jodoin, P.M. Spectral metric for dataset complexity assessment. In Proceedings of the IEEE Conference on Computer Vision and Pattern Recognition, Long Beach, CA, USA, 15–21 June 2019.
4. Hancock, J.M.; Zvelebil, M.J.; Cristianini, N. Fisher Discriminant Analysis (Linear Discriminant Analysis). *Dict. Bioinform. Comput. Biol.* Available online: https://doi.org/10.1002/9780471650126.dob0238.pub2 (accessed on 25 October 2020).
5. Bingham, E.; Mannila, H. Random projection in dimensionality reduction: Applications to image and text data. In Proceedings of the ACM Special Interest Group on Knowledge Discovery in Data, San Francisco, CA, USA, 26–29 August 2001.
6. Efron, B. Bootstrap Methods: Another look at the jackknife. *Ann. Stat.* **1979**, *7*, 1–26. [CrossRef]
7. Li, M.; Vitányi, P. *An Introduction to Kolmogorov Complexity and Its Applications*; Springer: Berlin, Germany, 2008.
8. Leyva, E.; González, A.; Pérez, R. A set of complexity measures designed for applying meta-learning to instance selection. *IEEE Trans. Knowl. Data Eng.* **2015**, *27*, 354–367. [CrossRef]
9. Sotoca, J.M.; Mollineda, R.A.; Sánchez, J.S. A meta-learning framework for pattern classification by means of data complexity measures. *Intel. Artif.* **2006**, *10*, 31–38.
10. Garcia, L.P.F.; Lorena, A.C.; de Souto, M.C.P.; Ho, T.K. Classifier recommendation using data complexity measures. In Proceedings of the International Conference on Pattern Recognition, Beijing, China, 20–24 August 2018.
11. de Melo, V.V.; Lorena, A.C. Using complexity measures to evolve synthetic classification datasets. In Proceedings of the IEEE International Joint Conference on Neural Network, Rio de Janeiro, Brazil, 8–13 July 2018.
12. Masci, J.; Meier, U.; Cireşan, D.; Schmidhuber, J. Stacked Convolutional Auto-Encoders for Hierarchical Feature Extraction. In Proceedings of the International Conference on Artificial Neural Networks, Espoo, Finland, 14–17 June 2011.
13. van der Maaten, L.; Hinton, G. Visualizing Data using t-SNE. *J. Mach. Learn. Res.* **2008**, *9*, 2579–2605.
14. Duin, R.P.W.; Pękalska, E. Object representation, sample size and dataset complexity. *Data Complexity in Pattern Recognition*; Springer: Berlin, Germany, 2006.
15. Li, C.; Farkhoor, H.; Liu, R.; Yosinski, J. Measuring the intrinsic dimension of object landscapes. In Proceedings of the International Conference on Learning Representations, Vancouver, BC, Canada, 30 April–3 May 2018.
16. Golub, G.H.; Loan, C.F.V. *Matrix Computations*. Baltimore; Johns Hopkins University Press: Baltimore, MD, USA, 1996; pp. 470–507.
17. Dasgupta, S.; Gupta, A. *An Elementary Proof of the Johnson-Lindenstrauss Lemma*; Technical Report; UC Berkeley: Berkeley, CA, USA, 1999.
18. Kaski, S. Dimensionality reduction by random mapping: Fast similarity computation for clustering. In Proceedings of the IEEE International Joint Conference on Neural Networks, Anchorage, AK, USA, 4–9 May 1998.
19. LeCun, Y.; Cortes, C. MNIST Handwritten Digit Database. Available online: http://yann.lecun.com/exdb/mnist/ (accessed on 25 October 2020).
20. Bulatov, Y. Notmnist Dataset. Technical Report, Google (Books/OCR). 2011. Available online: http://yaroslavvb.blogspot.it/2011/09/notmnist-dataset.html (accessed on 25 October 2020).
21. Chaladz, G.; Kalatozishvili, L. Linnaeus 5 Dataset for Machine Learning. Available online: http://chaladze.com/l5/ (accessed on 25 October 2020).
22. Krizhevsky, A. *Learning Multiple Layer of Features from Tiny Images*; Technical Report; Computer Science Department, University of Toronto: Toronto, ON, Canada, 2009.
23. Coates, A.; Lee, H.; Ng, A.Y. An analysis of single layer networks in unsupervised feature learning. *J. Mach. Learn. Res.* **2011**, *15*, 215–223

24. Netzer, Y.; Wang, T.; Coates, A.; Bissacco, A.; Wu, B.; Ng, A.Y. Reading Digits in Natural Images with Unsupervised Feature Learning. In Proceedings of the NIPS Workshop on Deep Learning and Unsupervised Feature Learning, Granada, Spain, 16–17 December 2011.
25. Deng, J.; Dong, W.; Socher, R.; Li, L.J.; Li, K.; Fei-Fei, L. ImageNet: A large-scale hierarchical image database. In Proceedings of the IEEE Conference on Computer Vision and Pattern Recognition, Miami, FL, USA, 20–25 June 2009; pp. 248–255.
26. Srivastava, N.; Hinton, G.; Krizhevsky, A.; Sutskever, I.; Salakhutdinov, R. Dropout: A Simple Way to Prevent Neural Networks from Overfitting. *J. Mach. Learn. Res.* **2014**, *15*, 1929–1958.
27. Ioffe, S.; Szegedy, C. Batch Normalization: Accelerating Deep Network Training by Reducing Internal Covariate Shift. *arXiv* **2015**, arXiv:1502.03167.
28. Opitz, D.; Maclin, R. Popular Ensemble Methods: An Empirical Study. *J. Artif. Intell. Res.* **1999**, *11*, 169–198. [CrossRef]

Article

SPEKS: Forward Private SGX-Based Public Key Encryption with Keyword Search

Hyundo Yoon [1], Soojung Moon [2], Youngki Kim [2], Changhee Hahn [1], Wonjun Lee [2] and Junbeom Hur [1],*

[1] Department of Computer Science and Engineering, Korea University, Seoul 02841, Korea; hdyoon@isslab.korea.ac.kr (H.Y.); hahn850514@korea.ac.kr (C.H.)

[2] School of Cybersecurity, Korea University, Seoul 02841, Korea; sjmoon28@korea.ac.kr (S.M.); kyk642@korea.ac.kr (Y.K.); wlee@korea.ac.kr (W.L.)

* Correspondence: jbhur@korea.ac.kr

Received: 15 September 2020; Accepted: 2 November 2020; Published: 5 November 2020

Abstract: Public key encryption with keyword search (PEKS) enables users to search over encrypted data outsourced to an untrusted server. Unfortunately, updates to the outsourced data may incur information leakage by exploiting the previously submitted queries. Prior works addressed this issue by means of forward privacy, but most of them suffer from significant performance degradation. In this paper, we present a novel forward private PEKS scheme leveraging Software Guard Extension (SGX), a trusted execution environment provided by Intel. The proposed scheme presents substantial performance improvements over prior work. Specifically, we reduce the query processing cost from $O(n)$ to $O(1)$, where n is the number of encrypted data. According to our performance analysis, the overall computation time is reduced by 80% on average. Lastly, we provide a formal security definition of SGX-based forward private PEKS, as well as a rigorous security proof of the proposed scheme.

Keywords: searchable encryption; PEKS; forward privacy; trusted execution environment; SGX

1. Introduction

Data outsourcing to cloud service providers is beneficial in terms of data management, but raises data security and privacy concerns. Encrypting data prior to outsourcing may solve the data privacy problems. However, it inevitably complicates, or sometimes hinders important data management operations such as searches over the outsourced data. Public key encryption with keyword search (PEKS) solves this dilemma, in which data senders are allowed to encrypt data using a public key such that the ciphertexts are searchable only by a data receiver whose secret key is associated with the public key [1].

Unfortunately, previous PEKS schemes are vulnerable to query leakage attacks. For example, in file injection attacks [2], an adversarial data sender generates maliciously crafted files of his choice, encrypts them with the public key of a data receiver, and then outsources it to the cloud storage. Then, the adversary observes file access patterns by monitoring which files are returned in response to queries submitted by a specific receiver, thereby leaking the receiver's queries.

As a countermeasure, forward private PEKS schemes have been proposed, which can guarantee that the past search queries cannot be used for newly inserted files [3]. Unfortunately, the previous schemes are unsuitable for the multi-user environment where multiple data senders are existing for each receiver, which is the widespread setting in cloud-based applications (In this study, a multi-receiver environment is not considered. Thus, henceforth, a multi-user environment implies only a multi-sender environment in the paper). Thus, designing forward private PEKS that securely support multi-user setting in a scalable way is one of the challenging and important goals in the PEKS literature.

Moreover, prior works suffer from high communication overhead that degrades practicality. For example, Zhang et al. [4] achieved forward privacy by means of key revocation, which incurs costly key management tasks to distribute key update messages every time a query is processed. Zeng et al. [5] proposed a scheme to guarantee forward privacy without such key revocations. However, the scheme depends on computationally extensive cryptographic primitives, which incurs unacceptable computation costs in practice. Furthermore, the query size of their scheme depends on the time periods, leading to significant communication overheads.

To design secure and efficient schemes, one may utilize Trusted Execution Environments (TEEs) such as Intel Software Guard Extension (SGX) [6–10]. TEE provides memory isolation such that it loads data or code from (untrusted) main memory to the (trusted) isolated memory area, or enclave. Since TEE can protect data and processes from operating systems or hypervisors using enclaves, it can guarantee confidentiality and integrity of them even when operating systems or hypervisors are compromised. Recently, Amjad et al. [11] introduced an SGX-supported dynamic searchable symmetric encryption scheme that is forward private. However, it is also not applicable to the multi-user settings.

In this paper, we propose SPEKS, a forward private SGX-based public key encryption with keyword search scheme. To the best of our knowledge, it is the first SGX-based PEKS that achieves forward privacy in a multi-user setting. The proposed scheme uses a search counter to achieve forward privacy by unlinking the current data status with the previous queries. Specifically, both the data receiver and the cloud server share the same search counter, which is updated per each data update. Since the current data is encrypted using the latest search counter, the previous queries cannot be associated with subsequently updated data. Thus, forward privacy is guaranteed in the proposed scheme. In addition, SPEKS significantly outperforms prior works [4,5,12] and preserves forward privacy against stronger attack model by utilizing Intel SGX.

The contributions of this work are as follows:

- We propose a forward secure public key encryption with keyword search using Intel SGX, the first SGX-based PEKS scheme that achieves forward privacy in multi-user settings.
- The communication cost is significantly reduced as a single query is sufficient to search over multiple encrypted data, while prior works require numerous queries in proportional to the number of encrypted data.
- We define a security model of SGX-based forward private PEKS, and formally prove the security of our scheme.
- We implement our scheme using SGX, and evaluate the performance of our scheme and the previous schemes. According to the experiment with implementations, our scheme is significantly more efficient then the previous schemes without security degradation.

2. Background

Intel Software Guard Extension (SGX) is used for designing our construction for forward secure searchable encryption. SGX is an extension of the x86 instruction set architecture (ISA) introduced since the 6th generation Intel Skylake Processor. SGX provides Memory Isolation, Enclave Page Cache, and Software Attestation, which are major functionalities that we rely on to construct our scheme. In this section, we briefly introduce the SGX structures and basic PEKS algorithms upon which our scheme is built.

2.1. Intel Software Guard Extensions (SGX)

Memory Isolation. SGX platform can be divided into untrusted parts and trusted parts. Enclaves are trusted parts, or private regions of the physical memory whose contents are protected. The memory space for enclave is isolated from any process outside the enclave itself, including processes running at higher privilege levels. Thus, any access by other processes such as privileged operating systems, firmware, hypervisor and code in system management mode (SMM) to the enclave memory is disallowed.

The enclave memory is mapped into virtual memory of the untrusted part, and the untrusted part is executed on the ordinary process within the virtual address space. The mapping of the enclave memory is crucial, because this enables the enclave to access the host process's entire virtual memory. However, the host process is only allowed to call enclave through certain interface. In addition, the executed code and data inside the enclave are encrypted when they reside in the untrusted part of the memory. When loaded into the enclave, on the other hand, the enclave is decrypted on the fly within the CPU. Thus, the processor protects the code from being examined by other processes, which treated as potentially hostile.

Enclave Page Cache (EPC): Enclave page cache (EPC) is memory area where the enclave code and data are placed. Using the Memory Encryption Engine (MEE), the EPC is encrypted and external reads on that memory bus can only monitor encrypted data. For EPC, a fixed amount of the main memory, limited to 128 MB, of the system is allocated to store enclave and related metadata. Since the dedicated memory is shared between enclave itself and related metadata, the enclave cache, on average, is able to use 96 MB [13]. Because of the memory limitation, enclaves sometimes need to swap pages when dealing with large data of which size exceeds the dedicated memory. During the boot phase, the SGX memory is reserved statically throughout the runtime of the system. If there are multiple enclaves, the memory is supposed to be dynamically managed by the OS and allocated to each enclave. When the page swapping occurs, the key generated at the boot-time is used for both encryption and decryption of the page. In the page swapping operations, confidentiality and integrity of the swapped-out pages can be guaranteed.

Software Attestation [14]: SGX supports software attestation feature that verifies the validity of locally or remotely created enclaves. The enclave measurement, which is the initial code loaded when the enclave is created, is used to verify the correctness of the enclave. Provided by the SGX attestation functionality, it can be assured that the measurements are authentic and associated with the benign enclave. For local attestation, EREPORT and EGETKEY instructions are used to generate the signed report and verify it at the target enclave. For remote attestation, the signature is provided by the Quoting Enclave (QE), a component of SGX. Before generating the signature, QE only accepts measurements from the hardware itself, which ensures that only legitimate enclave is measured.

2.2. Public Key Encryption with Keyword Search (PEKS)

Boneh et al. [1] first introduced the notion of public key encryption with keyword search (PEKS). Compared to symmetric searchable encryption, PEKS has better performance in data sharing. Abdalla et al. [15] gives a generic framework of PEKS and shows how to obtain public key based searchable encryption from anonymous identity-based encryption. In the PEKS scheme, a data receiver provides a gateway with a trapdoor function for keywords. Then, a data sender uses the data receiver's public key for encrypting a keyword and sends the ciphertext to the server or the gateway. The latter applies search or test function to the search token and the ciphertext. When the keywords within the search token and the ciphertext match, the search or the test function returns 1; otherwise, 0. The scheme is proven to be secure in the standard model, but under the condition where the number of malicious clients is smaller than a specified value.

3. SPEKS Overview and Definitions

In this section, we describe a high level design of our SPEKS scheme, and show the search processes over encrypted data by users. Then, we define algorithms for SPEKS scheme and security model.

3.1. Overview

The high level design of our scheme is shown in Figure 1. In the proposed scheme, there are three system entities: data receiver (DR), data sender (DS), SGX-enabled cloud server (CS).

During the setup phase, a DR initially generates his private key SK_u, public key PK_u, and symmetric key K_u. Using the SGX attestation protocol for enclave authentication, the DR establishes a secure channel with the enclave within the CS (shown in step ① in Figure 1). After establishing the secure connection, the DR provisions SK_u and K_u into the enclave (step ①). The enclave stores two provisioned keys for future processes. When enclave is unloaded or rebooted, the provisioned keys can be securely stored in the local memory.

For the *PEKS* algorithm, a DS gets search counter of the DR, encrypts data that includes predefined keyword with the search counter, and uploads the encrypted data to the server (see step ② and ③). Then, the DR generates a search query, encrypts it with symmetric key SK_u, and transfers it to enclave within the CS using the *Trapdoor* algorithm (step ④). The enclave has provisioned keys required for decryption and the search query from the DR. For the *Search* algorithm, the data record is loaded to the enclave (step ⑤). If the data record size is greater than the EPC, the record are separated into smaller pieces and partial records are loaded multiple times to the enclave. The enclave decrypts the search query using the symmetric key and searches the matching record (step ⑥). Finally, if there is a matched result, then the enclave returns the result to the DR (step ⑦).

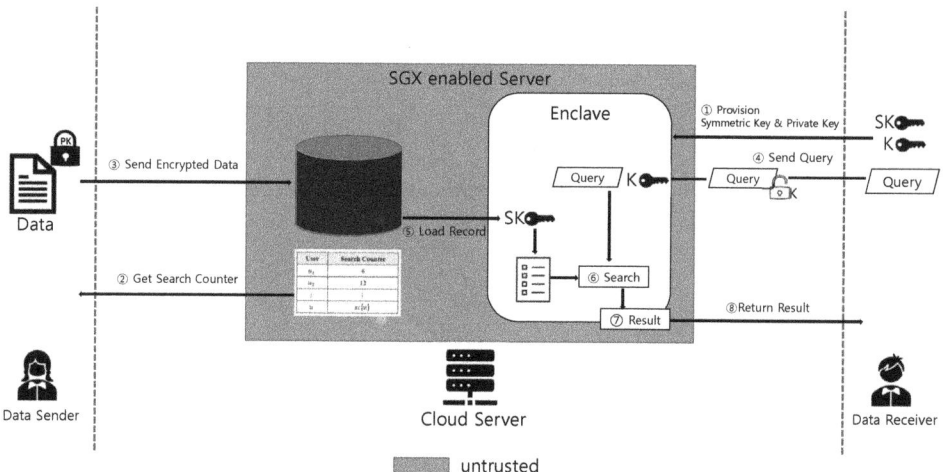

Figure 1. High level design overview.

3.2. Algorithms and Security Definitions

SPEKS consists of four polynomial-time algorithms: $SPEKS = (Setup(1^\lambda, \lambda), PEKS(PK_u, w, u, F), Trapdoor(K_u, w, sc[u]), Search(SK_u, \mathcal{R}, t_w))$.

Definition 1. *(SPEKS). A secure SPEKS is a tuple of four polynomial-time algorithms (Setup, PEKS, Trapdoor, Search) as follows:*

- $(PK_u, SK_u, K) \leftarrow Setup(1^\lambda, \lambda)$: It takes the security parameter 1^λ as input for generating a key pair for private key SK_u and public key PK_u, and takes λ as input for generating symmetric key K_u.
- $t_w \leftarrow Trapdoor(K_u, w, sc[u])$: It takes the symmetric key K_u, keyword w, and search counter $sc[u]$ as input. It then outputs encrypted search token t_w.
- $\mathcal{R} \leftarrow PEKS(PK_u, w, u, F)$: It takes the public key PK_u, keyword w, user index u, and a set of data F as input. It then outputs a record $\mathcal{R}$.
- $(F/\perp) \leftarrow Search(SK_u, \mathcal{R}, t_w)$: It takes the private key SK_u, record $\mathcal{R}$, and search token t_w as input. It then outputs F if there is a match; otherwise, $\perp$.

Definition 2. *(Correctness) Let $\mathcal{D}$ denote a SPEKS-scheme consisting of the four algorithms described in Definition 1. For any correctly generated public key pair (PK, SK) and symmetric K of the data receiver, and for any keyword w, $Search(SK_u, \mathcal{R}, t_w) = 1$ holds with probability 1, where ciphertext $\mathcal{R} \leftarrow PEKS(PK_u, w, u, F)$ and $t_w \leftarrow Trapdoor(K_u, w, sc[u])$.*

We define our security model based on the three steps framework introduced in [16]. For the first step, we need to formulate a leakage which means an upper bound of the information that an adversary may gather from the protocol. Second step is defining the $\textbf{Real}_\mathcal{A}(\lambda)$ and $\textbf{Ideal}_{\mathcal{A},\mathcal{S}}(\lambda)$ games for an adaptive adversary $\mathcal{A}$ and a polynomial-time simulator $\mathcal{S}$. $\textbf{Real}_\mathcal{A}(\lambda)$ is the actual protocol and $\textbf{Ideal}_{\mathcal{A},\mathcal{S}}(\lambda)$ is the simulated protocol for the real game by utilizing $\mathcal{S}$ using only the formulated leakage. Information learned in the previously executed protocols can be used by an adaptive adversary for its subsequent queries. Third step is proving that a scheme is CKA2-secure by showing that $\mathcal{A}$ can distinguish the outputs of the games with probability close to 0. When the probability is negligibly close to 0, $\mathcal{A}$ does not learn anything more than just the leakage stated in the first step.

Similar to the scheme introduced by Fuhry et al. [13], our scheme has an additional transaction between the cloud server and the trusted hardware, SGX. This additional transaction can be monitored by the adversary; therefore, we extended the original security model to hardware-security model. $\mathcal{L}_{hw}$ denotes the leakage on the CKA2-HW-security.

Definition 3. *(CKA2-HW-security). Let $\mathcal{D}$ denote a SPEKS scheme consisting of the four algorithms described in Definition 1. $\mathcal{A}$ is a stateful passive adversary, and $\mathcal{S}$ is a stateful simulator that gets the leakage functions $\mathcal{L}_{PEKS}$ and $\mathcal{L}_{hw}$. Two probabilistic experiments $\textbf{Real}_\mathcal{A}(\lambda)$ and $\textbf{Ideal}_{\mathcal{A},\mathcal{S}}(\lambda)$ are described as a follow.*

- **Real**$_\mathcal{A}(\lambda)$: The data receiver runs Setup $(1^\lambda, \lambda)$ and generates a key pair (PK, SK) and symmetric key K. $\mathcal{A}$ outputs a search counter of user, $sc[u]$. The data sender calculates $\mathcal{R} \leftarrow PEKS(PK_u, w, u, F)$ and passes $\mathcal{R}$ to $\mathcal{A}$. The data receiver returns search token t_w to $\mathcal{A}$ after calculating $t_w \leftarrow Trapdoor(K_u, w, sc[u])$. $\mathcal{A}$ can use $\mathcal{R}$ and the returned tokens at any time to make a query to the trusted hardware. The trusted hardware answers the query by running $(F/\perp) \leftarrow Search(SK_u, \mathcal{R}, t_w)$. If the query matches, then the search counter is incremented and $\mathcal{A}$ returns a bit **b** as a result of the experiment.
- **Ideal**$_{\mathcal{A},\mathcal{S}}(\lambda)$: The adversary $\mathcal{A}$ outputs search counter sc to the data sender. Using $\mathcal{L}_{PEKS}$, the data sender creates $\mathcal{R}$ and sends it to $\mathcal{A}$. The simulator $\mathcal{S}$ creates search token t_w and passes it to $\mathcal{A}$. $\mathcal{A}$ can use $\mathcal{R}$ and search token t_w to make queries to $\mathcal{S}$, who simulates the trusted hardware. Next, with the given $\mathcal{L}_{hw}$, $\mathcal{S}$ returns the search result. At last, the adversary $\mathcal{A}$ returns an output bit **b** of the experiment.

We claim that $\mathcal{D}$ is $(\mathcal{L}_{PEKS}, \mathcal{L}_{hw})$-secure against adaptive chosen-keyword attacks if for any probabilistic, polynomial-time algorithms $\mathcal{A}$, there exists a probabilistic, polynomial-time $\mathcal{S}$ such that:

$$|\Pr[\textbf{Real}_\mathcal{A}(\lambda) = 1] - \Pr[\textbf{Ideal}_{\mathcal{A},\mathcal{S}}(\lambda) = 1]| \leq \text{negl}(\lambda).$$

4. Construction

4.1. Cryptographic Primitive

Let Enc_{PKE} and Dec_{PKE} refer to IND-CPA secure public key encryption and decryption algorithm respectively, and Enc_{SKE} and Dec_{SKE} refer to IND-CPA secure symmetric key encryption and decryption algorithm respectively. The proposed scheme is constructed based on these symmetric and public key encryption/decryption algorithms.

4.2. Provisioning

For key sharing between the enclave and the data receiver, the data receiver provisions his private key and symmetric key to the enclave. Since the keys should not be revealed to any untrusted entity, secure connection between the data receiver and the enclave should be established using the attestation feature of SGX. During the creation of the enclave, the key pair (sk_E) and (pk_E) are created. The hardware random number generator (rdrand [17]) available in current CPUs can provide the sufficient randomness required for the key generation in practice.

Subsequently, the enclave sends the created pk_E to the quoting enclave (QE). The QE creates the signature used for verification of the measurement of the initial memory content of the enclave M_E and the public key $\sigma_{QE}(M_E \parallel pk_E)$. With the given Intel's public key, the data receiver verifies the signature of M_E, pk_E, and $\sigma_{QE}(M_E \parallel pk_E)$. The data receiver is now able to encrypt SK_u and K_u with pk_E and sends them back to the enclave. As a result, the enclave and the data receiver share the SK_u and K_u, which they use for secure communication.

4.3. Algorithms

The proposed forward secure searchable encryption scheme with keyword search (SPEKS) consists of the following four algorithms: (Setup, PEKS, Trapdoor, Search).

Algorithm 1 gives a formal description of Setup of our SPEKS scheme. In $(PK_u, SK_u, K) \leftarrow Setup(1^\lambda, \lambda)$ algorithm, a data receiver (DR) generates PK_u, SK_u, and K_u. Next, the DR provisions the SK_u and K_u to the enclave within the cloud server, $Enclave_{CS}$, through a secure channel. The secure channel can be established by the attestation feature provided by Intel SGX as explained in Section 4.2.

Next, Algorithm 2 provides a formal description of PEKS. In $\mathcal{R} \leftarrow PEKS(PK_u, w, u, F)$, where F denotes a set of data, a data sender (DS) first requests search counter $sc[u]$ from the cloud server (CS). Using the retrieved $sc[u]$, the DS runs $Enc_{PKE}(PK_u, (w, sc[u]))$ and generates searchable ciphertext ct. A record $\mathcal{R}$ consists of three components (d, ind, ct), where d refers to the data, ind refers to the index, and ct refers to the searchable ciphertext. The generated record $\mathcal{R}$ is sent to the CS.

Algorithm 3 describes the Trapdoor algorithm of our scheme. In the algorithm, the DR creates a search token with the keyword. Specifically, in the execution of $t_w \leftarrow Trapdoor(K_u, w, sc[u])$, the DR uses the search counter $sc[u]$ and keyword, and generates the search token. Then, using symmetric key encryption (SKE), the DS encrypts the search token with symmetric key K. The encrypted search token t_w is now transferred to $Enclave_{CS}$. After transferring the search token, the DR increments his or her own search counter by 1.

Algorithm 4 describes the Search algorithm of our scheme. In Algorithm 4, $Enclave_{CS}$ checks whether search token t_w matches $\mathcal{R}$. $Enclave_{CS}$ runs $Dec_{SKE}(K_u, t_w)$ and retrieves keyword w' and search counter sc'. Next, using the key SK, keyword w and search counter sc are retrieved from the ciphertext ct_i. The ind_i from $\mathcal{R}$ is returned. $sc[u]$ is then incremented by one, and F with returned ind_i is returned to the DR, when matched; else, $\perp$ is returned.

Algorithm 1: $(PK_u, SK_u, K) \leftarrow Setup(1^\lambda, \lambda)$

DR:

$(PK_u, SK_u) \leftarrow Setup(\lambda)$

Symmetric key $K_u \leftarrow Setup(1^\lambda)$

Provision Private Key SK_u

and Symmetric K_u to $Enclave_{CS}$

Algorithm 2: $\mathcal{R} \leftarrow PEKS(PK_u, w, u, F)$

DS:
Request the search counter of u from the CS

CS:
Return $sc[u]$ to DS

DS:
for $i = 1$ to $|F|$ do
  $ct_i \leftarrow Enc_{PKE}(PK_u, (w, sc[u]))$
  $\mathcal{R} \leftarrow \mathcal{R} \cup \{(d_i, ind_i, ct_i)\}$
end for
Transfer $\mathcal{R}$ to CS

CS:
for $i = 1$ to $|\mathcal{R}|$ do
  $ED \leftarrow ED \cup \{(d_i, ind_i, ct_i)\}$
end for

Algorithm 3: $t_w \leftarrow Trapdoor(K_u, w, sc[u])$

DR:
$\tau_w \leftarrow (w, sc[u])$
$t_w \leftarrow Enc_{SKE}(K_u, \tau_w)$
Transfer t_w to $Enclave_{CS}$
$sc[u] \leftarrow sc[u] + 1$

Algorithm 4: $(F/\perp) \leftarrow Search(SK_u, \mathcal{R}, t_w)$

CS:
$Enclave_{CS}$:
$(w', sc') \leftarrow Dec_{SKE}(K_u, t_w)$
for i=1 to sc' do
  $(w, sc) \leftarrow Dec_{PKE}(SK_u, ct_i)$
  if $(w = w')$ and $(i = sc)$ then
    return ind_i
  end if
end for
$sc[u] \leftarrow sc[u] + 1$
Return F to DR if match; else, $\perp$

5. Analysis

5.1. Security Analysis

We will prove the security of our scheme by defining the leakage functions related to access pattern. Then, we will explain how our SPEKS scheme guarantees the forward privacy.

We define two leakage functions: $\mathcal{L}_{PEKS}(sc)$ and $\mathcal{L}_{hw}(sc, \mathcal{R})$. $\mathcal{L}_{PEKS}(sc)$ function outputs a record $\mathcal{R}$ given the search counter sc, which consists of encrypted data, indices, and searchable ciphertexts. Given sc and $\mathcal{R}$, $\mathcal{L}_{hw}(sc, \mathcal{R})$ function outputs the access pattern $\mathcal{P}(sc, \mathcal{R})$.

The access pattern $\mathcal{P}(sc, \mathcal{R})$ contains information of search counter sc and records $\mathcal{R}$, which are stored in the untrusted memory region of the server. When the data receiver requests sc, the server can see which value is being returned. $\mathcal{R}$ also leaks which record is being sent to enclave or the data receiver. In our analysis, we further utilize values access pattern $\Delta(sc, \mathcal{R})$ [13], which, in our analysis, describes the pointers to the result values that specifically points the record with index ind.

Theorem 1. (Security). The SPEKS construction is $(\mathcal{L}_{PEKS}, \mathcal{L}_{hw})$-secure.

Proof. We consider a polynomial-time simulator $\mathcal{S}$ for which probabilistic, polynomial-time adversary $\mathcal{A}$ can distinguish between $\mathbf{Real}_{\mathcal{A}}(\lambda)$ and $\mathbf{Ideal}_{\mathcal{A},\mathcal{S}}(\lambda)$ with negligible probability.

- *Setup*: $\mathcal{S}$ creates a new random keys $(\tilde{PK}, \tilde{SK}, \tilde{K}) = Setup(1^\lambda, \lambda)$ and stores them.
- *Simulating $\mathcal{R}$*: $\mathcal{S}$ gets $\mathcal{L}_{PEKS}$ and receives search counter sc. Furthermore, $\mathcal{S}$ creates $|F|$ (the size of data set) encryption of keyword $C = \left(C_1, ..., C_{|F|}\right)$ using $Enc_{PKE}(PK, (w, sc))$. All encrypted value is given a distinct index value ind. $\mathcal{S}$ outputs $\mathcal{R} = (ind_i, C_i)$. Since the value of search counter and the size of the record are included in the leakage, the operations above are possible. The simulation of $\mathcal{R}$ has the same size with the output of $\mathbf{Real}_{\mathcal{A}}(\lambda)$. In addition, the simulation result is indistinguishable from the output of $\mathbf{Real}_{\mathcal{A}}(\lambda)$ due to IND-CPA-security of public key encryption scheme.
- *Simulating t_w*: The simulator $\mathcal{S}$ creates value $\tau_w = (w, sc)$ and encrypts it as $Enc_{SKE}(K_u, \tau_w)$. $\mathcal{S}$ outputs search token t_w. Since Enc_{SKE} is IND-CPA secure, the simulated t_w is indistinguishable from the output of $\mathbf{Real}_{\mathcal{A}}(\lambda)$.
- *Simulating secure hardware*: At a given time t, $\mathcal{S}$ receives search token and $\mathcal{L}_{hw}$. $\mathcal{S}$ uses $\mathcal{P}(sc, \mathcal{R}, t)$ to simulate the access pattern. $\mathcal{S}$ begins with the first record of $\mathcal{P}$ and follows the indices given by $\mathcal{R}$. The leakage Δ determines the specific point of the record with index ind.

□

The adversary $\mathcal{A}$ cannot distinguish access of $\mathbf{Real}_{\mathcal{A}}(\lambda)$ from simulated access due to the delivering of deterministic results. The results are consistent for each different requests made for the same keyword. Since $\Delta(sc, \mathcal{R})$ is explicit, the number of result pointers matches and the pointers are also consistent. The pointed values are indistinguishable, because those values are encrypted IND-CCA secure.

Forward Privacy. In order to guarantee forward privacy, the past search queries should not be directly associated with the updated files. In our SPEKS scheme, we use a search counter that is supposed to be updated after each search. The search queries are generated only with private key and the search counter. Since the ciphertexts are created with the current newly updated search counters, past queries generated with past search counter values cannot match with newly updated files. Therefore, forward privacy is guaranteed in our proposed scheme.

5.2. Performance Analysis

In this section, we analyze the performance of our scheme and provide a comparative analysis with previous forward secure public key encryption with keyword search (FS-PEKS) schemes such as Zeng at al.'s [5] and Kim et al.'s [12] schemes.

Our experiment is run on a system equipped with Intel(R) Core(TM) i7-9700K CPU at 3.60 GHz, 16G DDR4 RAM. 64-bit Ubuntu 18.04.4 LTS with enabled SGX is used as an operating system. Our scheme is implemented based on Intel's Software Guard Extension (SGX) Software Development Kit (SDK).

When considering the multi-user environment, it is important to evaluate the initial costs for key setup and key management. In order for general symmetric searchable encryption (SSE) schemes to support a multi-user environment, they need to set up the key multiple times in proportion to the number of users. For instance, if we define u as the number of data senders and $|DH|$ as the initial cost of Diffie–Hellman key exchange protocol between a data sender and a data receiver, then the initial cost for the key setup is

$$(initial\quad key\quad setup\quad cost) = u \cdot |DH|.$$

However, the proposed scheme does not require key exchange protocol for each data sender, thus the key setup cost remains constant.

Furthermore, since the data receiver also needs to manage each key corresponding to each data sender, storage overhead for storing the key is also increased in proportion to the number of data senders in the previous schemes. For the key management, SSE schemes require a data receiver to store all of the keys set up for data senders. If $|K|$ refers to the size of a key, the overall storage overhead is

$$(storage\quad cost) = u \cdot |K|.$$

Whereas, our scheme does not require a data receiver to store multiple keys for each sender. Therefore, our scheme has constant storage overhead for key management regardless of the number of data senders, which shows high scalability of our scheme in the multi-sender environment.

Computation overhead: As shown in Figure 2, the proposed scheme has lower computation cost compared to those of Kim et al.'s and Zeng at al.'s schemes. Specifically, for *PEKS* algorithm, while Kim at al.'s scheme takes 3.958 ms and Zeng at al.'s takes 8.123 ms, our scheme takes just 0.0919 ms, which is significantly less overhead. Next, for generating a search token using *Trapdoor* algorithm, our scheme takes 0.02 ms, which is constant independently of the search count. However, in Kim et al.'s scheme [12], it takes 4.85 ms for a single search token, and the computational cost increases in proportion to the number of search counters. Zeng at al.'s scheme takes 12.11 ms for running *Trapdoor*, which is orders of magnitude slower than ours. In addition, for the *Search* algorithm, as shown in Table 1, it has the same complexity as our scheme in terms of the search time. However, when measuring the actual computation time in practice, the *Search* algorithm of ours takes, in average, 0.0436 ms, while the computation cost of search process in [5] depends on a set of encoded time period. This causes unnecessary computational overhead for some cases. The search algorithm in Kim et al.'s scheme takes 0.863 ms as shown in Figure 2.

This reduction in computation cost is caused by the characteristic of the trusted execution environment, especially Intel SGX in our scheme. Previous PEKS schemes [5,12] are constructed based on the pairing based cryptographic operations which leads to high computation overhead. For instance, in *Trapdoor* algorithm, our proposed scheme uses AES-GCM that is included in the SGX SDK for encryption and decryption of search query. Compared to pairing-based operations, AES-GCM is much more efficient cryptographic primitive. In addition, For *Search* algorithm, previous schemes utilize the pairing-based cryptography for searching over ciphertext. RSA or Elliptic Curve Cryptography cannot be used in such software-only based schemes, because the comparison over ciphertexts for search is not possible. However, the trusted execution environment provided by SGX enables the search process over plaintext while still guaranteeing the data privacy.

Communication overhead: As the previous revocation-based FS-PEKS scheme [4], most of the search counter-based schemes including Kim et al.'s scheme [12] generate multiple search tokens. To be specific, since public and private keys are revoked for each search phase, revocation-based FS-PEKS scheme needs to create multiple search tokens for previous ciphertext, and the size of the token depends on the number of searches made beforehand. Such an overhead becomes devastating as a number of searches are made subsequently. For instance, after 1000 searches, data receiver needs to generate 1000 search tokens. Moreover, the revocation-based approach leads to sending re-encrypted data, incurring an additional communication overhead. Likewise, Kim et al.'s scheme [12] generates a number of search tokens as the search counter increases, shown in Figure 3. Therefore, communication overhead related to the query size depends on the number of search counters. As shown in Table 1, the query size is $O(1)$ in our scheme because it requires only a constant number of search tokens regardless of the search counter. However, in Kim et al.'s scheme [12], the number of generated search tokens increases as the search counter increases. Zeng at al,'s scheme, on the other hand, does not adopt counter-based mechanism, but still creates multiple search tokens for the search operations. As shown in Table 1, communication overhead related to query size in Zeng et al.'s scheme depends on the encoded time period. However, unlike the other previous schemes, our scheme only generates a single token regardless of the number of search counters, thus the proposed scheme is more scalable in practice.

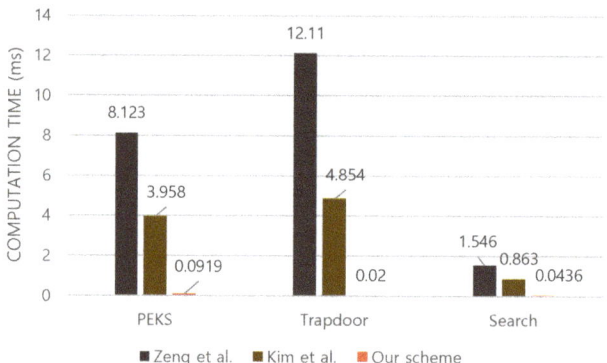

Figure 2. Computational cost of each algorithm.

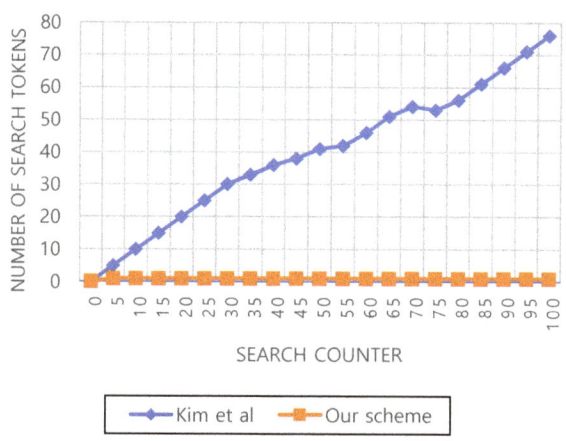

Figure 3. Communication cost of each scheme.

Overall, the proposed scheme significantly outperforms previous FS-PEKS schemes and achieves better security by exploiting trusted execution environment, specifically Intel SGX in our scheme.

Table 1. Efficiency comparison of public key encryption with keyword search (PEKS) schemes. ($|sc|$ refers to the value of search counter, n_d refers to the number of data, $|id|$ refers to size of identifier, $|S|$ denotes number of searches made, $|T|$ denotes a set of encoded time period.)

Scheme	Search Time	Query Size	Index Size
Zeng et al. [5]	$O(|T| \cdot n_d)$	$O(|T|)$	$O(n_d)$
Kim et al. [12]	$O(|sc| \cdot n_d)$	$O(|sc|)$	$O(n_d + |id|)$
Our scheme	$O(|sc| \cdot n_d)$	$O(1)$	$O(n_d)$

6. Related Work

In this section, we introduce the previous searchable encryption schemes and trusted execution environment (TEE).

6.1. Searchable Encryption

After the first searchable encryption (SE) was proposed by Song et al. [18], SE has been continuously studied to extend its functionality. Generally, the existing SE schemes can be classified into two types: searchable symmetric encryption (SSE) and public key encryption with keyword search (PEKS). By utilizing the symmetric key primitives [18–21], SSE schemes are generally more efficient than PEKS schemes. However, SSE schemes are not suitable for multiple data sender environments. PEKS schemes, based on the public key primitives [22,23], was first introduced by Boneh et al. [1], and it suits for multiple data sender environment due to the efficient key management. In PEKS schemes, generally, a data sender generates searchable ciphertext with a specific user's public key. Then, the data receiver creates a search queries and retrieves the data with secret key.

6.2. TEE Based Implementations

Fisch et al. [24] first introduced functional encryption scheme using Intel SGX and formally defined the security model. Since the first adoption of Intel SGX, many studies have been made to construct encryption schemes on Intel SGX platform. Fuhry et al. [13] used Intel SGX to design HardIDX, which is an encrypted database index. The functionality of search operation is implemented inside the enclave, but does not support the update operation. In addition, Zerotrace [25] proposed generic efficient ORAM primitives using Intel SGX, and Oblix [26] was designed for oblivious search. In Oblix, update process is designed to minimize the leakage of access pattern and result size of searches. Harnessing TEE such as Intel SGX as a building block for SE scheme construction is an effective way to increase efficiency and security of the schemes in practice.

7. Conclusions

In this paper, we proposed a public key encryption with keyword search scheme guaranteeing forward privacy using Intel SGX. We formally defined a security model for the proposed TEE-based scheme. Compared with the previous schemes, our scheme shows significantly higher efficiency because the proposed scheme generates a single search token regardless of conditions; while the previous schemes require multiple search tokens. Furthermore, the proposed scheme requires significantly less computation time for creating indices, generating search tokens, and searching processes.

Our scheme considers only a multi-sender environment. Extending our scheme to the multi-receiver environment is another important and challenging issue. In addition, preserving resilience against de-synchronization attack is also an important open problem in most of the cryptographic protocols or algorithms based on shared secret information such as IV (initial vector) or counter information. Since most of the forward secure PEKS schemes are constructed based on counter values, how to make an efficient countermeasure against the de-synchronization attack over the shared counter value is also a challenging topic in the PEKS literature as an important future work.

Author Contributions: Conceptualization, H.Y. and C.H.; methodology, H.Y. and J.H.; validation, H.Y., J.H. and W.L.; formal analysis, H.Y. and C.H.; investigation, H.Y., S.M., and Y.K.; data curation, S.M. and Y.K.; writing—original draft preparation, H.Y.; writing—review and editing, H.Y., C.H., and J.H.; visualization, H.Y., S.M., and Y.K.; supervision, J.H. and W.L.; project administration, H.Y., J.H. All authors have read and agreed to the published version of the manuscript.

Funding: This work was supported as part of Military Crypto Research Center (UD170109ED) funded by Defense Acquisition Program Administration (DAPA) and Agency for Defense Development (ADD).

Conflicts of Interest: The authors declare no conflict of interest.

Abbreviations

The following abbreviations are used in this manuscript:

PEKS	Public Key encryption with keyword search
FS-PEKS	Forward Secure PEKS
SE	Searchable encryption
TEE	Trusted Execution Environment
SGX	Software Guard Extension
IND-CPA	Indistinguishable under chosen-plaintext attack
PKE	Public key encryption
SKE	Symmetric key encryption
CS	Cloud server
DS	Data sender
DR	Data receiver

References

1. Boneh, D.; Di Crescenzo, G.; Ostrovsky, R.; Persiano, G. Public key encryption with keyword search. In *International Conference on the Theory and Applications of Cryptographic Techniques*; Springer: Berlin/Heidelberg, Germany, 2004; pp. 506–522.
2. Zhang, Y.; Katz, J.; Papamanthou, C. All your queries are belong to us: The power of file-injection attacks on searchable encryption. In Proceedings of the 25th {USENIX} Security Symposium ({USENIX} Security 16), Austin, TX, USA, 10–12 August 2016; pp. 707–720.
3. Bost, R. Σοφος: Forward secure searchable encryption. In Proceedings of the 2016 ACM SIGSAC Conference on Computer and Communications Security, Vienna, Austria, 24–28 October 2016; pp. 1143–1154.
4. Zhang, X.; Xu, C.; Wang, H.; Zhang, Y.; Wang, S. FS-PEKS: Lattice-based forward secure public-key encryption with keyword search for cloud-assisted industrial Internet of Things. *IEEE Trans. Depend. Secur. Comput.* **2019**. [CrossRef]
5. Zeng, M.; Qian, H.F.; Chen, J.; Zhang, K. Forward Secure Public Key Encryption with Keyword Search for Outsourced Cloud Storage. *IEEE Trans. Cloud Comput.* **2019**. [CrossRef]
6. Anati, I.; Gueron, S.; Johnson, S.; Scarlata, V. Innovative technology for CPU based attestation and sealing. In Proceedings of the 2nd International Workshop on Hardware and Architectural Support for Security and Privacy, Tel-Aviv, Israel, 23–24 June 2013; Volume 13, p. 7.
7. Costan, V.; Devadas, S. Intel SGX Explained. *IACR Cryptol. EPrint Arch.* **2016**, *2016*, 1–118.
8. Hoekstra, M.; Lal, R.; Pappachan, P.; Phegade, V.; Del Cuvillo, J. Using innovative instructions to create trustworthy software solutions. *HASP@ ISCA* **2013**, *11*, 2487726–2488370.
9. Intel, I. Software Guard Extensions Programming Reference, Revision 2. 2014. Available online: https://software.intel.com/sites/default/files/managed/48/88/329298-002.pdf (accessed on 15 September 2020).
10. Intel, R. Software Guard Extensions (Intel R SGX). 2018. Available online: https://www.intel.com/content/www/us/en/architecture-and-technology/software-guard-extensions.html (accessed on 15 September 2020).
11. Amjad, G.; Kamara, S.; Moataz, T. Forward and backward private searchable encryption with SGX. In Proceedings of the 12th European Workshop on Systems Security, Dresden, Germany, 2–5 March 2019; pp. 1–6.
12. Hyeongseob Kim, C.H.; Hur, J. Forward Secure Public Key Encryption with Keyword Search for Cloud-assisted IoT. In Proceedings of the 2020 IEEE International Conference on Cloud Computing, Beijing, China, 18–24 October 2020.
13. Fuhry, B.; Bahmani, R.; Brasser, F.; Hahn, F.; Kerschbaum, F.; Sadeghi, A.R. HardIDX: Practical and secure index with SGX. In *IFIP Annual Conference on Data and Applications Security and Privacy*; Springer: Berlin/Heidelberg, Germany, 2017; pp. 386–408.
14. Johnson, S.; Scarlata, V.; Rozas, C.; Brickell, E.; Mckeen, F. Intel® software guard extensions: Epid provisioning and attestation services. *White Pap.* **2016**, *1*, 119.

15. Abdalla, M.; Bellare, M.; Catalano, D.; Kiltz, E.; Kohno, T.; Lange, T.; Malone-Lee, J.; Neven, G.; Paillier, P.; Shi, H. Searchable encryption revisited: Consistency properties, relation to anonymous IBE, and extensions. In *Annual International Cryptology Conference*; Springer: Berlin/Heidelberg, Germany, 2005; pp. 205–222.
16. Stefanov, E.; Papamanthou, C.; Shi, E. Practical Dynamic Searchable Encryption with Small Leakage. *NDSS* **2014**, *71*, 72–75.
17. Guide, P. Intel® 64 and ia-32 Architectures Software Developer's Manual. In *Volume 3B: System Programming Guide Part*; 2011; Volume 2, p. 11. Available online: file:///C:/Users/MDPI/AppData/Local/Temp/253669-sdm-vol-3b.pdf (accessed on 15 September 2020).
18. Song, D.X.; Wagner, D.; Perrig, A. Practical techniques for searches on encrypted data. In Proceeding of the 2000 IEEE Symposium on Security and Privacy (S&P 2000), Berkeley, CA, USA, 14–17 May 2000; IEEE: Piscataway, NJ, USA, 2000; pp. 44–55.
19. Curtmola, R.; Garay, J.; Kamara, S.; Ostrovsky, R. Searchable symmetric encryption: Improved definitions and efficient constructions. *J. Comput. Secur.* **2011**, *19*, 895–934. [CrossRef]
20. Islam, M.S.; Kuzu, M.; Kantarcioglu, M. Access pattern disclosure on searchable encryption: Ramification, attack and mitigation. *Ndss* **2012**, *20*, 12.
21. Cash, D.; Jarecki, S.; Jutla, C.; Krawczyk, H.; Roşu, M.C.; Steiner, M. Highly-scalable searchable symmetric encryption with support for boolean queries. In *Annual Cryptology Conference*; Springer: Berlin/Heidelberg, Germany, 2013; pp. 353–373.
22. Xu, P.; Jin, H.; Wu, Q.; Wang, W. Public-key encryption with fuzzy keyword search: A provably secure scheme under keyword guessing attack. *IEEE Trans. Comput.* **2012**, *62*, 2266–2277. [CrossRef]
23. Bösch, C.; Hartel, P.; Jonker, W.; Peter, A. A survey of provably secure searchable encryption. *ACM Comput. Surv. (CSUR)* **2014**, *47*, 1–51. [CrossRef]
24. Fisch, B.; Vinayagamurthy, D.; Boneh, D.; Gorbunov, S. Iron: Functional encryption using Intel SGX. In Proceedings of the 2017 ACM SIGSAC Conference on Computer and Communications Security, Dallas, TX, USA, 30 October–3 November 2017; pp. 765–782.
25. Sasy, S.; Gorbunov, S.; Fletcher, C.W. ZeroTrace: Oblivious Memory Primitives from Intel SGX. *IACR Cryptol. EPrint Arch.* **2017**, *2017*, 549.
26. Mishra, P.; Poddar, R.; Chen, J.; Chiesa, A.; Popa, R.A. Oblix: An efficient oblivious search index. In Proceedings of the 2018 IEEE Symposium on Security and Privacy (SP), San Francisco, CA, USA, 21–23 May 2018; IEEE: Piscataway, NJ, USA, 2018; pp. 279–296.

Publisher's Note: MDPI stays neutral with regard to jurisdictional claims in published maps and institutional affiliations.

© 2020 by the authors. Licensee MDPI, Basel, Switzerland. This article is an open access article distributed under the terms and conditions of the Creative Commons Attribution (CC BY) license (http://creativecommons.org/licenses/by/4.0/).

Article

A Taxonomy for Security Flaws in Event-Based Systems

Youn Kyu Lee [1] and Dohoon Kim [2,*]

[1] Department of Information Security, Seoul Women's University, Seoul 01797, Korea; younkyul@swu.ac.kr
[2] Department of Computer Science, Kyonggi University, Suwon-si 16227, Korea
* Correspondence: karmy01@kgu.ac.kr

Received: 1 September 2020; Accepted: 14 October 2020; Published: 20 October 2020

Abstract: Event-based system (EBS) is prevalent in various systems including mobile cyber physical systems (MCPSs), Internet of Things (IoT) applications, mobile applications, and web applications, because of its particular communication model that uses implicit invocation and concurrency between components. However, an EBS's non-determinism in event processing can introduce inherent security vulnerabilities into the system. Multiple types of attacks can incapacitate and damage a target EBS by exploiting this event-based communication model. To minimize the risk of security threats in EBSs, security efforts are required by determining the types of security flaws in the system, the relationship between the flaws, and feasible techniques for dealing with each flaw. However, existing security flaw taxonomies do not appropriately reflect the security issues that originate from an EBS's characteristics. In this paper, we introduce a new taxonomy that defines and classifies the particular types of inherent security flaws in an EBS, which can serve as a basis for resolving its specific security problems. We also correlate our taxonomy with security attacks that can exploit each flaw and identify existing solutions that can be applied to preventing such attacks. We demonstrate that our taxonomy handles particular aspects of EBSs not covered by existing taxonomies.

Keywords: security taxonomies; event-based systems; mobile cyber physical systems; security flaws

1. Introduction

Event-based systems (EBSs) developed by using message-oriented middleware (MOM) platforms [1] have been widely used in mobile cyber physical systems (MCPSs) as well as a wide range of applications including Internet of Things (IoT) [2–5], financial markets, logistics, and web apps [6], including those that directly interfaced with users (e.g., Android apps [7]). In the case of MCPSs, for example, since they integrate distributed entities including computational, communication, and physical components [8], event-based architecture has been considered as an appropriate mechanism for their implementation [8–11]. MCPSs' inherent heterogeneity and integration of multiple processes make event-based architecture as a relevant approach for their modeling and application [12–15]. Specifically, EBSs are highly scalable, easily evolvable, and have a low coupling that makes them especially suitable for highly heterogeneous distributed systems [16–21].

EBSs' popular attributes are led by their communication model. For example, in EBSs, components (interchangeably referred to as "event-clients" or "event-agents") invoke each other implicitly by publishing event messages (simply referred to as "events") instead of directly calling other components via explicit references. Accordingly, the components may not know the consumers of the events they publish, and may not necessarily know the producers of the events they consume as well. Although this communication mechanism provides several advantages, as its operation is based on non-determinism in event processing, it exposes EBSs to security threats such as event spoofing, interception, and eavesdropping [22–24] (called event attacks). To minimize the risk of such threats on EBSs, security efforts are required.

When working on software security efforts, developers or administrators are required to determine the types of security flaws that exist in the system, the relative importance of each flaw, and the types of techniques that can be employed to handle each flaw. A security flaw taxonomy (an ordered system that indicates the natural relationships of security flaws [25,26]) can provide a basis for developers to make better decisions in securing their target software system. For the past three decades, many such lists and taxonomies of security problems have been studied [25–38]. However, despite the prevalence of EBSs, systematic identification and classification of EBSs' security flaws have not been extensively studied yet. Existing security flaw taxonomies do not adequately reflect the security issues that originate from the EBSs' characteristics or have been found in recent types of EBSs such as Android (Android is a mobile operating system (OS), but it also has been studied as a particular type of EBS because it supports event-based communication model. In this research, we consider Android not only as an OS, but also as a software system encompassing from middleware to applications. We will discuss the details in Section 2.2). Because EBSs have particular attributes that general software systems do not bear (e.g., implicit invocation in event communication), the existing lists or taxonomies are not directly applicable for securing EBSs. Therefore, it is inherently necessary to first systematically identify and classify EBSs' fundamental security flaws to negate any vulnerabilities in the system.

In this paper, we introduce a new taxonomy that classifies the security flaws within EBSs [22,39–47]. Built upon previously identified security flaws present in general software systems [25], our taxonomy classifies particular types of inherent flaws in EBSs, and is distinguished from the existing taxonomies because (1) it clarifies and classifies the inherently present security flaws in EBSs, (2) it covers all types of security flaws in the EBSs domain that have been identified so far, and (3) it considers different types of EBSs configurations (e.g., commercial or open-source MOM platforms). We also correlate our taxonomy with security attacks that can exploit these flaws and existing solutions that are applicable to preventing corresponding attacks. We evaluated our taxonomy in terms of its coverage by comparing it with the existing security flaw taxonomies. Our taxonomy covers all types of security flaws discovered in EBSs so far and even handles additional security flaws not covered by existing taxonomies.

The remainder of paper is structured as follows: Section 2 illustrates the background and definitions, Section 3 describes the methodology that we followed and the resulting taxonomy, Section 4 describes its evaluation, and Section 6 presents the conclusions.

2. Background

In this section, we clarify the underlying concepts and terminology that we will use later to describe our taxonomy in Section 3. We first provide the definitions of key concepts that our taxonomy uses. We then introduce the fundamental mechanism of EBSs and the different types of event attacks.

2.1. Key Concepts

In this paper, our use of the terms "flaw", "vulnerability", and "attack" are based on the terms defined in the existing literature [25,26]. A flaw is a defect of a software system, which can result in a security violation [25]. A vulnerability is caused by at least one flaw and can be exploited by attacks. An attack refers to the techniques that an attacker uses for attempting to detect and exploit a vulnerability. Attack or vulnerability taxonomies might be useful when developers (or administrators or testers) need to clarify the ways their target system can be attacked and the parts of the system that should be protected. However, considering the fact that a flaw is the root cause of security violations and can be masked by another part of the system, its identification is more useful for making a target system robust to security threats. Hence, in this paper, we focus on flaws, rather than attacks or vulnerabilities.

2.2. Event-Based Systems

The EBSs' popular attributes (e.g., scalability, evolvability, and low coupling [16–20]) are fundamentally enabled by their communication model. In EBSs, the components (i.e., the units of computation and data) communicate asynchronously with each other by using messages [48]. A message typically describes one or more observed events. An event is any occurrence that can be observed by a component (e.g., a change of the component's state or a change in the environment of the system) [49]. An event and its corresponding message are often conflated in literature for convenience. In this paper, the term "event" will be used to refer to these concepts broadly. A connector is an architectural element tasked with effecting and regulating interactions among the components [1]. Although there exist several connector types, in this paper, a connector will always refer to an event-based distribution connector [1] that distributes events to associated components. We will use the term "event broker" to refer to this concept broadly.

In EBSs, the components do not have explicit references to each other and are only able to invoke an event broker directly [49]. Consequently, the addition, removal, and updating of components can be achieved relatively easily during runtime [50]. A component can be an event producer or a consumer, or both. Communication between the components is processed via "source" and "sink" [51]—a source is an event interface invoked to publish events by a producer component; a sink is an event interface that an event broker invokes to transfer an event to a consumer component. When a producer publishes an event, the event broker routes the event to the appropriate consumers based on the system configuration, along with the routing and filtering policies [49]. When the event broker transfers an event to a component's sink, the component consumes the event. Each sink declares an event type and only allows the processing of events that match its declared type. In this paper, we will target the following three event types commonly used in today's EBSs [48]: (1) nominal, (2) subject-based and (3) attribute-based. Nominal event types are explicitly declared in a system's programming language and subsequently enforced at compile-time. In subject-based event typing, each event type is defined through a string value that captures an event's name. Similar subject-based event types can be organized into naming hierarchies (e.g., Weather/Country/City). In attribute-based event typing, an event type is defined through a set of attributes, where each attribute is a pair of name and value. Event types can be further defined into more specific event subtypes.

2.3. Event Attacks

Event attacks represent the security problems caused by non-determinism in an EBS's event processing encountered by developers and end-users. Event attacks abuse, incapacitate, and damage the system by exploiting event-based communication. Different types of event attacks have been identified throughout various domains, such as mobile and web apps [22,24,47,52–61]. The research to date has identified the following types of event attacks: *Spoofing* (A1): A malicious component can send an event that spoofs a target component to exploit the target's functionality/data [22]; *Interception* (A2): A malicious component can intercept an event that is supposed to be sent to other components and can send back inappropriate replies to make a target component malfunction or to exploit the target's functionality/data [22,24]; *Eavesdropping* (A3): A malicious component can eavesdrop on an event, which contains sensitive data, and is supposed to be open only for particular components [24,60]; *Confused deputy* (A4): A malicious component can indirectly access a target component, by accessing another component that has access to the target component, to exploit the target's functionality/data [47]; *Collusion* (A5): Two or more malicious components can collude by exchanging events to exploit the functionalities or resources of a target component [47]; *Flooding* (A6): A malicious component can send an overwhelming amount of events that makes a target component malfunction [55]; *Delaying* (A7): A malicious component (or event broker) can intentionally delay a series of event interactions to make a target component malfunction [54]. We have formally defined each type of event attack as listed in Table 1.

Table 1. Types of Event Attacks.

No.	Attack Type	Definition
A1	Spoofing	For $V_1, V_2, M_1 \in C$ where $V_1 \neq V_2 \neq M_1$ and $\exists (V_1 \xrightarrow{e} V_2)$ and (V_2 contains f) and $(M_1 \xRightarrow{e} V_2)$: M_1 sent a spoofed e to V_2 to exploit f in V_2
A2	Interception	For $V_1, V_2, M_1 \in C$ where $V_1 \neq V_2 \neq M_1$ and $\exists (V_1 \xrightarrow{e} V_2)$ and (e contains s) and $(V_1 \xRightarrow{e} M_1) \land \neg(V_1 \xRightarrow{e} V_2)$: M_1 intercepted e, which was supposed to be sent to V_2, to obtain s
A3	Eavesdropping	For $V_1, V_2, M_1 \in C$ where $V_1 \neq V_2 \neq M_1$ and $\exists (V_1 \xrightarrow{e} V_2)$ and (e contains s) and $(V_1 \xRightarrow{e} M_1) \land (V_1 \xRightarrow{e} V_2)$: M_1 eavesdropped on e, which was supposed to be open only to V_2, to obtain s
A4	Confused deputy	For $V_1, V_2, M_1 \in C$ where $V_1 \neq V_2 \neq M_1$ and $\nexists(M_1 \xrightarrow{e} V_1)$ and (V_1 contains f) and $(M_1 \xRightarrow{e_1} V_2) \land (V_2 \xRightarrow{e_2} V_1)$: M_1 accessed V_1 by accessing V_2, which can access V_1, to exploit f in V_1
A5	Collusion	For $V_1, M_1, M_2 \in C$ where $V_1 \neq M_1 \neq M_2$ and $\nexists(M_1 \xrightarrow{e} V_1)$ and (V_1 contains f) and $(M_1 \xRightarrow{e_1} M_2) \land (M_2 \xRightarrow{e_2} V_1)$: M_1 colluded with M_2, which can access V_1, to exploit f in V_1
A6	Flooding	For $V_1, V_2, M_1 \in C$ where $V_1 \neq V_2 \neq M_1$ and $\exists(V_1 \xrightarrow{e} V_2)$ and $(M_1 \xRightarrow{e*} V_2) \land \neg(V_1 \xRightarrow{e} V_2) \land$ (the number of $e*$ is overwhelmingly greater than the average number of e): M_1 sent an overwhelming number of $e*$ to hinder V_1 from accessing V_2
A7	Delaying	For $V_1, V_2, V_3, M_1 \in C$ where $V_1 \neq V_2 \neq V_3 \neq M_1$ and $\exists(V_1 \xrightarrow{e} M_1 \xrightarrow{e_1} V_2 \xrightarrow{e_2} V_3)$ and $(V_1 \xRightarrow{e} M_1 \xRightarrow{e_1} V_2 \xRightarrow{e_1} V_3) \land$ (the time interval between e and e_1 is overwhelmingly larger than the time interval between e_1 and e_2): M_1 delayed the publication of e_1 to make V_2 and V_3 malfunction

C: a set of components, V: a victim component, M: a malicious component, f: sensitive functionality, s: sensitive information, e: an event, $x \xrightarrow{\alpha} y$: an event communication channel for sending an event α from x to y, $x \xRightarrow{\alpha} y$: an event α sent from x to y.

As event attacks are administered in the same manner as ordinary event exchanges and the malicious components disguise themselves as benign, it is difficult to identify and block event attacks. Preventing event attacks becomes more challenging especially when it is not possible to predict which component will compromise the system (e.g., as in the case in Android and J2EE apps). For example, in Android systems, depending on the apps installed according to different users' preferences, the components comprising the system would be different. In such a case, as it is hard to guarantee that all components in the system are benign or safe from security threats, existing techniques that require pre-defined access distribution (e.g., role-based access control [39]) cannot be used to prevent event attacks. Although the Android system was designed to enforce permission-based access control [7], some types of event attacks can bypass the permission checks (i.e., confused deputy and collusion [47,53,61]). Putting a strict limitation on event communication may address some of these security threats, but it can reduce the flexibility of and hamper the benefits of the EBSs. Although developers are required to follow security policies while building a system, they tend to lack attention and make mistakes [62]. Practice has also shown that developers are often completely unaware of potential threats or underestimate the framework's capabilities, thus placing the responsibility on the end-users to protect themselves while using the system [63].

3. Taxonomy

3.1. Literature Review Methodology

To analyze the security flaws in the EBS domain, we inspected the results of 84 literatures published in reputable journals and conferences [22,24,39–47,52,56,60,61,64–132]. We carefully followed the general guidelines for a systematic literature review process [133]. Specifically, we formulated our taxonomy by performing a content analysis over a set of literatures. The literatures were initially collected by using reliable literature search engines, such as IEEE Explore, ACM Digital Library, Springer Link, and Google Scholar. As shown in Table 2, our search query was formed as a conjunction of the domain keywords (i.e., "distributed event-based systems", "event-based systems", "android intent", and "android event") and attribute keywords (i.e., "security vulnerability", "security attack", "security flaw", and "security error"). Specifically, our search query was defined as the following formula: $\forall d \in D \land \forall a \in A$, where D is the set of domain keywords and A is the set of attribute keywords as specified in Table 2. Note that, to cover a larger number of literatures, synonyms were considered for the attribute keywords during the search process. For example, regarding "vulnerability", we also considered similar keywords such as "flaw" and "error". Because the scope of search for Android keywords is too large, in order to effectively collect the Android literature dealing with the characteristics of EBSs, we used "android event" and "android intent" as domain keywords. The selected keywords were applied to the search for the literatures' titles, abstracts, and tags. To exclude outdated literatures, we limited the scope of the search to literatures published from 2000 to 2020. Although the majority of the literatures regarding EBSs were almost a decade old, we decided to keep them if they had appeared in top-tier conferences or journals with significant contributions (H5-index $\geq$ 20 or citation counts $\geq$ 50). Table 2 shows the number of initially searched literatures (IEEE Explore = 104, ACM Digital Library = 624, Springer Link = 1188, Google Scholar = 3078, Total = 4994) processed by keyword-based search over the aforementioned databases. After the initial searching, because the search engines in each database may have processed our queries differently, we performed a consistent keyword validation on the searched literatures based on the same keywords (1st filtering = 2018). After the first filtering, as not all the searched literatures fit within the scope of this research, we performed a brief review based on the title and abstract of each literature (2nd filtering = 780). Our review criteria included whether they handled security issues in EBSs. After the second filtering, we performed a detailed review on the filtered literatures by inspecting if they fit within the scope of this research. Finally, 84 literatures were selected as the base ingredient for our taxonomy.

Table 2. Number of Collected References during Literature Review Process.

D: Domain Keyword	A: Attribute Keyword	IEEE	ACM	Springer	Google Scholar
distributed event-based systems, event-based systems, android event, android intent	security vulnerability, security attack, security flaw, security error	104	624	1188	3078
Initially Searched				4994	
After 1st Filtering				2018	
After 2nd Filtering				780	
After Final Filtering				84	

3.2. Taxonomy Construction Methodology

Although EBSs have particular attributes that general software systems do not bear, they may still inherit security issues from them. Hence, we decided to build a taxonomy upon existing taxonomies that targeted general software systems.

First, we targeted the taxonomies that classify software security flaws. The advantage of this type of taxonomy lies in the convenience of creating a common language for sharing security flaws, allowing an efficient organization of security flaws across information sources, and ultimately identifying strategies to remedy security problems, which is the final goal of this research. For example, depending on the type of flaw, developers can figure out applicable solutions from among the existing ones and also for flaws that lack appropriate solutions. According to the review of security flaw taxonomies [37,38,134], the outdated taxonomies (i.e., before the year 2000) tend to be less elaborate than recently published ones [26,33] or some of them have been adapted to the latest ones [25,27,29,37,38]. Thus, among the selected taxonomies, we filtered out the taxonomies published before the year 2000. The taxonomies that only focused on implementation-level errors were also excluded to consider design-oriented security flaws.

Consequently, from among the remaining set of candidates, "software security flaw taxonomy" by Weber et al. [25] was selected as the starting point to create a taxonomy, because it has been designed to adequately reflect the nature of security issues in an EBS. Weber's taxonomy classifies the flaws based on genesis (i.e., how they were introduced to the system). Specifically, this taxonomy is distinguished from others due to its major division between "intentional" and "inadvertent" flaws, which is pertinent to classifying security flaws in EBS. As an EBS generally provides an extensible infrastructure, unintended external source code can be included in the system, which implies that a developer's intention is an important determinant for classifying an EBS's security flaws. For example, although the Android framework was not originally designed to contain security flaws, if an Android app, intentionally designed as malicious, is installed on the system, the system will contain "intentional" security flaws. We adapted Weber's taxonomy based on 84 selected literatures on security issues in EBSs [39–44,64–77,127] as well as on Android security issues that originated from its event-based communication [22,24,45–47,52,56,60,61,78–126,128–132]. From those publications, we first extracted the security flaws each approach tries to address or introduce as an example. Then we clustered the flaws based on the similarity of ways they can be exploited. Finally, we examined if any of those flaws is related to its counterpart in Weber's taxonomy. The detailed process is as follows:

According to the existing research [40,45,79,87,105,118,121], an EBS may contain malicious code that allows different types of external access, such as a piece of code directed to unsafe URL. These types of flaws belong in the same category as "Trapdoor" in Weber's taxonomy. Prior research has defined and introduced a particular concurrency problem that only exists in EBSs, referred to as event anomalies [81,127,128]. Weber's taxonomy does define "Concurrency" flaws, but only includes time-of-check to time-of-use (TOCTTOU) errors; therefore, we expanded the scope of their characteristics and changed the name of the category to "Inadequate Concurrency" to present a more precise definition. The existing approaches indicated that the components in an EBS may communicate via covert (i.e., non-system-standard) communication channels [47,100,119]. Although some types of "Covert Channels" flaws were defined in Weber's taxonomy, we extended them to include newly identified covert channels such as the battery and vibrator in mobile devices. Authentication issues were also identified in EBSs, in the form of permission grant and authentication in a multi-domain EBS—a particular type of EBS comprising multiple event-brokers from different domains [65,80,86,90,108,118–120,135]. We extended the "Inadequate Authentication" category in Weber's taxonomy to include those authentication-related flaws. From Android apps, new types of resource leaks such as resource leaks via wifi and SQLite database were introduced [40,45,88,104,106,114,115,126,129,132], which can be added to "Resource Leak" in Weber's taxonomy. We changed the name of the category "Inadequate Resource Management" to define the scope more broadly. We also found that the flaws that existing approaches try to resolve fall under "Logic/Time Bomb" in Weber's taxonomy [56,103,115]. The existing EBS research introduced the knowledge of flaws where multiple components collude to exploit the system [45,47,61,88,100,104,106,109,117,131]. Moreover, the majority of security attacks in EBS are basically caused by its extensible event communication channels [22,24,39–41,45,47,52,60,68,70,71, 77,94,97,99,130,135]. As Weber's taxonomy does not include them, we extended the definitions of "Conspirator" and "Open Event Channels," respectively. We also added "Unsafe Events" and "Unsafe Event Interface" for including cases where those open event channels are unintentionally introduced to the system [22,24,39,41,68–70,75,77,79,84,85,87,95,102,110,123,130]. Note that, to guarantee the completeness of taxonomy, all the flaws extracted from the existing publications were incorporated in the new taxonomy. However, drawing from the flaws in the Weber's taxonomy, we excluded those that were not introduced in the existing literatures under review to build a taxonomy specialized for EBSs.

3.3. Taxonomy

The security flaw taxonomy for EBSs is shown in Figure 1. As an EBS is a particular type of software system, it incorporates some flaws from general software systems. Note that the boxes highlighted in *red* (F1, F4, F6, F9, F10) indicate the flaws adapted from the existing ones [25] to better reflect the system's event-based characteristics, and the boxes highlighted in *blue* (F2, F5, F7, F8) indicate the flaws we added because they are specifically caused by event-based communication. Finally, the *green* box (F3) indicates a flaw whose definition remains unchanged from the existing one [25]. In particular, the dashed boxes (F2, F5, F6, F7, F8, F10) indicate the flaws that can be exploited by event attacks. It is important to note that every flaw in this taxonomy was validated by existing publications regarding the security of EBS and Android [22,24,39–47,52,56,60,61,64–132] In this taxonomy, a software system is defined as a combined system that comprises both application-level and framework-level elements (i.e., middleware) where an operating system is considered as a sub-component of the system. As the taxonomy considers both the design and implementation-level flaws, we will use "developer" as a term that represents both system designer and programmer. Moreover, a component is defined as an architectural unit that can communicate with other components using system-defined events.

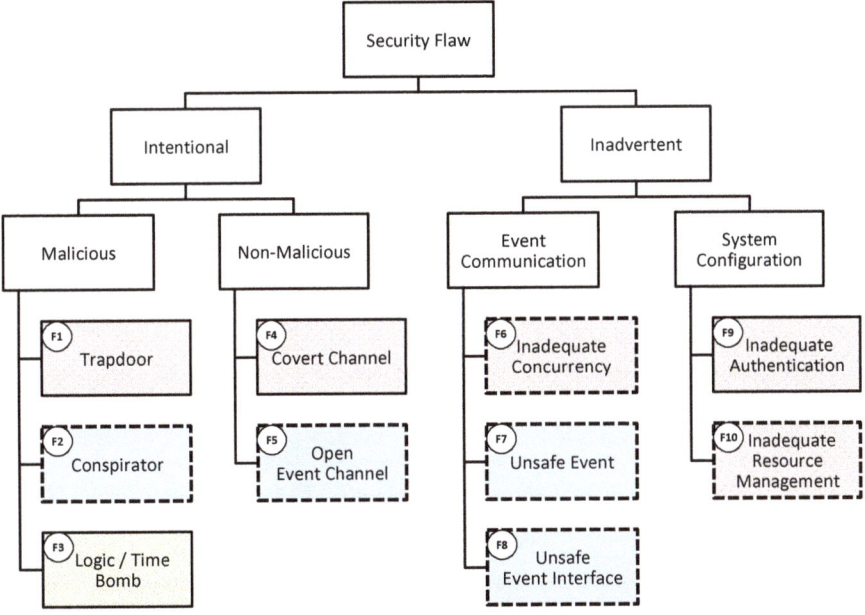

Figure 1. Security Flaw Taxonomy for event-based system (EBS). The *Red* boxes indicate the flaws adapted from the original taxonomy. The *Blue* boxes indicate the newly added flaws. The *Green* box indicates the flaw unchanged from the original taxonomy. The circled labels indicate the assigned number for each flaw.

The goal of this classification is to provide a basis for determining the appropriate security strategies to be used in a particular context. The taxonomy is first classified according to the developer's intention (*Intentional* and *Inadvertent*) because different security strategies can be used to reduce each type of flaw. For example, in a target EBS, if most of the security flaws are unintentionally and inadvertently introduced, exhaustive source code reviews and testing can be utilized to reduce the flaws [26]. However, in case most of the security flaws are intentionally introduced to an EBS, it would be more effective to minimize the proportion of externally-developed source code in the system by restricting the external components access (e.g., restrictive installation of third-party apps on Android system) or by incorporating more trustable message oriented middleware (MOM) platforms.

Intentional flaws are classified as *Malicious* and *Non-Malicious*. The *Malicious* flaws indicate the flaws that were deliberately inserted. If any part of the system was incorporated from an unreliable source, it might intentionally contain the following flaws:

- **F1. *Trapdoor*** [40,45,47,56,72,79,86,87,89,90,92,93,103,105,109–113,115,117–122,125,126]: Due to an EBS's flexibility and scalability, the system may contain the source code that allows someone to gain illicit access to the system, possibly at both the application and framework level. For example, a user may install an Android app comprising malicious code which directs to undesirable web site. Furthermore, an externally-developed framework for event-based communication may contain malicious code for allowing access to the system.
- **F2. *Conspirator*** [40,43,45,47,61,88,97,100,103,104,106,107,109,117,119,123,124,131,135,136]: EBSs may comprise components that collude by exchanging events to exploit the system functionalities or access sensitive resources. For example, in an Android system, a component belonging to an app that can access the Internet and a component belonging to an app that can access contact information could collude to send out the contact information over the Internet [47]. Furthermore, a component can help the other component indirectly access sensitive resources, such as photos, contacts, or text messages.

Non-Malicious flaws are the side-effects of features that were deliberately added to the system. These flaws are not recognized by developers in general, but we categorize them as intentional because they were designed into the system by essential system requirements. For example, functional requirements created without considering security requirements can lead to these flaws.

- **F4. *Covert Channel*** [47,100,119,123]: Two components that are not permitted to communicate via system-standard communication channels (e.g., event-based communication) communicate through the side-effects of the operations authorized for them. Covert channels are classified as intentional and non-malicious because they are not due to bugs in the system's implementation, but due to the system's design. Moreover, they mainly appeared in resource-sharing that are not maliciously designed in the system. This can happen either by means of manipulating storage, or by modulating the time which various operations take to perform. As EBSs can be deployed in various environments, such as mobile devices, the types of covert channels are diversified. For example, in Android systems, shared hardware resources such as audio volume, vibrator, and battery can be used as a communication channel between malicious components [137].
- **F5. *Open Event Channel*** [22,24,39–41,45–47,52,60,65,68,70,71,75,77,78,84,85,87,94,95,97–99,104, 106,107,110,116,117,119,123,130,135,138,139]: This flaw exists when a component intentionally exposes its event communication channel to communicate with other components. Specifically, a component can advertise the types of event it can dispatch or open its event interfaces to share its functionality or data with other components. Although it would make a system more scalable and expandable, there exists a threat where malicious components can exploit the event communication channels in undesirable ways. For example, Android components can dispatch system-defined events to share their functionalities with others, but malicious components can intercept those events and exploit the functionalities [22].

Inadvertent flaws indicate software bugs. Although they can be detected and removed through testing, some flaws may remain undetected and later cause problems during the operation and maintenance stages of the system. Inadvertent flaws are classified based on the parts where the flaws reside. *Event-Based Communication* flaws represent the flaws that can be caused by the design or implementation of a system's event-based communication.

- **F6. *Inadequate Concurrency*** [22,81,127,128]: A particular form of concurrency flaw exists in EBSs, called event anomalies [81]. In general, EBSs' components randomly process the events that were received simultaneously. Specifically, if two different components simultaneously send the events that can access the same memory location (e.g., a variable containing state or data) of the target component, there is no guarantee that any one of the two events will be processed prior to the other. This flaw may allow spoofed events sent from malicious components to corrupt the victim component's memory location [81].

- **F7. Unsafe Event** [22,24,39–41,45,46,52,60,64,68–71,75,77–79,82,85,94,95,97,98,101,102,107,110,117, 130,135,138,139]: This flaw is caused when an event containing sensitive information is insufficiently protected. For example, if a component broadcasts an event containing sensitive information without any particular protection (e.g., encryption), malicious components may intercept or eavesdrop on the event and peek at the sensitive information [22].
- **F8. Unsafe Event Interface** [22,24,39–41,45–47,52,65,68,70,71,75,77,78,82,84,87,94,97,99,104,106,107, 110,116,117,119,123,130,135,138,139]: If an event interface of a component has inadequate for filtering for handling received events, the component can be exposed to spoofed events. In case a component contains sensitive functionalities that can be triggered in response to receiving events through the unsafe interface, a malicious component can inject spoofed events to the exposed event interface thereby causing the target component to malfunction or operate in undesirable ways [22].

System Configuration flaws are the ones that can be caused by a system's defective configurations or deployments.

- **F9. Inadequate Authentication** [65,80,86,90,108,118–120]: Because of a low coupling between components in EBSs, this flaw exists when a system does not completely authenticate each component (e.g., checking if each component has sufficient permissions to send or receive events). This may allow malicious components to exploit event interactions in the system (e.g., intercepting or corrupting events). Moreover, in a multi-domain EBS, as the system may comprise multiple event brokers from different domains, the identification and authentication of components may not be uniform across the event broker networks [135], which may allow unsafe access between components.
- **F10. Inadequate Resource Management** [39–41,43,45,56,64,69,72,77,88,101,103,104,106,108,114,115, 124,126,129,132,135]: To achieve scalability, EBSs can be deployed on distributed clusters of heterogeneous nodes, which causes complex resource management. This flaw is caused when a system allocates resources to a component and releases them in an untimely manner. For example, if resource allocation is not appropriately designed, a malicious component can monopolize the system resources, which can result in denial of service. Furthermore, inadequate dynamic allocation may lead to convert channels where malicious components can communicate with each other [140].

The remaining flaw in *green* box indicates a flaw inherited from Weber's taxonomy [25]: *Logic/Time Bomb* [56,103,115] flaw indicates a piece of source code designed to disrupt the system when certain conditions are satisfied.

3.4. Relationship between Security Flaws and Event Attacks

The identified security flaws in EBSs can be exploited by different types of attacks including event attacks. To effectively counter each type of event attack, we identified the relationship between the flaws and the event attacks. Then we examined existing solutions that have been proposed to protect the flaws from event attacks. In this section, we demonstrate the relationship between the flaws and event attacks, and assess existing solutions for resolving those attacks.

As discussed in Section 2.3, event attacks represent the security problems faced by developers or end-users due to an EBS's non-determinism in event processing. Recall the seven types of event attacks: *Spoofing* (A1), *Interception* (A2), *Eavesdropping* (A3), *Confused deputy* (A4), *Collusion* (A5), *Flooding* (A6), and *Delaying* (A7).

Each security flaw in an EBS can be exploited by different types of event attacks as depicted in Table 3. To protect each type of security flaw from event attacks, various solutions have been studied across different EBS platforms (e.g., OASIS [77] and Android [141]). Table 3 also presents the representative solutions that prevent event attacks from exploiting each type of security flaw.

Table 3. EBS Security Flaws, Event Attacks, and Existing Solutions.

No.	Security Flaw in EBS	Event Attack	Existing Solution
F1	Trapdoor	-	-
F2	Conspirator	A5	- Detection of information leaks [46,60,142] - Detection and control of colluding apps [47]
F3	Logic/Time Bomb	-	-
F4	Covert Channel	-	-
F5	Open Event Channel	A1-7	- Encryption of events [41] - Policy enforcement [46,47,71,143]
F6	Inadequate Concurrency	A1	- Detection of event anomalies [68]
F7	Unsafe Event	A2,3,7	- Role-based access control [39,135] - Encryption of events [41] - Detection of vulnerable components [22,45,46,142] - Policy enforcement [46,47,71,143]
F8	Unsafe Event Interface	A1,4,6	- Role-based access control [39,135] - Detection of vulnerable components [22,45,46,142] - Policy enforcement [46,47,71,143]
F9	Inadequate Authentication	A1-7	- Security policy validation [39,144]
F10	Inadequate Resource Management	A6-7	- Analysis of runtime events and resources [145,146]

As indicated in Table 3, neither security flaw F1 nor F4 are the targets of event attacks. They can be resolved by general security solutions such as a signature-based detection [147–149] or identification of covert channels [47]. Flaw F2 can be exploited by the attack A5, but the threat can be minimized by detecting sensitive information flows between the components [46,60,142] or controlling unsafe event communication between components [47,53]. Flaw F5 can be exploited by multiple types of event attacks (A1-7). Existing research has tried to minimize the threat using encryption of events, but it requires safe key distribution between the components and additional resources that may become a burden for an environment with limited resources (e.g., mobile devices) [41]. While enforcement of security policies [46,47,71,143] has also been proposed, a coarse-grained policy may fail to prevent event attacks. For flaw F6, which is vulnerable to the attack A1, a static analysis for event anomalies detection [81,127,128] can help developers identify and fix the flaw. Flaw F7 can be a target for the attacks A2, A3, and A7. Although role-based access control and encryption of events [39,41,135] may prevent the attacks, those techniques require certain assumptions about the components engaged in event-based interactions, namely, they assume that "benign" components will be known. In other words, these approaches cannot properly deal with event-related security threats when the types of components are not clearly delineated and a malicious component can behave as a legitimate component. Though existing research has focused on the detection of attacks A2 and A3 in Android apps [22,45,46,142], they either target limited types of attacks or do not provide actual prevention mechanisms. Flaw F8, which is vulnerable to the attacks A1, A4, and A6, can be resolved by the same solutions that are applicable for flaw F7. Flaw F9 is exposed to all types of event attacks, because the possibility of a malicious component's existence in a system can be increased if the system's authentication mechanism is not well-defined. This threat can be minimized by validating a system's security policies [39,144]. Flaw F10, which is vulnerable to the attacks A6 and A7, can be resolved by analyzing and monitoring a system's runtime event interactions or resource usages [145,146].

Overall, existing solutions belong to prevention- or detection-type and each type has its limitations. As the prevention-type solutions are based on the assumption that the types of components are clearly delineated, they can be coarse-grained in case it is unclear how to pinpoint the benign components. Although detection-type solutions provide relatively finer-grained results for identifying the flaws vulnerable to event attacks, they suffer from inaccuracy and scalability issues in their analysis. To further secure EBSs, advanced approaches that combine detecting flaws and preventing attacks are required.

4. Evaluation

To validate our taxonomy in terms of coverage, two different types of evaluation were required: (1) completeness: if it covers all types of security flaws in EBSs; and (2) originality: if it handles particular types of security flaws not covered by existing listings or taxonomies.

Regarding the completeness of our taxonomy, as mentioned in Section 3.2, all types of flaws extracted from existing publications were incorporated in our taxonomy. We carefully collected 80 existing publications dealing with security issues in EBSs as well as Android security issues that originated from its event-based communication feature. We then derived different types of security flaws from those literature and classified them, which guarantees that our taxonomy covers all types of security flaws identified in the EBS domain so far.

To evaluate the originality of our taxonomy, we performed an analytic comparison with existing listings and taxonomies for security flaws. Among a number of studies for classifying security issues, we targeted the most cited or recently published taxonomies. To the best of our knowledge, four existing works share our taxonomy's goal of classifying security issues—Weber's [25], OWASP [36], Tsipneuk's [29], and Linares-Vásquez's [35]. The first three taxonomies mainly target general software systems and the last one targets the Android system. Considering the fact that Android is widely used and is a particular type of EBS, we included Linares-Vásquez's taxonomy in this evaluation. Although the selected taxonomies target different types of security issues (i.e., risks, errors, and vulnerabilities), they also serve the same purpose as our taxonomy in that they classify the cause of the security violations. We analyzed if each type of security issue in the selected taxonomies can be mapped to any flaw type in our taxonomy in terms of its definition. If the definitions of any two types were identical, we classified them as "*completely mapped,*" and if they were partially matched in broad terms, then as "*partially mapped.*" As each taxonomy has different levels in its classification, we correlated the security issues regardless of the levels of classification.

As mentioned in Section 3.2, out of 16 flaws in Weber's taxonomy [25], we adapted five in terms of their definition and added four related to event-based communication. We excluded ten flaws that mainly focused on implementation-level security issues in general software systems (e.g., aliasing and error handling).

Compared with the Open Web Application Security Project (OWASP) Top Ten 2017 [36], which is a list of the 10 most critical web application security risks, three risk types can be mapped to the flaws in our taxonomy (see Table 4). Specifically, "*Injection*" in the OWASP list can be partially mapped to the flaws F1 and F8 in our taxonomy. It represents an exploitation of a victim to perform unintended behaviors, which can be implemented via flaws F1 and F8. In a broad sense, "*Sensitive data exposure*" in the OWASP list can be partially mapped to the flaw F7, because an unsafe event may expose sensitive data. To be more exact, however, the flaws F7 and F8 are more specific to event-based communication. The remaining seven types of risks in the OWASP list such as "*Cross site scripting*" and "*Insecure deserialization*" are more focused on the inherent characteristics of web applications.

Table 4. Correlation with Existing Security Flaw Taxonomies.

No.	Security Flaw in EBS	Weber's [25]	OWASP [36]	Tsipenyuk's [29]	Linares-Vásquez's [35]
F1	Trap door	○	○	○	○
F2	Conspirator				
F3	Logic/Time Bomb	●			
F4	Covert Channel	○			
F5	Open Event Channel				
F6	Inadequate Concurrency	○			
F7	Unsafe Event		○		○
F8	Unsafe Event Interface		○	○	○
F9	Inadequate Authentication	○			
F10	Inadequate Resource Management	○		○	●

○ : partially mapped, ● : completely mapped

Tsipenyuk's taxonomy [29] handles implementation-level errors that affect a system's security. It classifies seven main categories and 76 underlying errors. Among those errors, three types can be mapped to the flaws in our taxonomy (see Table 4). Specifically, both *"Command injection"* and *"Process control"* can be partially mapped to the flaws F1 and F8 in our taxonomy. They also represent the exploitation of a victim to perform unintended behaviors, which can be implemented via flaws F1 and F8. *"Unreleased resource"* can be partially mapped to the flaw F10 in our taxonomy. It represents a system's failure to release system resources, which can be caused by inadequate resource allocation. However, none of these error types consider the inherent characteristics of EBSs, such as event-based communication. The remaining 73 types of errors in Tsipenyuk's taxonomy do not correlate with the flaws in our taxonomy.

Linares-Vásquez's taxonomy [35] targets security vulnerabilities in Android, and classifies 15 main categories with 126 underlying vulnerabilities. Similar to the aforementioned taxonomies, both *"Code injection"* and *"Command injection"* in Linares-Vásquez's taxonomy can be partially mapped to the flaws F1 and F8 in our taxonomy. *"Resource management errors"* can be completely mapped to our flaw F10 in terms of its definition. Although *"Race condition"* in Linares-Vásquez's can be partially mapped to flaw F6, it does not consider event anomalies [81]. *"Missing encryption of sensitive data"* and *"Insufficient verification of data authenticity"* can be partially mapped to flaw F7 to consider an event containing sensitive information without any particular protection. The remaining 120 types of vulnerabilities in Linares-Vásquez's taxonomy are more focused on Android-specific security issues.

Overall, although existing taxonomies for security issues handle some of the flaws in our taxonomy, most of them are partially matched. Our taxonomy covers additional security flaws related to the inherent characteristics of EBSs, which are not covered by existing listings or taxonomies. However, it is important to note that existing taxonomies cover the flaws related to general software systems that are not the focus on our taxonomy.

5. Discussion

In this paper, we analyzed security flaw patterns and trends in the existing literature, and underlined challenges that will shape the focus of future research. Our taxonomy can help engineers assessing security problems in EBSs they built. A finer-grained classification of the most common flaws or attacks is useful because system administrators need to anticipate what they will experience in their system. It also provides a baseline for collecting and organizing security-related data, and consequently the information can help engineers strengthen their EBSs. Furthermore, our taxonomy will be useful for security practitioners to organize the problem space. Security problems are caused by an unexpected combination of flaws in general. In these cases, finer-grained distinctions between security flaws can help define a specific problem space. Our taxonomy will be useful for researchers to develop and evaluate potential research directions. Despite significant research efforts to mitigate the security threats in EBSs, solutions targeting these types of systems still lack. We believe that the results of our review (see Section 3.4) will help initiate the required research in this area.

In this research, we carefully followed the general guidelines for a systematic literature review (SLR) process in order to minimize the threats to validity. Nevertheless, there exist inherent threats that require further discussion. Our SLR process includes the utilization of search engine and keyword construction. To maximize the completeness of our taxonomy—whether all of the appropriate literature was included—, we adopted multiple search engines and employed an iterative approach for keyword construction. Furthermore, our SLR process inevitably relies on the interpretation of individual reviewers. To address any resulting bias, we additionally conducted the crosschecking of the literatures, such that no paper reviewed by a single reviewer. Although new variations of security flaws in EBSs can be encountered, to mitigate this threat, our taxonomy has adapted existing classification method which has proven to be rich enough to adequately classify the characteristics of security flaws. This implies that our taxonomy can be adapted to counter new types of security flaws in EBSs.

6. Conclusions

Event-based systems (EBSs) have become popular in mobile cyber physical systems, IoT applications, mobile applications, and web applications because of their inherent advantages. However, their reliance on non-determinism in event processing can be exploited by different types of attacks (e.g., event attacks). In the light of current interest in the security threats within EBSs, we developed a novel security flaw taxonomy for EBS. Each flaw is categorized based on the common factors present among flaws, enabling a systematic approach to resolving the security problems in an EBS. We showed the correlations between each flaw and different types of attacks as well as between each flaw and the applicable existing solutions for preventing the corresponding attacks. We also demonstrated that our taxonomy covers all types of security flaws identified in EBSs so far and even handles additional security flaws not covered by existing taxonomies.

Our taxonomy will help developers determine the types of security flaws existing in their target system and decide the appropriate techniques suitable to resolve each one. In addition, our taxonomy will shed light on potential research directions for securing EBSs.

Author Contributions: Y.K.L. was the main researcher who initiated and organized research reported in the paper, and all authors including Y.K.L. and D.K. were responsible for analyzing the literatures and writing the paper. D.K. performed detailed writing-review and validation. All authors have read and agreed to the published version of the manuscript.

Funding: This work was supported by the National Research Foundation of Korea(NRF) grant funded by the Korea government(MSIT) (No. 2020R1F1A1068774) and a research grant from Seoul Women's University (2020-0451).

Acknowledgments: Dohoon Kim is the corresponding author of this paper.

Conflicts of Interest: The authors declare no conflict of interest.

References

1. Taylor, R.; Medvidovic, N.; Dashofy, E. *Software Architecture: Foundations, Theory, and Practice*; John Wiley & Sons: Hoboken, NJ, USA, 2009.
2. Bonte, P.; Ongenae, F.; De Turck, F. Subset Reasoning for Event-Based Systems. *IEEE Access* **2019**, *7*, 107533–107549. [CrossRef]
3. Kędzierski, D.; Matuszak, P. *IoT System for Sensors Data Acquisition and Controlling Devices via Web*; Technical Report; Wrocław University of Science and Technology: Wrocław, Poland, 2019.
4. Ma, M.; Wang, P. Efficient Event Inference and Context-Awareness in Internet of Things Edge Systems. *IEEE Trans. Big Data* **2019**. [CrossRef]
5. Koldehofe, B. *Principles of Building Scalable and Robust Event-Based Systems*; Technical Report; Technische Universität Darmstadt: Darmstadt, Germany, 2019.

6. Java Message Service (JMS). 2016. Available online: http://www.oracle.com/technetwork/java/jms/index.html (accessed on 16 September 2016).
7. Android Open Source Project. 2015. Available online: https://source.android.com (accessed on 16 September 2016).
8. Lee, E.A. Cyber Physical Systems: Design Challenges. In Proceedings of the IEEE International Symposium on Object and Component-Oriented Real-Time Distributed Computing (ISORC), Orlando, FL, USA, 5–7 May 2008; pp. 363–369.
9. Li, X.; Wang, Y.; Zhou, X. An event-based architecture for cyber physical systems. In Proceedings of the IEEE International Conference on Information Science and Technology (ICITS), Shenzhen, China, 26–28 April 2014; pp. 96–99.
10. Ochoa, S.F.; Fortino, G.; Di Fatta, G. Cyber-Physical Systems, Internet of Things and Big Data. *Future Gener. Comput. Syst.* **2017**, *5*, 40. [CrossRef]
11. Pu, C. A World of Opportunities: CPS, IOT, and Beyond. In Proceedings of the IEEE International Symposium on Object and Component-Oriented Real-Time Distributed Computing, New York, NY, USA, 11–14 July 2011; pp. 229–230.
12. Tan, Y.; Vuran, M.C.; Goddard, S.; Yu, Y.; Song, M.; Ren, S. A Concept Lattice-Based Event Model for Cyber-Physical Systems. In Proceedings of the ACM/IEEE International Conference on Cyber-Physical Systems (ICCPS), Stockholm, Sweden, 12–15 April 2010; pp. 50–60.
13. Ollesch, J.; Hesenius, M.; Gruhn, V. Engineering Events in CPS-Experiences and Lessons Learned. In Proceedings of the 2017 IEEE/ACM 3rd International Workshop on Software Engineering for Smart Cyber-Physical Systems (SEsCPS), Buenos Aires, Argentina, 21 May 2017; pp. 3–9.
14. Rosenthal, F.; Jung, M.; Zitterbart, M.; Hanebeck, U.D. CoCPN–Towards Flexible and Adaptive Cyber-Physical Systems Through Cooperation. In Proceedings of the 2019 16th IEEE Annual Consumer Communications & Networking Conference (CCNC), Las Vegas, NV, USA, 11–14 January 2019; pp. 1–6.
15. Ollesch, J.; Hesenius, M.; Gruhn, V.; Alias, C. The Requirements Engineering Perspective on Events in Cyber-Physical Systems: Poster. In Proceedings of the 11th ACM International Conference on Distributed and Event-based Systems, Barcelona, Spain, 19–23 June 2017; pp. 349–350.
16. Eugster, P.; Felber, P.A.; Guerraoui, R.; Kermarrec, A.M. The Many Faces of Publish/Subscribe. *ACM Comput. Surv.* **2003**, *35*, 114–131. [CrossRef]
17. Taylor, R.N.; Medvidovic, N.; Anderson, K.M.; Whitehead, E.J.; Robbins, J.E.; Nies, K.A.; Oreizy, P.; Dubrow, D.L. A Component- and Message-Based Architectural Style for GUI Software. *IEEE Trans. Softw. Eng.* **1996**, *22*, 390–406. [CrossRef]
18. Cugola, G.; Di Nitto, E.; Fuggetta, A. The JEDI Event-Based Infrastructure and Its Application to the Development of the OPSS WFMS. *ACM Comput. Surv.* **2001**, *27*, 827–850. [CrossRef]
19. Correira, J. *Market Share: AIM and Portal Software, Worldwide, 2005*; Gartner Market Research Report; Gartner Research: Stamford, CT, USA, 2006.
20. Biscotti, F.; Raina, A. *Market Share Analysis: Application Infrastructure and Middleware Software, Worldwide, 2011*; Gartner Market Research Report; Gartner Research: Stamford, CT, USA, 2012.
21. Mohamed, S.; Forshaw, M.; Thomas, N.; Dinn, A. Performance and Dependability Evaluation of Distributed Event-based Systems: A Dynamic Code-injection Approach. In Proceedings of the 8th ACM/SPEC on International Conference on Performance Engineering (ICPE), L'Aquila, Italy, 22–27 April 2017; pp. 349–352
22. Chin, E.; Felt, A.P.; Greenwood, K.; Wagner, D. Analyzing Inter-Application Communication in Android. In Proceedings of the 9th International Conference on Mobile Systems, Applications, and Services (MobiSys), Washington, DC, USA, 28 June–1 July 2011; pp. 239–252.
23. Lee, Y.K. Detecting Inter-Component Vulnerabilities in Event-based Systems. *Int. J. Adv. Comput. Sci. Appl.* **2019**, *10*, 22–28. [CrossRef]
24. Salvia, R.; Cortesi, A.; Ferrara, P.; Spoto, F. Intents Analysis of Android Apps for Confidentiality Leakage Detection. In *Advanced Computing and Systems for Security*; Springer: Berlin/Heidelberg, Germany, 2020; pp. 43–65.
25. Weber, S.; Karger, P.A.; Paradkar, A. A Software Flaw Taxonomy: Aiming Tools at Security. *SIGSOFT Softw. Eng. Notes* **2005**, *30*, 1–7. [CrossRef]
26. Landwehr, C.E.; Bull, A.R.; McDermott, J.P.; Choi, W.S. A Taxonomy of Computer Program Security Flaws. *ACM Comput. Surv.* **1994**, *26*, 211–254. [CrossRef]

27. Sufatrio; Tan, D.J.J.; Chua, T.W.; Thing, V.L.L. Securing Android: A Survey, Taxonomy, and Challenges. *ACM Comput. Surv.* **2015**, *47*, 58:1–58:45. [CrossRef]
28. Simmons, C.; Ellis, C.; Shiva, S.; Dasgupta, D.; Wu, Q. *AVOIDIT: A Cyber Attack Taxonomy*; Technical Report; University of Memphis: Memphis, TN, USA, 2009.
29. Tsipenyuk, K.; Chess, B.; McGraw, G. Seven Pernicious Kingdoms: A Taxonomy of Software Security Errors. *IEEE Secur. Priv.* **2005**, *3*, 81–84. [CrossRef]
30. Jiwnani, K.; Zelkowitz, M. Susceptibility Matrix: A New Aid to Software Auditing. *IEEE Secur. Priv.* **2004**, *2*, 16–21. [CrossRef]
31. Igure, V.M.; Williams, R.D. Taxonomies of Attacks and Vulnerabilities in Computer Systems. *IEEE Commun. Surv. Tutor.* **2008**, *10*, 6–19. [CrossRef]
32. Joshi, C.; Singh, U.K. ADMIT- A Five Dimensional Approach towards Standardization of Network and Computer Attack Taxonomies. *Int. J. Comput. Appl.* **2014**, *100*, 30–36. [CrossRef]
33. Aslam, T. A taxonomy of Security Faults in the Unix Operating System. Master's Thesis, Purdue University, West Lafayette, IN, USA, 1995.
34. Piessens, F. A Taxonomy of Causes of Software Vulnerabilities in Internet Software. In Proceedings of the Supplementary 13th International Symposium on Software Reliability Engineering (ISSRE), Annapolis, MD, USA, 12–15 November 2002; pp. 47–52.
35. Linares-Vásquez, M.; Bavota, G.; Escobar-Velásquez, C. An Empirical Study on Android-related Vulnerabilities. In Proceedings of the 14th International Conference on Mining Software Repositories (MSR), Buenos Aires, Argentina, 20–21 May 2017; pp. 2–13. [CrossRef]
36. Category:OWASP Top Ten 2017 Project. 2017. Available online: https://owasp.org/www-project-top-ten/ (accessed on 9 October 2017).
37. Joshi, C.; Singh, U. A Review on Taxonomies of Attacks and Vulnerability in Computer and Network System. *Int. J.* **2015**, *5*, 742–747.
38. Hui, Z.; Huang, S.; Ren, Z.; Yao, Y. Review of Software Security Defects Taxonomy. In Proceedings of the 5th International Conference on Rough Set and Knowledge Technology (RSKT), Beijing, China, 15–17 October 2010; pp. 310–321.
39. Belokosztolszki, A.; Eyers, D.M.; Pietzuch, P.R.; Bacon, J.; Moody, K. Role-Based Access Control for Publish/Subscribe Middleware Architectures. In Proceedings of the 2nd International Workshop on Distributed Event-Based Systems (DEBS), San Diego, CA, USA, 8 June 2003; pp. 1–8.
40. Shand, B.; Pietzuch, P.; Papagiannis, I.; Moody, K.; Migliavacca, M.; Eyers, D.; Bacon, J. Security Policy and Information Sharing in Distributed Event-Based Systems. In *Reasoning in Event-Based Distributed Systems*; Springer: Berlin/Heidelberg, Germany, 2011; pp. 151–172.
41. Pesonen, L.I.W.; Eyers, D.M.; Bacon, J. Encryption-Enforced Access Control in Dynamic Multi-Domain Publish/Subscribe Networks. In Proceedings of the Inaugural International Conference on Distributed Event-based Systems (DEBS), Toronto, ON, Canada, 20–22 June 2007; pp. 104–115.
42. Srivatsa, M.; Liu, L.; Iyengar, A. EventGuard: A System Architecture for Securing Publish-Subscribe Networks. *ACM Trans. Comput. Syst. (TOCS)* **2011**, *29*, 10:1–10:40. [CrossRef]
43. Fiege, L.; Mezini, M.; Mühl, G.; Buchmann, A.P. Engineering Event-Based Systems with Scopes. In Proceedings of the 16th European Conference on Object-Oriented Programming (ECOOP), Malaga, Spain, 10–14 June 2002; pp. 309–333.
44. Templeton, S.J.; Levitt, K.E. Detecting Spoofed Packets. In Proceedings of the DARPA Information Survivability Conference and Exposition, Washington, DC, USA, 22–24 April 2003; Volume 1, pp. 164–175.
45. Bagheri, H.; Sadeghi, A.; Garcia, J.; Malek, S. COVERT: Compositional Analysis of Android Inter-App Permission Leakage. *IEEE Trans. Softw. Eng.* **2015**, *41*, 866–886. [CrossRef]
46. Bagheri, H.; Sadeghi, A.; Jabbarvand, R.; Malek, S. *Automated Dynamic Enforcement of Synthesized Security Policies in Android*; Technical Report GMU-CS-TR-2015-5; George Mason University: Fairfax, VA, USA, 2015.
47. Bugiel, S.; Davi, L.; Dmitrienko, R.; Fischer, T. Towards Taming Privilege-Escalation Attacks on Android. In Proceedings of the 19th Annual Network & Distributed System Security Symposium (NDSS), San Diego, CA, USA, 5–8 February 2012.
48. Mühl, G.; Fiege, L.; Pietzuch, P. *Distributed Event-Based Systems*; Springer Inc.: New York, NY, USA, 2006.

49. Popescu, D.; Garcia, J.; Bierhoff, K.; Medvidovic, N. Impact Analysis for Distributed Event-based Systems. In Proceedings of the 6th ACM International Conference on Distributed Event-Based Systems (DEBS), Berlin, Germany, 16–20 July 2012; pp. 241–251.
50. Oreizy, P.; Medvidovic, N.; Taylor, R.N. Architecture-based Runtime Software Evolution. In Proceedings of the 20th International Conference on Software Engineering (ICSE), Kyoto, Japan, 19–25 April 1998; pp. 177–186.
51. Garcia, J.; Popescu, D.; Safi, G.; Halfond, W.G.J.; Medvidovic, N. Identifying Message Flow in Distributed Event-Based Systems. In Proceedings of the 9th Joint Meeting on Foundations of Software Engineering (ESEC/FSE), Saint Petersburg, Russia, 18–26 August 2013; pp. 367–377.
52. Bagheri, H.; Sadeghi, A.; Jabbarvand, R.; Malek, S. Practical, Formal Synthesis and Automatic Enforcement of Security Policies for Android. In Proceedings of the 46th IEEE/IFIP International Conference on Dependable Systems and Networks (DSN), Toulouse, France, 28 June–1 July 2016; pp. 514–525.
53. Bugiel, S.; Davi, L.; Dmitrienko, A.; Fischer, T.; Sadeghi, A.R. *XManDroid: A New Android Evolution to Mitigate Privilege Escalation Attacks*; Technical Report TR-2011-04; Technische Universität Darmstadt: Darmstadt, Germany, 2011 .
54. Zhang, R.; Cai, K.; Wonham, W.M. Delay-robustness in distributed control of timed discrete-event systems based on supervisor localization. In Proceedings of the 53rd IEEE Conference on Decision and Control, Los Angeles, CA, USA, 15–17 December 2014; pp. 6719–6724.
55. Dolk, V.S.; Tesi, P.; Persis, C.D.; Heemels, W.P.M.H. Event-Triggered Control Systems Under Denial-of-Service Attacks. *IEEE Trans. Control Netw. Syst.* **2017**, *4*, 93–105. [CrossRef]
56. Rasthofer, S.; Arzt, S.; Lovat, E.; Bodden, E. DroidForce: Enforcing Complex, Data-centric, System-wide Policies in Android. In Proceedings of the 9th International Conference on Availability, Reliability, and Security (ARES), Fribourg, Switzerland, 8–12 September 2014; pp. 40–49.
57. Tripp, O.; Pistoia, M.; Cousot, P.; Cousot, R.; Guarnieri, S. ANDROMEDA: Accurate and Scalable Security Analysis of Web Applications. In Proceedings of the 16th International Conference on Fundamental Approaches to Software Engineering (FASE), Rome, Italy, 16–24 March 2013; pp. 210–225. [CrossRef]
58. Sridharan, M.; Artzi, S.; Pistoia, M.; Guarnieri, S.; Tripp, O.; Berg, R. F4F: Taint Analysis of Framework-based Web Applications. In Proceedings of the 2011 ACM International Conference on Object Oriented Programming Systems Languages and Applications (OOPSLA), Portland, OR, USA, 22–27 October 2011; pp. 1053–1068. [CrossRef]
59. Pietzuch, P. Building Secure Event Processing Applications. In Proceedings of the First International Workshop on Algorithms and Models for Distributed Event Processing (AlMoDEP), Rome, Italy, 19 September 2011; p. 11. [CrossRef]
60. Li, L.; Bartel, A.; Bissyandé, T.F.; Klein, J.; Le Traon, Y.; Arzt, S.; Rasthofer, S.; Bodden, E.; Octeau, D.; Mcdaniel, P. IccTA: Detecting Inter-Component Privacy Leaks in Android App. In Proceedings of the 37th International Conference on Software Engineering (ICSE), Florence, Italy, 16–24 May 2015; pp. 280–291.
61. Demissie, B.F.; Ceccato, M.; Shar, L.K. Security analysis of permission re-delegation vulnerabilities in Android apps. In *Empirical Software Engineering*; Springer: Berlin/Heidelberg, Germany, 2020; pp. 1–53.
62. Developer Error: The Most Dangerous Programming Mistakes | InfoWorld. 2016. Available online: http://www.infoworld.com/article/2622611/application-security/developer-error--the-most-dangerous-programming-mistakes.html (accessed on 25 September 2016).
63. End User Device (EUD) Security Guidance. 2018. Available online: https://www.ncsc.gov.uk/collection/end-user-device-security/ (accessed on 17 November 2018).
64. Petroni, F.; Querzoni, L.; Beraldi, R.; Paolucci, M. Exploiting User Feedback for Online Filtering in Event-based Systems. In Proceedings of the 31st Annual ACM Symposium on Applied Computing (SAC), Pisa, Italy, 4–8 April 2016; pp. 2021–2026. [CrossRef]
65. Aniello, L.; Baldoni, R.; Ciccotelli, C.; Di Luna, G.A.; Frontali, F.; Querzoni, L. The Overlay Scan Attack: Inferring Topologies of Distributed Pub/Sub Systems Through Broker Saturation. In Proceedings of the 8th ACM International Conference on Distributed Event-Based Systems (DEBS), Mumbai, India, 26–29 May 2014; pp. 107–117. [CrossRef]
66. Tariq, M.A.; Koldehofe, B.; Altaweel, A.; Rothermel, K. Providing Basic Security Mechanisms in Broker-less Publish/Subscribe Systems. In Proceedings of the Fourth ACM International Conference on Distributed Event-Based Systems (DEBS), Cambridge, UK, 12–15 July 2010; pp. 38–49. [CrossRef]

67. Srivatsa, M.; Liu, L. Secure Event Dissemination in Publish-Subscribe Networks. In Proceedings of the 27th International Conference on Distributed Computing Systems (ICDCS), Toronto, ON, Canada, 25–29 June 2007; p. 22. [CrossRef]
68. Raiciu, C.; Rosenblum, D.S. Enabling Confidentiality in Content-Based Publish/Subscribe Infrastructures. In Proceedings of the Securecomm and Workshops (SecureComm), Baltimore, MD, USA, 28 August–1 September 2006; pp. 1–11.
69. Nabeel, M.; Shang, N.; Bertino, E. Efficient Privacy Preserving Content Based Publish Subscribe Systems. In Proceedings of the 17th ACM Symposium on Access Control Models and Technologies (SACMAT), Newark, NJ, USA, 20–22 June 2012; pp. 133–144. [CrossRef]
70. Bacon, J.; Eyers, D.M.; Singh, J.; Pietzuch, P.R. Access Control in Publish/Subscribe Systems. In Proceedings of the Second International Conference on Distributed Event-Based Systems (DEBS), Rome, Italy, 1–4 July 2008; pp. 23–34. [CrossRef]
71. Singh, J.; Bacon, J.; Eyers, D. Policy Enforcement Within Emerging Distributed, Event-based Systems. In Proceedings of the 8th ACM International Conference on Distributed Event-Based Systems (DEBS), Bombay, Mumbai, India, 26–29 May 2014; pp. 246–255. [CrossRef]
72. Dave, S.; Mahadevia, J.; Trivedi, B. Security Policy Implementation Using Connection and Event Log to Achieve Network Access Control. In Proceedings of the International Conference on Advances in Computing and Artificial Intelligence (ACAI), Freiburg, Germany, 7–10 June 2011; pp. 29–33. [CrossRef]
73. Wun, A.; Jacobsen, H.A. A Policy Management Framework for Content-based Publish/Subscribe Middleware. In Proceedings of the ACM/IFIP/USENIX 2007 International Conference on Middleware (Middleware), Newport Beach, CA, USA, 26–30 November 2007; pp. 368–388.
74. Singh, J.; Eyers, D.M.; Bacon, J. Disclosure Control in Multi-domain Publish/Subscribe Systems. In Proceedings of the 5th ACM International Conference on Distributed Event-based System (DEBS), Yorktown Heights, NY, USA, 11–14 July 2011; pp. 159–170. [CrossRef]
75. Papagiannis, I.; Migliavacca, M.; Pietzuch, P.; Shand, B.; Eyers, D.; Bacon, J. PrivateFlow: Decentralised Information Flow Control in Event Based Middleware. In Proceedings of the Third ACM International Conference on Distributed Event-Based Systems (DEBS), Nashville, TN, USA, 6–9 July 2009; pp. 38:1–38:2. [CrossRef]
76. Pietzuch, P.; Migliavacca, M.; Bacon, J.; Eyers, D.; Sigh, J.; Shand, B. Security in Multi-domain Event-based Systems. *IT Inf. Technol.* **2009**, *51*. [CrossRef]
77. Bacon, J.; Moody, K.; Yao, W. A Model of OASIS Role-based Access Control and Its Support for Active Security. *ACM Trans. Inf. Syst. Secur.* **2002**, *5*, 492–540. [CrossRef]
78. Fuchs, A.P.; Chaudhuri, A.; Foster, J.S. SCanDroid: *Automated Security Certification of Android Applications*; Technical Report; University of Maryland: College Park, MD, USA, 2009 .
79. Gibler, C.; Crussell, J.; Erickson, J.; Chen, H. AndroidLeaks: Automatically Detecting Potential Privacy Leaks in Android Applications on a Large Scale. In Proceedings of the 5th International Conference on Trust and Trustworthy Computing (TRUST), Vienna, Austria, 13–15 June 2012; pp. 291–307.
80. Zhou, Y.; Jiang, X. Detecting Passive Content Leaks and Pollution in Android Applications. In Proceedings of the 19th Annual Network & Distributed System Security Symposium (NDSS), San Diego, CA, USA, 24–27 February 2013.
81. Safi, G.; Shahbazian, A.; Halfond, W.G.; Medvidovic, N. Detecting Event Anomalies in Event-Based Systems. In Proceedings of the 10th Joint Meeting of the European Software Engineering Conference and the ACM SIGSOFT Symposium on the Foundations of Software Engineering (ESEC/FSE), Bergamo, Italy, 30 August–4 September 2015; pp. 25–37.
82. Enck, W.; Gilbert, P.; Chun, B.G.; Cox, L.P.; Jung, J.; McDaniel, P.; Sheth, A.N. TaintDroid: An Information-flow Tracking System for Realtime Privacy Monitoring on Smartphones. In Proceedings of the 9th USENIX Conference on Operating Systems Design and Implementation (OSDI), Vancouver, BC, Canada, 4–6 October 2010; pp. 393–407.
83. Arzt, S.; Rasthofer, S.; Fritz, C.; Bodden, E.; Bartel, A.; Klein, J.; Le Traon, Y.; Octeau, D.; McDaniel, P. Flowdroid: Precise Context, Flow, Field, Object-Sensitive and Lifecycle-Aware Taint Analysis for Android Apps. In Proceedings of the 35th Annual ACM SIGPLAN Conference on Programming Language Design and Implementation (PLDI), Edinburgh, UK, 9–11 June 2014; pp. 259–269.

84. Grace, M.C.; Zhou, Y.; Wang, Z.; Jiang, X. Systematic Detection of Capability Leaks in Stock Android Smartphones. In Proceedings of the 19th Annual Network & Distributed System Security Symposium (NDSS), San Diego, CA, USA, 5–8 February 2012.
85. Gordon, M.I.; Kim, D.; Perkins, J.H.; Gilham, L.; Nguyen, N.; Rinard, M.C. Information Flow Analysis of Android Applications in DroidSafe. In Proceedings of the 22nd Annual Network & Distributed System Security Symposium (NDSS), San Diego, CA, USA, 8–11 February 2015.
86. Yang, Z.; Yang, M.; Zhang, Y.; Gu, G.; Ning, P.; Wang, X.S. AppIntent: Analyzing Sensitive Data Transmission in Android for Privacy Leakage Detection. In Proceedings of the ACM SIGSAC Conference on Computer Communications Security (CCS), Berlin, Germany, 4–8 November 2013; pp. 1043–1054.
87. Chan, P.P.; Hui, L.C.; Yiu, S.M. DroidChecker: Analyzing Android Applications for Capability Leak. In Proceedings of the 5th Conference on Security and Privacy in Wireless and Mobile Networks (WISEC), Tucson, AZ, USA, 16–18 April 2012; pp. 125–136.
88. Felt, A.P.; Chin, E.; Hanna, S.; Song, D.; Wagner, D. Android Permissions Demystified. In Proceedings of the 18th ACM Conference on Computer and Communications Security (CCS), Chicago, IL, USA, 17–21 October 2011; pp. 627–638.
89. Kim, J.; Yoon, Y.; Yi, K.; Shin, J. ScanDal: Static Analyzer for Detecting Privacy Leaks in Android Applications. In Proceedings of the Mob. Secur. Technol. (MoST), San Francisco, CA, USA, 24 May 2012.
90. Yang, Z.; Yang, M. LeakMiner: Detect Information Leakage on Android with Static Taint Analysis. In Proceedings of the 3rd World Congress on Software Engineering (WCSE), London, UK, 4–6 July 2012; pp. 101–104.
91. Yang, S.; Yan, D.; Wu, H.; Wang, Y.; Rountev, A. Static Control-Flow Analysis of User-driven Callbacks in Android Applications. In Proceedings of the 37th International Conference on Software Engineering (ICSE), Florence, Italy, 16–24 May 2015; pp. 89–99.
92. Mann, C.; Starostin, A. A Framework for Static Detection of Privacy Leaks in Android Applications. In Proceedings of the 27th Symposium on Applied Computing (SAC), Trento, Italy, 26–30 March 2012; pp. 1457–1462.
93. Huang, J.; Zhang, X.; Tan, L.; Wang, P.; Liang, B. AsDroid: Detecting Stealthy Behaviors in Android Applications by User Interface and Program Behavior Contradiction. In Proceedings of the 36th International Conference on Software Engineering (ICSE), Hyderabad, India, 31 May–7 June 2014; pp. 1036–1046.
94. Wei, F.; Roy, S.; Ou, X.; Robby. Amandroid: A Precise and General Inter-Component Data Flow Analysis Framework for Security Vetting of Android Apps. ACM Trans. Priv. Secur. 2018, 21, 1–32. [CrossRef]
95. Klieber, W.; Flynn, L.; Bhosale, A.; Jia, L.; Bauer, L. Android Taint Flow Analysis for App Sets. In Proceedings of the 3rd International Workshop on the State of the Art in Java Program Analysis (SOAP), Santa Barbara, CA, USA, 14 June 2016; pp. 1–6.
96. Octeau, D.; Luchaup, D.; Dering, M.; Jha, S.; McDaniel, P. Composite Constant Propagation: Application to Android Inter-Component Communication Analysis. In Proceedings of the 37th International Conference on Software Engineering (ICSE), Florence, Italy, 16–24 May 2015; pp. 77–88.
97. Octeau, D.; McDaniel, P.; Jha, S.; Bartel, A.; Bodden, E.; Klein, J.; Le Traon, Y. Effective Inter-component Communication Mapping in Android with Epicc: An Essential Step Towards Holistic Security Analysis. In Proceedings of the 22nd USENIX Conference on Security (SEC), Washington, DC, USA, 14–16 August 2013; pp. 543–558.
98. Li, L.; Bartel, A.; Klein, J.; Traon, Y.L.; Arzt, S.; Rasthofer, S.; Bodden, E.; Octeau, D.; Mcdaniel, P. I know what leaked in your pocket: Uncovering privacy leaks on Android Apps with Static Taint Analysis. *arXiv* **2014**, arXiv:1404.7431.
99. Li, L.; Bartel, A.; Klein, J.; Traon, Y.L. Automatically Exploiting Potential Component Leaks in Android Applications. In Proceedings of the 13th International Conference on Trust, Security and Privacy in Computing and Communications (TRUSTCOM), Beijing, China, 24–26 September 2014; pp. 388–397.
100. Ravitch, T.; Creswick, E.R.; Tomb, A.; Foltzer, A.; Elliott, T.; Casburn, L. Multi-App Security Analysis with FUSE: Statically Detecting Android App Collusion. In Proceedings of the 4th Program Protection and Reverse Engineering Workshop (PPREW), San Diego, CA, USA, 24 January 2014; pp. 4:1–4:10.

101. Shen, F.; Vishnubhotla, N.; Todarka, C.; Arora, M.; Dhandapani, B.; Lehner, E.J.; Ko, S.Y.; Ziarek, L. Information Flows As a Permission Mechanism. In Proceedings of the 29th ACM/IEEE International Conference on Automated Software Engineering (ASE), Vasteras, Sweden, 15–19 September 2014; pp. 515–526.
102. Choi, K.; Chang, B.M. A Type and Effect System for Activation Flow of Components in Android Programs. *Inf. Process. Lett.* **2014**, *114*, 620–627. [CrossRef]
103. Bartsch, S.; Berger, B.; Bunke, M.; Sohr, K. The Transitivity-of-Trust Problem in Android Application Interaction. In Proceedings of the 8th International Conference on Availability, Reliability and Security (ARES), Regensburg, Bavaria, Germany, 2–6 September 2013; pp. 291–296.
104. Zhongyang, Y.; Xin, Z.; Mao, B.; Xie, L. DroidAlarm: An All-Sided Static Analysis Tool for Android Privilege-Escalation Malware. In Proceedings of the 8th ACM SIGSAC Symposium on Information, Computer and Communications Security (CCS), Hangzhou, China, 7–10 May 2013; pp. 353–358.
105. Ernst, M.D.; Just, R.; Millstein, S.; Dietl, W.; Pernsteiner, S.; Roesner, F.; Koscher, K.; Barros, P.B.; Bhoraskar, R.; Han, S.; Vines, P.; Wu, E.X. Collaborative Verification of Information Flow for a High-Assurance App Store. In Proceedings of the 2014 ACM SIGSAC Conference on Computer and Communications Security (CCS), Scottsdale, AZ, USA, 3–7 November 2014; pp. 1092–1104.
106. Wu, J.; Cui, T.; Ban, T.; Guo, S.; Cui, L. PaddyFrog: Systematically Detecting Confused Deputy Vulnerability in Android Applications. *Secur. Commun. Netw.* **2015**, *8*, 2338–2349. [CrossRef]
107. Octeau, D.; Jha, S.; Dering, M.; McDaniel, P.; Bartel, A.; Li, L.; Klein, J.; Traon, Y.L. Combining Static Analysis with Probabilistic Models to Enable Market-Scale Android Inter-Component Analysis. In Proceedings of the 43rd Symposium on Principles of Programming Languages (POPL), St. Petersburg, FL, USA, 20–22 January 2016; pp. 469–484.
108. Wu, L.; Grace, M.; Zhou, Y.; Wu, C.; Jiang, X. The Impact of Vendor Customizations on Android Security. In Proceedings of the 2013 ACM SIGSAC Conference on Computer and Communications Security (CCS), Berlin, Germany, 4–8 November 2013; pp. 623–634.
109. Elish, K.O.; Yao, D.; Ryder, B.G. On the Need of Precise Inter-App ICC Classification for Detecting Android Malware Collusions. In Proceedings of the IEEE Mobile Security Technologies (MoST), in Conjunction with the IEEE Symposium on Security and Privacy, San Jose, CA, USA, 21 May 2015.
110. Backes, M.; Gerling, S.; Hammer, C.; Maffei, M.; von Styp-Rekowsky, P. AppGuard: Enforcing User Requirements on Android Apps. In Proceedings of the 19th International Conference on Tools and Algorithms for the Construction and Analysis of Systems (TACAS), Rome, Italy, 16–24 March 2013; pp. 543–548.
111. Xu, R.; Saïdi, H.; Anderson, R. Aurasium: Practical Policy Enforcement for Android Applications. In Proceedings of the 21st USENIX Conference on Security Symposium (USENIX), Bellevue, WA, USA, 8–10 August 2012; pp. 539–552.
112. Davis, B.; Sanders, B.; Khodaverdian, A.; Chen, H. I-ARM-Droid: A Rewriting Framework for In-App Reference Monitors for Android Applications. In Proceedings of the Mobile Security Technologies (MoST), San Francisco, CA, USA, 24 May 2012.
113. Davis, B.; Chen, H. RetroSkeleton: Retrofitting Android Apps. In Proceedings of the 11th Annual International Conference on Mobile Systems, Applications, and Services (MobiSys), Taipei, Taiwan, 25–28 June 2013; pp. 181–192.
114. Jeon, J.; Micinski, K.K.; Vaughan, J.A.; Fogel, A.; Reddy, N.; Foster, J.S.; Millstein, T. Dr. Android and Mr. Hide: Fine-grained Permissions in Android Applications. In Proceedings of the 2nd ACM Workshop on Security and Privacy in Smartphones and Mobile Devices (SPSM), Raleigh, NC, USA, 19 October 2012; pp. 3–14.
115. Chen, K.Z.; Johnson, N.; Dai, S.; Macnamara, K.; Magrino, T.; Wu, E.; Rinard, M.; Song, D. Contextual Policy Enforcement in Android Applications with Permission Event Graphs. In Proceedings of the 20th Annual Network & Distributed System Security Symposium (NDSS), San Diego, CA, USA, 24–27 February 2013.
116. Zhang, M.; Yin, H. Appsealer: Automatic Generation of Vulnerability-Specific Patches for Preventing Component Hijacking Attacks in Android Applications. In Proceedings of the 21st Annual Network & Distributed System Security Symposium (NDSS), San Diego, CA, USA, 23–26 February 2014.
117. Bartel, A.; Klein, J.; Monperrus, M.; Allix, K.; Le Traon, Y. *Improving Privacy on Android Smartphones through In-Vivo Bytecode Instrumentation*; Technical Report; University of Luxembourg: Luxembourg, 2012.

118. Ongtang, M.; McLaughlin, S.; Enck, W.; McDaniel, P. Semantically rich application-centric security in Android. *Secur. Commun. Netw.* **2012**, *5*, 658–673. [CrossRef]
119. Bugiel, S.; Heuser, S.; Sadeghi, A.R. Flexible and Fine-grained Mandatory Access Control on Android for Diverse Security and Privacy Policies. In Proceedings of the 22nd USENIX Conference on Security (USENIX Security), Washington, DC, USA, 14–16 August 2013; pp. 131–146.
120. Zhao, Z.; Colon Osono, F.C. "TrustDroid™": Preventing the Use of Smartphones for Information Leaking in Corporate Networks Through the Used of Static Analysis Taint Tracking. In Proceedings of the 7th International Conference on Malicious and Unwanted Software (MALWARE), Fajardo, PR, USA, 16–18 October 2012; pp. 135–143.
121. Enck, W.; Ongtang, M.; McDaniel, P. On Lightweight Mobile Phone Application Certification. In Proceedings of the 16th ACM Conference on Computer and Communications Security (CCS), Chicago, IL, USA, 9–13 November 2009; pp. 235–245.
122. Schreckling, D.; Posegga, J.; Köstler, J.; Schaff, M. Kynoid: Real-Time Enforcement of Fine-Grained, User-Defined, and Data-Centric Security Policies for Android. In Proceedings of the 6th IFIP International Conference on Information Security Theory and Practice: Security, Privacy and Trust in Computing Systems and Ambient Intelligent (WISTP), Egham, UK, 20–22 June 2012; pp. 208–223.
123. Dietz, M.; Shekhar, S.; Pisetsky, Y.; Shu, A.; Wallach, D.S. Quire: Lightweight Provenance for Smart Phone Operating Systems. In Proceedings of the 20th USENIX Conference on Security (SEC), San Francisco, CA, USA, 8–11 August 2011; p. 23.
124. Felt, A.P.; Wang, H.J.; Moshchuk, A.; Hanna, S.; Chin, E. Permission Re-delegation: Attacks and Defenses. In Proceedings of the 20th USENIX Conference on Security (SEC), San Francisco, CA, USA, 8–11 August 2011; p. 22.
125. Hornyack, P.; Han, S.; Jung, J.; Schechter, S.; Wetherall, D. These Aren't the Droids You're Looking for: Retrofitting Android to Protect Data from Imperious Applications. In Proceedings of the 18th ACM Conference on Computer and Communications Security (CCS), Chicago, IL, USA, 17–21 October 2011; pp. 639–652.
126. Wang, X.; Sun, K.; Wang, Y.; Jing, J. DeepDroid: Dynamically Enforcing Enterprise Policy on Android Devices. In Proceedings of the 22nd Annual Network & Distributed System Security Symposium (NDSS), San Diego, CA, USA, 8–11 February 2015.
127. Hu, Y.; Neamtiu, I. Static Detection of Event-Based Races in Android Apps. In Proceedings of the Twenty-Third International Conference on Architectural Support for Programming Languages and Operating Systems (ASPLOS), Williamsburg, VA, USA, 24–28 March 2018; pp. 257–270.
128. Lau, P.T. Static detection of event-driven races in HTML5-based mobile apps. In *International Conference on Verification and Evaluation of Computer and Communication Systems*; Springer: Berlin/Heidelberg, Germany, 2019; pp. 32–46.
129. Wu, H.; Qin, Z.; Tian, X.; Sun, E.; Xu, F.; Zhong, S. Broken Relationship of Mobile User Intentions and Permission Control of Shared System Resources. In Proceedings of the 2019 IEEE Conference on Dependable and Secure Computing (DSC), Hangzhou, China, 18–20 November 2019; pp. 1–8.
130. El-Zawawy, M.A.; Losiouk, E.; Conti, M. Do not let Next-Intent Vulnerability be your next nightmare: Type system-based approach to detect it in Android apps. *Int. J. Inf. Sec.* **2020**, 1–20. [CrossRef]
131. Casolare, R.; Martinelli, F.; Mercaldo, F.; Nardone, V.; Santone, A. Colluding Android Apps Detection via Model Checking. In *Workshops of the International Conference on Advanced Information Networking and Applications*; Springer: Berlin/Heidelberg, Germany, 2020; pp. 776–786.
132. Mahesh, P.S.; Muthumanickam, K. A Security Scheme for Discovering Battery Draining Attacks in Android Smartphone. In *ICDSMLA 2019*; Springer: Berlin/Heidelberg, Germany, 2020; pp. 1908–1915.
133. Kitchenham, B. *Procedures for Performing Systematic Reviews*; Keele University: Keele, UK, 2004; Volume 33, pp. 1–26.
134. Howard, J.D. *An Analysis of Security Incidents on the Internet 1989–1995*; Technical Report; Carnegie-Mellon Univiersity: Pittsburgh, PA, USA, 1997.
135. Bacon, J.; Eyers, D.; Singh, J.; Shand, B.; Migliavacca, M.; Pietzuch, P. Security in Multi-domain Event-based Systems Sicherheit in ereignis-basierten Mehrdomänensystemen. *IT Inf. Technol.* **2009**, *51*, 277–284.
136. Chen, H.; Su, J.; Qiao, L.; Xin, Q. Malware collusion attack against SVM: Issues and countermeasures. *Appl. Sci.* **2018**, *8*, 1718. [CrossRef]

137. Rangwala, M.; Zhang, P.; Zou, X.; Li, F. A Taxonomy of Privilege Escalation Attacks in Android Applications. *Int. J. Secur. Netw.* **2014**, *9*, 40–55. [CrossRef]
138. Roy, S.; Chaulagain, D.; Bhusal, S. Static Analysis for Security Vetting of Android Apps. In *From Database to Cyber Security*; Springer: Berlin/Heidelberg, Germany, 2018; pp. 375–404.
139. Garcia, J.; Hammad, M.; Ghorbani, N.; Malek, S. Automatic Generation of Inter-Component Communication Exploits for Android Applications. In Proceedings of the 2017 11th Joint Meeting on Foundations of Software Engineering (ESEC/FSE), Paderborn, Germany, 6–8 September 2017; pp. 661–671.
140. Portokalidis, G.; Homburg, P.; Anagnostakis, K.; Bos, H. Paranoid Android: Versatile protection for smartphones. In Proceedings of the 26th Annual Computer Security Applications Conference (ACSAC), Austin, TX, USA, 6–10 December 2010; pp. 347–356.
141. android.App | Android Developers. 2016. Available online: http://developer.android.com/reference/android/app/package-summary.html (accessed on 16 August 2016).
142. Li, L.; Bissyandé, T.F.; Papadakis, M.; Rasthofer, S.; Bartel, A.; Octeau, D.; Klein, J.; Traon, L. Static analysis of android apps: A systematic literature review. *Inf. Softw. Technol.* **2017**, *88*, 67–95. [CrossRef]
143. Fuentes Carranza, J.C.; Fong, P.W.L. Brokering Policies and Execution Monitors for IoT Middleware. In Proceedings of the 24th ACM Symposium on Access Control Models and Technologies (SACMAT), Toronto, ON, Canada, 4–6 June 2019; Association for Computing Machinery: New York, NY, USA; pp. 49–60.
144. Pistoia, M.; Fink, S.J.; Flynn, R.J.; Yahav, E. When Role Models Have Flaws: Static Validation of Enterprise Security Policies. In Proceedings of the 29th International Conference on Software Engineering (ICSE), Minneapolis, MN, USA, 19–27 May 2007; pp. 478–488. [CrossRef]
145. Lee, B.; Kim, S.M.; Park, E.; Han, D. MemScope: Analyzing Memory Duplication on Android Systems. In Proceedings of the 6th Asia-Pacific Workshop on Systems (APSys), Tokyo, Japan, 27–28 July 2015; pp. 19:1–19:7.
146. Silva, A.; Simmonds, J. BehaviorDroid: Monitoring Android Applications. In Proceedings of the International Conference on Mobile Software Engineering and Systems (MOBILESoft), Austin, TX, USA, 16–17 May 2016; pp. 19–20.
147. Sahu, M.K.; Ahirwar, M.; Hemlata, A. A Review of Malware Detection Based on Pattern Matching Technique. *Int. J. Comput. Sci. Inf. Technol.* **2014**, *5*, 944–947.
148. Wu, H.; Schwab, S.; Peckham, R.L. Signature Based Network Intrusion Detection System and Method. U.S. Patent 7,424,744, 9 September, 2008.
149. Anjum, F.; Subhadrabandhu, D.; Sarkar, S. Signature based intrusion detection for wireless ad-hoc networks: A comparative study of various routing protocols. In Proceedings of the Vehicular Technology Conference (VTC), Jeju, Korea, 22–25 April 2003; Volume 3, pp. 2152–2156.

Publisher's Note: MDPI stays neutral with regard to jurisdictional claims in published maps and institutional affiliations.

© 2020 by the authors. Licensee MDPI, Basel, Switzerland. This article is an open access article distributed under the terms and conditions of the Creative Commons Attribution (CC BY) license (http://creativecommons.org/licenses/by/4.0/).

Article

Reducing Dynamic Power Consumption in Mixed-Critical Real-Time Systems

Ijaz Ali [1], Yong-Il Jo [2], Seonah Lee [2,3], Wan Yeon Lee [4] and Kyong Hoon Kim [5,*]

1. Department of Informatics, Gyeongsang National University, Jinju 52828, Korea; ijazali1984@gnu.ac.kr
2. Department of AI Convergence Engineering, Gyeongsang National University, Jinju 52828, Korea; crues@gnu.ac.kr (Y.-I.J.); saleese@gnu.ac.kr (S.L.)
3. Department of Aerospace and Software Engineering, Gyeongsang National University, Jinju 52828, Korea
4. Department of Computer Science, Dongduk Women's University, Seoul 02748, Korea; wanlee@dongduk.ac.kr
5. School of Computer Science and Engineering, Kyungpook National University, Daegu 41566, Korea
* Correspondence: kyong.kim@knu.ac.kr

Received: 8 September 2020; Accepted: 12 October 2020; Published: 16 October 2020

Abstract: In this paper, we study energy minimization consumption of a mixed criticality real-time system on uni-core. Our focus is on a new scheduling scheme to decrease the frequency level in order to conserve power. Since many systems are equipped with dynamic power and frequency level memory, power can be saved by decreasing the system frequency. In this paper, we provide new dynamic energy minimization consumption in mixed-criticality real-time systems. Recent research has been done on low-criticality mode for power reduction. Thus, the proposed scheme can reduce the energy both in high-criticality and low-criticality modes. The effectiveness of our proposed scheme in energy reduction is clearly shown through simulations results.

Keywords: mixed-criticality; power-aware; real-time scheduling; DVFS

1. Introduction

Real-time systems take some inputs and produce outputs in a time-bound manner. Meeting deadline is the core concept of a real-time system such that missing a deadline may collapse the whole system. A real-time system has fragile uses such as an airline command system, which is so highly critical that a single failure can cause a major explosion. Similarly, a real-time system is employed in satellite receivers for collecting highly important information and failures can misguide and result in a major collapse [1]. Daily home appliances such as microwave, AC, electric power system, and refrigerator, etc. can also employ a real-time system.

In a real-time system, the term mixed-critically means that high-critical tasks must meet their deadlines at the cost of missing deadlines for certain low-criticality tasks. Therefore mixed-criticality can be used as a tool for assuring the system failure needed for different components. In the literature, mixed-criticality is identified as mission-criticality and LO- (low-criticality) criticality. The mission-criticality (hard real-time) failures can cause major damage in the systems such as loss of flight control, receiving wrong information via radar system, and misguiding satellite data. On the other hand, LO-criticality (soft real-time) is relaxed critical and can be considered less destructive such that deadlines can be violated occasionally.

A mixed-criticality system (MCS) is characterized to execute in each of two modes, high and low critical mode [2]. Each task is described by the shortest arrival time of a task (period denoted by P), deadline (denoted by D), and Worst case execution time $WCET$ one per criticality level, denoted by

($C_i(LO)$ and $C_i(HI)$). The condition of the basic *MCS* model is the system beginning in the LO-criticality mode and can stay in that mode given all jobs execute within their low-criticality computation times ($C_i(LO)$). If any job executes for its ($C_i(LO)$) execution time without any signal, the system directly moves to high-criticality (HI)-criticality mode. In HI-criticality mode, LO-criticality jobs should not be executed but some level of service should be maintained if at all possible as LO-criticality tasks are still critical.

In this scheme Guan, Emberson, and Pedro [3–5] consider a simple protocol for mode switch situations for controlling the time of the change of mode back to low-criticality, which is to wait until the CPU is idle and then safely be made. Producing a somewhat more efficient scheme, Santy [6] extends this approach that can be applied to a globally scheduling multi-processor system in which the CPU may never get to an ideal tick. In a dual criticality level that has just shifted into a HI-criticality mode and hence no LO-criticality tasks are computed, its protocol is to first wait when the HI-criticality task has completed its high computation time and then wait for the next high priority task, and this continues until the lowest priority job is inactive and it is then safe to reintroduce all low-criticality jobs. If there is a further misbehavior of low computation bound the protocol drops all low-criticality jobs if any jobs compute more then its ($C_i(LO)$) value.

Dynamic voltage and frequency scaling (DVFS) is a commonly-used technique for reducing the overall energy consumption, which is minimized in a large-scale data processing environment. This technique is based on utilizing two common parameters such as processor voltage and processor frequency to reduce power consumption. DVFS enable processor maximum power consumption, which can be accomplished by decreasing the operating frequency level of a processor. However, a scale-down of the processor's CPU frequency causes a delay in task completion time. Much of the literature has been focused on reducing power consumption in embedded systems. A similar technique, real-time dynamic voltage and frequency scaling (RT-DVFS), studied reducing power consumption for periodic and aperiodic tasks. In the RT-DVFS technique, slack time is used as a parameter for adjusting the processor speed such that tasks deadlines will be guaranteed.

In the proposed work, we scheduled a single-processor which support variable frequency and voltage scaling. Our aim is to schedule the given jobs that a CPU speeds all jobs achieved to meet its deadline and minimize energy. Few research has been done on minimizing the energy in a mixed-criticality (MC) real-time system, in [7] CPU acceleration is a deterioration algorithm that adds for given mixed-criticality aperiodic real-time tasks. They characterize an optimization issue of power consumption in MC real-time systems under extended frequency scaling. As the same time each job is performed under the derived frequency scaling. So we enhanced the dynamic approach where the frequency level accommodates under the derived frequency scaling for the plain power decline. The main grant in this research is that we reduced energy in HI-criticality mode dynamically.

2. Related Work and Problem Description

Initially, an MC system is considered by Vestal [8] for scheduling and since then it has gained increasing interest in real-time scheduling. S. Barauch and P. Ekberg consider [9] the mixed-criticality system in a way that all LO-criticality jobs are discarded when the system mode switches to HI-criticality [10–12]. In [13], they showed that the scheme of Vestal is optimal for fixed-priority scheduling systems. In [14], they provided response-time analysis of mixed-criticality tasks in order to increase the schedulability of fixed-priority tasks. In [10], they provided a heuristic scheduling algorithm based on Audsley priority assignment strategy for efficient scheduling.

Audsley approach [15] is used to assign priority from the lowest to highest level. At each priority level, the lowest priority job from the low criticality task set is tried first, if it is schedulable then the job moves up to the next priority level if it is schedulable, then the lowest search can be abandoned as the task set is unscheduled. In [16], they considered how these time-triggered tables can be produced via first simulation.

The energy-minimization consumption of a processor is generally classified into dynamic and static techniques in terms of the consideration of dynamic frequency adjustment. They are also classified into continuous or discrete frequency level schemes according to the assumption of frequency continuity. Yao et al. [17] and Aydin et al. [18] also proposed a static (or offline) scheduling method to reduce energy minimization in a real-time system, in this paper [19] Jejurikar and Gupta study the energy saving of a periodic real-time job. Gruian determined proposed stochastic data to derive a energy-efficient schedules scheme in [20]. In [21], they provided minimum power consumption in periodic task scheduling for discrete frequency-level systems. On the contrary, the dynamic scheduling scheme adjusts the CPU frequency or speed levels depending on the current system load in order to fully utilized the CPU slack time.

The Audsley scheme for assigning priority to mixed-criticality jobs is based on their criticality level in this paper [15], and priority is given to jobs manner high to low scheduling priorities so that priorities are given to lowest priorities task, the schedule difficulty of the MC real-time system is investigated by Baruah, the author proof when all jobs are released at the same time is when these jobs are set to NP-complete [9]. In this scheme, they investigated the optimal schedule algorithm for the MC system scheduling performing well in practice.

The own criticality base priority (OCBP) to MC sporadic jobs by Li and Baruah [22] considers criticality for priority assignment. When a new job arrives to the system, a new priority is assigned to the job. In [3], they presented a scheduling scheme known as priority-list reuse scheduling based on the OCBP scheduler. In [23], they assumed a likewise realistic energy model and presented an optimal static scheme for minimizing the energy of multi-component with adjusting individual frequencies main memory and processor system bus.

The connection between multiple-choice knap sack problem (MCKP) and dynamic voltage scaling (DVS) for periodic task and energy optimization was at first proven by Mejia-Alvarez and Mosse [24]. In this paper Aydin et al. consider [18] the dynamic voltage frequency scaling scheme for periodic jobs that complete before their worst-case execution times (WCETs). In [25], they proposed the elastic scheduling for the purpose of utilizing CPU with discrete frequencies. In [26], they presented a dynamic slack algorithm allocation for real time that consider both the loss energy minimization and frequency scaling overhead. The cycle conservation approach was proposed by Mei et al. [27]. They suggested a novel power aware scheduling scheme named cycle conservation DVFS for sporadic jobs. In this algorithm P.Pillai and K.G.Shin [28] proposed real-time DVS, the OS's real time scheduler, and jobs managing service to allocate minimum power consumption while maintaining that the deadlines must always be met.

More recently researches on a power-aware mixed-criticality real-time system have been presented by [7,29]. The major technique is used for a power-aware mixed-criticality system and they consider only a set job with no periodical jobs. They determine possible CPU speed degraded for MCS jobs. In this algorithm [29], they show that minimizing the energy of power-aware mixed-criticality real-time scheduling for periodic jobs under continuous frequency scaling. The early deadline first with the virtual deadline (EDF-VD) algorithm [11] provide the most favorable virtual deadline (VD) and frequency scaling of jobs, and do not adjust during run time the derived frequency levels of jobs. In [30], when high-critical jobs do not finish low computation time, all low-critical jobs are terminated and the system frequency level is set to maximum, in this paper they only reduce frequency in low-critical mode.

In our work we provide an efficient power-aware scheduling algorithm in MC real-time systems and adjust the optimal frequency level of high-criticality mode, to the best of our knowledge this is the first work that introduces optimal energy consumption of high-criticality mode in a mixed-criticality real-time system, the main grant our scheme is that we minimize energy in high-criticality mode dynamically and show the experimental results in simulations.

3. System Model

3.1. Task Model

In this subsection, we provide an overview of the task model. In the mixed-criticality real-time systems, a low-criticality periodic task releases an order of jobs only in low criticality mode, while high-criticality tasks release their jobs in both high- and low-criticality mode. Thus a mixed-criticality task τ_i consists of four parameters: Period (P_i), computation time of low-criticality jobs, $C_i(LO)$, computation time of high-criticality jobs, $C_i(HI)$, and tasks level (X_i) as follows:

- P_i: The task period. The task releases a job every period (minimum interval arrival time);
- $C_i(LO)$: The worst-case execution time in low-criticality mode. The task requires $C_i(LO)$ times in low-criticality mode;
- $C_i(HI)$: The worst-case execution time in high-criticality mode. The task requires $C_i(HI)$ times in high-criticality mode;
- X_i: The criticality level of task. The system can be either in high-criticality (HI) mode or in low-criticality (LO) mode.

The task τ_i is a periodic real-time task, so that jobs are released at every P_i time units. The j-th instance or job of a task τ_i is denoted as the $\tau_{i,j}$. In the mixed-criticality system, tasks are categorized into low-criticality and high-criticality tasks. In addition, the system mode is also divided into low-criticality and high-criticality mode. In low-criticality mode, all tasks release their jobs so that each task's job τ_i requires the worst-case execution time of $C_i(LO)$. On the contrary, in high-criticality mode, only the high-criticality tasks release their jobs with $C_i(HI)$ execution time $(C_i(HI) \leq C_i(LO))$. Thus, each task has its criticality mode X_i.

The mixed-criticality system is an integrated suit of hardware, middleware service, operating system, and application software that support the execution of non-criticality, mission-criticality, and safety-critical functions. The system starts in low-criticality mode. However, if there is a possibility that any low-critical job interrupts in high-criticality jobs' execution time, then the system criticality mode changes. In such a situation, all low-criticality tasks are dropped in the system. In mixed-criticality systems, such a possibility occurs when a high-criticality job does not complete its computation time, which is the condition of switching from low-criticality mode to high-criticality mode.

On the contrary, the system returns to low-criticality mode when there is no possibility of overrun. While high-criticality tasks are executed in high-criticality mode, the system changes its criticality to low mode as long as there is no task ready in the queue [29].

For example, Figure 1 shows an example of three mixed-criticality tasks of $\tau_1(2, 2, 5, LO)$, $\tau_2(1, 3, 6, HI)$, and $\tau_3(2, 3, 8, HI)$. The system starts in low-criticality mode, where each task requires $C_i(LO)$ execution time. Each task releases its job every P_i time units. The scheduling algorithm used in Figure 1 is EDF (earliest deadline first).

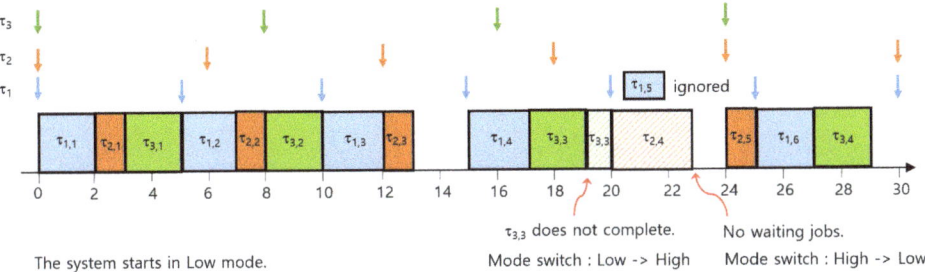

Figure 1. An example of mixed-criticality scheduling.

Let us assume that the job $\tau_{3,3}$ does not complete its execution at time 19. Then, the system changes the criticality mode to high-criticality. After then, the system executes only high-criticality tasks (τ_2 and τ_3) with their $C_i(HI)$ execution times. The execution times of $\tau_{3,3}$ and $\tau_{2,4}$ become 3 in each. When the system is in high-criticality mode, all low-criticality jobs are ignored or removed from the queue. For instance, the job $\tau_{1,5}$ released at time 20 is removed from the scheduling queue since it is a low-criticality job.

The systems returns to low-criticality mode if there is no high-criticality jobs waiting in the scheduling queue. For example, the system returns back to the low-criticality mode at time 23 because there are no jobs available. After then, the system executes low-criticality jobs again as before.

3.2. Power Model

In this paper, we assume the DVFS-enabled CPU system where the CPU frequency is adjusted dynamically during run-time. The number of discrete frequency levels is given by m while the frequency levels are defined as a set F.

Let us assume that a task requires t execution time on the CPU at its maximum frequency level. For a given frequency level f of the CPU, the relative speed level s is defined by f/f_{max}, where f_{max} is the maximum frequency level. Then, the task execution time is defined by t/s.

Since the dynamic power consumption is a major issue in the power consumption of systems, we take dynamic power consumption into account in the paper. Generally, the dynamic power is in proportion to f^3 or f^4 for a frequency level f, we use Equation (1) for the execution time model of a task with t execution time on the relative speed level s [31].

$$E = \alpha \cdot \frac{t}{s} \cdot s^3 = \alpha \cdot t \cdot s^2, \qquad (1)$$

where α is a coefficient. In this paper we assume $\alpha = 1$ for the sake of simplicity.

Figure 2 shows an DVFS scheme for real-time task scheduling. For example, a real-time task requires 3 time unit for its execution, while its result requires 10 time units (Figure 2a). If there is no other task, the system has 7 time-unit slack time to the task deadline. Thus, the task can be executed on the relative speed level of 0.3, as shown in Figure 2b. In the reduced CPU speed level, the system can reduce the power consumption without violating the task deadline.

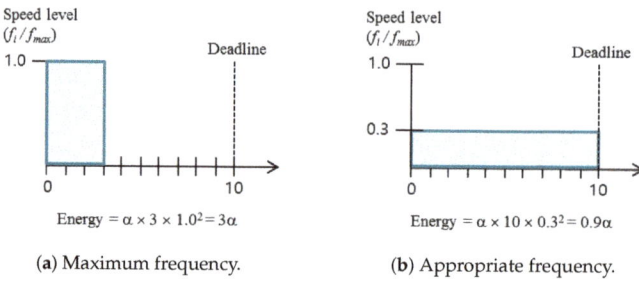

Figure 2. Dynamic voltage scaling (DVS) for real-time tasks.

4. Research Motivations

4.1. Recap of EDF-VD for Power-Aware Mixed-Criticality Real-Time Tasks

In this subsection, we describe a brief explanation of the previous work on power-aware mixed-criticality tasks scheduling [29]. The base scheduling algorithm is early deadline first with the virtual deadline (EDF-VD) which is a mode-switched EDF scheduling technique developed for mixed-criticality task sets [22,32,33]. The reservation of time budgets for HI criticality tasks is done in the LO mode. This is achieved by shortening the deadline of HI criticality tasks. Intuitively, shortening the deadline of HI criticality tasks will push them to finish earlier in the LO mode, leaving more time until their actual deadlines to accommodate extra workloads. Indeed, this form of safety preparation (i.e., shortening deadlines of HI criticality tasks in the LO mode) has proven to be effective in improving system schedulability [34].

In EDF-VD, the value of x in a system determines the virtual deadline VD_i as $P_i \cdot x$, where $0 < x \leq 1$. In order to guarantee the schedulability of task sets both in LO mode and HI mode, the value of x should satisfy the two equations of Equations (2) and (3):

$$\frac{U_{LO}^{HI}}{x} + U_{LO}^{LO} \leq 1 \qquad (2)$$

$$U_{HI}^{HI} + xU_{LO}^{LO} \leq 1 \qquad (3)$$

In [29], EDF-VD is adjusted in order to provided power-awareness for mixed-criticality real-time systems. They defined a problem of power-aware scheduling in MC systems. The objective is to minimize power consumption satisfying both Equations (4) and (5):

$$\sum_{\tau_i \in T_{HI}} \frac{C_i(LO)/f_{LO}^{HI}}{P_i} \cdot \frac{1}{x} + \sum_{\tau_i \in T_{LO}} \frac{C_i(LO)/f_{LO}^{LO}}{P_i} \leq 1 \qquad (4)$$

$$\sum_{\tau_i \in T_{HI}} \frac{C_i(HI)}{P_i} + x \cdot \sum_{\tau_i \in T_{LO}} \frac{C_i(LO)/f_{LO}^{LO}}{P_i} \leq 1 \qquad (5)$$

where T_{HI} and T_{LO} are sets of high-criticality tasks and low-criticality tasks, in each. In Equations (4) and (5), f_{LO}^{LO} and f_{LO}^{HI} indicate optimal frequency levels of HI-criticality tasks and LO-criticality tasks in low mode. They provided an optimal solution to derive x, f_{LO}^{LO}, and f_{LO}^{HI} for the formulated problem.

For example, Table 1 shows an example of a task set. The optimal values of x, f_{LO}^{LO}, and f_{LO}^{HI} are given by 0.56, 0.6, and 0.8, respectively from the method in [29]. The right three columns of Table 1 shows the virtual deadline and the execution time in low-criticality mode. Figure 3 shows the scheduling example of Table 1 based on EDF-VD.

Table 1. An example of tasks.

Task	P_i	$C_i(LO)$	$C_i(HI)$	X_i	$VD_i = x \cdot P_i$	$C_i(LO)/f_{LO}^{LO}$	$C_i(HI)/f_{LO}^{HI}$
τ_1	6	1	2	HI	3.36	-	1.25
τ_2	8	1	3	HI	4.48	-	1.25
τ_3	12	1	1	LO	-	1.67	-
τ_4	16	2	2	LO	-	2.33	-

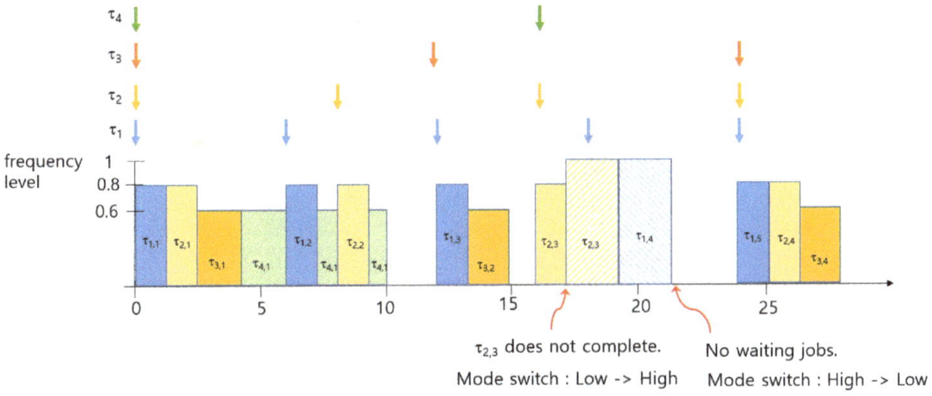

Figure 3. An example of power-aware mixed-criticality Scheduling of Table 1.

As shown in Figure 3, high-criticality tasks, τ_1 and τ_2, are run at a f_{LO}^{HI} frequency level in low-criticality mode, while low-criticality tasks of τ_3 and τ_4 run at f_{LO}^{LO}. Let us assume that $\tau_{2,3}$ does not complete $C_i(LO)$ at time 17.25. Then, the system mode changes to high-criticality mode so that two low-criticality jobs of τ_3 and τ_4 are ignored after the mode switch event. In high-criticality mode, the frequency level is set as the maximum frequency in order to guarantee the schedulability of high-criticality tasks. The system mode returns back to low-criticality mode after executing all high-criticality jobs.

4.2. Motivations

As discussed in the previous subsection, the previous work focused on low-criticality mode. However, we can further reduce the power in high-criticality mode without violating the schedulability. For example, we can reduce the frequency level while executing $\tau_{2,3}$ and $\tau_{1,4}$ in the high-criticality mode of Figure 3.

In order to guarantee the schedulability in both criticality modes, we need appropriate frequency levels in each mode. The main problem of this paper is to determine optimal frequency levels that consider both modes.

5. The Proposed Scheme

5.1. Dynamic Power Aware Scheme MCS Jobs

The proposed scheme dynamically adjusts the CPU frequency level depending on both the system mode and task mode. The baseline frequency levels are derived from static analysis so that x, f_{LO}^{LO}, f_{LO}^{HI}, and f_{HI}^{HI} are obtained before run-time. Throughout the optimization problem, we solve those values in the initial step.

The power-consumption with consideration of both high- and low-crticality modes in defined by the following three equations. The unit-time power consumption in low-crticality mode is derived by Equation (6), where LCM is the least common multiplier of all periods. In Equation (6), the total power consumption during LCM is computed by adding the power consumption of task τ_i in low mode using Equation (1). The number of τ_i's jobs is LCM/P_i. Thus, the unit-time power consumption is obtained by dividing the total sum with LCM.

Similarly, the unit-time power consumption in high-criticality mode is defined by Equation (7). Thus, the average unit-time power consumption can be obtained as the expected value in each mode, as in Equation (8), where P_{LO} and P_{HI} denote the probabilities of the system mode in low- and high-crticality, respectively.

$$\begin{aligned} UP_{LO} &= \frac{1}{LCM} \left(\sum_{\tau_i \in T_{LO}} \frac{LCM}{P_i} \cdot \frac{C_i(LO)}{f_{LO}^{LO}} \cdot (f_{LO}^{LO})^3 + \sum_{\tau_i \in T_{HI}} \frac{LCM}{P_i} \cdot \frac{C_i(LO)}{f_{LO}^{HI}} \cdot (f_{LO}^{HI})^3 \right) \\ &= \sum_{\tau_i \in T_{LO}} \frac{C_i(LO)}{P_i} \cdot (f_{LO}^{LO})^2 + \sum_{\tau_i \in T_{HI}} \frac{C_i(LO)}{P_i} \cdot (f_{LO}^{HI})^2 \\ &= U_{LO}^{LO} \cdot (f_{LO}^{LO})^2 + U_{LO}^{HI} \cdot (f_{LO}^{HI})^2 \end{aligned} \quad (6)$$

$$\begin{aligned} UP_{HI} &= \frac{1}{LCM} \sum_{\tau_i \in T_{HI}} \frac{LCM}{P_i} \cdot \frac{C_i(HI)}{f_{HI}^{HI}} \cdot (f_{HI}^{HI})^3 \\ &= \sum_{\tau_i \in T_{HI}} \frac{C_i(HI)}{P_i} \cdot (f_{HI}^{HI})^2 \\ &= U_{HI}^{HI} \cdot (f_{HI}^{HI})^2 \end{aligned} \quad (7)$$

$$\begin{aligned} UAP &= UP_{LO} \cdot P_{LO} + UP_{HI} \cdot P_{HI} \\ &= \left(U_{LO}^{LO} \cdot (f_{LO}^{LO})^2 + U_{LO}^{HI} \cdot (f_{LO}^{HI})^2 \right) \cdot P_{LO} + U_{HI}^{HI} \cdot (f_{HI}^{HI})^2 \cdot P_{HI} \end{aligned} \quad (8)$$

For the given probabilities of P_{LO} and P_{HI}, the problem of deciding the optimal frequency levels and x of EDF-VD is: to minimize

$$\left(U_{LO}^{LO} \cdot (f_{LO}^{LO})^2 + U_{LO}^{HI} \cdot (f_{LO}^{HI})^2 \right) \cdot P_{LO} + U_{HI}^{HI} \cdot (f_{HI}^{HI})^2 \cdot P_{HI} \quad (9)$$

subject to

$$\frac{U_{LO}^{HI}}{f_{LO}^{HI}} \cdot \frac{1}{x} + \frac{U_{LO}^{LO}}{f_{LO}^{LO}} \leq 1 \quad (10)$$

$$\frac{U_{HI}^{HI}}{f_{HI}^{HI}} + x \cdot \frac{U_{LO}^{LO}}{f_{LO}^{LO}} \leq 1. \quad (11)$$

The scheduling system flow in low mode is shown in Figure 4a. Each task releases jobs with $C_i(LO)$ execution time every period. Since we use EDF-VD, the virtual deadline of a high-criticality job released at time t is given by $t + VD_i$. The deadline of low-criticality job is set as $t + p_i$. These new jobs are waiting in the ready queue.

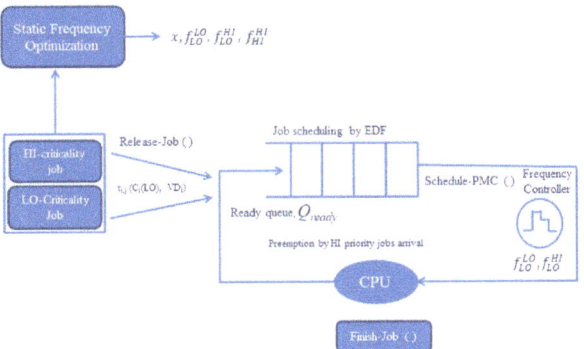

(a) Scheduling flow in low mode.

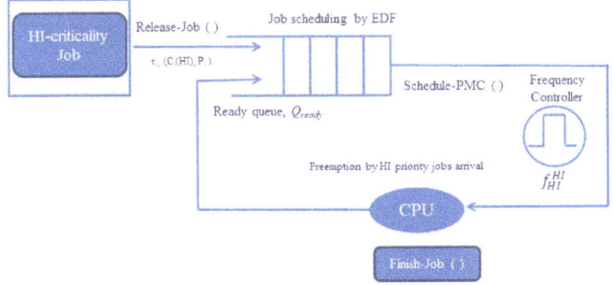

(b) Scheduling flow in high mode.

Figure 4. The proposed scheduling framework.

The scheduling algorithm for jobs is based on early deadline first so that the job with the earliest deadline is scheduled first. At the time of dispatching a high-criticality job, the CPU frequency level is set as f_{LO}^{HI}. On the contrary, the frequency level is adjusted with f_{LO}^{LO} for low-criticality job execution.

When a high-criticality job does not complete its low-mode execution time, then the system switches to high-criticality mode. At that time, all low-criticality jobs are dropped in order to guarantee high-criticality tasks as shown in Figure 4b. However, the system can switch back to low-mode at any time when there is no pending task.

5.2. DVFS Scheduling

The notation for the scheduling algorithm is shown in Table 2. The task utilization of τ_i is denoted as U_i. Each job, denoted as J_k, in the waiting queue is defined by (C_k, D_k) so that a job requires C_k execution time by the deadline D_k. The values are determined at the time of job release.

Table 2. Notations.

Notation	Meaning
U_i	The utilization of the task τ_i
$J_k = (C_k, D_k)$	The job of task τ_i
t	The current time
Q_{ready}	The CPU ready queue
J_{curr}	current job of execution

The proposed scheme is defined by functions that are called at a certain event. The algorithms are given in the followings pseudo-code in Algorithms 1 and 2.

- *Job-Release (τ_i):* Every P_i period, a task τ_i releases a job. The function *Job-Release* is called;
- *Job-Finish (J_i):* The function is called when a job completes its execution or over-runs the execution time;
- *Power-aware Schedule ():* At the time of a job release or completion, the function re-schedules jobs in the queue;
- *Frequency-Adjust ():* The CPU frequency is adjusted at the time of job allocation to the CPU.

When a job is released in low mode, the job is inserted in the ready queue. The task utilization is also updated. Since the frequency-level of a LO-criticality task is given by f_{LO}^{LO}, the task utilization is determined by the equation in line 5 of Algorithm 1. In case of a high-critical job of $C_i(HI) - C_i(LO)$ every period so that the utilization is given by the equation in line 7. If the current system mode is low, we terminate or ignore the low-criticality job. If the current mode is high, we execute the high-criticality job (line 14). The job is inserted in the ready queue, we call the scheduling algorithm in line 19.

When the job J_i finishes its computation, if the current system mode is low, nothing is executed. We only check $X_i = HI$. We have two cases if J_i finishes. If J_i does not complete, the system mode becomes high. When the ready queue is empty and there is no high-criticality job in the ready queue, the system mode is changed from high to low (lines 29–31).

The function *Power-aware Schedule ()* dispatches jobs using EDF (line 38–43 of Algorithm 1). At each scheduling event, *Frequency-Adjust ()* function is called so as to adjust the CPU frequency dynamically. As shown in Algorithm 2, if the system is in high-criticality mode, we minimize the frequency of high-criticality mode which is set as f_{HI}^{HI}. The frequency level is set as the frequency level sufficient to schedule current jobs. Thus, the relative speed level of the frequency is greater than or equal to the current utilization.

Algorithm 1 Algorithm of energy minimization consumption in mixed-criticality tasks.

1: **function** JOB-RELEASE(τ_i)
2:    **if** the current system mode is Low **then**
3:       Insert job $J_i(C_i(LO), t + VD_i)$ into Q_{ready}
4:       **if** $X_i =$ Low **then**   ▷ Low-criticality job
5:          $U_i \leftarrow (C_i(LO)/f_{LO}^{LO})/P_i$
6:       **else**
7:          $U_i \leftarrow (C_i(LO)/f_{LO}^{HI})/P_i + ((C_i(HI) - C_i(LO)/f_{HI}^{HI})/P_i$
8:       **end if**
9:    **else**   ▷ The current system mode is High
10:       **if** $X_i =$ Low **then**
11:          $U_i \leftarrow 0$
12:       **else**   ▷ $X_i =$ High
13:          $U_i \leftarrow (C_i(HI)/f_{HI}^{HI})/P_i$
14:          Insert job $J_i(C_i(HI), t + P_i)$ into Q_{ready}
15:       **end if**
16:    **end if**
17:    POWER-AWARE SCHEDULE( )
18: **end function**

19: **function** JOB-FINISH(J_i)
20:    **if** the current system mode is Low **then**
21:       **if** $X_i =$ High **then**   ▷ High-criticality job
22:          **if** J_i finish $C_i(LO)$ completely **then**
23:             $U_i \leftarrow (Ci(LO)/f_{LO}^{HI})/P_i$
24:          **else**
25:             The system mode changed to High   ▷ Mode switch to HI
26:          **end if**
27:       **end if**
28:    **else**   ▷ The current system mode is High
29:       **if** $Q_{ready} = \varnothing$ **then**
30:          The system mode is changed from High to Low   ▷ Mode switch back to LO
31:       **end if**
32:    **end if**
33:    POWER-AWARE SCHEDULE( )
34: **end function**

35: **function** POWER-AWARE SCHEDULE( )
36:    **if** $Q_{ready} \neq \varnothing$ **then**
37:       $J_k \leftarrow$ the job with the earliest deadline in Q_{ready}
38:       **if** $J_{curr} = \varnothing$ **then**   ▷ CPU idle
39:          $J_{curr} \leftarrow J_k$
40:       **else if** $D_k < D_{curr}$ **then**   ▷ Preemption by EDF
41:          J_{curr} is preempted and re-Inserted into Q_{ready}
42:          $J_{curr} \leftarrow J_k$
43:       **end if**
44:       FREQUENCY-ADJUST( )
45:    **end if**
46: **end function**

Algorithm 2 Algorithm of selecting frequency.

```
 1: function FREQUENCY-ADJUST( )
 2:     if The system is in High mode then
 3:         The frequency is set as f_HI^HI.
 4:     else                                              ▷ The system is in Low mode.
 5:         U ← min(∑_{i=1}^{n} U_i, 1.0)
 6:         if X_curr = LO then
 7:             U ← U × f_LO^LO
 8:         else
 9:             U ← U × f_LO^HI
10:         end if
11:         freq ← the minimum f_i ∈ F s.t. U ≤ f_i/f_max
12:         The frequency is set as freq.
13:     end if
14: end function
```

5.3. Example

Let us consider the task set in Table 1 as an example. The previous work derives the optimal value of f_{LO}^{LO} and f_{LO}^{HI} as 0.6 and 0.8, respectively. In high-criticality mode, the maximum frequency level is used. However, the proposed work derives the optimal frequency levels by solving Equation (9) with two constraints of Equations (10) and (11). Table 3 shows those values for given probabilities of high- and low-criticality mode.

For example, for a given $P_{HI} = 0.2$, the optimal frequency levels of f_{LO}^{LO}, f_{LO}^{HI}, and f_{HI}^{HI} are 0.7, 0.8, and 0.9. The scheduling example of Table 1 in the same scenario as Figure 3 is shown in Figure 5. The frequency level in high-criticality is set as 0.9, not as 1.0. As shown in Table 3, the proposed work can reduce more energy in higher probability of high-criticality mode.

Table 3. Optimal frequency levels and x of the example of Table 1.

		x	f_{LO}^{LO}	f_{LO}^{HI}	f_{HI}^{HI}	Power Improvement
Previous		0.56	0.6	0.8	1	-
Previous	$P_{HI} = 0.1$	0.56	0.6	0.8	1	0%
	$P_{HI} = 0.2$	0.52	0.7	0.8	0.9	1.5%
	$P_{HI} = 0.3$	0.47	0.7	0.9	0.8	6.3%
	$P_{HI} = 0.4$	0.47	0.7	0.9	0.8	14.6%

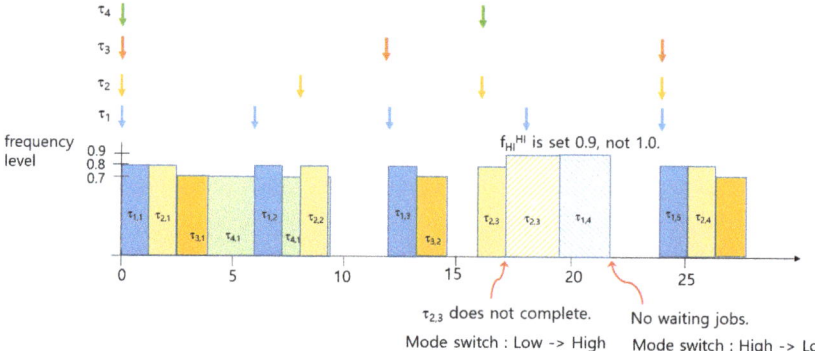

Figure 5. An example of proposed power-aware scheduling.

6. Performance Evaluation

6.1. Simulations Environment

We conduct extensive simulation to validate the proposed idea by utilizing random power-aware mixed-criticality task sets. Simulation parameters are shown in Table 4. We used six discrete frequency levels in the system. The execution time is randomly generated from 1 to 100. Then, the task period is defined in order to meet the target utilization. We have a different utilization of LO- and HI-criticality jobs which is 0.2, 0.25, 0.3, 0.35, 0.4, and 0.45. We have five different tasks in a set, where the numbers of LO-criticality and HI-criticality tasks are two and three in each. We generate 1000 random tasks sets to evaluate the effect of energy minimization consumption for a given tasks sets. We simulate each task set for the least common multiple of the tasks' periods.

Table 4. Simulation Parameters.

Parameters	Values
CPU Frequency levels	0.4, 0.5, 0.6, 0.7, 0.8, 0.9, 1.0
u_{LO}^{LO}	0.3, 0.35, 0.4, 0.45
u_{LO}^{HI}	0.3, 0.35, 0.4, 0.45,
Low-to-high rate (r)	1.5, 2.0, 2.5, 3.0
Low-criticality tasks	2
High-criticality tasks	3

6.2. Energy Consumption Results

We present energy consumption for different task sets as shown in Figure 6a–d. We measure the average value of 1000 task sets. The figure presents energy consumption as a function of system utilization for different probabilities. As shown in the figure, the proposed approach achieves better minimum energy consumption compared to that of existing approaches for the same task set. The main reason of minimum energy consumption is due to the task utilization at low and high criticality modes. The figure further shows that when the probability of high-criticality mode is increased, the impact of energy consumption gradually increases from 0.01 to 0.09. As shown in Figure 6c, the minimum energy consumption depends on the probability values for task utilization U = (0.2, 0.25, 0.3, 0.35, 0.4, 0.45).

We also present the impact of average x on energy minimization in Figure 7. We consider the same value of x for both previous and proposed approaches. When the value of utilization is increased by 0.35, the proposed approach achieves significant improvement in the performance. The impact of x in the probabilities is shown in Figure 7a. When the utilization is between 0.2 and 0.25, the average x is 0.4 but when the utilization is increased up to 0.35 and the value of x is increased by 0.56. When the utilization is between 0.35 and 0.4, then the average value of x goes to 0.65. This implies that in HI-criticality mode the energy consumption is not affected when we increase the value of x.

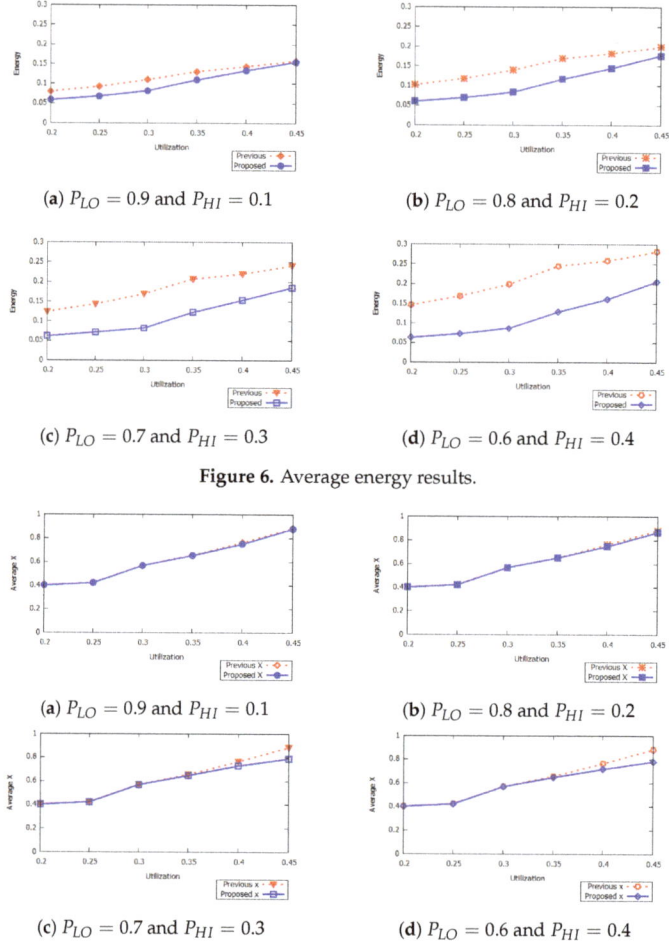

(a) $P_{LO} = 0.9$ and $P_{HI} = 0.1$

(b) $P_{LO} = 0.8$ and $P_{HI} = 0.2$

(c) $P_{LO} = 0.7$ and $P_{HI} = 0.3$

(d) $P_{LO} = 0.6$ and $P_{HI} = 0.4$

Figure 6. Average energy results.

(a) $P_{LO} = 0.9$ and $P_{HI} = 0.1$

(b) $P_{LO} = 0.8$ and $P_{HI} = 0.2$

(c) $P_{LO} = 0.7$ and $P_{HI} = 0.3$

(d) $P_{LO} = 0.6$ and $P_{HI} = 0.4$

Figure 7. The impact of x.

Figure 8 shows energy consumption as a function of different ratios of low- and high-computation times. The figure considers different values of r ranging from 1.5 to 3. The ratio between low-critical and high-critical execution time in the sequence in order to observe its effects on the scheduling of mixed-criticality tasks. As shown in Figure 8, the increasing ratio also leads to an increase in the average energy consumption. When the ratio is 1.5, the values of average energy for proposed and previous approaches are 0.082 and 0.136, respectively. Similarly, when the probability is between 0.6 to 0.4, the proposed approach minimizes energy consumption as compared to that of the previous approach as shown in Figure 8b. It is concluded that an increase in the ratio leads to increase in the average energy consumption of the mixed-criticality task sets.

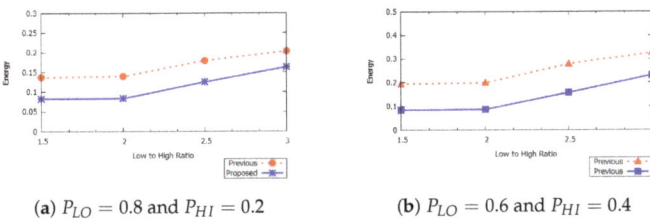

(a) $P_{LO} = 0.8$ and $P_{HI} = 0.2$ (b) $P_{LO} = 0.6$ and $P_{HI} = 0.4$

Figure 8. The impact of ratio r.

The result in Figure 9 shows the impact of different task sets in mixed-criticality systems. The figure presents the average energy as a function of seven task sets, i.e., (1LO/6HI, 2LO/5HI, 3LO/4HI, 4LO/3HI, 5LO/2HI, 6LO/1HI) ranging from low to high critical modes. It is observed that the average energy is increasing for the average number of 1000 task sets.

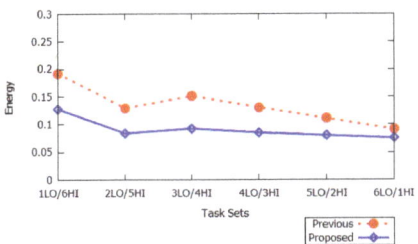

Figure 9. Impact of the number of low- and high-criticality tasks ($P_{HI} = 0.2$).

In Figure 10, the average energy consumption is presented for different frequency intervals. The figure shows the effects of the task-sets frequencies on minimum energy consumption. In the range between 0.4 and 0.5, we generate random task sets utilization for the sufficient number of tasks. When the frequency interval is between 0.05 and 1, the proposed approach outperforms the previous approach approach. Figure 10b shows that when the frequency interval is between 0.05 and 0.1, the value of x decreases. It is concluded that the proposed approach achieves a lower value of x compared to that of the previous approach.

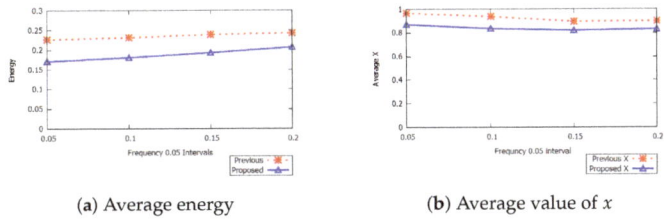

(a) Average energy (b) Average value of x

Figure 10. Impact of frequency intervals.

6.3. Comparison Summary

The following Table 5 describes a comparison with the previous work. Although the previous work sets the maximum frequency level in high-criticality mode, the proposed scheme adjusts the level.

When the probability of high-criticality mode is low, the performance of both work seems similar. However, the proposed work has more overhead for frequency scaling adjustment.

Table 5. Comparison summary.

	Previous	Proposed
Frequency in HI-mode	Maximum	Optimized
Performance at low P_{HI}	Near optimal	Optimal
Performance at high P_{HI}	Good	Optimal
Frequency switch overhead	Moderate	High

7. Discussion and Conclusions

7.1. Discussion

An issue of the proposed work is practicality in terms of the probability of high-criticality mode. Recent work [35,36] have considered the probability of execution times of tasks for mixed-criticality systems. In [37], they introduced the probabilistic confidence of a task and a system and provided statistical scheduling algorithm. In [35,36], probabilistic scheduling algorithms are analyzed for mixed-criticality real-time systems with a consideration of mode-switch probabilities.

As shown in Figure 6a, the proposed work shows the similar performance in low-P_{HI} systems. When the probability of high-criticality mode is extremely low (e.g., 10^{-8}), the effect of power reduction in high-criticality mode is negligible. However, the proposed work is still useful in terms of followings.

- Although the probability of mode-switch of an individual task is low, the probability of the system mode-switch can be increased for a larger number of tasks. Let us assume that f_i is defined by the probability of the task's τ_i mode-switch. Then, the probability of the system mode-switch of the task set T is derived by $1 - \Pi_{\tau_i \in T}(1 - f_i)$ [35]. Figure 11 shows the probability of the system mode-switch in terms of individual task's probability and the number of tasks (N). Let us note that the x-axis in Figure 11 is log-scale. In case of $N = 50$, the proposed work may affect the performance from the probability of task mode-switch of 0.002 because the proposed work shows performance gain where $P_{HI} \geq 0.1$. On the contrary, when the number of tasks is higher (e.g., $N = 200$), the probability of system mode-switch will become higher from lower task mode-switch probability (e.g., $f_i = 0.001$). Thus, the proposed work will be useful depending on the number of tasks and task's mode-switch probability;

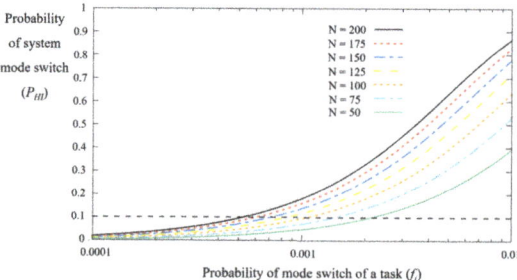

Figure 11. The probability of mode switch w.r.t. task mode switch probability and the number of tasks.

- The system mode-switch policy also affects the probability. In mixed-criticality systems, it is still an open issue on how long the system remains in high-criticality mode after the mode-switch occurrence. The proposed work performance is useful in mixed-criticality systems where the system should remain for a certain period after the mode-switch;
- Finally, the problem formulation with consideration of high-criticality mode is one contribution. Since the probability of mode-switch can be adjusted according to the system safety requirement, the proposed work will be useful when the system optimization is required in mixed-criticality systems.

7.2. Concluding Remark

In this paper, we designed a new dynamic power-aware scheduling scheme of mixed-criticality real-time tasks under high frequency scaling on unicore processors. To tackle the difficulty in trading off minimizing power in HI-criticality mode to reduce the overall average energy, we first proposed reducing the energy level in high-criticality mode. Furthermore, we switched to low-critical mode if there was idle time between high critical job executions.

Our experimental simulation results show that our scheme is more efficient in terms of reducing energy at the high critical mode as well as in low critical mode. Our proposed scheme outperformed the static scheme for reducing energy because the frequency scaling in the static scheme may not have been optimal in dynamic scheme. The results validated that our proposed scheme better performed by increasing the probability of the high critical tasks in comparison to low critical tasks.

We plan to investigate more on the proposed scheduling scheme and extend it to the multi-core processor systems. In addition, we will further analyze the probability of high-criticality mode in many applications and apply it to the proposed work. We will also apply the probabilistic scheduling approach in the proposed work in order to find the optimal power-aware scheduling.

Author Contributions: I.A. and K.H.K. proposed the main idea, implemented the simulations, and wrote the draft-version manuscript. Y.-I.J. verified the simulation program and analyzed the the simulation results. S.L. and W.Y.L. reviewed the manuscript. All the authors have reviewed and revised the final manuscript. All authors have read and agreed to the published version of the manuscript.

Funding: This work was supported partly by the Human Resources Development of the Korea Institute of Energy Technology Evaluation and Planning (KETEP) grant funded by the Ministry of Trade, Industry and Energy (No. 20194030202430), and by Basic Science Research Program through the National Research Foundation of Korea (NRF) funded by the Ministry of Education (grant NRF-2018R1D1A1B07050093).

Conflicts of Interest: The authors declare no conflict of interest.

References

1. Aeronautical Radio Inc. *Avionics Application Software Standard Interface Part 1 Required Services*; ARINC Specification 653P1-2; Aeronautical Radio Inc.: Annapolis, MD, USA, December 2005.
2. Burns, A.; Davis, R. Mixed Criticality Systems-A review. In Proceedings of the 2011 IEEE 32nd Real-Time Systems Symposium, Vienna, Austria, 29 November–2 December 2011; pp. 1–69.
3. Guan, N.; Ekberg, P.; Stigge, M.; Yi, W. Effective and Efficient Scheduling of Certifiable Mixed-Criticality Sporadic Task Systems. In Proceedings of the 2011 IEEE 32nd Real-Time Systems Symposium, Vienna, Austria, 29 November–2 December 2011; pp. 13–23.
4. Emberson, P.; Bate, I. Minimising Task Migration and Priority Changes in Mode Transitions. In Proceedings of the 13th IEEE Real Time and Embedded Technology and Applications Symposium, Bellevue, WA, USA, 3–6 April 2007; pp. 158–167.
5. Pedro, P.; Burns, A. Schedulability Analysis for Mode Changes in Flexible Real-Time Systems. In Proceedings of the 10th Euromicro Workshop on Real-Time Systems, Berlin, Germany, 17–19 June 1998; pp. 172–179.

6. Santy, F.; Raravi, G.; Nelissen, G.; Nelis, V.; Kumar, P.; Goossens, J.; Tovar, E. Two Protocols to Reduce The Criticality Level of Multiprocessor Mixed-Criticality Systems. In Proceedings of the 21st International Conference on Real-Time Networks and Systems, Sophia Antipolis, France, 17–18 October 2013; pp. 183–192.
7. Baruah, S.; Guo, Z. Mixed-Criticality Scheduling upon Varying-speed Processors. In Proceedings of the 2013 IEEE 34th Real-Time Systems Symposium, Vancouver, BC, Canada, 3–6 December 2013; pp. 68–77.
8. Vestal, S. Preemptive Scheduling of Multi-Criticality Systems with Varying Degrees of Execution Time Assurance. In Proceedings of the 28th IEEE International Real-Time Systems Symposium, Tucson, AZ, USA, 3–6 December 2007; pp. 239–243.
9. Baruah, S.; Bonifaci, V.; D'Angelo, G.; Li, H.; Marchetti-Spaccamela, A.; Megow, N.; Stougie, L. Scheduling Real-Time Mixed-Criticality Jobs. *IEEE Trans. Comput.* **2012**, *61*, 1140–1152. [CrossRef]
10. Baruah, S.K.; Burns, A.; Davis, R.I. Response-Time Analysis for Mixed Criticality Systems. In Proceedings of the 2011 IEEE 32nd Real-Time Systems Symposium, Vienna, Austria, 29 November–2 December 2011; pp. 34–43.
11. Baruah, S.K.; Bonifaci, V.; d'Angelo, G.; Marchetti-Spaccamela, A.; Van Der Ster, S.; Stougie, L. *Mixed-Criticality Scheduling of Sporadic Task Systems*; European Symposium on Algorithms: 2011; pp. 555–556.
12. Baruah, S.; Vestal, S. Schedulability Analysis of Sporadic Tasks with Multiple Criticality Specifications. In Proceedings of the 2008 Euromicro Conference on Real-Time Systems, Prague, Czech Republic, 2–4 July 2008; pp. 147–155.
13. Dorin, F.; Richard, P.; Richard, M.; Goossens, J. Schedulability and Sensitivity Analysis of Multiple Criticality Tasks with Fixed-Priorities. *Real Time Syst.* **2010**, *46*, 305–331. [CrossRef]
14. Baruah, S.; Li, H.; Stougie, L. Towards The Design of Certifiable Mixed-Criticality Systems. In Proceedings of the 2010 16th IEEE Real-Time and Embedded Technology and Applications Symposium, Stockholm, Sweden, 12–15 April 2010; pp. 13–22.
15. Audsley, N.C. *Optimal Priority Assignment and Feasibility of Static Priority Tasks with Arbitrary Start Times*; Department of Computer Science, University of York: York, UK, 1991.
16. Socci, D.; Poplavko, P.; Bensalem, S.; Bozga, M. Time-Triggered Mixed-Critical Scheduler on Single and Multi-Processor Platforms. In Proceedings of the 2015 IEEE 17th International Conference on High Performance Computing and Communications, New York, NY, USA, 24–26 August 2015; pp. 684–687.
17. Yao, F.; Demers, A.; Shenker, S. A Scheduling Model for Reduced CPU Energy. In Proceedings of the IEEE 36th Annual Foundations of Computer Science, Milwaukee, WI, USA, 23–25 October 1995; pp. 374–382.
18. Aydin, H.; Melhem, R.; Mossé, D.; Mejía-Alvarez, P. Power-aware Scheduling for Periodic Real-Time Tasks. *IEEE Trans. Comput.* **2004**, *53*, 584–600. [CrossRef]
19. Jejurikar, R.; Gupta, R. Optimized Slowdown in Real-time Task Systems. *IEEE Trans. Comput.* **2006**, *55*, 1588–1598. [CrossRef]
20. Gruian, F. Hard Real-Time Scheduling for Low-Energy using Stochastic Data and DVS Processors. In Proceedings of the 2001 International Symposium on Low Power Electronics and esign, Huntington Beach, CA, USA, 6–7 August 2001; pp. 46–51.
21. Zhong, X.; Xu, C.Z. System-Wide Energy Minimization for Real-Time Tasks: Lower Bound and Approximation. *ACM Trans. Embed. Comput. Syst.* **2008**, *7*, 1–24. [CrossRef]
22. Li, H.; Baruah, S. An Algorithm for Scheduling Certifiable Mixed-Criticality Sporadic Task Systems. In Proceedings of the 2010 31st IEEE Real-Time Systems Symposium, San Diego, CA, USA, 30 November–3 December 2010; pp. 183–192.
23. Yun, H.; Wu, P.L.; Arya, A.; Kim, C.; Abdelzaher, T.; Sha, L. System-Wide Energy Optimization for Multiple DVS Components and Real-Time Tasks. *Real Time Syst.* **2011**, *47*, 489–515. [CrossRef]
24. Mejia-Alvarez, P.; Levner, E.; Mossé, D. Adaptive Scheduling Server for Power-Aware Real-Time Tasks. *ACM Trans. Embed. Comput. Syst.* **2004**, *3*, 284–306. [CrossRef]
25. Marinoni, M.; Buttazzo, G. Elastic DVS Management in Processors with Discrete Voltage/Frequency Modes. *IEEE Trans. Ind. Inform.* **2007**, *3*, 51–62. [CrossRef]
26. Wang, W.; Ranka, S.; Mishra, P. Energy-Aware Dynamic Slack Allocation for Real-Time Multitasking Systems. *Sustain. Comput. Inform. Syst.* **2012**, *2*, 128–137. [CrossRef]

27. Mei, J.; Li, K.; Hu, J.; Yin, S.; Sha, E.H.M. Energy-Aware Preemptive Scheduling Algorithm for Sporadic Tasks on DVS Platform. *Microprocess. Microsyst.* **2013**, *37*, 99–112. [CrossRef]
28. Pillai, P.; Shin, K.G. Real-Time Dynamic Voltage Scaling for Low-Power Embedded Operating Systems. In Proceedings of the Eighteenth ACM Symposium on Operating Systems Principles, Banff, AB, Canada, 21–24 October 2001; pp. 89–102.
29. Huang, P.; Kumar, P.; Giannopoulou, G.; Thiele, L. Energy Efficient DVFS Scheduling for Mixed-Criticality Systems. In Proceedings of the 2014 International Conference on Embedded Software, Jaypee Greens, India, 12–17 October 2014; pp. 1–10.
30. Ijaz, A.; Jun-ho, S.; Kyong, H.K. A Dynamic Power-aware Scheduling of Mixed-Criticality Real-time Systems. In Proceedings of the 2015 IEEE International Conference on Computer and Information Technology, Ubiquitous Computing and Communications; Dependable, Autonomic and Secure Computing; Pervasive Intelligence and Computing, Liverpool, UK, 26–28 October 2015; pp. 438–445.
31. Niu, L.; Quan, G. Reducing Both Dynamic and Leakage Energy Consumption for Hard Real-Time Systems. In Proceedings of the 2004 International Conference on Compilers, Architecture, and Synthesis for Embedded Systems, Washington, DC, USA, 22–25 September 2004; pp. 140–148.
32. Ekberg, P.; Yi, W. Bounding and Shaping The Demand of Generalized Mixed-Criticality Sporadic Task Systems. *Real Time Syst.* **2014**, *50*, 48–86. [CrossRef]
33. Liu, D.; Spasic, J.; Guan, N.; Chen, G.; Liu, S.; Stefanov, T.; Yi, W. EDF-VD Scheduling of Mixed-Criticality Systems with Degraded Quality Guarantees. In Proceedings of the 2016 IEEE Real-Time Systems Symposium, Porto, Portugal, 29 November–2 December 2016; pp. 35–46.
34. Baruah, S.; Bonifaci, V.; D'Angelo, G.; Li, H.; Marchetti-Spaccamela, A.; Van Der Ster, S.; Stougie, L. The Preemptive Uniprocessor Scheduling of Mixed-Criticality Implicit-Deadline Sporadic Task Systems. In Proceedings of the 2012 24th Euromicro Conference on Real-Time Systems, Pisa, Italy, 11–13 July 2012; pp. 145–154.
35. Guo, Z.; Santinalli, L.; Yang, K. EDF Schedulability Analysis on Mixed-Criticality Systems with Permitted Failure Probability. In Proceedings of the 21st IEEE International Conference on Embedded and Real-Time Computing Systems and Applications (RTCSA), Hong Kong, China, 19–21 August 2015.
36. Maxim, D.; Davis, R.I.; Cucu-Grosjean, L.; Easwaran, A. Probabilistic Analysis for Mixed Criticality Systems using Fixed Priority Preemptive Scheduling. In Proceedings of the 25th International Conference on Real-Time Networks and Systems, Grenoble, France, 4–6 October 2017.
37. Edgar, S.; Burns, A. Statistical analysis of WCET for scheduling. In Proceedings of the 2001 IEEE Real-Time Systems Symposium, London, UK, 3–6 December 2001.

Publisher's Note: MDPI stays neutral with regard to jurisdictional claims in published maps and institutional affiliations.

© 2020 by the authors. Licensee MDPI, Basel, Switzerland. This article is an open access article distributed under the terms and conditions of the Creative Commons Attribution (CC BY) license (http://creativecommons.org/licenses/by/4.0/).

Article

Dynamic All-Red Signal Control Based on Deep Neural Network Considering Red Light Runner Characteristics

Seong Kyung Kwon [†], Hojin Jung [†] and Kyoung-Dae Kim *

Daegu Gyeongbuk Institute of Science & Technology, Daegu 41000, Korea; sk_kwon@dgist.ac.kr (S.K.K.); hojinwkd@dgist.ac.kr (H.J.)
* Correspondence: kkim@dgist.ac.kr
† These authors contributed equally to this work.

Received: 31 July 2020; Accepted: 24 August 2020; Published: 1 September 2020

Abstract: Despite recent advances in technologies for intelligent transportation systems, the safety of intersection traffic is still threatened by traffic signal violation, called the Red Light Runner (RLR). The conventional approach to ensure the intersection safety under the threat of an RLR is to extend the length of the all-red signal when an RLR is detected. Therefore, the selection of all-red signal length is an important factor for intersection safety as well as traffic efficiency. In this paper, for better safety and efficiency of intersection traffic, we propose a framework for dynamic all-red signal control that adjusts the length of all-red signal time according to the driving characteristics of the detected RLR. In this work, we define RLRs into four different classes based on the clustering results using the Dynamic Time Wrapping (DTW) and the Hierarchical Clustering Analysis (HCA). The proposed system uses a Multi-Channel Deep Convolutional Neural Network (MC-DCNN) for online detection of RLR and also classification of RLR class. For dynamic all-red signal control, the proposed system uses a multi-level regression model to estimate the necessary all-red signal extension time more accurately and hence improves the overall intersection traffic safety as well as efficiency.

Keywords: Intelligent Transportation System (ITS); deep neural network; Red Light Runner (RLR); dynamic signal control; intersection safety

1. Introduction

As the traffic volume in urban areas has increased significantly over the last decades, there has been many demands and efforts to develop and deploy technologies for intelligent transportation systems in order to address issues of traffic congestion, safety, efficiency, and also environmental improvements [1]. Undoubtedly, one of the most complex, dangerous, and important traffic environments on the road is the intersection, where traffic flows from different directions overlap in a common space, and it also has substantial impacts on the overall urban traffic efficiency and safety [2]. At intersections, traffic flows from different directions are typically coordinated through traffic light systems to prevent conflicting traffic flows passing the intersection simultaneously. Therefore, if a traffic participant violates the traffic rules imposed by the traffic light, the other participants in the intersection inevitably face the risk of an accident. The most representative example of such a traffic participant that violates the traffic signal is the Red Light Runner (RLR) [3].

An RLR is a vehicle passing through an intersection, ignoring the traffic signal when the traffic light is red. According to the AAA Foundation for Traffic Safety, the number of deaths from RLRs increased by 31% from 2009 to 2017. In addition, the Insurance Institute for Highway Safety (IIHS) reported in 2017 that approximately 132,000 casualties were caused by the RLR. Also, the Manual on

Uniform Traffic Control Devices (MUTCD), a standard for maintaining and installing traffic control devices, provides the control of intersection signals to reduce RLR accidents [4]. In general, intersection traffic lights consist of green, yellow, red and all-red signals. All-red signals exist when the intersection traffic light changes from yellow to red and red to green, and is used to prevent accidents caused by vehicles entering the intersection with the yellow signal [5]. MUTCD proposes the construction of a system that extends the all-red signal of intersection traffic lights when an RLR is detected. The length of the all-red signal needs to be determined so that collision by RLR does not occur in the intersection. One of the methods of determining the signal extension time is to use a statistical method to extend a constant time regardless of the current state of the vehicle. Another method extends the all-red signal by dividing the distance to the collision prediction point by the speed of the current vehicle.

The current all-red signal extension system depends only on the vehicle speed at the moment when an RLR is detected. However, if the RLR does not move at a fixed speed as expected, the safety in the intersection cannot be ensured. Therefore, in this paper, we propose a framework for a dynamic all-red signal control system that determines the signal extension time according to the driving pattern of the detected RLR. In this proposed system, driving patterns of RLR vehicles are distinguished through the Multi-Channel Deep Convolutional Neural Network (MC-DCNN) [6]. Also, a multi-level regression strategy, consisting of the Hougen–Watson nonlinear regression model [7] and a quadratic polynomial regression model, is used to estimate the necessary all-red signal extension time with improved accuracy.

The structure of the paper is organized as follows. Section 2 introduces conventional RLR prediction and signal extension methodologies. An overview of the proposed system is presented in Section 3. Clustering and classification based on the characteristics of RLRs are covered in Section 4. The proposed dynamic signal control model is described in Section 5. We validate the performance of the proposed system in Sections 6 and 7. Finally, conclusions are discussed in Section 8.

2. Related Works

RLR is an action that threatens the traffic system passing through by ignoring the signaling system at a signaled intersection. RLR is a serious problem that can lead to fatal traffic accidents as well as minor traffic violations. A collision between a violating vehicle and another vehicle legally passing through an intersection and a green traffic light is called an RLR collision. To avoid RLR-related collisions, it is important to identify factors that have a significant impact on the behavior of RLR drivers and to predict RLR likelihood in real-time [8].

Li et al. [9] proposed a connected vehicle based dynamic all-red extension (DARE) framework to prevent potential collisions due to RLR. The proposed method performs binary classification of RLR and Non-RLR based on non-weighted and weighted least square support vector machines (LS-SVM) using continuous trajectories measured by radar sensors. As a result, RLR and Non-RLR were classified with higher accuracy compared to other techniques based on conventional inductive loop detection. In [10], RLR prediction consists of two parts: arrival time and vehicle behaviors when the vehicle reaches the stop line. The proposed technique is a Bayesian network (BN) probability model based on continuous trajectories collected by radar sensors for RLR prediction. Based on the vehicle's speed, acceleration, and car-following behavior, and the causality of BN, RLR prediction performance was improved. In addition, the driving decision maker was provided with the predicted RLR probability and contributed to the improvement of traffic safety. de Goma et al. [11] proposed a camera-based RLR detection technique using a Single Shot Detector (SSD). In this study, researchers use cameras to collect data at intersections. The proposed system achieved RLR detection performance of 92.1% by applying a deep learning based approach. However, despite the high detection performance, the proposed technique focused on detection rather than the prediction of RLR as a camera-based technique. In [12], a random forest-based learning model was proposed to predict RLR violation. In addition, observation data and driver simulator data were used to analyze factors affecting RLR. According to the results of the proposed prediction model, the important factors for predicting RLR violations are the distance between the vehicle and the intersection, time to intersection (TTI) and the speed of the vehicle at the yellow onset.

In order to reduce accidents at intersections, techniques to control the traffic signal when RLR is detected has been proposed. In [13], a traffic signal countdown (CT) auxiliary device is used in order to reduce the RLR. The CT-based traffic light system aims to reduce RLR by providing the driver with the remaining time of green light. However, at the end of the green light's duration, the RLR may increase as the driver accelerates through the intersection before the signal changes. Likewise, if there is little red light remaining when reaching the intersection, the driver will not decelerate and may enter the intersection early and an RLR may occur. Control of the yellow signal interval had a positive effect on the reduction of RLR [14]. Control of the yellow signal interval helped the driver to make a driving decision at the intersection. According to the study, the time duration of the yellow signal that most effectively reduces RLR is 5 s, and when the duration of the yellow signal exceeds 5 s, RLR is increased again. Since this method is a fixed yellow signal setting, the effect is reduced if the driver gets used to the yellow signal in the long term. Retting et al. [15] proposed an extension of the yellow signal and an enforcement system using a Red Light Camera (RLC). The incidence of RLR was reduced by 36% by increasing the duration of the yellow stop light by 1 s. In addition, by applying an enforcement system using RLC, the RLR incidence rate was reduced by more than 96%. Collotta et al. [16] proposed a method to reduce RLR violations by dynamically allocating signal periods through a Wireless Sensor Network (WSN). The main goal is to dynamically change the green time based on the queue length, allocating a larger green time to the road with the longest queue. Experiments conducted in Philadelphia reduced RLR violations through dynamic assignment of traffic signal periods. However, changing signal settings under the influence of RLR can lead to an asymmetric traffic assignment problem. In [17], authors argued that two distinct problems can be formulated to address the asymmetric traffic assignment problem: First, the global optimization of signal setting and traffic assignment (GOSSTA) combined problem and second, the local optimization of signal setting and traffic assignment (LOSSTA) combined problem. Related to these problems, Adacher et al. [18] transformed the GOSSTA problem into a surrogate continuous optimization problem via a generalized surrogate problem methodology based on an online control scheme and solved the latter using a standard gradient-based approach. On the other hand, D'Acierno et al. [19] proposed an Ant Colony Optimization (ACO) algorithm to solve LOSSTA. The results of the proposed ACO algorithm for real networks were able to get the solution in a shorter time with the same accuracy as the conventional method of the successive averages (MSA) approach [20].

Kashani et al. [21] identified driver and vehicle characteristics that affect accidents using classification and regression tree techniques based on the 2012–2016 Isfahan crash database. In this study, the tree model divided drivers into three age groups: under 22.5 years old, 22.5 to 51.5 years old, and over 51.5 years old. It also suggested improving driver education, increasing traffic fines, and banning drivers with poor driving history to reduce RLR. Fu et al. [22] proposed a step-by-step penalty strategy to prevent the re-offending of RLR vehicles. Despite the rigorous penalty strategy to reduce RLR, its effectiveness was limited. The reason is that traffic delays for other vehicles due to the potential risk of collision with RLR vehicles are not included. In addition, both unintentional and intentional RLRs are subject to the same penalties because the proposed system cannot make a clear distinction between unintentional RLR and intentional RLR. This may be unfair for unintended RLR violators.

Conventional studies have focused on the binary classification of RLR and Non-RLR, and the extension of fixed time signals. Penalties were also effective in reducing RLR. Additionally, some studies have discussed penalty policies to reduce RLR. However, excessive penalties for unintended RLR are a problem to be solved. Our proposed system performs a specific classification of RLR based on features rather than binary classification of RLR and Non-RLR. This can contribute to the classification of unintended RLRs based on the characteristics of RLRs, and is expected to positively help in constructing a stronger RLR fines system. In addition, our proposed system can contribute to the improvement of safety and efficiency of the intersection traffic system based on the dynamic all-red signal extension conforming to the specified RLR class. As discussed above, while it is still possible that the proposed dynamic all-red signal extension may cause an asymmetric traffic assignment problem, it is not the primary focus of this paper to improve the overall traffic efficiency by solving the asymmetric traffic assignment problem as done in many aforementioned related works. Instead, we focus more on improving the safety of intersection traffic by preventing accidents due to RLRs and also the efficiency of it by overcoming the problem of conventional fixed signal extension mechanisms.

3. System Overview

For better intersection safety, a dynamic all-red signal control is necessary to avoid collisions due to sudden appearances of RLRs. To address the issues with conventional fixed signal extension approach, the proposed system identifies first which incoming vehicles are likely to be RLRs and then utilizes the driving characteristics of the detected RLR to adjust the length of the all-red signal accordingly. Hence, the proposed system improves the overall safety as well as efficiency of intersection traffic.

Figure 1 shows the overall architecture of the proposed dynamic all-red signal control system. The first step of the process begins with traffic data collection from the intersection traffic environment. Traffic data to be collected includes traffic signal as well as all incoming vehicles' movement data such as each vehicle's speed, acceleration, distance to the intersection (DTI) and headway during a certain time duration. Note that, for the purpose of all-red signal length control, the system requires traffic data measured while the traffic signal is in the yellow state. The next step of the process is to identify which incoming vehicles are likely to be RLR. As shown in Figure 1, we use the MC-DCNN classifier for this purpose. The proposed MC-DCNN classifier classifies not only whether an incoming vehicle is likely to be an RLR or not but it also classifies into several different types of RLR based on the vehicle's driving characteristics if the vehicle is likely to be an RLR. Then the last step of the process is to determine the length of all-red signal extension based on the detailed classification result from the MC-DCNN. For this step, we use a multi-level regression approach consisting of the Hougen–Watson nonlinear regression and a quadratic polynomial fitting to determine the necessary all-red signal extension time. More details on each of the steps in the process are covered in the following sections.

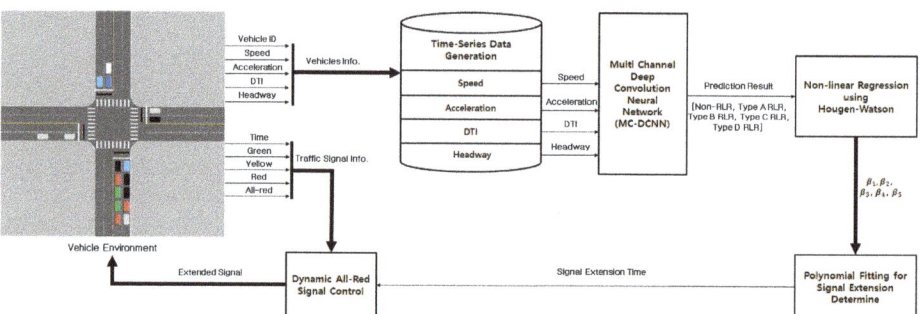

Figure 1. The proposed dynamic all-red signal control architecture.

4. Clustering and Classification

In general, the intersection is considered as the most complex road traffic environment. Furthermore, each vehicle on the road shows very different driving characteristics depending on the driving style or physical/mental conditions of the driver in the vehicle. Hence, the movements of vehicles approaching an intersection to cross are very different from each other and are affected by various factors. Thus, for safer intersection traffic through traffic light control, it is not enough to identify which vehicle is likely to be an RLR. To determine the length of the all-red signal appropriately, it is also necessary to identify the characteristics of the vehicle movement and determine the necessary all-red signal time for the vehicle accordingly. Our approach to addressing this issue is to utilize techniques for time-series clustering for characterization of RLRs into several clusters according to their movements. Then, the identified groups of clusters are used as labels for the generation of the traffic dataset to be used for training the MC-DCNN classifier.

Figure 2 shows the overall procedure for dataset generation. The data collected from the traffic environment includes traffic signal data, vehicle movement data, and also whether each vehicle is RLR or non-RLR. In the collected raw traffic data, RLR vehicles are not distinguished according to their characteristics. Therefore, clusters for each RLR characteristic are generated through Dynamic Time Wrapping (DTW) and Hierarchical Clustering Analysis (HCA) processes. After this process, a dataset for training MC-DCNN is constructed based on the traffic data together with RLR cluster labels so that each vehicle in the dataset is now labeled with a cluster ID according to its driving characteristics.

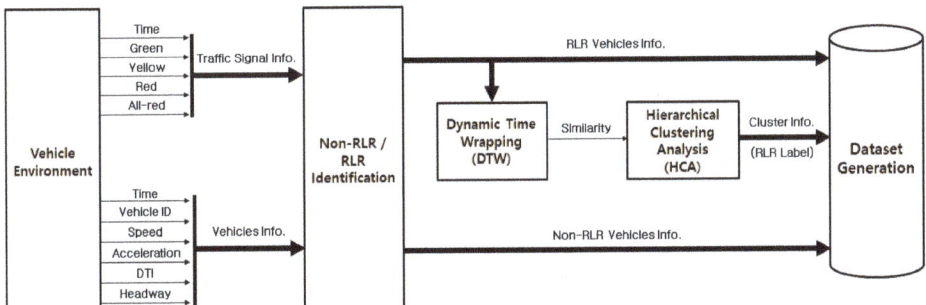

Figure 2. Dataset preparation process for classification.

4.1. Time-Series Clustering

Conventional studies are based on the assumption that the RLR passes through the intersection at a fixed speed. However, RLR vehicles have a variety of driving characteristics in the real world. Therefore, we adopt the clustering method to define the driving characteristics of RLR. The clustering method performs merging into one group when the similarity between data is high, and splits into another group when the similarity is low. However, driving characteristics are difficult to define with one moment of data. Therefore, driving data continuously measured over a certain period of time and a clustering method for time-series data are required. In general, the time-series clustering method consists of a representation of continuous-time trajectories in time-series form, calculation of similarity or distance measure between every pair of time-series data, and then clustering all time-series data into several groups according to the similarity measure.

At an intersection, a vehicle's speed profile changes dramatically in response to traffic signals. Vehicles with no intention of signal violations and RLR vehicles typically show different movement from the start of the yellow signal [23]. Furthermore, it is well known that the speed profile of a vehicle represents the driving pattern of the vehicle and also reflects various factors affecting the vehicle motion such as driving condition and driving style [24,25]. As an illustration of how other factors affect the speed profile of a vehicle, Figure 3 shows a comparison between driving profiles of two different RLR clusters. Figure 3a shows a pattern in which the speed and acceleration are maintained without significant change after 1 s of yellow onset. The DTI shows a decreasing pattern because it is moving toward the intersection. The headway has a value of 1, which means that there is no preceding vehicle. On the other hand, the headway shown in Figure 3b changes from 1 to 0 around 1.5 s after the yellow onset. This means that a preceding vehicle suddenly appeared in front of the vehicle from the other lane. With its influence, the speed and acceleration of the RLR decreases rapidly and then increases as the headway increases again.

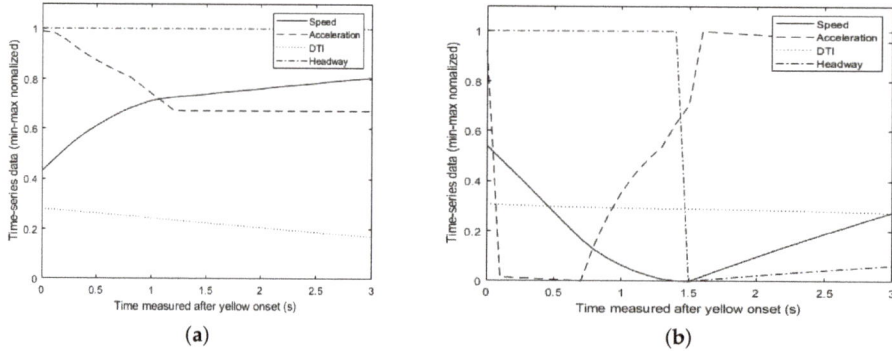

Figure 3. Comparison of driving profiles from two different Red Light Runner (RLR) clusters. (**a**) Speed maintenance pattern; (**b**) Acceleration after deceleration by the preceding vehicle pattern.

Similarity measure is a way to check the similarity between time-series data. We calculate the similarity measure based on the speed profile of each vehicle and utilize it to create a cluster as the speed profile of a vehicle is one of the representative time-series data used to distinguish RLR vehicles. The most commonly used methods for calculating the similarity measure are the Euclidian distance and DTW. Euclidian distance is a technique to calculate the distance between two time-series in each time slice by one-to-one matching. This technique is simple and fast, but there is a limitation when there exists a time shift between sequences. In comparison, DTW performs one-to-many or many-to-one matching and is more robust than the Euclidian distance technique for time shifts between sequences [26]. Therefore, we use DTW to calculate the similarity measure in the speed profiles of various vehicles.

Once the similarity measures are calculated through DTW, clustering is performed through Hierarchical Clustering Analysis (HCA) [27]. HCA is an algorithm that performs clustering using a hierarchical tree structure. Since the number of clusters of driving characteristics of RLR cannot be pre-defined easily, we determine the number of clusters by investigating the tree structure where the difference in similarity measure calculated by DTW increases rapidly. Through the HCA process, the driving characteristics of RLR vehicles are divided into four groups which are (i) acceleration (Type A RLR), (ii) acceleration after deceleration (Type B RLR), (iii) speed maintenance (Type C RLR), and (iv) acceleration after deceleration by preceding vehicle (Type D RLR). Here, the created clusters are used for the training process of the classification model.

4.2. Classification

A traditional technique for RLR detection and classification is the Support Vector Machine (SVM) [28,29]. SVM is a technique that classifies into two classes by obtaining a decision boundary that separates several sample points. The decision boundary separates two classes of clusters, and the sample closest to the boundary becomes the support vector. SVM classifies the binary classes by finding the decision boundary that maximizes the margin between the support vector and the decision boundary. Multi-class SVM for multi-class classification obtains sub-SVMs for classifying each class, and performs multi-class classification based on this idea [30,31]. Recently, deep learning models with higher classification accuracy than SVM have been proposed [32]. A representative deep learning model is the Convolutional Neural Network (CNN). In general, CNN consists of a convolutional layer, Rectified Linear Unit (ReLU) layer, pooling layer, and fully-connected layer [33]. The convolutional layer extracts the features of the input, while the ReLU layer increases the non-linearity properties of the convolutional layer. The pooling layer prevents overfitting through down-sampling. Finally, scores are calculated for each class of output in the fully connected layer. However, the general CNN is an image-based model but not for the time-series data. Therefore, a deep learning model using time-series data as input is needed.

We use the Multi-Channel Deep Convolutional Neural Network (MC-DCNN), a signal data-based model for time-series classification [34,35]. MC-DCNN is a model that uses time-series data of each sensor as the input of multi-channels. The proposed MC-DCNN model uses the speed, acceleration, headway, and DTI as input signals. Since the driving pattern obtained from the speed profile of the vehicle is affected by various driving conditions, the headway and DTI are also selected as inputs to consider the front vehicle and the distance to the intersection. In addition, speed and acceleration are selected to analyze the driving pattern of the RLR. Since the input signal used for MC-DCNN is time-series data, a window length and a prediction time after yellow onset are also required to determine the time interval of traffic data measurement and also to determine when to perform the classification. Prediction time after yellow initiation refers to the point at which RLR is predicted after the start of the yellow signal. If the window length is 2 s and the prediction time after the onset of yellow is 3 s, 2 s of data are collected from 1 to 3 s after the yellow onset.

The proposed network structure consists of two convolutional, ReLU, pooling layers and the last fully connected layer. The convolution layer is composed of a 1D convolution because the driving pattern is identified through the feature over time [36]. The last layer is a softmax, which outputs a distribution over classes. The classes are defined in five categories: Non-RLR, Type A RLR, Type B RLR, Type C RLR, and Type D RLR.

5. Dynamic All-Red Signal Control

In order to dynamically control the length of the all-red signal considering the driving characteristics of RLRs, it is necessary to predict the time at which the RLR under consideration can completely pass the intersection. For this purpose, we use multi-level regression to predict the necessary time duration for the RLR to completely get out of the intersection from the moment of prediction, which we call the *intersection passing time* in the sequel. The input data for the regression model is composed of the speed, DTI, and headway of the RLR at the prediction time. As the first level of regression for prediction, we use the Hougen–Watson model in (1), one of the nonlinear regression models, to roughly estimate the intersection passing time.

$$\hat{y} = \frac{\beta_1 x_2 - x_3/\beta_5}{1 + \beta_2 x_1 + \beta_3 x_2 + \beta_4 x_3} \qquad (1)$$

where $\hat{y}$ is the predicted intersection passing time and variables x_1, x_2, x_3 are the DTI, the speed, the headway of a vehicle, respectively. $\beta_1, \cdots, \beta_5$ in (1) are parameters to be determined through regression using data. In our study, we determined these parameters by the Levenberg–Marquardt nonlinear least squares algorithm [37,38]. The Levenberg–Marquardt algorithm is a combination of two minimization methods, which are known as gradient descent and Gauss–Newton. The Levenberg–Marquardt operates in a gradient descent method when it is far from the solution, and finds the solution in a Gauss–Newton method near the solution. In addition, the Levenberg–Marquardt method is more stable than the Gauss–Newton method and converges to the solution relatively quickly, so the Levenberg–Marquardt method is mostly used in the nonlinear least square problem. The Levenberg–Marquardt nonlinear least squares algorithm optimizes the model by iteratively reducing the sum of squares of errors between the model and the measured data through an update process to the parameters.

As the prediction of intersection passing time of RLR through the Hougen–Watson model is a rough estimate of actual intersection passing time required for the RLR, the predicted time can be much shorter than necessary for some cases. This means that if the length of all-red signal is adjusted according to this estimated intersection passing time, then vehicles from other direction may enter the intersection before the RLR completely clears the intersection. Thus, it is necessary to address such safety issue caused by using only the Hough–Watson model in predicting intersection passing time. For this purpose, we also use the quadratic polynomial fitting model as the second level of regression based on the prediction results of the Hougen–Watson model for better safety of intersection traffic. Furthermore, since prediction of the intersection passing time of RLR without considering the driving characteristics of the RLR, the predicted intersection passing time can be too conservative in some cases. Therefore, to address this issue and improve the overall traffic efficiency, we build separate multi-level regression models according to RLR classes, as described in Section 4.2, and predict the intersection passing time of an RLR according to its RLR class. More details on this multi-level regression framework and results are given in Section 7.3.

6. Traffic Simulation

The system proposed in this paper requires data collection for clustering and classification. However, it is difficult to collect traffic data in a real environment. Therefore, we use the Vissim traffic simulator, which is widely used in transportation engineering for microscopic traffic simulation, to collect intersection traffic data and also to evaluate the performance of the proposed system.

Figure 4 shows the intersection traffic environment configured in Vissim and also shows the traffic signal phases. A standard intersection model is used, which has three input lanes and two output lanes for each ramp way. The leftmost input lane is for left turning, and the center lane is for straight traffic. The far right lane is used for both straight and also for right turning with 20% probability. The traffic signal cycle at the intersection consists of four phases. The signal duration is set to be 27 s for straight traffic and 15 s for left turning traffic according to the traditional Webster's method [39]. On the other hand, the signal duration for yellow and red in each phase are set differently according to the traffic speed based on the FHWA's Traffic Signal Timing Manual [40]. Traffic flow includes car-following and lane change motion.

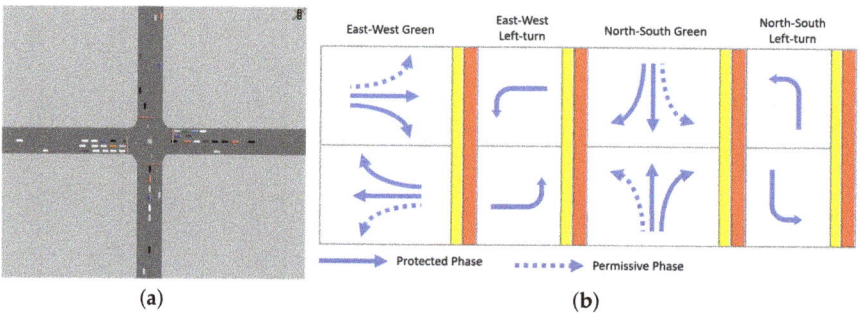

Figure 4. Intersection traffic simulation in Vissim. (**a**) Simulated intersection traffic; (**b**) Traffic signal phase.

Since Vissim provides two different models, called the *continuous decision model* and *one decision model*, to mimic the reaction patterns of real drivers at an intersection when the traffic signal changes from green to yellow, we utilize both of these models in our simulations to generate a more realistic intersection traffic data.

In a continuous decision model, there are two options available. First, a vehicle will not brake, if even the maximum deceleration would not allow for a stop at the stop line. Second, a vehicle brakes if a vehicle cannot pass the traffic light within 2 s when continuing at its current speed rate. On the other hand, in one decision model, the decision made at the time of the yellow onset is kept until the vehicle has passed the stop line. A vehicle stops according to the following probability

$$p = \frac{1}{1 + e^{-\alpha_1 - \alpha_2 v - \alpha_3 dx}} \qquad (2)$$

where v is the vehicle's current speed, dx is the DTI, and α_1, α_2, α_3 are fitting parameters. In our simulation, we use the default values for these fitting parameters, which are $\alpha_1 = 1.59$, $\alpha_2 = 0.27$, and $\alpha_3 = -0.26$ provided in Vissim.

Figure 5 shows representative reaction patterns of traffic observed in simulation according to two decision models. Depending on the state of a vehicle such as current speed, DTI at the time of yellow onset, the vehicle reacts into three different patterns. First, *Go* is the case when a vehicle enters the intersection before the red signal, *Stop* is the case when a vehicle stops at the stop line on the red signal, and finally, *RLR* means the case when a vehicle is entering the intersection at the red signal [9]. Figure 5a shows the change in speed for each reaction of continuous decision traffic. The vehicle with Go reaction does not have a red signal before the distance to the intersection becomes 0 m. The vehicle with Stop reaction stops gradually with a yellow signal starting at a distance more than 60 m from the intersection. However, vehicles with the RLR reaction show that they start to accelerate rapidly between about 15 to 20 m before the intersection. Figure 5b shows the speed change for each reaction of one decision model. In one decision model, Go and Stop reactions are similar to those in the continuous decision model. On the other hand, one of the vehicles with RLR reaction maintains speed without significant change in its speed even when the yellow signal starts. Thus, for the purpose of our study in this paper, we can confirm that the intersection traffic simulated in Vissim according to two decision models can provide a close enough representation to actual intersection traffic.

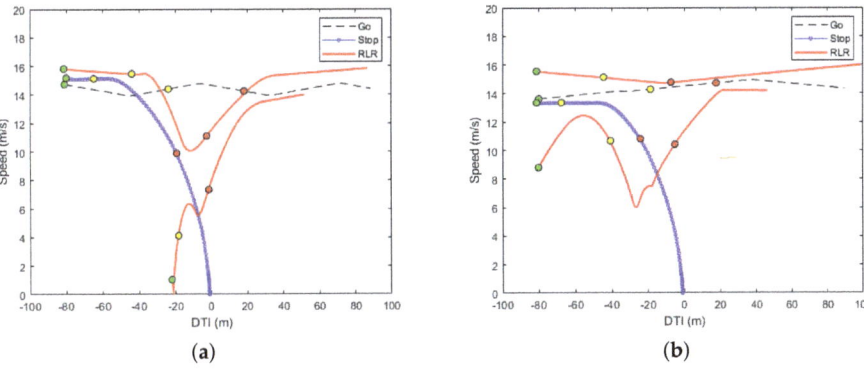

Figure 5. Comparison of vehicle reaction pattern between continuous decision model and one decision model where colored circles in the images indicate the traffic light signals. (**a**) Examples of velocity profiles with continuous decision model; (**b**) Examples of velocity profiles with one decision model.

Table 1 shows the statistical result of 2567 vehicle data (RLR: 1710 and non-RLR:857) collected over 24 h simulation in Vissim. This result is obtained with vehicles of which DTI is less than 100 m at the time of yellow onset. In the case of the continuous decision model, acceleration of RLR is relatively high compared to that of Non-RLR. This means that RLR vehicles attempt to pass the intersection faster than non-RLR vehicles. In the case of RLR in one decision model, acceleration is the lowest but it has a high headway on average. In addition, the mean and standard deviation of acceleration are the smallest and thus the movement of maintaining the speed is observed. In the results, we can also observe that RLR vehicles of the two decision models have higher mean speed than other reaction patterns. In addition, the mean of DTI in both decision models is farther than that with the Go reaction but closer than that of the Stop reaction.

Table 1. Statistical results of traffic simulation data collected at the time of yellow onset.

Variable	Decision Model	Behavior	Mean	Standard Deviation
Speed (m/s)	Continuous	RLR	14.1337	1.5924
		Go	13.6342	1.3388
		Stop	12.2642	4.4733
	One	RLR	15.2914	1.3388
		Go	13.8057	2.7491
		Stop	12.3939	4.3449
Acceleration (m/s^2)	Continuous	RLR	0.3404	0.7978
		Go	0.2910	0.6586
		Stop	0.1817	0.8693
	One	RLR	−0.0500	0.4520
		Go	0.2076	0.5830
		Stop	0.1709	0.7996
DTI (m)	Continuous	RLR	37.6579	3.7382
		Go	16.0680	10.6932
		Stop	63.8649	21.3053
	One	RLR	51.3914	6.3918
		Go	19.1971	12.2729
		Stop	65.6994	21.5267
Headway (m)	Continuous	RLR	88.8779	76.6408
		Go	88.9833	81.1717
		Stop	86.4493	78.2994
	One	RLR	106.6986	77.8763
		Go	95.3744	83.9599
		Stop	89.2601	79.3263

7. Results

In this section, we present results of the proposed clustering, classification, and dynamic all-red signal control approach obtained through traffic simulations in Vissim.

7.1. Clustering

As described in Section 4.1, we use the DTW algorithm to measure the similarity between a pair of speed profile time-series. Figure 6 shows several examples of speed profile time-series data, selected from different clusters which are determined later through the HCA clustering process, to illustrate the effect of the DTW algorithm for optimal alignment of two time-series data and the similarity measure calculated between them. Figure 6a shows a comparison between speed profiles from Type A RLR and Type B RLR clusters. The similarity measure between these two time-series data, calculated as the accumulated pairwise Euclidean distance, is 131.26 in this case. Similarly, Figure 6b,c also show the similarity results from different RLR clusters where similarity measures calculated from the DTW algorithm are 87.85 and 71.23, respectively. On the other hand, Figure 6d shows the similarity result between a pair of speed profile time-series selected from the same cluster, which is Type B RLR in this case. For these speed profile time-series data, the similarity measure from the DTW algorithm is less than 25, which is substantially lower than the other three cases in the figure and hence clearly indicates that these two time-series are quite similar to each other in terms of their shapes while they may be in slightly different phases.

Next, to determine the number of clusters via HCA based on the similarity measures, it is necessary to choose a threshold appropriately for the value of a similarity measure. If the threshold for cluster separation is too low, then there will be too many clusters formed and the driving characteristics of RLRs between clusters are not clearly distinguishable. Therefore, we investigate the hierarchical structure of clusters generated from HCA for all RLR traffic datasets and choose to separate clusters when the similarity measure suddenly increases more than 50 in the HCA process since clusters formed from this are most reasonably distinguishable in terms of their driving characteristics. As a result, there are four different clusters formed for RLRs, as described in Section 4.1.

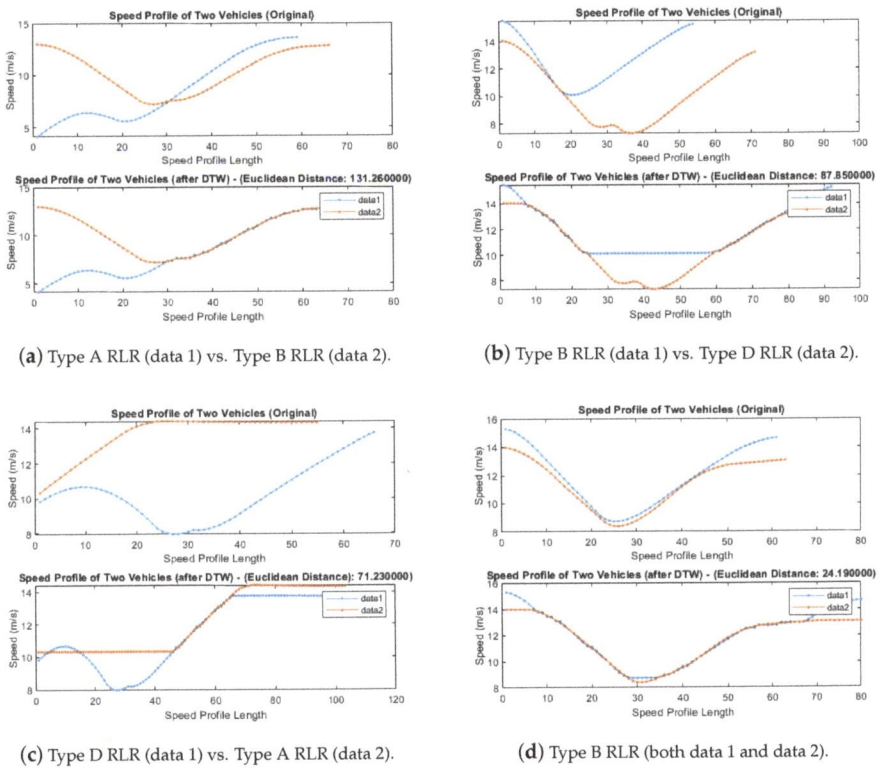

Figure 6. Examples of similarity results through the Dynamic Time Wrapping (DTW) algorithm.

Figure 7 shows the result of clustering generated through the HCA process for all RLR traffic data collected from the Vissim simulation. Figure 7a–d shows RLR speed profiles of each cluster. As shown in the figure, four RLR clusters show different driving characteristics where RLR in Type A keeps accelerating to cross an intersection, RLR in Type B first decelerates and then accelerates, RLR in Type C is mostly maintaining its speed, and finally, RLR in Type D exhibits similar behavior as Type B in the beginning but decelerates rapidly shortly after accelerating due to the sudden appearance of a proceeding vehicle in front of the RLR.

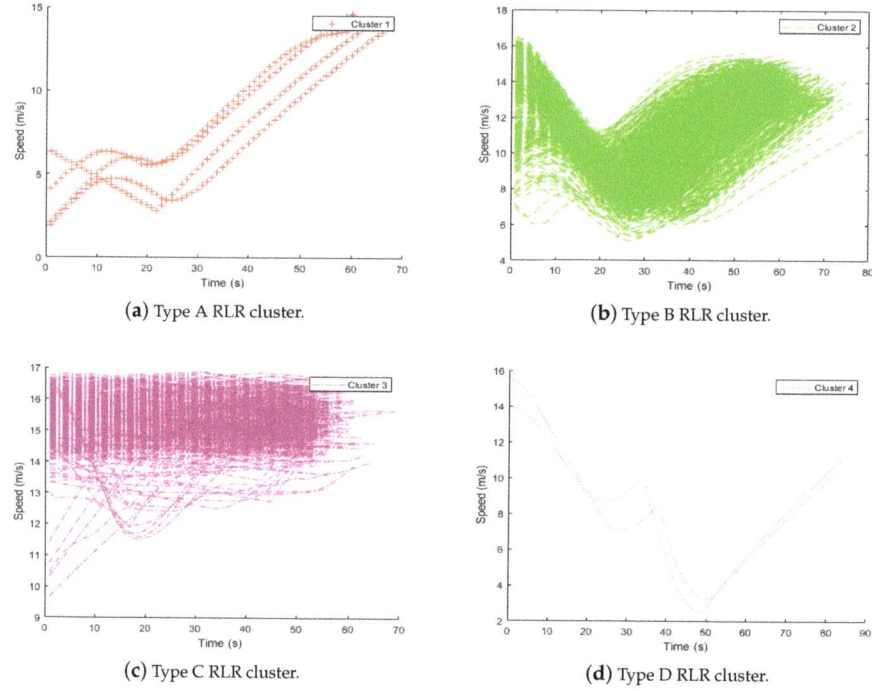

Figure 7. Clustering of RLR traffic dataset through Hierarchical Clustering Analysis (HCA).

7.2. Classification

For online classification of an incoming vehicle to predict whether the vehicle is a Non-RLR or one of the four RLR types, we use MC-DCNN as described in Section 4.2. For training of the MC-DCNN model, we built a training dataset from traffic data consisting of time-series of vehicle speed, acceleration, DTI, and headways with cluster type determined through HCA so that each vehicle in the training dataset is labeled whether it is a Non-RLR, Type A RLR, Type B RLR, Type C RLR, and Type D RLR. Therefore, as shown in Figure 1, the trained MC-DCNN model gives a prediction to which class out of the above five classes an incoming vehicle is classified.

To evaluate the classification performance MC-DCNN, we compare the classification accuracy of MC-DCNN with that of SVM using the validation dataset. Tables 2 and 3 are classification accuracy results using SVM and MC-DCNN, respectively. In the results, the classification accuracy is 100% if the classifier classifies all five classes, Non-RLR, Type A, B, C, D RLR correctly. The "window size" means the time-series length of input data, and the "prediction time after yellow onset" means the time when a classifier performs classification after yellow onset. In the case of SVM, if the window size is 0 s (i.e., there is only one data point in the input time-series), the accuracy is lower than about 60% regardless of prediction time. Table 2 also shows that the longer the input time-series length, the better the classification performance. The highest accuracy appears when the window size is 3 s and the prediction time is 2.5 or 3 s after yellow onset.

Compared to the result from SVM, the classification accuracy of the MC-DCNN model is substantially better than that of SVM especially when the windows size is small. For instance, even the classification accuracies of MC-DCNN with 0 s window size in all prediction time cases are comparable to those of SVM with a 2 s window size. Also, the highest accuracy achieved by MC-DCNN with 1 s window size is 99.9% at 3 s prediction time while SVM with the same window size and prediction time can achieve only up to 87.5%. It is interesting to see that this 99.9% accuracy with 1 s window size is even better than the highest classification accuracy of SVM achieved with the longest window size. As a result of this comparison, it is shown that the MC-DCNN classification model proposed in this work can classify the class of an incoming vehicle more accurately than SVM even with shorter duration of vehicle motion measurement and also at a slightly earlier time after yellow onset. Furthermore, it is expected that the proposed MC-DCNN model can be applied to improve the performance of the system for imposing fines for vehicles violating traffic signals based on the accurate classification performance.

Table 2. Classification accuracy of Support Vector Machine (SVM) classifier.

		Prediction Time after Yellow Onset (Sec)						
		0	0.5	1	1.5	2	2.5	3
Window size (sec)	0	56.6%	57.5%	58.6%	57.1%	57.4%	57.7%	59%
	0.5	79.8%	85.4%	85%	85.2%	84.6%	85.4%	85.1%
	1	84.3%	86.5%	87.7%	87.2%	87%	87.3%	87.5%
	1.5	88.4%	88.6%	89%	90%	90.2%	90.3%	90%
	2	90.6%	92.2%	92.6%	93.3%	93.3%	93.4%	93.3%
	2.5	94%	94.7%	95.6%	95.9%	95.8%	95.8%	96%
	3	98.9%	98.9%	99.2%	99.3%	99.3%	99.4%	99.4%

Table 3. Classification accuracy of the Multi-Channel Deep Convolutional Neural Networks (MC-DCNN) classifier.

		Prediction Time after Yellow Onset (Sec)						
		0	0.5	1	1.5	2	2.5	3
Window size (sec)	0	87.3%	92.5%	92.9%	90.7%	89.2%	95.4%	99.5%
	0.5	90.7%	95.2%	96.4%	97.4%	98.1%	98%	99.6%
	1	93.5%	96.4%	97.1%	97.8%	98.3%	98.4%	99.9%
	1.5	93.5%	96.9%	97.4%	98.4%	98.6%	99.1%	99.9%
	2	93.8%	96.2%	97.1%	99%	98.9%	99.3%	99.9%
	2.5	94.3%	96.7%	97.2%	98.7%	98.2%	98.9%	99.9%
	3	94.5%	97.3%	97.5%	98.6%	98.6%	99.3%	99.9%

7.3. Dynamic All-Red Signal Control

For the safety of intersection traffic under the threat of RLRs, an approach of all-red signal extension has been proposed to extend the all-red signal to a *pre-fixed* time duration, which is typically less than 5 s, in order to prevent vehicles from other directions entering the intersection when an RLR is detected. However, the fixed-time all-red signal extension may not be effective as drivers can adapt easily to the fixed extension time. In addition, it may reduce the intersection traffic efficiency in case the all-red signal extension time is chosen too conservatively and it may also reduce the traffic safety in case the all-red signal extension time is too short.

To address such issues related to the fixed-time all-red signal extension approach, we incorporate the driving characteristics of RLR to determine the necessary all-red extension time. For this purpose, we adopt a nonlinear regression model, called the Hougen–Watson model, to develop an all-red extension time prediction model based on the traffic data collected from the Vissim simulation. The Hougen–Watson model performs nonlinear fitting through multivariate input of speed, DTI and headway, and has the advantage of being easily usable because it is provided as a Matlab function.

Figure 8 shows the comparison between the actual intersection passing time calculated from the traffic data and the predicted intersection passing time by the Hougen–Watson prediction model for all RLRs traffic data. In the figure, circular points represent RLRs. For each RLR, the actual and the predicted intersection passing times for the vehicle can be compared between the values in the vertical and horizontal axis. The diagonal line, called the *Base line* in the figure, represents when the actual and predicted time matches. Thus RLRs above the base line actually take longer time than the predicted intersection passing time to completely cross an intersection. As shown in the figure, a large number of RLRs are shown above the base line. Therefore, for such RLRs, the Hougen–Watson prediction model alone is not enough to predict the necessary all-red signal extension time for all types of RLRs. To address this issue, we identified RLRs, called the *Outliers*, from the dataset in which actual intersection passing times are larger and also maximally deviated from their predicted intersection passing times. In Figure 8b, red colored circular points represent those outliers identified from the dataset and the dashed line represents the quadratic polynomial curve fitted to the outliers. Hence, if we use the quadratic curve model on top of the Hougen–Watson model to predict the intersection passing time, then the predicted time will be long enough for *most* RLRs so that they can completely clear an intersection within the time interval, which is much safer than using the Hougen–Watson model alone.

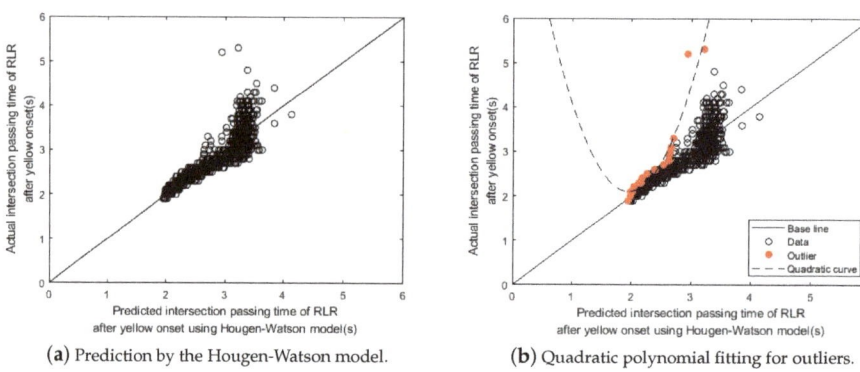

(a) Prediction by the Hougen-Watson model. (b) Quadratic polynomial fitting for outliers.

Figure 8. All-red signal extension time for RLRs: Actual vs. Prediction.

However, as one can notice, it may be too conservative sometimes to use only one prediction model to predict intersection passing times for all types of RLRs. For a certain class of RLRs, the predicted intersection passing time predicted by the model may be unnecessarily longer than needed for such RLRs. Thus, for better traffic efficiency, we develop and use different prediction models for different RLR classes to predict the intersection passing time more precisely. Figure 9 shows the prediction model of each RLR class developed by the same framework of using Hougen–Watson model and quadratic polynomial curve fitting. Having these four different prediction models corresponding to each RLR types, it is now possible to determine the necessary all-red signal extension time more effectively than using only one prediction model once the type of RLR of an incoming vehicle is correctly classified by the MC-DCNN classifier. Table 4 shows the values of the Hougen–Watson model parameters determined by the Levenberg–Marquardt algorithm for each prediction model and also the values of the coefficients for the quadratic polynomial curve fitting of outliers. Regarding the values of the quadratic polynomial curve fitting shown in the table, p_1 represents the second-order coefficient, p_2 is the first-order coefficient, and p_3 is the polynomial constant of a quadratic polynomial equation.

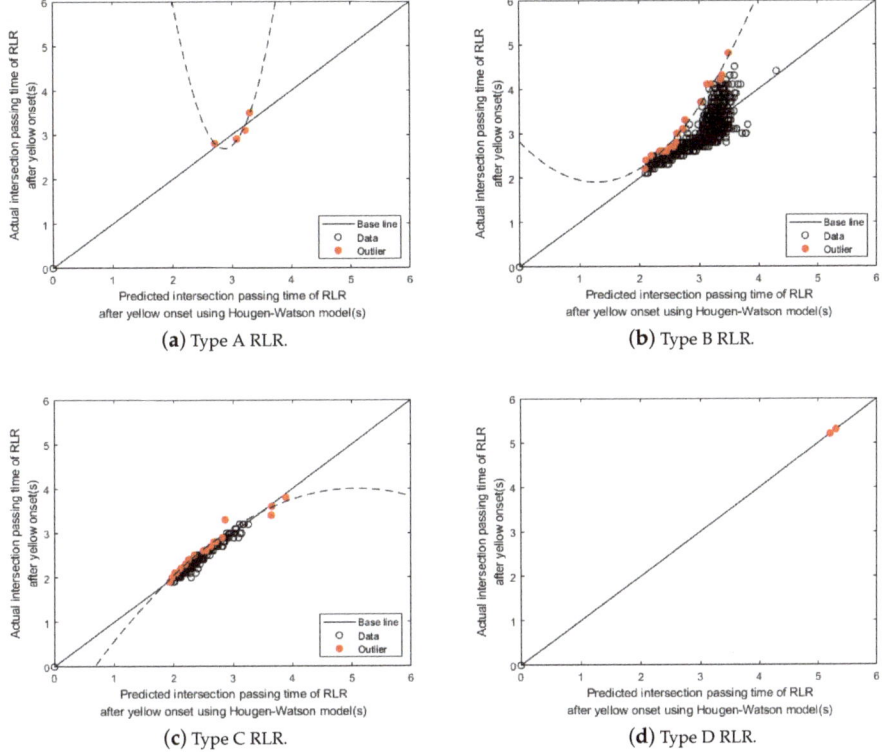

Figure 9. Prediction models of all red-light extension time for each RLR class type.

Table 4. Coefficients of prediction models for all-red signal extension time. (Mixed RLR represents the prediction model shown in Figure 8 and others are corresponding to models shown in Figure 9).

	Hougen–Watson Model					Polynomial Fitting		
	β_1	β_2	β_3	β_4	β_5	p_1	p_2	p_3
Type A RLR	2.83×10^{27}	-7.33×10^{26}	1.15×10^{27}	4.24×10^{27}	5.1×10^6	4.39	-25.03	39.06
Type B RLR	0.0642	0.1003	-0.0205	0.0382	-8.89×10^5	0.57	-1.45	2.83
Type C RLR	0.1625	0.2340	-0.0210	0.1941	-2.19×10^5	-0.21	2.1	-1.32
Type D RLR	2.8061	-0.6884	0.7655	-1.3043	0.0644	0	1	0
Mixed RLR	0.0733	0.0828	-0.0133	0.0510	-7.00×10^5	2.17	-8.48	10.39

To evaluate the accuracy of the proposed multi-class intersection passing time prediction framework compared to the case of using only one prediction model, the *mixed* RLR model in Table 4, we use the following standard deviation of residual σ_{est} defined as

$$\sigma_{est} = \sqrt{\frac{\sum (y - \hat{y})^2}{N}} \qquad (3)$$

where N is the number of RLRs, y is the actual intersection passing time of an RLR, and $\hat{y}$ is the predicted intersection passing time of the RLR. Table 5 is the result of the prediction accuracy of intersection passing time of RLRs measured by σ_{est} for the two prediction models in the case where the prediction time after yellow onset is 3 s. As shown in the result, the proposed multi-class model has a much smaller residual standard deviation of residual compared to the case of using the mixed RLR model. This result shows that the proposed model can predict the time more accurately when an RLR will completely cross an intersection.

Table 5. Comparison of residual between mixed RLR model and proposed model.

	Mixed RLR Model	Proposed Multi-Class Model
σ_{est} defined in (3) for $N = 1517$	0.03133	0.0166

Once the intersection passing time of an RLR $\hat{y}$ is estimated precisely, then it is relatively straightforward to determine the necessary all-red signal extension time for the RLR. A simple strategy for dynamic all-red signal extension control is as follows: If the length of the all-red signal is greater than 1 s, which is the default all-red signal length, then the length of the all-red signal is set to $\hat{y}$ unless it is larger 5 s. In case the value of $\hat{y}$ exceeds 5 s, then the all-red signal length is set to 5 s according to the standard.

8. Conclusions

In this paper, we proposed a system that dynamically controls all-red signal length based on the driving characteristics of Red Light Runner (RLR) vehicles to improve the overall intersection safety and efficiency. The main components of the proposed system are the Multi-Channel Deep Convolutional Neural Networks (MC-DCNN) classifier that classifies an approaching vehicle into five classes according the vehicle's driving characteristics and the multi-level nonlinear regression model that can predict the necessary all-red signal extension time more accurately. We used the Dynamic Time Wrapping (DTW) and the Hierarchical Clustering Analysis (HCA) to carefully determine the types of clusters to be classified via MC-DCNN so that each class can be reasonably distinguishable by their driving characteristics. As a result of this multi-step classification and regression process, we validated that the proposed system can predict the actual intersection passing time of RLRs with very small prediction error and thereby it can improve both the safety as well as the efficiency of intersection traffic. In the future, we will build vehicle surveillance systems at some sections of real road intersections to collect real traffic data. Synchronized data of vehicle data and signal information will be collected, and the proposed system will be verified in a real environment. In addition, we will conduct a quantitative assessment of intersection safety and economic loss through the analysis of traffic flow due to signal extension.

Author Contributions: Conceptualization, H.J. and K.-D.K.; methodology, software, simulation, H.J.; investigation, formal analysis, validation, simulation, writing—original draft preparation, S.K.K.; supervision, project administration, writing—review and editing, K.-D.K. All authors have read and agreed to the published version of the manuscript.

Funding: This work was supported by the National Research Foundation of Korea(NRF) grant funded by the Korea government(MSIT) (No.2019R1F1A1059496) and the DGIST R&D Program of the Ministry of Science and ICT (20-CoE-IT-01).

Conflicts of Interest: The authors declare no conflict of interest.

References

1. Betz, J.; Heilmeier, A.; Wischnewski, A.; Stahl, T.; Lienkamp, M. Autonomous Driving—A Crash Explained in Detail. *Appl. Sci.* **2019**, *9*, 5126. [CrossRef]
2. Alajali, W.; Zhou, W.; Wen, S. Traffic flow prediction for road intersection safety. In Proceedings of the 2018 IEEE SmartWorld, Ubiquitous Intelligence & Computing, Advanced & Trusted Computing, Scalable Computing & Communications, Cloud & Big Data Computing, Internet of People and Smart City Innovation (SmartWorld/SCALCOM/UIC/ATC/CBDCom/IOP/SCI), Guangzhou, China, 8–12 October 2018; pp. 812–820.

3. Porter, B.E.; Berry, T.D.; Harlow, J.; Vandecar, T. A Nationwide Survey of Red Light Running: Measuring Driver Behaviors for the 'Stop Red Light Running Program'. 1999. Available online: http://citeseerx.ist.psu.edu/viewdoc/download?doi=10.1.1.468.6543&rep=rep1&type=pdf (accessed on 31 July 2020).
4. McGee, H., Sr.; Moriarty, K.; Gates, T.J. Guidelines for timing yellow and red intervals at signalized intersections. *Transp. Res. Rec.* **2012**, *2298*, 1–8. [CrossRef]
5. Retting, R.A.; Greene, M.A. Influence of traffic signal timing on red-light running and potential vehicle conflicts at urban intersections. *Transp. Res. Rec.* **1997**, *1595*, 1–7. [CrossRef]
6. Zheng, Y.; Liu, Q.; Chen, E.; Ge, Y.; Zhao, J.L. Exploiting multi-channels deep convolutional neural networks for multivariate time series classification. *Front. Comput. Sci.* **2016**, *10*, 96–112. [CrossRef]
7. Ferraris, G.B.; Donati, G. A powerful method for Hougen—Watson model parameter estimation with integral conversion data. *Chem. Eng. Sci.* **1974**, *29*, 1504–1509. [CrossRef]
8. Ren, Y.; Wang, Y.; Wu, X.; Yu, G.; Ding, C. Influential factors of red-light running at signalized intersection and prediction using a rare events logistic regression model. *Accid. Anal. Prev.* **2016**, *95*, 266–273. [CrossRef]
9. Li, M.; Chen, X.; Lin, X.; Xu, D.; Wang, Y. Connected vehicle-based red-light running prediction for adaptive signalized intersections. *J. Intell. Transp. Syst.* **2018**, *22*, 229–243. [CrossRef]
10. Chen, X.; Zhou, L.; Li, L. Bayesian network for red-light-running prediction at signalized intersections. *J. Intell. Transp. Syst.* **2019**, *23*, 120–132. [CrossRef]
11. de Goma, J.C.; Bautista, R.J.; Eviota, M.A.J.; Lopena, V.P. Detecting Red-Light Runners (RLR) and Speeding Violation through Video Capture. In Proceedings of the 2020 IEEE 7th International Conference on Industrial Engineering and Applications (ICIEA), Bangkok, Thailand, 16–21 April 2020; pp. 774–778.
12. Jahangiri, A.; Rakha, H.; Dingus, T.A. Red-light running violation prediction using observational and simulator data. *Accid. Anal. Prev.* **2016**, *96*, 316–328. [CrossRef]
13. Elias, S.; Ghafurian, M.; Samuel, S. Effectiveness of Red-Light Running Countermeasures: A Systematic Review. In Proceedings of the 11th International Conference on Automotive User Interfaces and Interactive Vehicular Applications, Utrecht, The Netherlands, 21–25 September 2019; pp. 91–100.
14. Quiroga, C.; Kraus, E.; van Schalkwyk, I.; Bonneson, J. Red Light Running: A Policy Review. 2003. Available online: https://citeseerx.ist.psu.edu/viewdoc/download?doi=10.1.1.198.4032&rep=rep1&type=pdf (accessed on 31 July 2020)
15. Retting, R.A.; Ferguson, S.A.; Farmer, C.M. Reducing red light running through longer yellow signal timing and red light camera enforcement: Results of a field investigation. *Accid. Anal. Prev.* **2008**, *40*, 327–333. [CrossRef]
16. Collotta, M.; Pau, G.; Scatà, G.; Campisi, T. A dynamic traffic light management system based on wireless sensor networks for the reduction of the red-light running phenomenon. *Transp. Telecommun. J.* **2014**, *15*, 1–11. [CrossRef]
17. Cascetta, E.; Gallo, M.; Montella, B. Optimal signal setting on traffic networks with stochastic equilibrium assignment. In Proceedings of the TRISTAN III-Triennial Symposium on Transportation Analysis, San Juan, Puerto Rico, 17–23 June 1998; Volume 2.
18. Adacher, L.; Cipriani, E. A surrogate approach for the global optimization of signal settings and traffic assignment problem. In Proceedings of the 13th International IEEE Conference on Intelligent Transportation Systems, Funchal, Portugal, 19 September 2010; pp. 60–65.
19. D'Acierno, L.; Gallo, M.; Montella, B. An ant colony optimisation algorithm for solving the asymmetric traffic assignment problem. *Eur. J. Oper. Res.* **2012**, *217*, 459–469. [CrossRef]
20. Sbayti, H.; Lu, C.C.; Mahmassani, H.S. Efficient implementation of method of successive averages in simulation-based dynamic traffic assignment models for large-scale network applications. *Transp. Res. Rec.* **2007**, *2029*, 22–30. [CrossRef]
21. Kashani, A.T.; Amirifar, S.; Bondarabadi, M.A. Analysis of Driver and Vehicle Characteristics Involved in Red-Light Running Crashes: Isfahan, Iran. *Iran. J. Sci. Technol. Trans. Civ. Eng.* **2020**, 1–7. [CrossRef]
22. Fu, C.; Xiong, Y.; Zhang, Y.; Zhang, W.; Liu, Y. A novel model of increasing block fine for red-light running recidivism. *Adv. Mech. Eng.* **2019**, *11*, 1687814019828047. [CrossRef]
23. Zhang, L.; Zhou, K.; Zhang, W.B.; Misener, J.A. Prediction of red light running based on statistics of discrete point sensors. *Transp. Res. Rec.* **2009**, *2128*, 132–142. [CrossRef]
24. Zhu, X.; Yuan, Y.; Hu, X.; Chiu, Y.C.; Ma, Y.L. A Bayesian Network model for contextual versus non-contextual driving behavior assessment. *Transp. Res. Part C Emerg. Technol.* **2017**, *81*, 172–187. [CrossRef]

25. Karl, I.; Berg, G.; Ruger, F.; Farber, B. Driving behavior and simulator sickness while driving the vehicle in the loop: Validation of longitudinal driving behavior. *IEEE Intell. Transp. Syst. Mag.* **2013**, *5*, 42–57. [CrossRef]
26. Senin, P. *Dynamic Time Warping Algorithm Review*; Information and Computer Science Department University of Hawaii at Manoa: Honolulu, HI, USA, 2008.
27. Khan, L.; Awad, M.; Thuraisingham, B. A new intrusion detection system using support vector machines and hierarchical clustering. *VLDB J.* **2007**, *16*, 507–521. [CrossRef]
28. Chang, C.C.; Lin, C.J. LIBSVM: A library for support vector machines. *ACM Trans. Intell. Syst. Technol. (TIST)* **2011**, *2*, 1–27. [CrossRef]
29. Huang, K.S.; Chiu, P.J.; Tsai, H.M.; Kuo, C.C.; Lee, H.Y.; Wang, Y.C.F. Redeye: Preventing collisions caused by red-light running scooters with smartphones. *IEEE Trans. Intell. Transp. Syst.* **2015**, *17*, 1243–1257. [CrossRef]
30. Franc, V.; Hlaváč, V. Multi-class support vector machine. In Proceedings of the Object Recognition Supported by User Interaction for Service Robots, Quebec City, QC, Canada, 11–15 August 2002; Volume 2, pp. 236–239.
31. Debnath, R.; Takahide, N.; Takahashi, H. A decision based one-against-one method for multi-class support vector machine. *Pattern Anal. Appl.* **2004**, *7*, 164–175. [CrossRef]
32. Setiowati, S.; Zulfanahri; Franita, E.L.; Ardiyanto, I. A review of optimization method in face recognition: Comparison deep learning and non-deep learning methods. In Proceedings of the 2017 9th International Conference on Information Technology and Electrical Engineering (ICITEE), Phuket, Thailand, 12–13 October 2017; pp. 1–6.
33. Wang, C.; Han, Y.; Wang, W. An end-to-end deep learning image compression framework based on semantic analysis. *Appl. Sci.* **2019**, *9*, 3580. [CrossRef]
34. Fawaz, H.I.; Forestier, G.; Weber, J.; Idoumghar, L.; Muller, P.A. Deep learning for time series classification: A review. *Data Min. Knowl. Discov.* **2019**, *33*, 917–963. [CrossRef]
35. Sainath, T.N.; Weiss, R.J.; Wilson, K.W.; Li, B.; Narayanan, A.; Variani, E.; Bacchiani, M.; Shafran, I.; Senior, A.; Chin, K.; et al. Multichannel signal processing with deep neural networks for automatic speech recognition. *IEEE/ACM Trans. Audio Speech Lang. Process.* **2017**, *25*, 965–979. [CrossRef]
36. Nugraha, A.A.; Liutkus, A.; Vincent, E. Multichannel audio source separation with deep neural networks. *IEEE/ACM Trans. Audio Speech Lang. Process.* **2016**, *24*, 1652–1664. [CrossRef]
37. Dennis, J.E., Jr.; Gay, D.M.; Walsh, R.E. An adaptive nonlinear least-squares algorithm. *ACM Trans. Math. Softw. (TOMS)* **1981**, *7*, 348–368. [CrossRef]
38. Newville, M.; Stensitzki, T.; Allen, D.B.; Rawlik, M.; Ingargiola, A.; Nelson, A. *LMFIT: Non-Linear Least-Square Minimization and Curve-Fitting for Python*; Astrophysics Source Code Library (ASCL): Houghton, MI, USA, 2016.
39. Radhakrishnan, P.; Mathew, T.V. Passenger car units and saturation flow models for highly heterogeneous traffic at urban signalised intersections. *Transportmetrica* **2011**, *7*, 141–162. [CrossRef]
40. Koonce, P.; Rodegerdts, L. *Traffic Signal Timing Manual*; Technical Report; Federal Highway Administration: Washington, DC, USA, 2008.

© 2020 by the authors. Licensee MDPI, Basel, Switzerland. This article is an open access article distributed under the terms and conditions of the Creative Commons Attribution (CC BY) license (http://creativecommons.org/licenses/by/4.0/).

Article

A Real-Time Data Delivery for Mobile Sinks Group on Mobile Cyber-Physical Systems

Seungmin Oh [1], Yoonsoo Choi [2], Sangdae Kim [1], Cheonyong Kim [3], Kwansoo Jung [4] and Seok-Hun Kim [5],*

1. Division of Computer Science and Engineering, Kongju National University, Cheonan, Chungnam 31080, Korea; smoh@kongju.ac.kr (S.O.); sdkim.cse@gmail.com (S.K.)
2. Department of Computer Science and Engineering, Chungnam National University, Daejeon 34134, Korea; ch.yoons92@gmail.com
3. Advanced KREONET Center, Korea Institute of Science and Technology Information, Daejeon 34141, Korea; cykim0807@kisti.re.kr
4. Department of Fintech, Daejeon University, Daejeon 34519, Korea; ksjung@dju.ac.kr
5. Department of Electronic Commerce, Paichai University, Daejeon 35345, Korea
* Correspondence: kimshn@pcu.ac.kr

Received: 4 August 2020; Accepted: 26 August 2020; Published: 27 August 2020

Abstract: Mobile Cyber-Physical Systems (MCPS) have extended the application domains by exploiting the advantages of Cyber-Physical Systems (CPS) through the mobile devices. The cooperation of various mobile equipment and workers based on the MCPS further improved efficiency and productivity in the industry. To support this cooperation of groups of workers (hereafter referred to as the Mobile Sink Groups), data should be delivered to appropriate groups of workers in a timely manner. Traditionally, the data dissemination for MSG relies on flooding-based geocasting into the movable area of the group due to frequent movements of each group member. However, the flooding-based data dissemination could not be directly applied to real-time data delivery that demands the required time deadline and the end-to-end delivery distance, because the flooding could not define the end-to-end distance and progress to each member in a group. This paper proposes a real-time data delivery mechanism for supporting MSG in time-critical applications. In our mechanism, a ring-based modeling and data transfer scheme on a virtual grid in the ring for group mobility provides the end-to-end distance and the progress to forward real-time data to each member. Simulation results show our mechanism is superior to the existing ones in terms of real-time communication for MSG.

Keywords: Mobile Cyber-Physical Systems (MCPS); industry; Mobile Sink Groups (MSG); group mobility; real-time data delivery

1. Introduction

As Cyber-Physical Systems (CPS) are collectively a technology for managing systems that interlink real-world assets, such as various sensors and actuators, with computing power in the information world [1], and it has recently become a key research area in industry, which utilized in various applications such as smart factory, digital manufacturing, and digital twin [2]. For example, CPS exploit sufficient computing resources to process information that has not been addressed in the physical world in the past to promote economic benefits such as improved energy efficiency and productivity in the industry [3]. In addition, by transferring the experimental environment of the physical world to the virtual world, various prototypes could be tested in the virtual environment in advance as performing error diagnosis, predictive maintenance, and product performance measurement very efficiently [4].

Nowadays, with the development of pervasive mobile devices, Mobile Cyber-Physical Systems (MCPS) have attracted more and more attention. MCPS have extended the application domains by exploiting the advantages of CPS through mobile devices [5]. In other words, MCPS could embrace not only CPS, which mainly deal with static equipment and stable networks, but also a network consisting of a number of mobile devices, such as vehicle networks. As the networks with mobile devices are unstable, unlike the networks assumed by the CPS, and the computing power of each mobile device is very different, many studies have been proposed from various aspects for their efficient cooperation. In particular, the timeliness of the data is very important because delay and failures due to bottlenecks, etc., which could be caused by variable network environments, adversely affect the entire system [6,7]. In addition, the various mobile equipment and groups of workers (Mobile Sink Groups (MSG)) performing the collaboration should be able to receive data within a valid time because they must be operated in a mutually collaborative manner.

In the past, the spatiotemporal approach was exploited for real-time data transmission [8,9]. The spatiotemporal approach forwards data with the required delivery speed. The end-to-end delay is proportional to the distance between the devices. By maintaining the delivery speed across the network, this approach could provide a predictable real-time service according to the distance. For multihop communication, each node selects one node among its neighbor nodes, which has faster delivery speed than the required delivery speed. To apply the spatiotemporal approach, per-hop data forwarding requires the delivery speed, the coordinates of the specific destination, and the progress to the destination by each of the 1-hop neighbor nodes.

This traditional spatiotemporal approach has been able to successfully transmit data for individual mobile sinks through virtual infrastructure; however, data dissemination to a group of mobile sinks causes duplicated location management of all sinks and duplicated data delivery to all sinks. Therefore, the group mobility support scheme, divided into two steps, has been proposed: member information gathering and data forwarding to group members [10–12]. Typically, a leader gathers the location of member sinks and reports the representative location of the group (i.e., center point and radius) as the location information of each members might be changed frequently. After gathering, M-Geocasting [10] causes data packets to be flooded into the region (a circle) for active data delivery. In [10], a source node sends its data toward the center point of the movable area of a group. Once one of the boundary nodes gets the data, it starts flooding them only in the area. Flooding data could reduce the cost for trivial movement of sinks within the region. The authors of [11] exploit the internal movement of each member sink. They put data in a virtual rectangular area passing the center point of the group so that member sinks passively get the data when the sinks encounter the area. However, flooding-based dissemination has still a problem regarding application into the spatiotemporal approach for real-time data. The data flooding could not define the final destination for a mobile sink group. Without the final destination, the source node could not calculate the delivery distance and the required delivery speed. Furthermore, each node on the delivery path is not able to calculate the progress to the destination via its neighbor node. Moreover, the passive data dissemination also could not define the end-to-end distance and the progress. VTS [12] exploits a virtual tube storage to deliver data to mobile sink group. As this scheme requires the process of storing data and acquiring data through queries in the sink, it is difficult to achieve real-time data transmission.

To overcome the problem, we propose a real-time data delivery mechanism for supporting a mobile sink group. First, the proposed scheme calculates the movable area of mobile sink group based on the virtual grid structure. Based on the structure, the maximum (farthest) distance for the real-time communication is calculated to find the minimum speed that should be satisfied in the process of data transmission. Finally, the proposed scheme could transfer data to all sinks in the group in a valid time by performing main forwarding and branch forwarding process which along nodes that meet the previously calculated minimum speed. The simulation results verify that the proposed mechanism achieves better performance than the existing ones to support real-time communication for mobile sink groups.

The remainder of this paper is organized as follows. In Section 2, we explain the real-time data delivery for mobile sink groups. The performance evaluation results are provided in Section 3. Finally, the proposed scheme and simulation results are summarized in Section 4.

2. The Proposed Mechanism

2.1. Overview

In this section, we describe the overview of the our proposed scheme through Figure 1. As the group moves collectively, our mechanism puts data in a ring-based movable area of the group. In order to define the delivery distance, we construct a grid-based virtual structure in the movable area. Based on the virtual structure, our proposed scheme is largely divided into two forwarding steps: main forwarding and branch forwarding. In the main forwarding process, the data are forwarded along a straight line between the source node and center point of the group sinks (the solid line in Figure 1). The branch forwarding is performed at each branch point in the process of main forwarding. When any branch point receives data through the main forwarding process, each branch point forwards the data through the line to the previously anticipated boundary of the movable area of mobile sinks (the dotted line in Figure 1). In addition, the proposed mechanism calculates the maximum (farthest) distance for the real-time communication based on the virtual structure. Then, each destination and the progress toward the destination could be provided according to either main forwarding or branch forwarding.

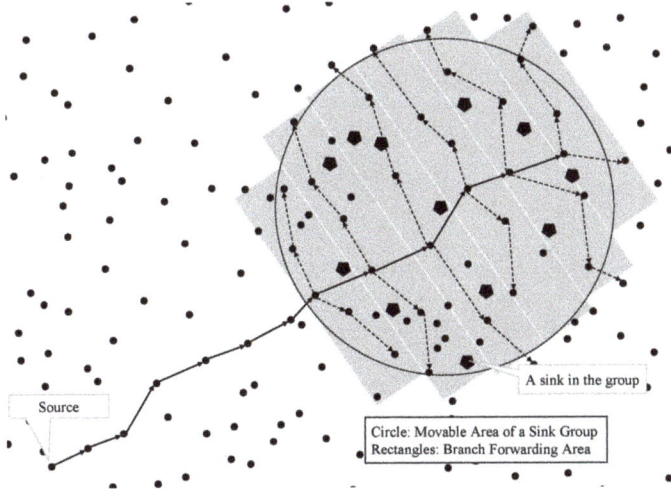

Figure 1. Overview of the proposed scheme.

2.2. Group Sink Modeling

In the MCPS environment, a group of mobile sinks usually have a common goal such as maintenance or production work in a restrict region. However, they have different roles for individuals. Thus, we assume that the group of mobile sinks collectively moves, but each member sink in the group moves independently in a restrict region. Each sink receives data from the nearest sensor as an agent node. To forward data to a sink, the coordinates of the sink are needed. However, in the case of a mobile sink group, per-sink movement management causes excessive energy consumption. M-Geocasting [10] offers an effective data delivery to mobile sink groups. We can gather the geographical information of member sinks and report the group information by a leader sink of the group that is responsible for gathering the location of all member sinks and periodically advertising coordinates of center point and a radius of the area. With the information of the mobile sink group, a source node sends its data using the geographic routing toward the center point. Once the data enter the area, it is flooded within the area. Using the flooding, the protocols do not need to independently manage the locations of each members. The group has a ring-based movable area with the center point and the radius. Each member sink selects one of the sensor nodes as an agent to access the network since the mobile sinks in the group exist on an infrastructureless field.

2.3. Calculation of the Delivery Speed of a Mobile Sink Group

In the spatiotemporal approach for the real-time communication, the delivery speed concept is applied. The delivery speed is maintained in order for all relay nodes to evenly distribute the real-time requirement of applications that have a dynamic topology and error-prone nodes. The selected next-hop node must have a relay speed that is faster than the required delivery speed to meet the requirement. The speed concept includes the spatial requirement and the temporal requirement for the data delivery. The temporal requirement can be given by the application, whereas the spatial requirement might be calculated with the Euclidean distance between the source node and the destination node, as we assume each sensor node could get its own coordinates from either GPS or any localization algorithms. However, in the mobile sink group, the end-to-end distance between a source node and each sink node could not be defined as the data delivery towards each sink node is based on flooding within the area.

A source node defines the distance and calculates the delivery speed after getting the location information of a mobile sink group from sink location server [10,11]. From the server, the source gets the center point P_C and the radius of movable area R_C. P_C is the central coordinate calculated based on the position of all sinks in the group, and when a circle is drawn around P_C, the radius of the circle that can contain all member sinks is R_C. R_C could vary depending on the requirement of application.

Equation (1) is a formula for calculating P_C, and Equation (2) is a formula for obtaining R_C.

$$P_C(x,y) = \frac{1}{n(P)} \sum_{i=1}^{n(P)} P_i, \quad P = \{(x,y) \mid (x,y) = \text{coordinate of member sinks}\} \quad (1)$$

$$R_C = MAX(D), \quad D = \{d \mid d = \text{distance between } P_C \text{ and member sinks}\} \quad (2)$$

To define the distance and calculate the delivery speed, main forwarding and branch forwarding are applied. In the main forwarding, we follow the longest straight line of the area, passing the center point. Branching the longest straight line could reduce the total length of the grid structure and increase the probability of path merging.

The total transmission distance for each sink is the summation of the main forwarding and the branching forwarding. The main forwarding operates on the straight line between a source (x_s, y_s) and the center point (x_c, y_c). The branching forwarding for each sink i (x_{si}, y_{si}) could be defined by the distance between the sink and the straight line:

$$\frac{|kx_{si} - y_{si} + y_c - kx_c|}{\sqrt{k^2 + 1}} \quad (3)$$

where $k = (y_s - y_c)/(x_s - x_c), (x_s \neq x_c)$.

In order to derive the delivery speed for every member in a mobile sink group, we consider the maximum (farthest) distance in the movable area. In the area, as the farthest point from the entry point might be located on the ring, we calculate the distance between two points on the ring. In Figure 2, we assume that the center point and the source node are on the coordinate (0,0) and (D,0), respectively. Each point on the circle can be represented with the angle θ: (Rcos θ, Rsin θ). The distance to each point is presented as follows.

$$f(\theta) = (D - R\cos\theta) + |R\sin\theta|. \quad (4)$$

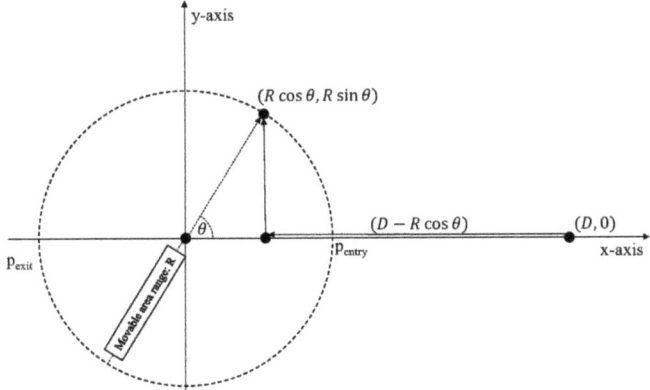

Figure 2. Longest distance in the movable area.

With a differential equation from the Equation (4), we can get the farthest points on the circle: $(\theta = 3/4\pi \text{ or } 5/4\pi)$ as $f'(3/4\pi) = f'(5/4\pi) = 0$ and $f''(3/4\pi) < 0, f''(5/4\pi) < 0$. Therefore, the maximum distance is $(D + \sqrt{2}R)$. With the maximum distance, the source node makes the delivery speed which will be maintained during the data delivery.

2.4. Real-Time Data Transfer via Branch Points

From a source node to the exit point of the movable area (via the entry point of the movable area), data are transferred by the main forwarding. During the main forwarding, the destination of the data packets for geographic routing is the coordinate of the exit point of the movable area.

Each branch forwarding is repeated in every radio-range. For each branch forwarding, multiple branch zones are virtually constructed. The reason to construct the branch zone is to reduce energy consumption by allowing only a flow of data in a zone and avoiding every node participating in communication. There are $\lceil 2R/r \rceil$ branching points in the main forwarding in a movable zone, where the radius is R and the radio range of the sensor nodes is r. The branching point set is represented as follows.

$$BP = \{b_i = (x_i, y_i) | \begin{aligned} x_i &= x_c + i(x_s - x_c)r/D, \\ y_i &= y_c + i(y_s - y_c)r/D, \\ i &= [-\lceil R/r \rceil, \lfloor R/r \rfloor] \} \end{aligned} \quad (5)$$

Each branch point is on the straight line between the entry point and the exit point. The entry point P_{EN} and the exit point P_{EX} can be represented as follows.

$$\begin{aligned} P_{EN} &= (x_c + R(x_s - x_c)/D, y_c + R(y_s - y_c)/D) \\ P_{EX} &= (x_c + R(x_c - x_s)/D, y_c + R(y_c - y_s)/D) \end{aligned} \quad (6)$$

In each branch point, three nodes could be selected at most as the next-hop nodes as shown in Figure 3. One is selected for the main forwarding, the others for branching toward orthogonal directions. To transfer data to the multiple next-hop nodes, we exploit the broadcast nature in wireless transmission. However, there might be interference and concurrent transmission among the selected nodes in the radio-range of the node holding a data packet. To avoid this problem, we apply time slot-based transmission for branching. It divides the time slot and assigns the nodes to each slot. The slot-based transmission is needed for sharing opportunity to relay among the branch nodes. Each node can relay its data packet from its hop delay to time deadline for the real-time packet.

The temporal duration can be called real-time tolerable time. As the tolerable times of the selected next-hop nodes might be overlapped to each other, controlled relaying is needed.

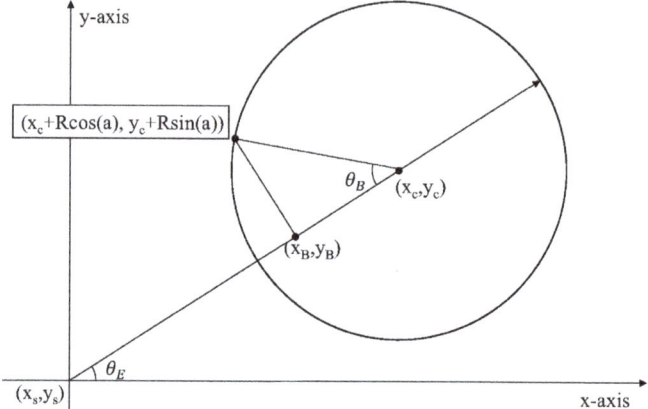

Figure 3. Branching point and termination of branching.

The nodes are assumed to timely synchronize by the time synchronization schemes [13,14]. Each next-hop node has its own and different available time until time deadline in real-time data transmission. We call it the tolerable time. However, in the branch node, the multiple next-hop nodes can relay their data packet independently, thus causing serious packet collision. In order to avoid this problem, an additional scheduling procedure is needed by the branch nodes. The branch node divides the real-time tolerable time to multiple time slots and assigns the time slots to its next-hop candidates. As the maximum number of the next-hop candidates is three, we divide it into three time slots. Each next-hop node could forward data packet in the assigned slot. The duration of the time slot should be longer than the minimum relaying time. For assignment of the time slots, we apply the following rules.

- The first time slot is assigned to the node which has the shortest hop delay.
- The last time slot is assigned to the node which has the longest time deadline.
- The remaining time slot is assigned to the node which has not been assigned to any time slot.

After branching, the destination of the data packet is modified toward the orthogonal direction. The destination could be calculated with the coordination of branch point and source node, and the information of the movable area. The destinations of branch points are needed to calculate because of the two orthogonal direction in shown in Figure 4. As the destination points locate on the circle of the movable area, the destination could be presented as follows:,

$$(x_c + R\cos(a), y_c + R\sin(a)), \qquad (7)$$

where $a = \pi + \theta_E + \theta_B$. The θ_E is the angle of the straight line of the source node and the center point and presented as

$$\theta_E = arctan((y_c - y_s)/(x_c - x_s)). \qquad (8)$$

The θ_B is the angle between two line from the branch point and the destination point to the center point. To the point, data packet is transferred via the geographic routing. Finally, the destination of each branch zone is presented as follows,

$$(x_c - R\cos(\theta_E + \theta_B), y_c - R\sin(\theta_E + \theta_B)). \tag{9}$$

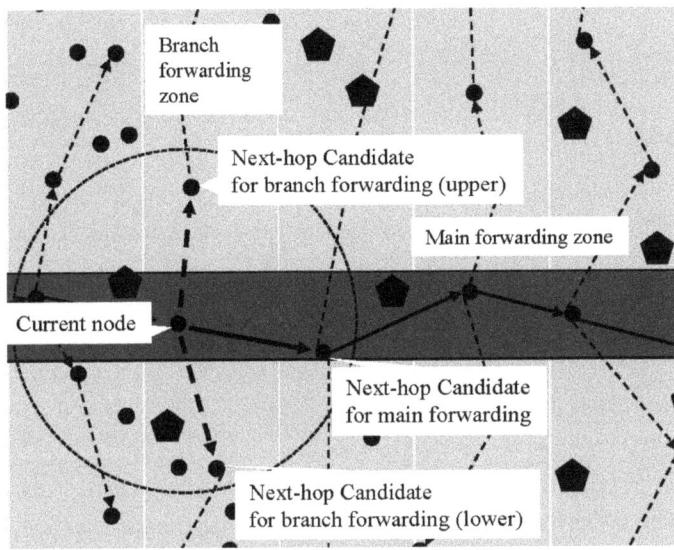

Figure 4. Real-time scheduling in branch points.

2.5. Management of Mobile Sinks by Sensor Nodes

Typically, mobile sink selects a sensor node as its communication agent node and gets data from the agent node. The procedure of data transfer starts in source node, via main forwarding, branch forwarding, and agent, ends in the mobile sink. For the real-time data transmission, the agent should relay the holding data with the highest priority (almost no delay).

Sometimes, each individual mobile sink might temporally be out of the movable area due to obstacles on the path. That is, deviations from environmental factors could be occur. When the mobile sink leaves the movable area, the sink selects the node closest to the edge of the movable areas as inner agent to report its location. In addition, if the sink is out of the communication range of inner agent, the node that exists within the communication range of inner agent is selected as outer agent. It ensures that the sink has a connectivity to receive data even if it is out of the movable area. When the inner agent receives a data packet, the agent forwards the packet to the outer agent using geographic routing. It is possible to relay with more distance because there might be remaining distance to the maximum distance $(D + \sqrt{2}R)$. The remaining distance could be represented as follows,

$$f_r(\theta) = \sqrt{2}R + R\cos\theta - |R\sin\theta|. \tag{10}$$

Although the remaining distance is positive, it cannot be enough to support the out-of-range mobile sink. In order to support the mobile sink with higher remaining distance and higher probability, the location of the out-of-range mobile sink is shared with neighbor boundary nodes and the data packet is relayed via one of the multiple boundary nodes by multipath routing as shown in Figure 5.

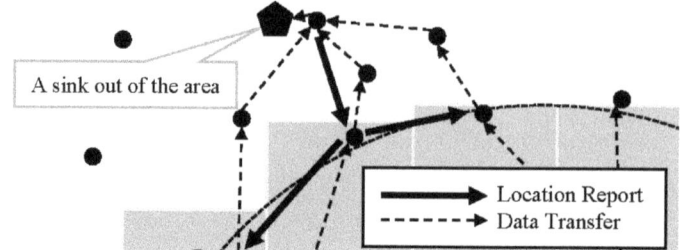

Figure 5. Mobility support for sinks out of the region.

3. Performance Evaluation

3.1. Analysis

We analyze the energy consumption of the flooding based scheme and the proposed protocol to define our routing protocol. To analyze the energy-efficiency of the proposed scheme, we focus on the worst-case communication overhead of each protocol. We consider a square area A in which N sensor nodes are uniformly distributed. There is a mobile sink group which has k multiple mobile sinks. The group moves at an average speed, while receiving d data packets from a source. The communication overhead to flood an area is proportional to the number of sensor nodes in the area, and that to send a message along a path by greedy geographical forwarding is proportional to the number of sensor nodes in the path. In this analysis, the mobile sink group has a radius R. There are $n = N/A * \pi * R^2$ sensor nodes in the group region.

A sink group is assumed to update its location m times, and receive d/m data packets between two consecutive location updates. A radius of the expected group region is $2R$. The overhead for group information calculation and advertisement is $5n+kR+\sqrt{2A}$, where n is the number of sensor nodes in the group region, kR is the update cost from each sink to the leader sink, and $\sqrt{2A}$ is the update cost from the leader sink to the location server in the sensor field. The communication overhead for location update is $m(5n+kR+\sqrt{2A}))$.

To deliver a data packet, we have two communication modes: unicasting from the source the entry point of the sink group and delivery mode within the group area. The length of the unicasting is $(D - R)$, where D is the average length between a source and the center of the group area and R is the radius of the area. Thus, the energy consumption of the unicasting is $(D - R)/r$. For delivery in the group area, the energy consumption is based on the number of sensor nodes in the area: $N\pi R^2/A$. It is exponential to the radius of the area R. Our protocol divides the delivery before and after the branch. There are $b = \lceil 2R/r \rceil$ branch points on the straight line $2R$. After the branch, energy consumption is $2bR$, where the constant 2 is for the two branches in the opposite directions. Totally, the energy consumption is presented as follows,

$$\begin{aligned} CO_{Flooding} &= m((5(N\pi R^2/A) + kR + \sqrt{2A}) + \\ &\quad d((D-R)/r + N\pi R^2/A), \\ CO_{Proposal} &= m((5(N\pi R^2/A) + kR + \sqrt{2A}) + \\ &\quad d((D-R)/r + \lceil 2R/r \rceil + (\lceil 2R/r \rceil)^2) \end{aligned}$$

As a result, the energy consumption of the flooding based scheme depends on the density and the radius of the area, whereas that of the proposed scheme is affected only by the radius of the area.

3.2. Simulation Environment and Results

We have implemented the proposed mechanism in the network simulator NS-3. For application to industrial area, sensor nodes follow the reference of the Wireless HART [15], one of the well-known standards in IWSNs which employs an IEEE 802.15.4-based radio, frequency hopping, and retry mechanisms. We compare with M-Geocasting [10] and VLDD [11], which are group mobility support protocols. The simulation network space consists of 1000 sensor nodes uniformly deployed in a 500 m × 500 m square area. Fifteen mobile sinks are in a group and the radio range of each sensor nodes is ~20 m. The source node generates 30 byte data packets with an interval of 400ms and the time deadline for each packet is 400 ms. The simulation time is 50 s. We measure the in-time data delivery ratio, which means how many of data packets are received by the mobile sinks within the time deadline. The result in the figures is the average value of 100 times of simulation.

Figure 6 shows the in-time data delivery ratio according to the end-to-end (E2E) distance. In this graph, the E2E distance indicates the Euclidean geographical distance between a source and the center of a movable area. In M-Geocasting, a number of packets are lost due to the fact that it exploits flooding and flooding makes broadcast storm. As VLDD is a passive forwarding for supporting group mobility based on the internal movement of each member sink, it causes temporal-useless data packets. In addition, we conduct a simulation with SPEED applying multiple destinations. With these simulation, as SPEED constructs multiple paths for each sink, the interference between multiple paths is frequently occurred. In our scheme, more than 80% of the packets could be received by the sinks of the mobile sink group via unicasting in movable area.

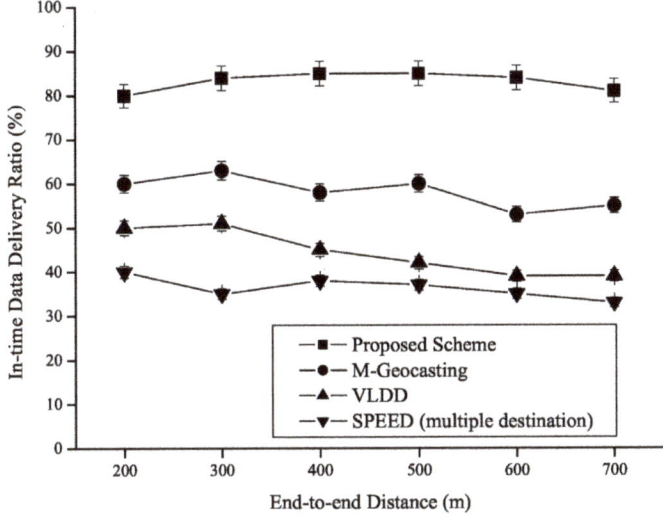

Figure 6. Comparison of in-time data delivery ratio according to end-to-end distance.

In Figure 7, the in-time data delivery ratio is presented according to the movable area range of a mobile sink group. In M-Geocasting, as the movable area spans, a larger number of sensor nodes should participate in communication and the interference is more frequently occurred. When the range of the area is 70 m, in M-Geocasting, approximately 61 sensor nodes participate in its flooding area; however, there are only about 39 participating nodes in our scheme. In VLDD, as the area is wider, it might have a lower possibility to receive an in-time data packet due to its passive data forwarding. With the performance of the proposed scheme, we show that our proposed scheme could cover the wider movable area by multiple unicast forwarding.

Appl. Sci. **2020**, *10*, 5950

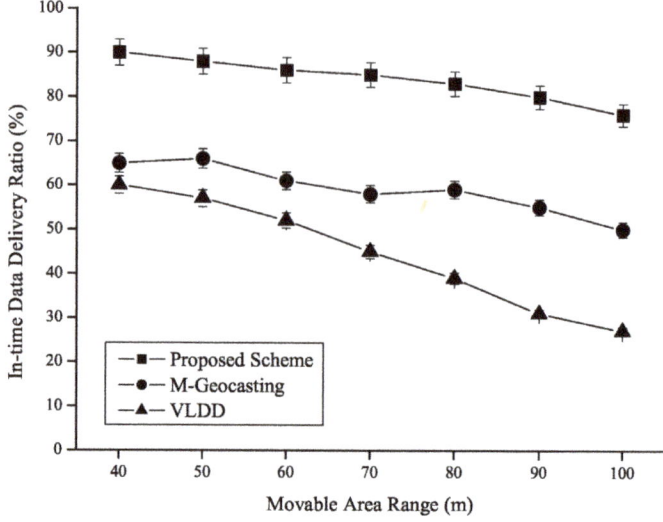

Figure 7. Comparison of in-time data delivery ratio according to movable area range.

Figure 8 shows that the in-time data delivery ratio is affected by the radio range of the sensor node. We vary the range from 15 m to 30 m. Our mechanism and VLDD show almost constant performance, although the range is varied. It is because that our mechanism and VLDD do not exploit the flooding. In M-Geocasting, as the range is wider, the number of one-hop neighbor nodes is increased. With the larger number of neighbor nodes, the number of branches in flooding is increased; however, the possibility of interference for each neighbors also increases dramatically. Therefore, the performance of data delivery ratio is rapidly degraded.

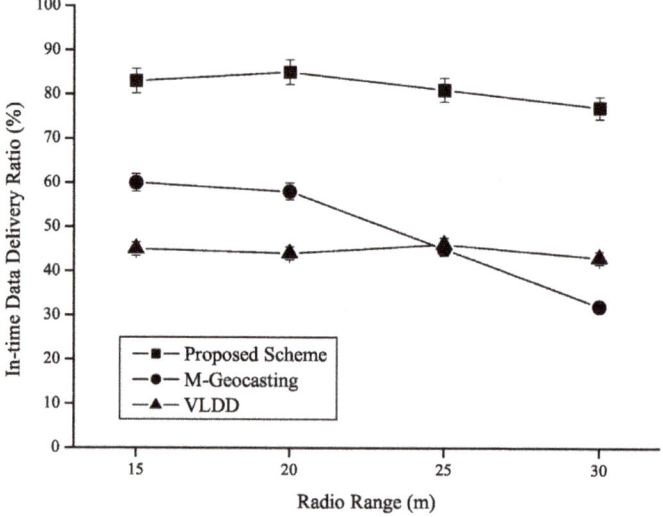

Figure 8. Comparison of total in-time data delivery ratio according to radio range.

4. Conclusions

Nowadays, Mobile Cyber-Physical Systems (MCPS) are widely exploited in various domains. In this environment, the Mobile Sink Groups (MSG) perform collaborative work with a common goal. Thus, data should be delivered to all mobile sinks in the group within a valid time. Traditionally, data delivery schemes for MSG have been proposed; however, as the existing flooding-based data delivery schemes have not been able to define end-to-end distance for each mobile sink, they struggle to satisfy the real-time requirement. To solve this problem, we proposed a scheme to model the MSG in a circular form, and to satisfy the real-time requirement for each member sink through data delivery using virtual grids. First, the proposed scheme models the MSG as one center point and radius, and defines the end-to-end distance based on the member sink furthest from the source node. Through this definition, the source node could could calculate the delivery speed which will be maintained during the data delivery. The data delivery process is largely divided into two phases: the main forwarding phase, which passing through the center of the mobile sinks from source node, and the branch forwarding phase at the branch point, which received the data through the main forwarding phase. In addition, even if some mobile sinks deviate from the initially calculated radius due to various environmental factors of MCPS, the connection of the sinks is ensured through the inner/outer agent concept. Through this process, the proposed scheme could deliver data to all member sinks in a timely manner. The performance evaluation results shows that the proposed scheme is superior to the existing schemes in terms of real-time communication for MSG.

The proposed scheme could have achieved real-time data delivery for a single MSG; however, there could be more than two MSG, independent single mobile sinks, and static sinks in the actual MCPS environment depending on the application. Therefore, further studies on methods such as multicasting are required to deal with the numerous applications of MCPS environments.

Author Contributions: S.O., Y.C., S.K., C.K., K.J., and S.-H.K. contributed to protocol design and detailed algorithms. They also conducted the performance analyses. All authors have read and agreed to the published version of the manuscript.

Funding: This work was supported by the research grant of Pai Chai University in 2020.

Conflicts of Interest: The authors declare no potential conflict of interests.

References

1. Lee, J.; Bagheri, B.; Kao, H.-A. A Cyber-Physical Systems architecture for Industry 4.0-based manufacturing systems. *Manuf. Lett.* **2015**, *3*, 18–23. [CrossRef]
2. Sha, L.; Gopalakrishnan, S.; Liu, X.; Wang, Q. Cyber-Physical Systems: A New Frontier. In Proceedings of the 2008 IEEE International Conference on Sensor Networks, Ubiquitous, and Trustworthy Computing, Taichung, Taiwan, 11–13 June 2008; pp. 1–9.
3. Ding, D.; Han, Q.; Wang, Z.; Ge, X. A Survey on Model-Based Distributed Control and Filtering for Industrial Cyber-Physical Systems. *IEEE Trans. Ind. Informatics* **2019**, *15*, 2483–2499. [CrossRef]
4. Tao, F.; Sui, F.; Liu, A.; Qi, Q.; Zhang, M.; Song, B.; Guo, Z.; Lu, S.C.-Y.; Nee, A.Y.C. Digital twin-driven product design framework. *Int. J. Prod. Res.* **2017**, *57*, 3935–3953. [CrossRef]
5. Guo, Y.; Hu, X.; Hu, B.; Cheng, J.; Zhou, M.; Kwok, R.Y.K. Mobile Cyber Physical Systems: Current Challenges and Future Networking Applications. *IEEE Access* **2018**, *6*, 12360–12368. [CrossRef]
6. Maurya, S.; Jain, V.K.; Chowdhury, D.R. Delay aware energy efficient reliable routing for data transmission in heterogeneous mobile sink wireless sensor network. *J. Netw. Comput. Appl.* **2019**, *144*, 118–137. [CrossRef]
7. Zhang, Y.; Xing, Z.; Wang, Y.; Chen, L.; Wang, Q.; Zhu, Y. Optimization Methods for Computing System in Mobile CPS. In Proceedings of the 2019 2nd International Conference on Big Data Technologies, Jinan, China, 28–30 August 2019; pp. 300–305.
8. He, T.; Stankovic, J.A.; Abdelzaher, T.F.; Lu, C. A spatiotemporal communication protocol for wireless sensor networks. *IEEE Trans. Parallel Distrib. Syst.* **2005**, *16*, 995–1006. [CrossRef]
9. Felemban, E.; Lee, C.-G.; Ekici, E. MMSPEED: Multipath Multi-SPEED protocol for QoS guarantee of reliability and. Timeliness in wireless sensor networks. *IEEE Trans. Mob. Comput.* **2006**, *5*, 738–754. [CrossRef]

10. Park, S.; Lee, E.; Park, H.; Lee, H.; Kim, S. Mobile Geocasting to Support Mobile Sink Groups in Wireless Sensor Networks. *IEEE Commun. Lett.* **2010**, *14*, 939–941. [CrossRef]
11. Mo, H.; Lee, E.; Park, S.; Kim, S. Virtual Line-Based Data Dissemination for Mobile Sink Groups in Wireless Sensor Networks. *IEEE Commun. Lett.* **2013**, *17*, 1864–1867. [CrossRef]
12. Yim, Y.; Mo, H.S.; Kim, C.; Kim, S.H.; Leung, V.C.; Lee, E. Virtual tube storage scheme for supporting mobile sink groups in wireless sensor networks. *Comput. Commun.* **2020**, *159*, 245–257. [CrossRef]
13. Lu, C.; Saifullah, A.; Li, B.; Sha, M.; Gonzalez, H.; Gunatilaka, D.; Wu, C.; Nie, L.; Chen, Y. Real-Time Wireless Sensor-Actuator Networks for Industrial Cyber-Physical Systems. *Proc. IEEE* **2016**, *104*, 1013–1024. [CrossRef]
14. Petersen, S.; Carlsen, S. WirelessHART Versus ISA100.11a: The Format War Hits the Factory Floor. *IEEE Ind. Electron. Mag.* **2011**, *5*, 23–34. [CrossRef]
15. Plc, I.G. WirelessHART Specification Released. *Control. Eng. Eur.* **2007**, *8*, 8–9.

© 2020 by the authors. Licensee MDPI, Basel, Switzerland. This article is an open access article distributed under the terms and conditions of the Creative Commons Attribution (CC BY) license (http://creativecommons.org/licenses/by/4.0/).

Article

AUTOSAR Runnable Periods Optimization for DAG-Based Complex Automobile Applications

Daeho Choi [1,†], Tae-Wook Kim [2,†] and Jong-Chan Kim [3,*]

1. Mobility Business Division, SWM.AI, Anyang-si, Gyeonggi-do 14055, Korea; daeho.choi@swm.ai
2. Graduate School of Automotive Engineering, Kookmin University, Seoul 02707, Korea; dsd8135@kookmin.ac.kr
3. Department of Automobile and IT Convergence, Kookmin University, Seoul 02707, Korea
* Correspondence: jongchank@kookmin.ac.kr; Tel.: +82-2-910-4288
† These authors contributed equally to this work.

Received: 13 July 2020; Accepted: 20 August 2020; Published: 23 August 2020

Abstract: When developing an automobile control application, its scheduling parameters as well as the control algorithm itself should be carefully optimized to achieve the best control performance from given computing resources. Moreover, since the wide acceptance of the AUTOSAR standard, where finer-granular scheduling entities (called runnables) rather than the traditional real-time tasks are used, the number of scheduling parameters to be optimized is far greater than the traditional task-based control systems. Hence, due to the vast problem space, it is not feasible to reuse existing time-consuming search-based optimization methods. With this motivation, this paper presents an analytical codesign method for deciding runnable periods that minimize given control cost functions. Our solution approach, based on the Lagrange multiplier method, can find optimized runnable periods in polynomial times due to its analytical nature. Moreover, our evaluation results for synthesized applications with varying complexities show that our method performs significantly better (12% to 59% of control cost reductions) than a state-of-the-art evolutionary algorithm. To the best of our knowledge, this study is one of the first attempts to find runnable periods that maximize a given system's control performance.

Keywords: AUTOSAR; DAG; runnable scheduling; control-scheduling codesign; lagrange multiplier

1. Introduction

AUTOSAR is the de facto standard software architecture for automobile control systems, covering a wide range of applications such as engine management, motor-driven power steering, and advanced driver assistance systems [1–3]. In the AUTOSAR standard, a control system is designed as a set of *software components*, which are the units of software packaging and deployment. Usually, multiple software components are connected and communicate through the AUTOSAR runtime environment (RTE). Each software component is also composed of a set of *runnables*, which are the smallest unit functions for software development and scheduling. Runnables communicate with each other within each software component and across different software components, using asynchronous message passing interfaces provided by the RTE. As a result, a system can be modeled as a directed acyclic graph (DAG) of runnables where data flow from sensors to actuators through the runnables in the DAG.

For runnable executions, each runnable is associated with an event source, which is usually a periodic timer, and runnables with the same periods are grouped into periodic tasks for scheduling on the AUTOSAR real-time operating system (RTOS). Runnable periods should be carefully optimized since they are control knobs for balancing the trade-off between a system's load and control performance. For example, imagine a system with extremely short runnable periods. The system will then be much too heavily loaded, hence not schedulable since the runnables should execute with extremely high frequencies. On the other hand, the short runnable periods, if realized, can produce a high control performance due to fast data flows and high control frequencies. At the opposite extreme, i.e., a system with extremely long runnable periods, it will be lightly loaded and hence easily schedulable; however, its control performance will be significantly degraded due to slow data flows and low control frequencies. In that sense, we need a method to find optimal runnable periods between those two extreme cases.

However, in the automotive industry, runnable periods are usually decided in an ad-hoc manner with time-consuming trials and errors [4], making it difficult to extract the optimal control performance out of given hardware resources. To cope with this problem, this paper formulates a runnable periods optimization problem for maximizing the control performance of a given system. Our previous work's initial approach was to use a simple combinatorial search method to find real optimal runnable periods [5]. However, our preliminary experiment revealed that even for a small system with a dozen runnables, since the optimization process cannot find solutions in polynomial times, it takes too much time, making it impractical for complex industry applications.

To deal with this scalability problem, our approach is to develop an analytical method that can find near-optimal solutions without time-consuming searches. For that, the first step is to pick an appropriate control performance model as the optimization objective. Among various models in the literature, we chose the linear control cost model from Bini and Cervin [6] that represents a control system's performance as an approximate linear cost function of its control period and delay [6]. This model has been used as a standard tool by many control-scheduling codesign studies [7–10]. The second step is to define the optimization constraint, that is, the schedulability constraint in our problem. Since the AUTOSAR standard assumes a priority-driven scheduling algorithm, we use the Liu and Layland (L&L) utilization bound method [11], which can be used for both the rate monotonic (RM) and the earliest deadline first (EDF) scheduling algorithms. For the explanation purpose, the EDF scheduling algorithm is mostly assumed throughout this paper, and later our method is extended to the RM scheduling algorithm.

Based on the control cost function and the schedulability constraint, our specific problem is to find the runnable periods that minimize the control cost while guaranteeing the schedulability constraint. Since the control cost function is a function of control period and delay, it should be transformed into a function of runnable periods. For that, we carefully investigate how runnable periods affect the temporal behavior, i.e., control period and delay, of a control system, and develop a generalized method for the transformation.

After the transformation, the Lagrange multiplier method is used to find the optimal runnable periods. Note that the Lagrange multiplier is a well-known optimization method for constrained optimization problems. As it provides an analytical method without any problem space search, our method can find the optimal runnable periods regardless of the size and the complexity of a target system. The detailed optimization process is explained in three steps beginning from the most uncomplicated application model to the general DAG model for the explanation purpose. Although our solution cannot find the real optimal solutions due to a heuristic applied during the optimization, our evaluation results for small systems show that the performance loss is marginal compared with the real optimal solutions. Moreover, even for large systems, our method performs better compared with a state-of-the-art optimization method.

This paper's contributions can be summarized as follows:

- We formulate a problem of AUTOSAR runnable periods optimization in the context of control-scheduling codesign, which we consider to be one of the first such attempts;
- For the above problem, we present a Lagrange multiplier-based analytical method for DAG-based AUTOSAR control applications, which can find near-optimal solutions in polynomial times.

The rest of this paper is organized as follows: Next section provides related work. In Section 3, the background is given and the problem is described. Sections 4 and 5 introduce our preliminary works for limited application models. Then, Section 6 describes our analytical solution for the general DAG model. Section 7 evaluates our method. Finally, Section 8 concludes this paper.

2. Related Work

Periods selection problem. Control-scheduling codesign methods have been developed in the literature to improve a control system's performance through optimizing its scheduling parameters. In this regard, Seto et al.'s seminal work [12] first presented a periods selection problem assuming that the control performance can be expressed as an exponential decay function of sampling periods and that the tasks are scheduled under a dynamic-priority scheduling algorithm. The periods selection problem was extended to fixed-priority systems by finding the finite set of feasible period ranges using a branch and bound-based integer programming method [13]. Later, Bini and Di Natale [14] proposed a faster algorithm that finds a sub-optimal periods assignment, which can be used for task sets of practical size that are not solvable by previous methods due to high computing demands. Du et al. [15] presented an analytical solution using the Lagrange multiplier method and an online algorithm for overloaded situations. Fu et al. [9] developed a heuristic algorithm for multicore processors.

Delay-aware approaches. A common assumption of the above studies regarding the periods selection problem is that the control performance is only affected by sampling rates, i.e., task periods, of a control system. However, delays between sensing and actuation also have significant effects on control performance. With this motivation, Bini and Cervin [6] incorporated each task's delay into their optimization cost function. In their work, to find the optimal periods assignment, cost functions are approximated as linear functions of control period and delay, and the delay is also approximated assuming the fluid model scheduler. Through the approximations, they proposed an analytical solution. Xu et al. [16] extended this approach for systems with harmonic periods.

Periods and deadlines selection problem. Wu et al. [8] formulated an optimization problem for selecting both task periods and deadlines simultaneously for EDF-scheduled systems. They showed that we can upper bound the amount of delays and jitters each task can experience by regulating relative deadlines of tasks. The cost function is assumed to be a nonlinear function of period and deadline of each task. Based on that, a two-step approach was proposed, which first fixes periods and later tries to minimize deadlines exploiting unused resources. Tan et al. [10] proposed an algorithm that simultaneously adjusts periods and deadlines assuming EDF-scheduled linear–quadratic–Gaussian (LQG) controllers. They showed that their algorithm is more robust with various workloads than the previous method. Cha et al. [17] proposed a heuristic algorithm for the periods and deadlines selection problem with arbitrary nonlinear control cost functions for systems scheduled by the RM scheduling algorithm.

Cause-effect chain analysis. The above studies commonly assume independent real-time tasks, where there is no data dependency among tasks and each task is responsible for its dedicated control target plant. To deal with practical automobile control applications composed of tasks with complex dependencies, DAG-based control applications had been studied in the context of cause-effect chain analyses of real-time tasks [18–21]. Even though they are using tasks instead of runnables, their system model is similar to ours. However, they address the opposite direction of our optimization problem, which is to analyze end-to-end delays for a DAG of tasks with given periods. Besides, [22] analyzed end-to-end delays of an engine management system, which is given as a DAG of runnables.

AUTOSAR system optimization. In automobile control systems based on the AUTOSAR standard, each control application is designed as a DAG of fine-granular runnables with more complex data dependencies compared with traditional real-time task-based systems. In this context, Long et al. [23] developed a runnable placement and scheduling method considering the inter-runnable communication overhead in an electronic control unit (ECU). Monot et al. [24] proposed an algorithm for sequencing and scheduling runnables for multicore ECUs. Saidi et al. [25] studied the runnable-to-core mapping problem using the integer linear programming (ILP) technique.

Kehr et al. [26] developed a method for migrating a legacy AUTOSAR application to a multicore processor while minimizing energy consumption.

AUTOSAR runnable scheduling. However, the above studies about AUTOSAR applications commonly assume that runnable periods are given a priori, which is not valid in the industry practice. With this motivation, runnable periods optimization problem was first formulated in our previous research paper by Kim et al. [5], which proposed a combinatorial search method that is useful only for small systems due to its high computing demands. Choi et al. [27] partly solved the scalability problem using an analytical method only for limited application structures. These two papers are precursors to this paper and will be thoroughly explained even in more depth and detail in Sections 4 and 5 for the self-completeness of this paper. This paper then further extends our previous works by presenting a more general solution that applies to arbitrarily-shaped complex DAG-based AUTOSAR applications.

3. Background and Problem Description

3.1. System Model

This paper assumes an automobile control application based on the AUTOSAR standard. Figure 1 shows an example system where the application is composed of N software components

$$\{C_1, C_2, \cdots, C_N\}. \tag{1}$$

Each software component C_i is also composed of $|C_i|$ runnables where $|C_i|$ denotes the number of runnables in C_i. Note that a runnable is the smallest unit function in the AUTOSAR standard. As shown in the figure, runnables, denoted by r_is, are connected with directed edges representing data dependencies among them. Thus, the whole system can be thought of as a DAG of runnables without explicitly specifying which software component each runnable belongs to. A DAG G is formally defined as

$$G = (V, E \subset V \times V) \tag{2}$$

where the set of vertices V is a set of n nodes or runnables $\{r_1, r_2, \cdots, r_n\}$ where $n = \sum_{i=1}^{N} |C_i|$ and E represents a set of directed edges or links among them. There exists a directed edge $(r_j, r_k) \in E$ if and only if the runnable r_k has a data dependency on the runnable r_j. Then, each i-th runnable r_i is defined by a tuple

$$r_i = (p_i, e_i) \tag{3}$$

where p_i is its period and e_i is the worst-case execution time. Among the runnables, we assume that r_1, the *sensor runnable*, plays a special role of collecting data from sensors, and r_n, the *actuator runnable*, is responsible for controlling actuators. Thus, G has only one source node r_1 and one sink node r_n. Our system model assumes that, in an ECU, there is only one CPU running a single control application described by G, where the ECU handles only a single control target plant, which is common in the automotive industry's federated architecture [28,29]. Note that e_is are given properties of the system, whereas p_is are controllable parameters. Thus, the runnable periods

$$(p_1, p_2, \cdots, p_n) \tag{4}$$

should be decided before integrating the runnables on the AUTOSAR platform. Once p_is are decided, runnables with the same p_is are grouped and consolidated into RTOS tasks, which are scheduled following the scheduling strategy of the RTOS.

For communications between runnables, an asynchronous sender-receiver communication is used [30]. In this communication method, a sender runnable periodically generates its output in a shared memory buffer with its own period, then a receiver runnable asynchronously reads the data in the memory buffer with its own period. When multiple writes occur to the same memory location without any reading operation from the receiver, the most recent data are always overwritten in the buffer. For further discussions afterward, we formally introduce the following definitions:

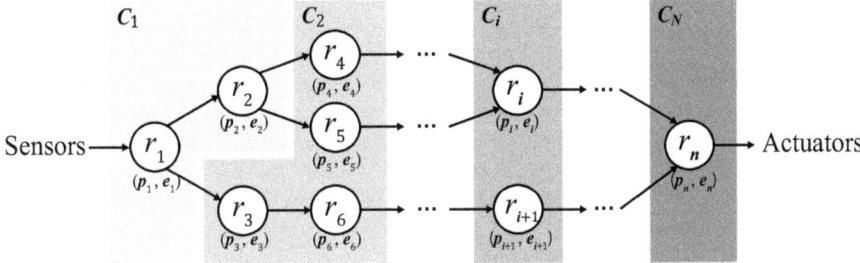

Figure 1. Our directed acyclic graph (DAG)-based system model with N software components and n runnables where each runnable r_i is annotated with its period p_i and worst-case execution time e_i.

Definition 1. **(Paths)** *For a DAG $G = (V, E)$, there is a finite number of directed paths from the source node r_1 to the sink node r_n. We assume that there are m paths in G, which is denoted by*

$$\mathbb{P}(G) = \{P_1, P_2, \cdots, P_m\}. \tag{5}$$

Then, a path is formally defined as an ordered set of runnables beginning with r_1 and ending with r_n in which all runnables are distinct and every pair of adjacent runnables is joined by a directed edge in E. From now on, for the notational convenience, when we refer to a path $P \in \mathbb{P}(G)$, it can denote the ordered set of runnable indexes $(1 \leq i \leq n)$ as well as the runnables themselves depending on the context.

Definition 2. **(Length)** *For a path $P \in \mathbb{P}(G)$, its length is defined as*

$$\sum_{i \in P} p_i, \tag{6}$$

which is the sum of runnable periods following a specific path P. When data flow through several paths in parallel, the speed of a data flow is collectively determined by the runnable periods in each path through which the data are flowing, considering our inter-runnable communication method.

Definition 3. **(Weight)** *For a path $P \in \mathbb{P}(G)$, its weight is defined as*

$$\sum_{i \in P} e_i, \tag{7}$$

which is the sum of runnable execution times following a specific path P. Thus, a path's weight is a representative metric for the amount of computing resource demand of the path.

Definition 4. **(Critical Path)** *Given a DAG G with its paths $\mathbb{P}(G)$, its critical path is defined by the path found in*

$$\operatorname*{argmax}_{P \in \mathbb{P}(G)} \sum_{i \in P} p_i, \tag{8}$$

which is the path with the longest length. Without loss of generality, we assume that there is only one critical path in each DAG.

Definition 5. **(Heaviest Path)** *Given a DAG G with its paths $\mathbb{P}(G)$, its heaviest path is defined by the path found in*

$$\operatorname*{argmax}_{P \in \mathbb{P}(G)} \sum_{i \in P} e_i, \tag{9}$$

which is the path maximizing the sum of e_is for the runnables in the path. The intuition behind the heaviest path is that it indicates the path that consumes the maximum amount of CPU time for a single execution of paths. Without loss of generality, we assume that there is only one heaviest path in each DAG.

3.2. Control Performance Model

A control system's performance can be defined in many different aspects. For example, its robustness to external disturbances, control stability, and control error can be such performance metrics. In general, a control system's performance is affected by its timing behavior as well as the control algorithm itself [31]. In this paper, we assume that the control algorithm is given as a fixed system property. Thus, our control performance model is about how the system's temporal properties affect the control performance. More specifically, we consider two distinct temporal properties: control period and end-to-end delay of the target control system.

In the AUTOSAR timing extensions, two latency constraints are defined: (i) data age timing constraint and (ii) reaction time constraint [20,32,33]. The specification states that when an actuator command is periodically produced, its source input (sensing) value's age should be maintained within a specified timing constraint. The reaction time constraint is also considered when an external event, such as pressing a button, should be reacted within a specified timing constraint. In this paper, since we are considering periodic workloads, the data age timing constraint is considered.

Based on the timing model, there are several ways to build a control performance model. One is to measure the resulting performance of the system by artificially controlling the temporal parameters. Simulation tools [34,35] can also be used to predict the control performance when we cannot directly measure the system under investigation. To provide a more general model, Bini and Cervin [6] introduced a linear control cost function as

$$J(T, \Delta) = \alpha T + \beta \Delta \tag{10}$$

where T is the control period, and Δ is the end-to-end delay from the sensors to the actuators. Note that α and β are constants that define the characteristics of the control target plant. Figure 2 shows an example control cost function. The intuition behind it is that if we give control commands to the actuator more often (frequently), its control cost gets smaller, and in the same manner, if we decide the control command with more fresh (recent) sensor data with shorter delays, the cost gets smaller, again. In general, the cost function J can be a nonlinear function of T and Δ, however, it can be approximated as a linear function as in [6–10,16]. In this paper, we use this linear approximate control cost function as the optimization objective.

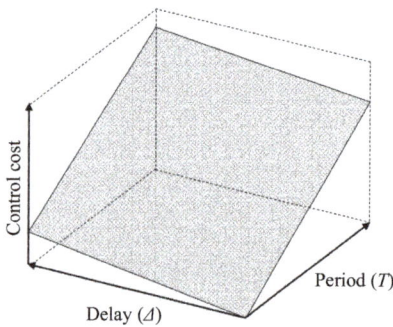

Figure 2. Control cost function, which is a linear function of the system's control period and delay [5].

3.3. Schedulability Constraint

The runnables $\{r_1, r_2, \cdots, r_n\}$ are implemented as RTOS tasks, where runnables with the same period are grouped together and sequentially executed inside a task body when the task is scheduled on a CPU. As most RTOSes only support implicit deadline tasks, their relative deadlines (= periods) should be guaranteed to satisfy runnable-level periodic timing requirements, i.e., p_is. For that, in this paper, we use the L&L utilization bound method, which guarantees the schedulability of a given system if the system utilization is less than or equal to a specific threshold value (i.e., utilization bound) for each scheduling algorithm. For example, the RM scheduling algorithm's utilization bound is roughly 69.3%, and the EDF scheduling algorithm's utilization bound is 100% [11]. We chose to use EDF for its simplicity, where its schedulability condition can be formally expressed as follows:

$$U(p_1, p_2, \cdots, p_n) = \sum_{i=1}^{n} \frac{e_i}{p_i} \leq 1. \tag{11}$$

Although we mainly use the EDF scheduling algorithm throughout this paper, since most scheduling algorithms support the utilization bound method for the schedulability test, we can easily apply our optimization method to other scheduling algorithms like the RM scheduling algorithm. Section 6.5 will deal with this issue in more detail.

3.4. Problem Description

With the system and control performance models and the schedulability constraint presented above, our problem can be defined as follows: With a given AUTOSAR control system composed of DAG-structured runnables $\{r_1, r_2, \cdots, r_n\}$ and a linear control cost function $J(T, \Delta)$ regarding the control target plant, find the optimal runnable periods $(p_1, p_2, \cdots, p_n)$ that minimize the control cost while satisfying the system's schedulability constraint. More formally, our problem is as follows:

$$\begin{aligned} & \underset{p_1, p_2, \cdots, p_n}{\text{minimize}} & & J(T, \Delta) \\ & \text{subject to} & & U(p_1, p_1, \cdots, p_n) \leq 1. \end{aligned} \tag{12}$$

In this paper, we try to find the theoretically optimal real numbered runnable periods, without explicitly considering neither the grouping of runnables into predefined periodic tasks nor the scheduling granularity (e.g., integer constraints) of a specific RTOS. However, our solution can be used as a baseline foundation for further practical applications after considering the implementation details imposed by a specific RTOS.

4. Analytical Solution for Linear Path Graphs

4.1. LPG Model

Instead of directly going for a general solution, let us begin by solving our optimization problem for a subset of the DAG model, and later extend the solution step by step towards a generalized one. This section specifically deals with the *linear path graph* (LPG) model, which is for graphs with runnables $\{r_1, r_2, \cdots, r_n\}$ such that the edges are given by $E = \{(r_i, r_{i+1}) | 1 \leq i \leq n-1\}$. Figure 3 shows an example LPG with n runnables and $n-1$ edges between them.

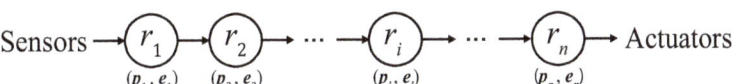

Figure 3. Linear path graph (LPG) model.

4.2. Transformation of Control Cost Function

When solving the optimization problem in the LPG model's scope, the first step is to redefine the control cost function as a function of the free variables of the optimization problem, i.e., runnable periods $(p_1, p_2, \cdots, p_n)$. For the transformation of $J(T, \Delta)$ in Equation (10) into a function of runnable periods, our strategy is to define both T and Δ using only runnable periods considering the LPG model's runnable execution and data flow patterns.

Control period T can be formally defined, from a plant's perspective, as a regular time interval between consecutive actuation instances. However, due to the jitter caused by preemption delays among concurrent runnables, the intervals may vary for each actuation instance. Thus, we consider the longest time interval as the worst-case period T. For LPG-based applications, T can be defined as double the actuator runnable r_n's period p_n, which is

$$T = 2p_n. \tag{13}$$

The worst-case scenario happens when a certain instance of r_n is scheduled at the beginning of its period, whereas, in the next instance, r_n is scheduled at the very end of its period. Assuming that actuation commands are emitted at each completion of r_n instances, the time interval between the actuation commands gets to the longest as possible in that particular scenario, which is $2p_n$. It can be argued that e_n should be considered, and the exact worst-case time interval should be $2p_n - e_n$. However, note that since e_n is the worst-case execution time, real execution times can be much smaller than e_n; thus, for simplicity's sake, we do not take e_n into consideration when defining T.

The end-to-end delay Δ is defined as the time taken for new sensor data to go through runnables until arriving at the actuator. According to the data flow architecture of our system model, the sensor runnable r_1 sends out its output to its neighboring runnables with its own period p_1. Then, the neighboring runnables also send out their outputs with their own periods. With these repeated transmissions, new sensor data originating from the source node r_1 gradually propagate through the runnables toward the sink node, i.e., the actuator runnable r_n. After r_n finally receives the updates, it can decide its actuation commands based on the new sensor data. In an LPG-based application where data flow through only a single path from r_1 to r_n, the worst-case end-to-end delay Δ can be calculated as

$$\Delta = 2p_1 + 2p_2 + \cdots + 2p_n = 2\sum_{i=1}^{n} p_i. \tag{14}$$

The worst case happens as in the following: a runnable r_{i-1} emits its output for r_i at a certain time t. Unfortunately, however, r_i begins just right before t, reading the previous (old) output of r_{i-1}. Let us assume that r_i is scheduled at the very beginning of its period at that time. Then, unfortunately again, the next instance of r_i is scheduled at the very end of its period, reading the new data and emitting its output at the end of the period (i.e., $t + 2p_i$). In the above scenario, the time taken for the data to go through r_i is double the r_i's period $2p_i$. Assuming this scenario happening for every runnable in the path, the end-to-end delay Δ becomes double the sum of all the runnable periods as in Equation (14). By combining Equations (13) and (14), the control cost function in Equation (10) is transformed into as follows:

$$J(p_1, p_2, \cdots, p_n) = 2\alpha p_n + 2\beta \sum_{i=1}^{n} p_i. \tag{15}$$

4.3. Finding the Optimal Runnable Periods

For visual understanding of the optimization process, let us pick an example system with only two runnables $\{r_1, r_2\}$. Then, the transformation of the control cost function is illustrated in Figure 4. In the left-hand side, the original control cost function is depicted, which is transformed into a function of p_1 and p_2 as in the right-hand side by Equation (15). Then, Figure 5 illustrates the optimization process where the schedulability constraint and the transformed control cost function are shown upon the two-dimensional problem space of p_1 and p_2. In the figure, our optimization objective is to find the lowest point in the control cost plane that is inside the green schedulable area. This concept can be generally extended to n-runnable systems in n-dimensional problem spaces. In general, our original optimization problem in Equation (12) can be transformed into the following using the transformed control cost function:

$$\begin{aligned}
\underset{p_1,p_2,\cdots,p_n}{\text{minimize}} \quad & J(p_1, p_2, \cdots, p_n) = 2\alpha p_n + 2\beta \sum_{i=1}^{n} p_i \\
\text{subject to} \quad & U(p_1, p_2, \cdots, p_n) = \sum_{i=1}^{n} \frac{e_i}{p_i} \leq 1.
\end{aligned} \quad (16)$$

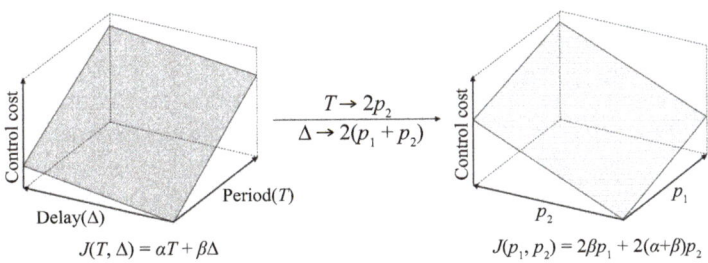

Figure 4. Visually illustrated transformation of control cost function [5].

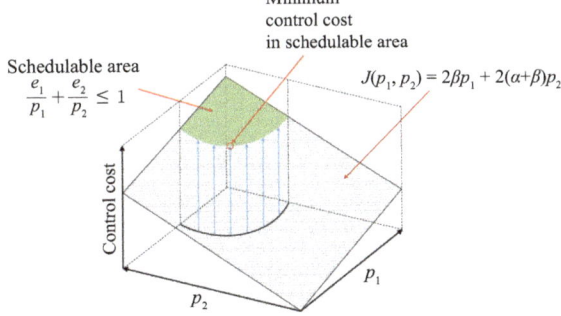

Figure 5. Visually illustrated constrained optimization process [5].

To analytically solve the transformed optimization problem, the Lagranage multiplier method is applied. For the first step, a Lagrange function is formulated as follows:

$$\mathcal{L} = 2\alpha p_n + 2\beta \sum_{i=1}^{n} p_i - \lambda \left(\sum_{i=1}^{n} \frac{e_i}{p_i} - 1 \right). \quad (17)$$

Then, we take the partial derivatives of $\mathcal{L}$ with respect to $p_1, p_2, \cdots, p_n$, and λ, respectively and set them to zeros as follows:

$$\nabla \mathcal{L} = \left(\frac{\partial \mathcal{L}}{\partial p_1}, \frac{\partial \mathcal{L}}{\partial p_2}, \cdots, \frac{\partial \mathcal{L}}{\partial p_n}, \frac{\partial \mathcal{L}}{\partial \lambda} \right) = 0, \quad (18)$$

which in turn is expanded to the followings:

$$\begin{aligned}
\frac{\partial \mathcal{L}}{\partial p_1} &= 2\beta + \frac{e_1}{p_1^2}\lambda = 0, \\
\frac{\partial \mathcal{L}}{\partial p_2} &= 2\beta + \frac{e_2}{p_2^2}\lambda = 0, \\
&\cdots, \\
\frac{\partial \mathcal{L}}{\partial p_n} &= 2(\alpha + \beta) + \frac{e_n}{p_n^2}\lambda = 0, \\
\frac{\partial \mathcal{L}}{\partial \lambda} &= -\left(\sum_{i=1}^n \frac{e_i}{p_i} - 1\right) = 0.
\end{aligned} \quad (19)$$

Then, by isolation λ in the left-hand side of the first in Equation (19), we have

$$\lambda = -\frac{2\beta p_1^2}{e_1}, \quad (20)$$

which can be applied to the remaining of Equation (19) except the last one. As a result, $p_2, p_3, \cdots$, and p_n are given in terms of p_1 as in the second to the last of the followings:

$$\begin{aligned}
p_1 &= \sum_{i=1}^{n-1} \sqrt{e_1 e_i} + \sqrt{\frac{(\alpha+\beta)e_1 e_n}{\beta}}, \\
p_2 &= p_1 \sqrt{\frac{e_2}{e_1}}, \\
&\cdots, \\
p_{n-1} &= p_1 \sqrt{\frac{e_{n-1}}{e_1}}, \\
p_n &= p_1 \sqrt{\frac{\beta e_n}{(\alpha+\beta)e_1}}.
\end{aligned} \quad (21)$$

Additionally, p_1 is given as the first of the above by replacing $p_2, p_3, \cdots$, and p_n in the last of Equation (19) with the second to the last of the above. Then, by Equation (21), we can find the real optimal runnable periods for arbitrary LPG-based applications.

5. Analytical Solution for Linear Multipath Graphs

Based on the method for the LPG model explained in Section 4, this section goes one step further to a more complex application model having multiple independent data flows from sensors to actuators.

5.1. LMG Model

When designing automobile control applications, there are cases where a simpler data flow model is preferred instead of using the complex DAG model. The most common such case is when there are several independent parallel data flows from sensors to actuators. In Figure 6, r_1 is the sensor runnable and r_n is the actuator runnable. Between them, there are m paths where each runnable in the middle part $\{r_2, r_3, \cdots, r_{n-1}\}$ belongs to only one specific path among them. To distinguish such a particular application architecture from general DAGs, we specifically call them the *linear multipath graph* (LMG) model. Although the LMG model can be applied to a limited range of applications, it is meaningful since there is an increasing need for integrating independent control algorithms to develop integrated control systems or multi-functional ECUs [36–38]. In such new systems, sensor data propagate through multiple independent paths of runnables to the actuators.

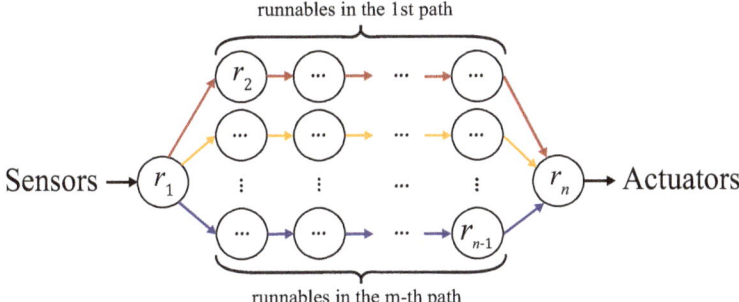

Figure 6. Linear multipath graph (LMG) model with m independent paths identified by edges with different colors [27].

5.2. Transformation of Control Cost Function

For the optimization, the objective function $J(T, \Delta)$ in Equation (10) should be transformed into a function of runnable periods $(p_1, p_2, \cdots, p_n)$. For that, in the same way in Section 4.2, the period T is transformed into as follows:

$$T = 2p_n. \tag{22}$$

For the end-to-end delay Δ, however, we cannot simply reuse the method in Section 4.2 since we have multiple paths with possibly different lengths. Thus, Δ should be defined as the length of the longest path among them to represent the worst-case end-to-end delay. More specifically, let us remind that P_i denotes the i-th path of m independent paths $\{P_1, P_2, \cdots, P_m\}$. Then, Δ is defined as follows:

$$\Delta = \max_{1 \leq i \leq m} \left(\sum_{j \in P_i} 2p_j \right). \tag{23}$$

Thus, our original optimization problem is transformed into as follows:

$$\begin{aligned} \underset{p_1, p_2, \cdots, p_n}{\text{minimize}} \quad & J(p_1, p_2, \cdots, p_n) = 2\alpha p_n + \beta \max_{1 \leq i \leq m} \left(\sum_{j \in P_i} 2p_j \right) \\ \text{subject to} \quad & U(p_1, p_2, \cdots, p_n) = \sum_{i=1}^{n} \frac{e_i}{p_i} \leq 1, \end{aligned} \tag{24}$$

where unlike the LPG model, the max operator introduces nonlinearity making it difficult to develop an analytical solution. Fortunately, however, due to the LMG model's workload characteristics, we can simplify the problem by defining an equilibrium state, which is to be obtained to find the optimal runnable periods in the LMG model. The equilibrium state of an LMG can be defined as follows:

Definition 6. (Equilibrium state) *For a set of m paths of a given LMG G, which is denoted by $\mathbb{P}(G) = \{P_1, P_2, \cdots, P_m\}$, G is in its equilibrium state if and only if*

$$\sum_{i \in P_1} p_i = \sum_{i \in P_2} p_i = \cdots = \sum_{i \in P_m} p_i. \tag{25}$$

Theorem 1. (Equilibrium state theorem) *If G is an LMG with its optimal runnable periods, G is always in its equilibrium state.*

Proof of Theorem 1. If G is with its optimal runnable periods while not in the equilibrium state, we can increase runnable periods that do not belong to the critical path, without affecting the end-to-end delay. Then, the increased runnable periods will make a lower system utilization, which can be used to further decrease the end-to-end delay by shortening runnable periods in the critical path. Thus, we can conclude that G is not with the optimal runnable periods, which is a contradiction. □

By the equilibrium state theorem, we can narrow down the problem space without sacrificing the optimality by excluding non-equilibrium states from the problem space. To express the equilibrium state more efficiently, Δ is re-expressed by breaking it into three parts as

$$\Delta = 2p_1 + \max_{1 \leq i \leq m} \left(\sum_{j \in \hat{P}_i} 2p_j \right) + 2p_n \tag{26}$$

with a helper notation $\hat{P}_i = P_i - \{1, n\}$. Then, to explicitly express the equilibrium state, we define a new notation p_* as in the following:

$$p_* = \sum_{i \in \hat{P}_1} p_i = \sum_{i \in \hat{P}_2} p_i = \cdots = \sum_{i \in \hat{P}_m} p_i, \tag{27}$$

which is an aggregate variable representing the path length of the middle part in the equilibrium state. Then, by using p_*, Δ can be re-expressed from Equations (26) and (27) as follows:

$$\Delta = 2(p_1 + p_* + p_n). \tag{28}$$

Finally, the control cost function $J(T, \Delta)$ from Equation (10) is rewritten as a function of (p_1, p_*, p_n) by Equations (22) and (28) as in the following:

$$J(p_1, p_*, p_n) = 2\alpha p_n + 2\beta(p_1 + p_* + p_n). \tag{29}$$

With this transformed control cost function $J(p_1, p_*, p_n)$, our original problem of n runnable periods is transformed into a problem of three free variables (p_1, p_*, p_n). Then, once they are decided, p_* is distributed to runnables along each path. For that, we use a heuristic that runnables with larger e_is are assigned with longer p_is. More specifically, we assign p_is strictly proportional to e_is. Following this assignment rule, runnable periods p_js for each $\hat{P}_i$ are decided as follows:

$$\forall i \in [1 .. m] \; \forall j \in \hat{P}_i : p_j = \frac{e_j}{\sum_{k \in \hat{P}_i} e_k} p_*. \tag{30}$$

5.3. Transformation of Schedulability Constraint Function

This subsection transforms the schedulability constraint function in Equation (11) to a function of (p_1, p_*, p_n). First, the original function $U(p_1, p_2, \cdots, p_n)$ is re-expressed by breaking it into three parts, and the middle part is arranged by grouping the runnables by the paths they belong to. The new expression can be simply comprehended as the sum of m per-path sums of utilizations as in the following:

$$\begin{aligned} U(p_1, p_2, \cdots, p_n) &= \frac{e_1}{p_1} + \left(\frac{e_2}{p_2} + \cdots + \frac{e_{n-1}}{p_{n-1}} \right) + \frac{e_n}{p_n} \\ &= \frac{e_1}{p_1} + \sum_{i=1}^{m} \left(\sum_{j \in \hat{P}_i} \frac{e_j}{p_j} \right) + \frac{e_n}{p_n}. \end{aligned} \tag{31}$$

Then, to transform each i-th per-path utilization sum into a function of p_*, Equation (30) is applied to eliminate p_j as in the following:

$$\sum_{j \in \hat{P}_i} \frac{e_j}{p_j} = \sum_{j \in \hat{P}_i} \frac{e_j}{\frac{e_j}{\sum_{k \in \hat{P}_i} e_k} p_*} = \sum_{j \in \hat{P}_i} \frac{\sum_{k \in \hat{P}_i} e_k}{p_*}$$
$$= |\hat{P}_i| \frac{\sum_{k \in \hat{P}_i} e_k}{p_*} = \frac{\sum_{k \in \hat{P}_i} |\hat{P}_i| e_k}{p_*} \quad (32)$$

where $|\hat{P}_i|$ denotes the number of elements in the ordered set $\hat{P}_i$. Finally, our utilization constraint is transformed into as follows:

$$U(p_1, p_*, p_n) = \frac{e_1}{p_1} + \frac{\sum_{i=1}^{m} \sum_{k \in \hat{P}_i} |\hat{P}_i| e_k}{p_*} + \frac{e_n}{p_n} \leq 1. \quad (33)$$

5.4. Finding the Optimal Runnable Periods

After the transformation of the control cost function and the schedulability constraint function, our runnable periods optimization problem for the LMG model can be formulated with the three free variables (p_1, p_*, p_n) as follows:

$$\begin{aligned}
\underset{p_1, p_*, p_n}{\text{minimize}} \quad & J(p_1, p_*, p_n) = 2\alpha p_n + 2\beta(p_1 + p_* + p_n) \\
\text{subject to} \quad & U(p_1, p_*, p_n) = \frac{e_1}{p_1} + \frac{\sum_{i=1}^{m} \sum_{k \in \hat{P}_i} |\hat{P}_i| e_k}{p_*} + \frac{e_n}{p_n} \leq 1.
\end{aligned} \quad (34)$$

To solve the optimization problem, a Lagrange function is formulated as follows:

$$\mathcal{L} = 2\alpha p_n + 2\beta(p_1 + p_* + p_n) - \lambda \left(\frac{e_1}{p_1} + \frac{\sum_{i=1}^{m} \sum_{k \in \hat{P}_i} |\hat{P}_i| e_k}{p_*} + \frac{e_n}{p_n} - 1 \right). \quad (35)$$

Then, we take the partial derivatives of $\mathcal{L}$ with respect to p_1, p_*, p_n, and λ, respectively and set them to zeros as follows:

$$\nabla \mathcal{L} = \left(\frac{\partial \mathcal{L}}{\partial p_1}, \frac{\partial \mathcal{L}}{\partial p_*}, \frac{\partial \mathcal{L}}{\partial p_n}, \frac{\partial \mathcal{L}}{\partial \lambda} \right) = 0, \quad (36)$$

which in turn is expanded to the followings:

$$\frac{\partial L}{\partial p_1} = 2\beta + \frac{e_1}{p_1^2}\lambda = 0,$$

$$\frac{\partial L}{\partial p_*} = 2\beta + \frac{\sum_{i=1}^{m}\sum_{k\in\hat{P}_i}|\hat{P}_i|e_k}{p_*^2}\lambda = 0,$$

$$\frac{\partial L}{\partial p_n} = 2(\alpha+\beta) + \frac{e_n}{p_n^2}\lambda = 0, \quad (37)$$

$$\frac{\partial L}{\partial \lambda} = -\left(\frac{e_1}{p_1} + \frac{\sum_{i=1}^{m}\sum_{k\in\hat{P}_i}|\hat{P}_i|e_k}{p_*} + \frac{e_n}{p_n} - 1\right) = 0.$$

Then, the first, second, and third of Equation (37) are rearranged by isolating λ in each left-hand side as follows:

$$\lambda = -2\beta\frac{p_1^2}{e_1},$$

$$\lambda = -2\beta\frac{p_*^2}{\sum_{i=1}^{m}\sum_{k\in\hat{P}_i}|\hat{P}_i|e_k}, \quad (38)$$

$$\lambda = -2(\alpha+\beta)\frac{p_n^2}{e_n}.$$

Then, by combining the first and second of Equation (38), we have the following:

$$2\beta\frac{p_1^2}{e_1} = 2\beta\frac{p_*^2}{\sum_{i=1}^{m}\sum_{k\in\hat{P}_i}|\hat{P}_i|e_k} \implies \frac{1}{p_*} = \frac{1}{p_1}\sqrt{\frac{e_1}{\sum_{i=1}^{m}\sum_{k\in\hat{P}_i}|\hat{P}_i|e_k}}. \quad (39)$$

By combining the first and third of Equation (38), we have the following:

$$2\beta\frac{p_1^2}{e_1} = 2(\alpha+\beta)\frac{p_n^2}{e_n} \implies \frac{1}{p_n} = \frac{1}{p_1}\sqrt{\frac{\alpha+\beta}{\beta}}\sqrt{\frac{e_1}{e_n}}. \quad (40)$$

By replacing $\frac{1}{p_*}$ and $\frac{1}{p_n}$ in the last of Equation (37) with the findings in Equations (39) and (40), we have the following:

$$\frac{1}{p_1}\left(e_1 + \sum_{i=1}^{m}\sum_{k\in\hat{P}_i}|\hat{P}_i|e_k\sqrt{\frac{e_1}{\sum_{i=1}^{m}\sum_{k\in\hat{P}_i}|\hat{P}_i|e_k}} + e_n\sqrt{\frac{(\alpha+\beta)e_1}{\beta e_n}}\right) = 1. \quad (41)$$

Finally, from Equations (39)–(41), we have the following solution:

$$p_1 = e_1 + \sqrt{e_1 \sum_{i=1}^{m} \sum_{k \in \hat{P}_i} |\hat{P}_i| e_k} + \sqrt{\frac{(\alpha+\beta) e_1 e_n}{\beta}}$$

$$p_* = p_1 \sqrt{\frac{\sum_{i=1}^{m} \sum_{k \in \hat{P}_i} |\hat{P}_i| e_k}{e_1}} \tag{42}$$

$$p_n = p_1 \sqrt{\frac{\beta e_n}{(\alpha+\beta) e_1}}.$$

We have one remaining step of deciding $(p_2, p_3, \cdots, p_{n-1})$. For that, we distribute p_* to runnables in each path in proportion to their e_is as in Equation (30). It is also worth noting that even with the equilibrium state theorem, we cannot find the real optimal solutions since we lose the optimality while distributing p_* with a heuristic. Nevertheless, we can find high-quality solutions close to the real optimal runnable periods. Interested readers are referred to our previous work [27].

6. Generalized Analytical Method for Directed Acyclic Graphs

This section generalizes the previously explained methods for the LPG model and the LMG model to the general DAG model. Both methods are not usable for a general DAG-based application for their limited applicability. In particular, since our method for the LMG model assumes that there is no such runnable that belongs to different paths at the same time, it is not applicable to DAGs with at least one such runnable. If we forcibly try it, Equation (30) may yield two different, hence, conflicting results for such runnables. Thus, we need a separate method for the DAG model.

6.1. DAG Model and Its Challenge

The DAG model is already explained in Section 3.1. Hence this subsection just highlights how it is different from the LPG model and the LMG model and presents a challenge that does not exist in the previous models. As noted earlier, there is only one path in the LPG model, making it easy to define the system's end-to-end delay. In the LMG model, even though there are multiple paths, we can use the equilibrium state theorem to simply represent them together by their identical path length in the middle part, denoted by p_*. Figure 7a shows a simple DAG that is not an LPG nor an LMG. In the figure, note that r_4 belongs to the following two different paths: $< r_1, r_2, r_4, r_7 >$ and $< r_1, r_4, r_7 >$. As a runnable period cannot be zero, the former is always longer than the latter. Thus, unlike the LMG model where we can always make an equilibrium state, we cannot always make an equilibrium state in the DAG model.

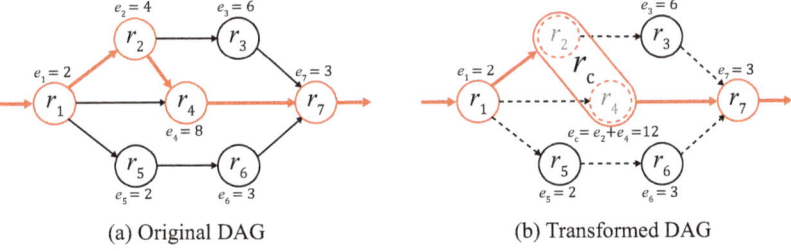

(a) Original DAG (b) Transformed DAG

Figure 7. An example of DAG explaining the concept of the critical path with r_c.

6.2. Transformation of Control Cost Function

With the above challenge, let us transform the control cost function to a function of runnable periods. For the period T, we can use the same method as for the LPG model and the LMG model since it is only concerned with the actuator runnable r_n. Thus, T is transformed into as follows:

$$T = 2p_n. \tag{43}$$

Unfortunately, however, when transforming the end-to-end delay Δ, we cannot simply reuse the method for the LMG model in Section 5.2 since we cannot be sure that an equilibrium state can be made. To handle this challenge, let us begin with the general definition of Δ as in the following, assuming m paths $\{P_1, P_2, \cdots, P_m\}$:

$$\Delta = \max_{1 \leq i \leq m} \left(\sum_{j \in P_i} 2p_j \right). \tag{44}$$

For example, in Figure 7a, there are four paths, $P_1 = <1,2,3,7>$, $P_2 = <1,2,4,7>$, $P_3 = <1,4,7>$, and $P_4 = <1,5,6,7>$. Among them, it is apparent that P_3 cannot be the critical path since it is always shorter than P_2. However, among P_1, P_2, and P_4, we cannot be sure which is the longest since all of them can be the critical path according to how we decide p_is.

To overcome this challenge, we propose to employ a heuristic with a clear rule regarding which path should be the critical path. For that, with given e_is, we employ a heuristic described by the following:

$$p_i \propto e_i, \text{ for } 2 \leq i \leq n-1. \tag{45}$$

Certainly, the most important benefit from making p_is simply proportional to e_is is that we can simply decide the critical path based on the path weights (See Definition 3) such that we can choose the heaviest path (See Definition 5) as the critical path. For example, in Figure 7a, the weights of paths, P_1 to P_4, are calculated as 15, 17, 13, and 10, respectively. Then, P_2, specified by the red color, turns out to be the heaviest path. By the heuristic, it is used as the critical path. The intuition behind this heuristic is that we give longer periods to runnables with longer execution times to evenly distribute the system utilization across runnables, eliminating possible bottlenecks. Note that p_1 and p_n are excluded in Equation (45) as they have no effect on deciding the critical path.

For further explanations, we introduce a new notation r_c, which is defined as the set of runnables in the critical path excluding r_1 and r_n. Figure 7b shows $r_c = \{r_2, r_4\}$. Then, let us think as if r_c is a virtual *composite runnable* combining its member runnables just like the ellipse covering r_2 and r_4 in the figure. Then, the critical path can be thought of as a three-runnable ordered set $<r_1, r_c, r_n>$. For r_c, let us also define e_c and p_c as in the followings:

$$e_c = \sum_{i \in r_c} e_i \tag{46}$$

and

$$p_c = \sum_{i \in r_c} p_i. \tag{47}$$

Based on the above notations, Δ can be defined as follows:

$$\Delta = 2(p_1 + p_c + p_n), \tag{48}$$

which makes the control cost function as follows with Equation (43):

$$J(p_1, p_c, p_n) = 2\alpha p_n + 2\beta(p_1 + p_c + p_n). \tag{49}$$

Then, regarding how to derive $p_2, p_3, \cdots,$ and p_{n-1} from p_c, we use the following assignment rule following Equation (45):

$$p_i = \frac{e_i}{e_c} p_c \text{ for } 2 \leq i \leq n-1. \tag{50}$$

Under the above assignment rule, the followings are ensured:

- p_is are always proportional to e_is;
- The length of the critical path excluding r_1 and r_n is equal to p_c;
- The length of any other path is always shorter than p_c.

As an example, in Figure 7b, we can find that $e_c = e_2 + e_4 = 12$ and $p_c = p_2 + p_4$. Once p_c is decided, each p_i can be derived as in the followings according to Equation (50):

$$p_2 = \frac{4}{12} p_c, \ p_3 = \frac{6}{e_c} p_c, \ p_4 = \frac{8}{12} p_c, \ p_5 = \frac{2}{12} p_c, \text{ and } p_6 = \frac{3}{12} p_c. \tag{51}$$

6.3. Transformation of Schedulability Constraint Function

The schedulability constraint in Equation (11) uses a function of n runnable periods. Thus, it is transformed into a function of the three free variables (p_1, p_c, p_n), following the rule in Equation (50) as follows:

$$\begin{aligned}
U(p_1, p_2, \cdots, p_n) &= \frac{e_1}{p_1} + \left(\frac{e_2}{p_2} + \cdots + \frac{e_{n-1}}{p_{n-1}} \right) + \frac{e_n}{p_n} = \\
&= \frac{e_1}{p_1} + \left(\frac{e_2}{\frac{e_2}{e_c} p_c} + \cdots + \frac{e_{n-1}}{\frac{e_{n-1}}{e_c} p_c} \right) + \frac{e_n}{p_n} \\
&= \frac{e_1}{p_1} + (n-2) \frac{e_c}{p_c} + \frac{e_n}{p_n}.
\end{aligned} \tag{52}$$

Now, the utilization function $U(p_1, p_2, \cdots, p_n)$ can be replaced by a function of (p_1, p_c, p_n) as in the following:

$$U(p_1, p_c, p_n) = \frac{e_1}{p_1} + (n-2) \frac{e_c}{p_c} + \frac{e_n}{p_n}. \tag{53}$$

6.4. Finding the Optimal Runnable Periods

Based on the control cost function in Equation (49) and the utilization function in Equation (53), our runnable periods optimization problem for the DAG model can be formulated with the three free variables (p_1, p_c, p_n) as follows:

$$\begin{aligned}
\underset{p_1, p_c, p_n}{\text{minimize}} \quad & J(p_1, p_c, p_n) = 2\alpha p_n + 2\beta (p_1 + p_c + p_n) \\
\text{subject to} \quad & U(p_1, p_c, p_n) = \frac{e_1}{p_1} + (n-2) \frac{e_c}{p_c} + \frac{e_n}{p_n} \leq 1.
\end{aligned} \tag{54}$$

To solve the optimization problem, a Lagrange function is formulated as follows:

$$\begin{aligned}
\mathcal{L} &= J(p_1, p_c, p_n) - \lambda (U(p_1, p_c, p_n) - 1) \\
&= 2\alpha p_n + 2\beta (p_1 + p_c + p_n) - \lambda \left(\frac{e_1}{p_1} + (n-2) \frac{e_c}{p_c} + \frac{e_n}{p_n} - 1 \right).
\end{aligned} \tag{55}$$

Then, we take the partial derivatives of $\mathcal{L}$ with respect to $p_1, p_c, p_n,$ and λ, respectively and set them to zeros as follows:

$$\nabla \mathcal{L} = \left(\frac{\partial \mathcal{L}}{\partial p_1}, \frac{\partial \mathcal{L}}{\partial p_c}, \frac{\partial \mathcal{L}}{\partial p_n}, \frac{\partial \mathcal{L}}{\partial \lambda} \right) = 0, \tag{56}$$

which in turn is expanded to the followings:

$$\begin{aligned}
\frac{\partial \mathcal{L}}{\partial p_1} &= 2\beta + \frac{e_1}{p_1^2}\lambda = 0, \\
\frac{\partial \mathcal{L}}{\partial p_c} &= 2\beta + (n-2)\frac{e_c}{p_c^2}\lambda = 0, \\
\frac{\partial \mathcal{L}}{\partial p_n} &= 2(\alpha + \beta) + \frac{e_n}{p_n^2}\lambda = 0, \\
\frac{\partial \mathcal{L}}{\partial \lambda} &= -\left(\frac{e_1}{p_1} + (n-2)\frac{e_c}{p_c} + \frac{e_n}{p_n} - 1\right) = 0.
\end{aligned} \quad (57)$$

Then, the first, second, and third of Equation (57) are rearranged by isolating λ in each left-hand side as follows:

$$\begin{aligned}
\lambda &= -2\beta \frac{p_1^2}{e_1}, \\
\lambda &= -2\beta \frac{p_c^2}{(n-2)e_c}, \\
\lambda &= -2(\alpha + \beta)\frac{p_n^2}{e_n}.
\end{aligned} \quad (58)$$

Then, by combining the first and second of Equation (58), we have the following:

$$2\beta \frac{p_1^2}{e_1} = 2\beta \frac{p_c^2}{(n-2)e_c} \implies \frac{1}{p_c} = \frac{1}{p_1}\sqrt{\frac{e_1}{(n-2)e_c}}. \quad (59)$$

By combining the first and third of Equation (58), we have the following:

$$2\beta \frac{p_1^2}{e_1} = 2(\alpha + \beta)\frac{p_n^2}{e_n} \implies \frac{1}{p_n} = \frac{1}{p_1}\sqrt{\frac{(\alpha+\beta)e_1}{\beta e_n}}. \quad (60)$$

By replacing $\frac{1}{p_c}$ and $\frac{1}{p_n}$ in the last of Equation (57) with the findings in Equations (59) and (60), we have the following:

$$\frac{1}{p_1}\left(e_1 + (n-2)e_c\sqrt{\frac{e_1}{(n-2)e_c}} + e_n\sqrt{\frac{(\alpha+\beta)e_1}{\beta e_n}}\right) = 1. \quad (61)$$

Finally, from Equations (59)–(61), we have the following solution:

$$\begin{aligned}
p_1 &= e_1 + \sqrt{(n-2)e_1 e_c} + \sqrt{\frac{(\alpha+\beta)e_1 e_n}{\beta}} \\
p_c &= p_1 \sqrt{\frac{(n-2)e_c}{e_1}} \\
p_n &= p_1 \sqrt{\frac{\beta e_n}{(\alpha+\beta)e_1}}.
\end{aligned} \quad (62)$$

After finding the optimal (p_1, p_c, p_n), the remaining runnable periods $(p_2, p_3, \cdots, p_{n-1})$ should be decided, too. For that, the assignment rule in Equation (50) is used.

6.5. Applying Our Method to Other Scheduling Algorithms

Thus far, we assumed the EDF scheduling algorithm for the underlying RTOS scheduling. However, other scheduling algorithms such as RM are also widely used in the automotive industry.

With this motivation, this subsection explains how we can apply our method to different scheduling algorithms. Fortunately, most real-time scheduling algorithms provide a schedulability analysis method based on the L&L utilization bound, where if the system utilization is less than or equal to a specific threshold value called a utilization bound, denoted by U_B, the system is guaranteed to be schedulable. As noted earlier, U_B for EDF is 100%, whereas U_B for RM is 69.3%. Then, the schedulability condition is formally expressed as follows:

$$U(p_1, p_2, \cdots, p_n) = \sum_{i=1}^{n} \frac{e_i}{p_i} \leq U_B. \tag{63}$$

Then, our optimization problem is slightly changed from Equation (54) to the following using U_B in the schedulability constraint:

$$\begin{aligned} \underset{p_1, p_c, p_n}{\text{minimize}} \quad & J(p_1, p_c, p_n) = 2\alpha p_n + 2\beta(p_1 + p_c + p_n) \\ \text{subject to} \quad & U(p_1, p_c, p_n) = \frac{e_1}{p_1} + (n-2)\frac{e_c}{p_c} + \frac{e_n}{p_n} \leq U_B. \end{aligned} \tag{64}$$

Then, its Lagrange function is also modified as follows:

$$\begin{aligned} \mathcal{L} &= J(p_1, p_c, p_n) - \lambda(U(p_1, p_c, p_n) - U_B) \\ &= 2\alpha p_n + 2\beta(p_1 + p_c + p_n) - \lambda\left(\frac{e_1}{p_1} + (n-2)\frac{e_c}{p_c} + \frac{e_n}{p_n} - U_B\right). \end{aligned} \tag{65}$$

Solving the above Lagrange function yields the following solution:

$$\begin{aligned} p_1 &= \frac{e_1 + \sqrt{(n-2)e_1 e_c} + \sqrt{\frac{(\alpha+\beta)e_1 e_n}{\beta}}}{U_B} \\ p_c &= p_1 \sqrt{\frac{(n-2)e_c}{e_1}} \\ p_n &= p_1 \sqrt{\frac{\beta e_n}{(\alpha+\beta)e_1}}. \end{aligned} \tag{66}$$

From the above, $(p_2, p_3, \cdots, p_{n-1})$ are decided by the assignment rule in Equation (50). Note that we can apply our method to any scheduling algorithm whose schedulability analysis can be conducted by the L&L utilization bound method.

6.6. Algorithm

Algorithm 1 shows a complete procedure for finding optimal runnable periods for a given DAG by our analytical method. As inputs, the algorithm accepts (i) a list of worst-case execution times for n runnables, (ii) a list of m paths in the DAG, (iii) α and β of a given control cost function, and (iv) a utilization bound U_B. The algorithm just needs a list of paths instead of the entire structure of the DAG. Thus, the algorithm itself does not consider generating paths from a DAG. As an output, the algorithm returns a list of optimal runnable periods. Note that the algorithm's computational complexity is just $\mathcal{O}(n \times m)$, which is caused when finding the heaviest path in line 3. This polynomial time complexity makes our analytical method practical for use with large systems.

Algorithm 1: Find optimal runnable periods for a DAG

Input: $\mathbb{E} = <e_1, e_2, \cdots, e_n>$: list of runnable execution times
Input: $\mathbb{P} = <P_1, P_2, \cdots, P_m>$: list of paths
Input: (α, β): coefficients of a control cost function
Input: U_B: utilization bound
Output: $<p_1, p_2, \cdots, p_n>$: optimal runnable periods
Function FindOptimalRunnablePeriods($\mathbb{E}, \mathbb{P}, \alpha, \beta, U_B$):

1. $n \leftarrow |\mathbb{E}|$ /* n: number of runnables */
2. $m \leftarrow |\mathbb{P}|$ /* m: number of paths */
3. $e_c \leftarrow \max_{P \in \mathbb{P}} \left(\sum_{i \in P} e_i \right) - (e_1 + e_n)$
4. $p_1 \leftarrow \dfrac{e_1 + \sqrt{(n-2)e_1 e_c} + \sqrt{\dfrac{(\alpha+\beta)e_1 e_n}{\beta}}}{U_B}$
5. $p_c \leftarrow p_1 \sqrt{\dfrac{(n-2)e_c}{e_1}}$
6. $p_n \leftarrow p_1 \sqrt{\dfrac{\beta e_n}{(\alpha+\beta)e_1}}$
7. **for** $i \leftarrow 2$ **to** $n-1$ **do**
8. $\quad p_i \leftarrow \dfrac{e_i}{e_c} p_c$
9. **return** $<p_1, p_2, \cdots, p_n>$

6.7. Applying Our Method to Conventional Task-Based Systems

Many control applications, but for the automotive industry, are still designed as a set of periodic real-time tasks. Thus, it can be beneficial if we can apply our runnable periods optimization method to such traditional control systems. For that, we first classify them into two different categories. The first is for systems with independent tasks with multiple target plants [12,14,15] and the second is for systems composed of periodic tasks with DAG-based data dependencies [18–20].

Note that the applications in the second category have a strong resemblance to our assumed system model. If we simply assume one-to-one mappings from runnables to tasks, our method for the runnable periods optimization can be applied to systems with periodic tasks without much modifications. However, the applications in the first category cannot make use of our method due to their disagreeing application model with ours. However, for those applications, traditional control-scheduling codesign methods [9,12–15] can be used instead.

7. Evaluation

This section specifically evaluates our optimization method for the general DAG model. Readers interested in the evaluation results for the LPG and LMG models are referred to [27]. More specifically, we evaluate our optimization method by answering the following questions:

- Q1: Is our analytical method able to find near-optimal runnable periods?
- Q2: Is it practical to find real optimal solutions by the exhaustive search method?
- Q3: Is our method practically competitive when optimizing large systems?

7.1. Evaluation Method

For the evaluation, we have to consider the following: (i) workload synthesis, (ii) control cost functions, (iii) optimization algorithms, and (iv) performance metrics. In the remainder of this subsection, the above topics are discussed to explain our evaluation method.

Workload synthesis. As representative AUTOSAR workloads, a total of nine DAGs are artificially synthesized. Among them, the first six DAGs in Figure 8 are relatively small ones with four to six runnables, whereas the remaining three DAGs in Figure 9 are with a relatively large number of runnables ranging from 12 to 25. Note that the DAGs are manually generated, however, understand that the resulting DAGs are purely random without any unfair bias. The small DAGs are used to test the optimality of our method since we can find the real optimal solutions for those small DAGs in Figure 8. On the other hand, we cannot find the real optimal solutions for the large DAGs in Figure 9 due to the vast problem space. However, although we cannot evaluate the optimality of our method with the large DAGs, they are still useful when evaluating our method in comparison to other heuristic optimization methods. Each DAG in the figures is labeled by a notation (nR, mL) representing its size and complexity, where nR denotes n runnables and mL denotes m links (or edges) between them. Basically, with larger n and m, DAGs become more and more complex. For example, the DAG in Figure 8a is labeled by $(4R, 5L)$, which has four runnables and five links, and the DAG in Figure 9c, labeled by $(25R, 34L)$, has 25 runnables and 34 links. For each DAG, we generate 100 sets of random runnable execution times uniformly distributed in the range of [20 ms, 150 ms].

Control cost functions. As our optimization objective, we use a linear control cost function as in Equation (10), which is a function of the control period (T) and the end-to-end delay (Δ). As a representative control cost function, we use the following as our default control cost function, unless otherwise stated:

$$J(T, \Delta) = 0.01T + 0.01\Delta. \tag{67}$$

Note the above control cost function has two coefficients $\alpha = 0.01$ and $\beta = 0.01$. Here, however, the relative ratio of α and β is more important than their absolute values since the ratio represents the control cost function's relative sensitivity to the control period and the end-to-end delay. By using the same values for α and β in our default control cost function, the control cost is equally sensitive to the control period and the end-to-end delay. To represent other scenarios with varying relative sensitivities, we also use varying αs and βs in the range of [0.01, 0.05].

Optimization algorithms. To evaluate the optimization performance of our method, for the comparison purpose, we specifically consider the following three optimization methods:

- *OUR:* Near-optimal solutions found by our analytical optimization method;
- *EXH:* Real optimal solutions found by the exhaustive combinatorial search method;
- *PSO:* Solutions optimized by the particle swarm optimization (PSO) method [39].

More specifically, the *EXH* method searches through the discrete integer problem space within [1 ms, 1000 ms] for each runnable period. We compare our method with the *EXH* method to evaluate the optimality of our optimization method with small DAGs to answer the question Q1. To evaluate the optimization performance with large DAGs as an answer to the question Q3, we compare our method with the *PSO* method.

Performance metrics. We mainly use two optimization performance metrics: (i) absolute control costs and (ii) normalized control costs. Absolute control costs are the raw control cost values resulting from an optimization process, whereas normalized control costs are used to compare our method with another algorithm, i.e., the *EXH* method and the *PSO* method. A normalized control cost is defined as the relative ratio of our resulting control cost by letting another method's result as 100%. Besides, to evaluate the practicality of each optimization method, the optimization times are measured with respect to varying application complexities. For the optimization, we use a workstation with an Intel i7-9700k CPU with 64 GB RAM (Dell, Round Rock, TX, USA)

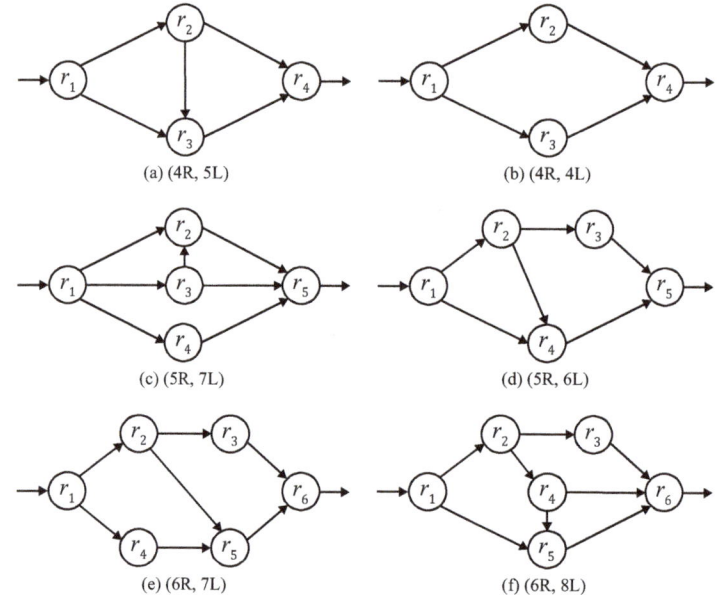

Figure 8. Small DAGs with varying number of runnables (denoted by nR) and links (denoted by mL).

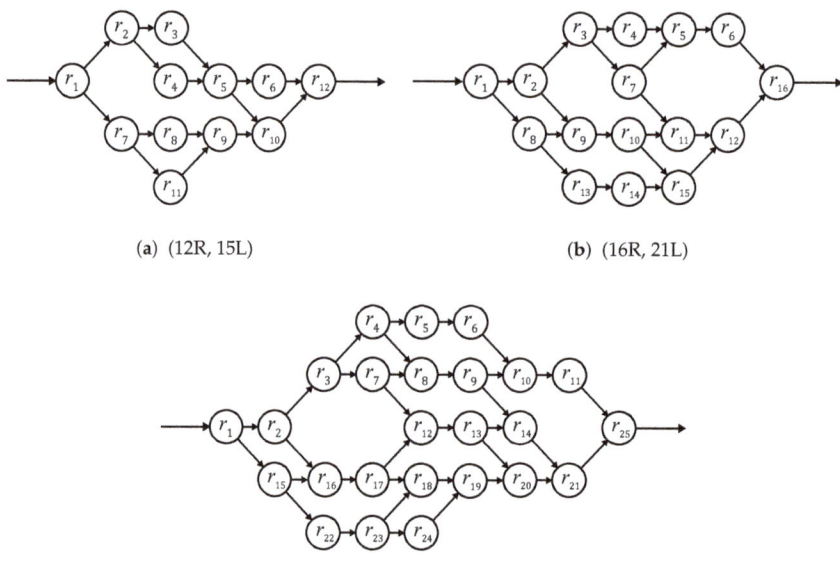

Figure 9. Large DAGs used for evaluating the practicality of our method.

7.2. Evaluation Results and Discussion

Q1: Is our analytical method able to find near-optimal runnable periods? For the six DAGs from Figure 8a–f, their normalized average control costs by the *EXH* method and our method are compared in Figure 10. In the figure, our method shows near-optimal control costs with marginal performance losses compared with the *EXH* method. The minimum control cost increase is just 1.1% and the maximum is 12.3%. One interesting point is that DAG (a) shows a significantly better performance than the other DAGs. That is because our heuristic for selecting the critical path is always valid in this particular DAG shape. Note that, in DAG (a), $< r_1, r_2, r_3, r_4 >$ will be correctly chosen as the critical path by our heuristic regardless of their execution times since every other path is a subset of it. On the other hand, in other DAGs, there are multiple choices for the critical path. Nonetheless, our method must bet on a certain path based on the given execution times. However, as shown in the figure, the performance losses from the real optimal solutions are marginal.

Thus far, we have assumed the EDF scheduling algorithm. However, in the automotive industry, the RM scheduling algorithm is also widely used for scheduling real-time tasks. In this regard, Figure 11 compares the EDF case where the utilization bound is 100% and the RM case where the utilization bound is 69.3%. More specifically, Figure 11a compares their normalized average control costs across the six DAGs, each of which represents the relative optimization performance compared with the *EXH* method. The figure shows that our method provides not much different optimization results across the two scheduling algorithms. Figure 11b compares their absolute average control costs where EDF shows a significantly lower average control cost since it can efficiently schedule workloads with its higher utilization bound.

To investigate how varying control cost functions affect the optimization performance, Figures 12a,b show normalized average control costs with varying αs and βs, respectively. As shown in the figures, our method provides a consistent optimization performance with varying control cost functions that represent various sensitivities to the control period and the end-to-end delay.

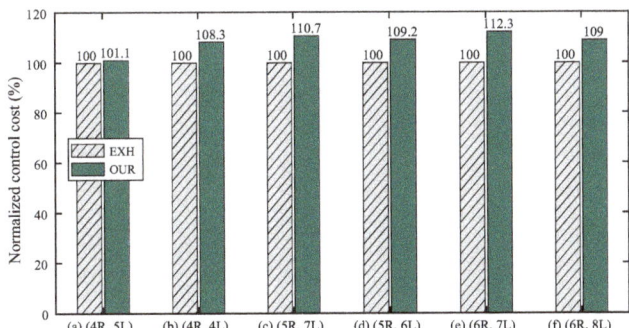

Figure 10. Normalized average control costs of our method compared with the *EXH* method.

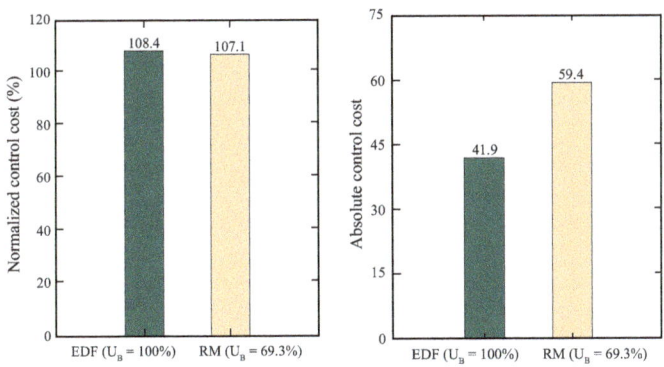

(**a**) Normalized average control costs. (**b**) Absolute average control costs.

Figure 11. Comparison of average control costs with the earliest deadline first (EDF) and rate monotonic (RM) scheduling algorithms.

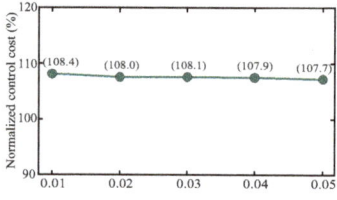
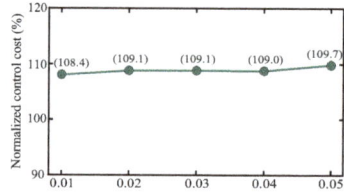

(a) With varying αs.   (b) With varying βs.

Figure 12. Normalized average control costs with varying control cost functions.

Q2: Is it practical to find real optimal solutions by the exhaustive search method? By looking at Q1's results, one can argue that if we can use the *EXH* method to find real optimal runnable periods, why not just use the *EXH* method instead of our method? However, this argument does not hold since the *EXH* method is not usable for large DAGs due to the vast search space when $n > 6$. To answer the question, we evaluate our optimization method in terms of the required time for the optimization process. Table 1 shows the required optimization times for our method and the *EXH* method with varying number of runnables. The numbers inside parentheses are projected numbers. As our method finds the runnable periods by an analytical method, it shows negligible computational complexities as predicted in Algorithm 1. With the *EXH* method, we can find optimal runnable periods in about one month when the numbers of runnables is seven. However, after seven runnables, it is not feasible to use the *EXH* method since it takes more than a year even for small and medium-size systems. Thus, due to the scalability problem, the *EXH* method cannot be used for practical industrial applications, whereas our analytical method can be used for large industry applications.

Table 1. Required optimization times.

Number of Runnables	OUR	EXH
4	0.012 ms	1 s
5	0.016 ms	90 s
6	0.022 ms	3 h
7	0.025 ms	21 days
8	0.031 ms	(350 days)
9	0.036 ms	(3.4 years)
10	0.042 ms	(3065 years)

Q3: Is our method practically competitive when optimizing large systems? From Q1 and Q2, we showed that (i) our analytical method works well with small systems and (ii) real optimal solutions cannot be found for large systems. One remaining question is whether we can apply our analytical method to large systems with sufficient optimization performance. To answer this question, we use the three large DAGs with n = 12, 16, and 25, as in Figure 9. For the comparison, we additionally use an evolutionary metaheuristic algorithm known as particle swarm optimization (denoted by *PSO*) that searches an unknown vast problem space efficiently with swarm intelligence. To implement the *PSO* method, we use the PySwarms library [40]. Figure 13 shows the normalized average control costs of our method compared with the *PSO* method, letting the resulting control costs by the *PSO* method as 100%. As shown in the figure, our method shows significantly better results than the *PSO* method, especially for the largest DAG case. We notice the decreasing trend of normalized average control costs with the increasing complexity of DAGs. With the above results, we can claim that our analytical method performs better than the traditional evolutionary optimization method.

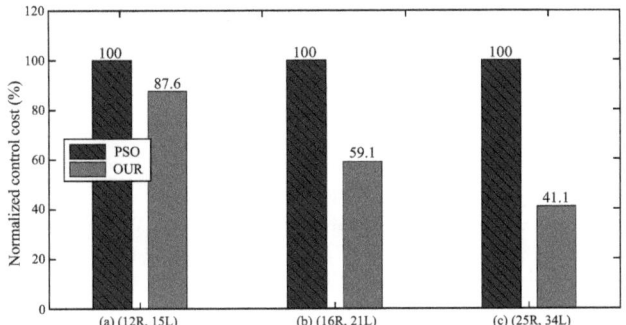

Figure 13. Normalized average control costs of our method for large DAGs compared with the PSO method.

8. Conclusions

This paper formulates a runnable periods optimization problem for AUTOSAR control applications and provides an analytical solution based on the Lagrange multiplier method. Our method can find near-optimal solutions that maximize a given system's control performance regardless of the size and complexity of the application. Since the complexity of automobile control applications is rapidly growing due to the recent development of various advanced driver assistance systems and autonomous driving applications, it is no longer feasible to use traditional ad-hoc methods or time-consuming search-based optimization algorithms. Due to the analytical nature of our proposed runnable periods optimization method, we consider that our solution can be readily used in the automotive industry when designing their complex industry-scale AUTOSAR control applications.

Although our method provides a promising solution for optimizing complex applications, our method is only usable when the control cost is given or approximated as a linear function. As the approximation can induce overestimated control costs, we plan to extend our optimization method to nonlinear control cost functions in our future work.

Author Contributions: Conceptualization, J.-C.K.; Data curation, D.C. and T.-W.K.; Methodology, D.C.; Software, D.C. and J.-C.K.; Supervision, J.-C.K.; Visualization, T.-W.K.; Writing—original draft, T.-W.K.; Writing—review & editing, J.-C.K. All authors have read and agreed to the published version of the manuscript.

Funding: This research was supported partly by the Ministry of Land, Infrastructure, and Transport (MOLIT), Korea, through the Transportation Logistics Development Program (20TLRP-B147674-03, Development of Operation Technology for V2X Truck Platooning) and partly by the National Research Foundation (NRF) grant funded by the Korea government (MSIT; Ministry of Science and ICT) (No. 2017R1C1B5018374) and partly by Institute for Information and communications Technology Promotion (IITP) grant funded by the Korea government (MSIT) (2014-0-00065, Resilient Cyber-Physical Systems Research).

Conflicts of Interest: The authors declare no conflicts of interest.

Abbreviations

The following abbreviations are used in this manuscript:

RTE	Runtime Environment
DAG	Directed Acyclic Graph
RTOS	Real-Time Operating System
L&L	Liu and Layland
RM	Rate Monotonic
EDF	Earliest Deadline First
LQG	Linear Quadratic Gaussian

ECU   Electronic Control Unit
ILP   Integer Linear Programming
LPG   Linear Path Graph
LMG   Linear Multipath Graph
PSO   Particle Swarm Optimization

References

1. Kehr, S.; Panić, M.; Quiñones, E.; Böddeker, B.; Sandoval, J.B.; Abella, J.; Cazorla, F.J.; Schäfer, G. Supertask: Maximizing runnable-level parallelism in AUTOSAR applications. In Proceedings of the 2016 Design, Automation & Test in Europe Conference & Exhibition (DATE), Dresden, Germany, 14–18 March 2016; pp. 25–30.
2. Kim, J.W.; Lee, K.J.; Ahn, H.S. Development of software component architecture for motor-driven power steering control system using AUTOSAR methodology. In Proceedings of the 2015 15th International Conference on Control, Automation and Systems (ICCAS), Busan, Korea, 13–16 October 2015; pp. 1995–1998.
3. Park, J.; Choi, B.W. Design and implementation procedure for an advanced driver assistance system based on an open source AUTOSAR. *Electronics* **2019**, *8*, 1025. [CrossRef]
4. AUTOSAR. Recommended Methods and Practices for Timing Analysis and Design within the AUTOSAR Development Process. AUTOSAR Classic Platform 4.3.1. Available online: https://www.autosar.org/fileadmin/user_upload/standards/classic/4-3/AUTOSAR_TR_TimingAnalysis.pdf (accessed on 13 July 2020).
5. Kim, T.W.; Lee, G.M.; Kim, J.C. AUTOSAR Runnable Scheduling for Optimal Tradeoff between Control Performance and CPU Utilization. In Proceedings of the 2018 18th International Conference on Control, Automation and Systems (ICCAS), PyeongChang, Korea, 17–20 October 2018; pp. 602–605.
6. Bini, E.; Cervin, A. Delay-aware period assignment in control systems. In Proceedings of the 2008 Real-Time Systems Symposium, Barcelona, Spain, 30 November–3 December 2008; pp. 291–300.
7. Wu, Y.; Bini, E.; Buttazzo, G. A framework for designing embedded real-time controllers. In Proceedings of the 2008 14th IEEE International Conference on Embedded and Real-Time Computing Systems and Applications, Kaohisung, Taiwan, 25–27 August 2008; pp. 303–311.
8. Wu, Y.; Buttazzo, G.; Bini, E.; Cervin, A. Parameter selection for real-time controllers in resource-constrained systems. *IEEE Trans. Ind. Inform.* **2010**, *6*, 610–620. [CrossRef]
9. Fu, H.; Liu, J.; Han, Z.; Shao, Z. A heuristic task periods selection algorithm for real-time control systems on a multi-core processor. *IEEE Access* **2017**, *5*, 24819–24829. [CrossRef]
10. Tan, L.; Du, C.; Dong, Y. Control-performance-driven period and deadline selection for cyber-physical systems. In Proceedings of the 2015 10th Asian Control Conference (ASCC), Kota Kinabalu, Malaysia, 31 May–3 June 2015; pp. 1–6.
11. Liu, C.L.; Layland, J.W. Scheduling algorithms for multiprogramming in a hard-real-time environment. *J. ACM* **1973**, *20*, 46–61. [CrossRef]
12. Seto, D.; Lehoczky, J.P.; Sha, L.; Shin, K.G. On task schedulability in real-time control systems. In Proceedings of the 17th IEEE Real-Time Systems Symposium, Washington, DC, USA, 4–6 December 1996; pp. 13–21.
13. Seto, D.; Lehoczky, J.P.; Sha, L. Task period selection and schedulability in real-time systems. In Proceedings of the 19th IEEE Real-Time Systems Symposium (Cat. No. 98CB36279), Madrid, Spain, 2–4 December 1998; pp. 188–198.
14. Enrico Bini, M.D.N. Optimal task rate selection in fixed priority systems. In Proceedings of the 26th IEEE International Real-Time Systems Symposium (RTSS'05), Miami, FL, USA, 6–8 December 2005; pp. 399–409.
15. Du, C.; Tan, L.; Dong, Y. Period selection for integrated controller tasks in cyber-physical systems. *Chin. J. Aeronaut.* **2015**, *28*, 894–902. [CrossRef]
16. Xu, Y.; Cervin, A.; Årzén, K.E. Harmonic scheduling and control co-design. In Proceedings of the 2016 IEEE 22nd International Conference on Embedded and Real-Time Computing Systems and Applications (RTCSA), Daegu, Korea, 17–19 August 2016; pp. 182–187.
17. Cha, H.J.; Jeong, W.H.; Kim, J.C. Control-scheduling codesign exploiting trade-off between task periods and deadlines. *Mob. Inf. Syst.* **2016**, *2016*, 3414816. [CrossRef]

18. Davare, A.; Zhu, Q.; Di Natale, M.; Pinello, C.; Kanajan, S.; Sangiovanni-Vincentelli, A. Period optimization for hard real-time distributed automotive systems. In Proceedings of the 44th annual Design Automation Conference, San Diego, CA, USA, 4–8 June 2007; pp. 278–283.
19. Feiertag, N.; Richter, K.; Nordlander, J.; Jonsson, J. A compositional framework for end-to-end path delay calculation of automotive systems under different path semantics. In Proceedings of the IEEE Real-Time Systems Symposium, Washington, DC, USA, 30 November–3 December 2009.
20. Schlatow, J.; Mostl, M.; Tobuschat, S.; Ishigooka, T.; Ernst, R. Data-age analysis and optimisation for cause-effect chains in automotive control systems. In Proceedings of the 2018 IEEE 13th International Symposium on Industrial Embedded Systems (SIES), Graz, Austria, 6–8 June 2018; pp. 1–9.
21. Dürr, M.; Brüggen, G.V.D.; Chen, K.H.; Chen, J.J. End-to-End Timing Analysis of Sporadic Cause-Effect Chains in Distributed Systems. *ACM Trans. Embed. Comput. Syst.* **2019**, *18*, 1–24. [CrossRef]
22. Choi, J.; Kang, D.; Ha, S. End-to-end latency analysis of cause-effect chains in an engine management system. In Proceedings of the 2018 Design, Automation & Test in Europe Conference & Exhibition (DATE), Dresden, Germany, 19–23 March 2018; pp. 1195–1198.
23. Long, R.; Li, H.; Peng, W.; Zhang, Y.; Zhao, M. An approach to optimize intra-ecu communication based on mapping of autosar runnable entities. In Proceedings of the 2009 International Conference on Embedded Software and Systems, Hangzhou, China, 25–27 May 2009; pp. 138–143.
24. Monot, A.; Navet, N.; Bavoux, B.; Simonot-Lion, F. Multisource software on multicore automotive ECUs—Combining runnable sequencing with task scheduling. *IEEE Trans. Ind. Electron.* **2012**, *59*, 3934–3942. [CrossRef]
25. Saidi, S.E.; Cotard, S.; Chaaban, K.; Marteil, K. An ILP approach for mapping autosar runnables on multi-core architectures. In Proceedings of the 2015 Workshop on Rapid Simulation and Performance Evaluation: Methods and Tools, Amsterdam, The Netherlands, 21 January 2015; p. 6.
26. Kehr, S.; Quiñones, E.; Langen, D.; Böddeker, B.; Schäfer, G. Parcus: Energy-aware and robust parallelization of AUTOSAR legacy applications. In Proceedings of the 2017 IEEE Real-Time and Embedded Technology and Applications Symposium (RTAS), Pittsburgh, PA, USA, 18–21 April 2017; pp. 343–352.
27. Choi, D.; Lee, G.M.; Jeon, W.; Kim, J.C. Control Performance-aware AUTOSAR Runnable Scheduling. *Trans. Korean Soc. Automot. Eng.* **2020**, *28*, 9–17. [CrossRef]
28. Obermaisser, R.; El Salloum, C.; Huber, B.; Kopetz, H. From a federated to an integrated automotive architecture. *IEEE Trans. Comput.-Aided Des. Integr. Circuits Syst.* **2009**, *28*, 956–965. [CrossRef]
29. Di Natale, M.; Sangiovanni-Vincentelli, A.L. Moving from federated to integrated architectures in automotive: The role of standards, methods and tools. *Proc. IEEE* **2010**, *98*, 603–620. [CrossRef]
30. AUTOSAR. Virtual Function Bus. AUTOSAR Classic Platform 4.3.1. Available online: https://www.autosar.org/fileadmin/user_upload/standards/classic/4-3/AUTOSAR_EXP_VFB.pdf (accessed on 13 July 2020).
31. Cervin, A.; Henriksson, D.; Lincoln, B.; Eker, J.; Arzen, K.E. How does control timing affect performance? Analysis and simulation of timing using Jitterbug and TrueTime. *IEEE Control. Syst. Mag.* **2003**, *23*, 16–30.
32. AUTOSAR. Specification of Timing Extensions. AUTOSAR Classic Platform 4.3.1. Available online: https://www.autosar.org/fileadmin/user_upload/standards/classic/4-3/AUTOSAR_TPS_TimingExtensions.pdf (accessed on 13 July 2020).
33. Peraldi-Frati, M.A.; Blom, H.; Karlsson, D.; Kuntz, S. Timing modeling with autosar-current state and future directions. In Proceedings of the 2012 Design, Automation & Test in Europe Conference & Exhibition (DATE), Dresden, Germany, 12–16 March 2012; pp. 805–809.
34. Lincoln, B.; Cervin, A. Jitterbug: A tool for analysis of real-time control performance. In Proceedings of the 41st IEEE Conference on Decision and Control, Las Vegas, NV, USA, 10–13 December 2002; Volume 2, pp. 1319–1324.
35. Henriksson, D.; Cervin, A.; Årzén, K.E. TrueTime: Simulation of control loops under shared computer resources. *IFAC Proc. Vol.* **2002**, *35*, 417–422. [CrossRef]
36. Yu, F.; Li, D.F.; Crolla, D. Integrated vehicle dynamics control—State-of-the art review. In Proceedings of the 2008 IEEE Vehicle Power and Propulsion Conference, Harbin, China, 3–5 September 2008; pp. 1–6.
37. Ono, E.; Hattori, Y.; Muragishi, Y.; Koibuchi, K. Vehicle dynamics integrated control for four-wheel-distributed steering and four-wheel-distributed traction/braking systems. *Veh. Syst. Dyn.* **2006**, *44*, 139–151. [CrossRef]
38. Akiyama, S.; Tashiro, T. Integrated Vehicle Control System. U.S. Patent 7,047,117, 16 May 2006.

39. Kennedy, J.; Eberhart, R. Particle swarm optimization. In Proceedings of the ICNN'95-International Conference on Neural Networks, Munich, Germany, 17–19 September 1995; Volume 4, pp. 1942–1948.
40. Miranda, L.J.V. PySwarms a Research Toolkit for Particle Swarm Optimization in Python. Available online: https://pyswarms.readthedocs.io/en/latest/index.html (accessed on 13 July 2020).

© 2020 by the authors. Licensee MDPI, Basel, Switzerland. This article is an open access article distributed under the terms and conditions of the Creative Commons Attribution (CC BY) license (http://creativecommons.org/licenses/by/4.0/).

MDPI
St. Alban-Anlage 66
4052 Basel
Switzerland
Tel. +41 61 683 77 34
Fax +41 61 302 89 18
www.mdpi.com

Applied Sciences Editorial Office
E-mail: applsci@mdpi.com
www.mdpi.com/journal/applsci

www.ingramcontent.com/pod-product-compliance
Lightning Source LLC
LaVergne TN
LVHW070153120526
838202LV00013BA/1060